❧

THE RUIN OF KASCH

Charles-Maurice de Talleyrand-Périgord, 1808, after
a portrait by François Gérard. Courtesy of
François Bonneau, Curator, Château de Valençay.

The Ruin of Kasch

ROBERTO CALASSO

❧

*Translated by William Weaver
and Stephen Sartarelli*

The BELKNAP PRESS *of*
HARVARD UNIVERSITY PRESS
Cambridge, Massachusetts

Author's Note

Having followed closely the long preparation of this book, I would like to say a word of heartfelt thanks to Maria Ascher of Harvard University Press, who helped in a very effective way to give the book its final form.

Second printing, 1994

Originally published as *La Rovina di Kasch* by Adelphi Edizioni, copyright © 1983 by Adelphi Edizioni, Milan.

This book is printed on acid-free paper, and its binding materials have been chosen for strength and durability.

Library of Congress cataloging information follows the Notes.

Contents

In the beginning, the mountains had great wings. Whenever they pleased, they would fly through the air and alight on the ground. Then the earth would tremble and quake. But Indra cut off the mountains' wings. He fastened the mountains to the earth, to steady it. The wings became clouds. Ever since that time, clouds have gathered around the mountaintops.

TALLEYRAND: I speak at the threshold of this book because I was the last man to know anything about ceremonies. And I speak, as always, to deceive. This book is not dedicated to me or to anyone else. This book is dedicated to dedication.

"Monsieur de Talleyrand is a difficult man to follow through the maze of his political life," says the Duchesse d'Abrantès, opening the doors to the *Salon de Monsieur de Talleyrand*. Over the entrance are stucco decorations redolent of the ancien régime. Near the exit is a bourgeois dining alcove. In the center, from the arms of every chair, the beasts of the Empire fix us with their hypnotic gaze. And in chambers off to the side, we encounter the guillotine and the forests of America. At the far end of the room, delegates to a congress stumble over ladies' trains as they dance. From every corner, the prince's witty remarks come reverberating toward the guests. A delicate tom-tom, an instrument heard for the first time at Mirabeau's funeral, disseminates them as billets-doux throughout the maze. Many different voices repeat them, though hardly ever that of the prince himself, who was so lazy when it came to writing. He would compress certain terrible truths into a flashing retort and would cast them into the hubbub of conversation, each time taking the chance that people would not understand them. But Talleyrand, *revenu de tout* even before he set out on a journey, had an abiding and magnanimous faith in at least one thing: in society as an echoing salon where at least one ear is always hiding, ready to receive the word. And thus his *mots*, enveloped in balm-steeped bandages, would be passed down through the years like so many folio volumes. There are some aristocrats who, as they grow old, begin to resemble their valets. In these pages the Grand Chamberlain will gradually become a mere master of ceremonies, the caretaker of a house full of ghosts, a guide for inquiring tourists. The maze of his life and of his salon will serve as the frame for an unholy performance that has been repeated countless times since, though with myriad variations, in place of the myth that society has allowed itself to forget.

.   .   .

In the drawing rooms that softly, gently enclosed the Congress of Vienna for the last time, in the conversations murmured in window niches and promptly transcribed by the secret police, there was much more at stake than flirtatious intrigues and something the history books would later call the new balance of Europe. One question arose before any other and after any other: that of definitively transforming the *ṛta*—the connection between heaven and earth that makes life possible and gives it order. It had all started one day when the gods, perhaps weary of the dense, opaque anguish of the primordial chaos, expressed a profound desire: "'How could these worlds of ours become farther apart from one another? How could there be more space for us?' They breathed through them [the worlds] with these three syllables [forming the word] 'vī-ta-ye'; and these worlds became far apart from one another, and there was then ampler space for the gods." And later for human beings. In the eighteenth century, there was no longer any point in discussing this issue; indeed, no one even remembered it clearly. But all the same, there was an urgent need to resolve once and for all a family matter which in fact dated back to the *ṛta:* the matter of legitimizing *legitimacy* as the *ṛta's* heir. Even law itself proved a troublesome topic. The word of the moment was really the other one—"legitimacy"—and the man to seize upon it could only be Talleyrand, whose relationship to the law had always been one of polite detachment. This change represented an enormous step and therefore had to pass unnoticed insofar as was possible, had to be submerged in gala balls and in tiresome dynastic wrangles, and sometimes also in domestic ones. "Legitimacy" was the last reassuring word, a picnic among the grassy ruins. But behind "legitimacy" lurked another noun, another realm: the realm of "convention," of arbitrary equivalences and agreements, which was finally attaining absolute power. Until then it had always been the cadet branch of the psyche. Its power had grown steadily, but in an unmentionable shadow, precisely because it lacked legitimacy. In order to acquire this, convention would have had to empty legitimacy of its contents and then assume its guise. Now legitimacy had to be recognized as fact, and the fact had to become sovereign. Political necessity had obviously led to this situation. With his campaign in Russia, Napoleon had summoned up the specter of unlimited war;

he was drawn to that land, which in itself represents the unlimited, the uncontrollable, the irremediable blend, the beside-itselfness of Europe, far from civilization and its *douceurs*. This same limitlessness was already about to emerge within Europe; diplomats, with their talent for euphemism, would call it "the social question." So the moment had come to yield authority to the only power that promised to negotiate with the unlimited as an equal, and perhaps even to dominate it (though even then few were convinced): Convention as Legitimacy. Time would take care of the bones of meanings—would clarify and bleach them. In the jungle on the border of Thailand and Cambodia, Pol Pot once roamed with his followers. Most of the surrounding world still viewed him as the only *legitimate* authority in his country. The plundered temples of his royal power expanded into the immense and numerous mass graves extending deep into the earth. The bodies contained there form layers that parallel our Canonical Phases: at the lowest level, the corpses still bear shreds of multicolored garments—they are the devotees of Lon Nol (the ancien régime); higher up, one sees the Buddhist bonzes (the refractory priests); then come a number of ordinary civilians, since the Public Safety police preyed on anyone and everyone; and finally appear the dark rags of the Khmer Rouge themselves (the true Jacobins, the true Bolsheviks, the plotters and renegades). The gravediggers heaped the skulls in piles shaped like those that the Cambodian peasants have used since ancient times for their annual harvest of pineapples. In such mass graves, history once again becomes natural history.

THE DUCHESSE D'ABRANTÈS: When was it that we all began wearing masks? Let me see . . . Yes, it was before I was allowed to go out in society, and my sharp-toothed cousins visited me and told me everything . . . It was during the reckless years of the Directory, when the purple togas that had been packaged in England were seized at Customs . . . when Bonaparte was received at the Luxembourg palace by the five Directors who were adorned with plumes, their cloaks covered with arabesques and cut in medieval style—yes, because they still had not quite decided to emulate Roman Virtue . . . They were pale with anxiety before the general, whom the sublime Ossian kept suspended two inches from the ground, . . . said our dear friend, our (and everyone's) perennial traitor, Talleyrand—the only one who has managed to betray everything, with the exception of style . . . and not, certainly not, out of delicacy, but because style is the golden scepter before which a vast kingdom, in both this world and another, ultimately bows down . . . A camp that was full of bewildered nomads and ornamented with bits of fabric stolen from unwitting travelers—such was Paris in those days . . . Everyone dreamed of the Court, but memories of the proper gestures were already beginning to fade . . . The Directors represented the people, but that was not enough. Actually, they resembled those traveling salesmen preparing to board stage-coaches and invade the provinces . . . with the new price lists . . .

An irresistible tropism turns the spirit toward Talleyrand: "Once, in my youth, and even in later years, when I loved adventure novels and melodramas, I saw that what enthralled me was *uncertainty about people's identity*." How could we not feel the same way toward Talleyrand's mask, which so many people have called "impenetrable" or "impassive" or "the mask of death," and to which so many others have ascribed the most diverse evils and the most unexpected virtues? A mask that had kept watch over the entire troubled history of the Canonical Phases, whose own identities were dubious: they did not know, would never know, whether to consider themselves propitious or unpropitious, all being marked *niveis atrisque lapillis*. Ultimately, the only thing that could be said of them was what Léon Bloy (in his typically blunt way) had noted: "Obviously God did not know what to do with this old world. He wanted new things; and to introduce them, a Napoleon was needed." Except for this harsh certitude, the whole was unstable. Subsequently, the features of a physiognomy presented themselves as a last mainstay. But then, all knowledge is physiognomic.

The last sage of physiognomy, Johann Kaspar Lavater, asked the young Goethe if he would collaborate on his *Physiognomische Fragmente*. Wasn't he perhaps already convinced of the "general homogeneity of all of nature's forms"? Of course, was Goethe's reply—and his contribution to Lavater's work went much further. In his opinion, even objects, clothes, and environments were part of physiognomic science: "Nature forms man, then man transforms himself, and this transformation is, in turn, natural. He who finds himself situated in the vast world creates another one inside himself—a little world enclosed and protected by walls, and fitted out in his own image."

More than half a century later, the aged Goethe found himself leafing through the *Collection des portraits historiques de Monsieur le baron Gérard,* published by Urbain Canel in Paris in 1826. The book contained some rather dubious etchings which Pierre Adam had made from sumptuous portraits scattered throughout Europe. Goethe's friend Boisserée once complained, during a visit, that the etchings had been crudely executed. "My dear boy," Goethe replied, "we in our Weimar modesty are content with such things. You are too refined and demanding." He spent many hours studying those etchings in private. In those days he didn't care for art; he was pursuing a physiognomic dream of his own. Once, as he was leafing through the album, he noticed the image of a man he had met on the now famous occasion at Erfurt, when he had been seated to the right of Napoleon (who had come out with that embarrassing remark, "Voilà un homme!"). Looking at the portrait of Talleyrand, he wrote: "The more one examines this collection, the more important it seems." Yet his comments on the portraits of Alexander I, Charles X, and Louis-Philippe d'Orléans had been amiably generic in their appreciation. Only when he is gazing at Talleyrand does he withdraw into the dark, contemplative stillness that gave rise to his most perfect pages: "Here we have before us the supreme diplomat of the century. Perfectly calm, he sits and confidently awaits all the events of the moment. In a setting that is stately but not ostentatious, he is dressed in simple and appropriate Court garb, his plumed hat on the divan just behind him, as if this man of *affaires* were waiting to hear that his carriage was ready to take him to a meeting. His left arm rests on a corner of the table, next to some papers and pens; his right arm is in his lap; his right leg is crossed over his left; and he appears perfectly impassive. One can't help thinking of the gods of Epicurus, who live 'where it never rains or snows and where storms never rage'; such is the serenity of this man, untouched by the tempests that howl around him. One can understand how he manages to assume such a demeanor, but not how he can maintain it. His gaze is utterly impenetrable. He looks straight ahead, but it is doubtful that he sees anyone who may be looking at him. His gaze is not directed inward, like a thinker's, or outward, like an observer's; the gaze rests within and on itself *[in und auf sich]*, as does his whole figure, which suggests not exactly complacency but surely some lack of rapport with his surroundings.

"But enough. Here we can pose as physiognomists and interpreters to our heart's content. In any case our comprehension will prove insufficient, our experience too brief, our imagination too limited for us to form an adequate idea of such a being. And the same will probably be true of future historians, who will see to what extent our views can be of use to them."

Buried in that essay, so superfluous, so marginal for the eighty-year-old Goethe, who still had to complete his Great Work, which was hovering among the archetypes (and for him, the organic and fulfilled being, it was essential not to leave that work in a fragmentary state), the lines on Talleyrand suggest that the *Dichter* was making a cautious revelation about himself. Goethe, too, knew the art of hiding everything on the surface. An album containing engravings of famous people—portraits in which the turmoil of history is already frozen and the gaze is already starting to grow dull, as in the illustrations that later appeared in the *Magasin Pittoresque*—was a suitable occasion for someone who claimed to be an "occasional poet." And it was precisely in his essay on this album, rather than in a conversation with Eckermann or some other devotee, that Goethe chose to allude to the long parallel life which had accompanied him through the land of upheavals. In essence, Goethe and Talleyrand were the only two beings of any absolute significance who had survived everything, from the early years of ice skating and boudoirs to that revered, ceremonious, and misunderstood old age—the old age of those who know too much. Goethe had already wormed his way inside the carapace of the Great Poet. Talleyrand at Valençay was receiving a writer sick with curiosity, Honoré de Balzac, who looked on him as some sort of ancient saurian, awesome and delicate; or, worse still, he was receiving the tempestuous George Sand and her gang. (Madame de Dino, who as usual was at the

Prince's side, noted: "All in all, very little grace; and the rest of the company utterly common.")

In that passage, Goethe was issuing a sharp warning: harbor no illusions, ye scholars, of understanding the gaze of Talleyrand; harbor no illusions of understanding the polished serenity of the aged councillor Goethe. And the game was carried to the point of provocation. Goethe the "Olympian" (as Germanic kitsch would say forever after) actually appealed to the "gods of Epicurus" in his effort to come to terms with Talleyrand's gaze. Yet he must have known that, according to common report, this gaze had witnessed almost every possible villainy—and had even planned some.

People soon perceived and commented on the bold superposition of the two impassive faces, which Goethe had tacitly suggested. It was Sainte-Beuve (who understood almost everything and did his best to keep this from being too noticeable) who ventured a few lines on the topic, in his introduction to one of the handsomest of the *illustrés romantiques*—an edition of Molière with vignettes by Tony Johannot, published by Paulin on the rue de Seine, Paris, in 1835 (Talleyrand was still living; Goethe had only recently died): "And all the same his [Molière's] lucidity, the habitual coldness of his character, at the center of such a lively work, did not in the least aspire to an icy, calculated impartiality of the sort found in Goethe, the Talleyrand of art. In those days, such critical refinements in poetry had not yet been invented." These lines, too, were hidden near the frame, so they would not be readily noticed. But they were noticed by the mischievous, overbearing Barbey d'Aurevilly, who could not pass up the opportunity to express his feudal contempt for Sainte-Beuve's carpet slippers ("Sainte-Beuve disliked argument; his ears would become red, and his usually sharp tongue would stammer in fury and vexation"), even as he credited him with merely an undeserved intuition: "One day Sainte-Beuve had a flash of inspiration: he called Goethe a literary Talleyrand. Today he regrets that correct idea." But at this point Barbey mounted his own slashing attack: "The *poseur* that Goethe may not have been by nature, but that his admirers have made of him with their excessive adulation, carefully concealed the emptiness of his being with his Olympian air, just as Talleyrand, who was equally vacuous, concealed his own beneath the indolent, mocking pose of a grand old man of the world *who had seen far worse . . .*

"In fact, there is a close resemblance between Goethe and Talleyrand, those two princely souls! Goethe is a literary Talleyrand, perching atop his cravat just like Talleyrand. But even if he did wear that famous cravat which had to be tied and retied eighteen times, Goethe lacked Talleyrand's impertinent tilt to the head and his fascinating, half-closed eye, the eye of a dying viper, because these were spontaneous and natural things in Talleyrand—gifts from God or the devil!—whereas there's nothing spontaneous and natural about Goethe, that opera actor who's always gazing at himself in a mirror."

How did the Revolution meet up with Talleyrand? "He loved the worldly life of the old days, as a man of his position and qualities could live it. He passionately loved women, gambling—everything that used to make a man of fashion. And so it was that 1789 found Monsieur de Talleyrand." Moreover, it found him endowed with an exceptionally keen grasp of the dynamics of his age. Here his political intelligence was already evident. "The benefits he enjoyed would have been taken from him in any case by the force of events; so, in his opinion, it was better to abandon them beforehand (but only *perhaps,* I must add)." In the irony of her *perhaps,* the Duchesse d'Abrantès is hinting at one of the few traits that can be attributed to Talleyrand with any certainty: the ability to sniff out the age. A beast in the boudoir. Deciding in aristocratic fashion to give away what a moment later would have been torn from him ("There was only one course to take: surrender before one had to, and while one could still take credit for it"). A Talleyrand cannot allow anything to be taken from him, but he will allow himself to give away everything. Especially if what he bestows is a *Gift-gift,* a poisoned present, an object of his private hatred—for example, ecclesiastical privileges, which came with a job (the job of being bishop) that the innate despotism of his parents had forced him to take. In donating those incomes and privileges to the nation, he was taking revenge on the demonic aspect of the nobility: its unassailable, absolute authority, which he had been obliged to submit to from birth.

Behind the welter of facts, behind the vows and betrayals, one also finds an obstinate *loyalty* in Talleyrand. Certain perceptions seem to have become fixed in him at the outset, and nothing that happened later could undermine them. First was his early awareness that the age of *bouleversements* and convulsions—in short, the "age of revolutions"—had begun; that every movement from then on would be a rippling of the prevailing currents; and that this would require an appropriate and definitive upheaval in all modes of action. Henceforth, certain signs of power would be ridiculously impotent, whereas certain other gestures would be more decisive than battles (for example, the ball given by Talleyrand for Madame Bonaparte at the Hôtel Galliffet on January 3, 1798). Second, he saw that now the *summum bonum*—the invisible, imperceptible sun of political action—would be not to impede or foster those convulsions (cruel childishness in either case), but rather to *soften the blow,* to coat the sharp edges in sweet essence of balm, to wrap them in noble gauze that had been abandoned in attics. And above all to dissociate those convulsions from *faith:* to refuse to credit them with that *extra something* which they always claim to represent—to refuse to believe, in short, that a massacre can easily be transformed into a sacrifice. Lacking any form of liturgy, people were already moving in a vast slaughterhouse.

Tat tvam asi: "that you are." This dictum—password to the gates of the cosmos and the mind, premise of all Vedantic premises—is not after all so far-fetched in relation to ordinary life. Surely no more than Descartes' *cogito.* But the civilized West, with the eighteenth century at center stage, seemed (and still seems) to be separated by a lead wall from everything that might turn one's gaze toward the *ātman-brahman.* Hermeticism was continuing to spread, but by then it had adapted to the practices of various sects and was getting ready for trembling séance-tables. If anything, it enjoys becoming involved with occult political designs that ultimately distract one from contemplation. *Clarté* teaches one above all not to see certain things. The important point, as Descartes insisted, is to define the field, to overcome the psyche-without-confines, to let the mind run free in a quivering golden cage of its own. But history is also accompanied by geological events—in this case the emergence within Europe of a new, wild continent: Germany. Caspar David Friedrich's painting of a land shrouded in fog, the *Nebelmeer,* is a posthumous tribute to that emergence, which had occurred under the auspices of the *Romantik*. "India wound up becoming Germany," Victor Hugo remarked as he watched the shadowplay that flickered on the "wall of the centuries." Every civilization must nourish within itself an Orient of its own. When the first notes of the romantic piano rang out, Europe found its Orient in that penetrating sound—an Orient that it had long tried to lose.

Talleyrand's function was first of all that of master of ceremonies—in a period that had forgotten what ceremonies meant and therefore claimed to get along without them, though it slid back clumsily at every step. And so Talleyrand impassively *offered his arm* and helped smooth over the embarrassment. But his distant gaze as he proffered this help should have alarmed everyone. For decades, except during the searing interlude of the Terror, Talleyrand, with some discreet prompting, had persisted in *introducing History into society*—ungainly History, ponderous, bloodstained, and awkward in her various toilettes. Thus, during the Directory, he had introduced the government of the parvenus, which marked the first time the demimonde had ever wielded power. And almost forty years later in London, at the age of eighty, he had introduced into society the government of the bourgeoisie, in which members of the middle class appeared in power *under their declared names:* lawyers and merchants, no longer *citoyens*. In his view, History seemed to display a progressive deterioration of tone. But it still needed help gliding smoothly over those long carpets. Talleyrand was justly horrified by the sudden stumblings of History, by its spasms. And so he placed a few drops of oil in the gears, expecting that others would clog them with sand. This Talleyrand foresaw, knew, had already seen, and it would happen again over and over. But he persisted all the same: *glissez, glissez,* something will remain in the end. A gesture, at least.

M***: The Napoleonic Court has been established in the equatorial forest; the merchants of the bazaar are discovering theocracy; Lenin dons a paratrooper's uniform and smokes Davidoff cigars; the Holy Experiments are littering the rice paddies with corpses. It appears more and more obvious that the stage for the future politics is Raymond Roussel's Africa. Henceforth, too, we shall be forced to rediscover many things that zeal has tried to eradicate. We believed that ideas were the most important thing; now they stand before us in rows, like dented cans of Coca-Cola. We thought the first requisite was generic knowledge ("The Evil of the world is ignorance" was the last banner, gnostic as always, of the conquering Clichés)—and now we realize that all education is magnetized by something tacit and implied, while instruction that is merely explicit sounds shrill and horrid, like a passage of Racine declaimed in a penitentiary on the warden's birthday. *Expressa nocent.*

Talleyrand never inspired respect. From his youth as an *abbé mauvais sujet* until his death agony, invective was heaped on him— denunciations, sarcasm, curses. For decades he was taunted because he was lame. Chateaubriand wrote that Talleyrand, "because he was the object of so much contempt, had become impregnated with it and had stored it away at the two sagging corners of his mouth." His mother begged Louis XVI not to nominate him for the episcopate, because he was unworthy of the vestments. As bishop, he had to defend himself against accusations of rather profane behavior (gambling, speculation, women). During his tenure as the Directory's foreign minister, the same Directors who had chosen him continually scorned him, and Rewbell kept saying that "Talleyrand is a collection of every vice, a model of betrayal and corruption. He's a powdered lackey of the ancien régime. At most he might do as a servant for display, if he were more sure-footed; but his feet are defective, like his heart." The newspapers wanted to excoriate him, and easily found reasons to do so. And one day even the emperor's fury rained down on him. Napoleon, actually wanting to strike him, to shatter his impassivity at least this once, resorted to a most ridiculous and offensive act: he grabbed Talleyrand by the chin and pushed him against the wall. As he does so, he coined a famous *mot:* "You are shit in a silk stocking!" The right-minded execration of Talleyrand reached its peak, however, with the Romantics: Chateaubriand, George Sand, Hugo. Devoted to the Ideal, they each wanted to give Talleyrand an eloquent kick, as if kicking a stray dog in an age that belonged no longer to him but to them. The moral trumpets blared, and indignation launched on vast wings into the future: it enveloped all those who in the years to come would be fathers of families; it spoke in the name of all young men with noble aspirations. Talleyrand, moreover, for anyone who was closely involved with literature as a profession, was an irresistible excuse for composing a malevolent bit of purple prose. Writers seemed to be competing like Alexandrian rhetoricians: Who could express his contempt for Talleyrand most elegantly? Who could best engrave it in the heavens as a new constellation of words? Meanwhile, Received Opinion assimilated, grateful and replete. Ultimately it would produce the purest crystal of Cliché—namely, Flaubert's: "Talleyrand, prince of. To be indignant against." It was an obligatory step, only one among many, in negotiating the alliance between Romanticism and kitsch—the first stage in the coarsening of the sensibilities that took place between the fever of 1830 and the desolation of 1850.

Compared to Talleyrand, Chateaubriand is the other path of the blood, the other way to make one's ancestors productive (and useful). Talleyrand discreetly guided all the powerful people who did not know how to walk on parquet; Chateaubriand, in contrast, wanted to steep the common psyche in a new liquid. Nameless sunsets, misty cataracts, hollow resonances. A patina of aesthetic retreat, a padding of death, a claustral cobweb, an invincible heather among the ancient stone slabs. Talleyrand was his enemy primarily because he was his main rival in cultivating the past and making it fruitful in the new age.

THE SENATOR FROM ST. PETERSBURG: As we look at this dying evening, this tattered glow, vestige of a Day that will never dawn again, as we wait for opaque night to lift our spirits and return us to the void, I wish to tell you, here where we Deviants are among ourselves, how glad I am to think that I was born in this hybrid place, in this shrill age which I pray every day will receive its punishment. But then I find myself once again with you on this terrace, which rests on its four little Chinese columns, and I abandon myself to my most cherished habit: the whims of conversation. Behind me I feel the tranquillity of my library. I have never written about, but have often described, the awe I still feel when contemplating the wicked doctrines I have always execrated.

I see in them the workings of Malice as well as a formal excellence, blended into a whole that inspires respect. A few ideas—but let us not use this inappropriate word—a few statements that lack all sense of what we really, truly are, a few superficial rules of behavior, have bridled the earth, and we cannot even say who proposed them or if they have ever appeared in a written work.

In their volatility and promiscuity, these statements are akin to what proverbs once were. They are the air we breathe without being aware of it. And their emptiness is linked to their vast authority—to their ability to expand power, to stir and blend the earth without anyone's being able to say how those remnants of words could produce such an incessant hum. And deep down, I savor these iniquities more faithfully than anyone—far more than those who frequent them as if they were making outings in the country. Thus it happened that when I met Fouché, we initially looked at each other like two libertines belonging to the same club. Perhaps it was then that I told him there was only one reason I was not on his side: because the Good was more of an adventure.

Empire: a moment of suspension, of concealed terror. Power is afraid of itself, and fear corrodes each day. A desire to enclose in zoomorphic stasis (Egypt on the furniture) the great *dégringolade,* the collapse, of the bourgeois age. The Empire tries once again to invent an aristocracy for itself (as the reign of the will, it must be able to invent *everything*); the Restoration, which returns aristocrats to their legitimate places, cannot hide even momentarily the fact that it is installing the Shopkeeper in power. Egypt: to stamp utter precariousness with the seal of utter fixity. Napoleonic Egypt marks the last time that terror in the face of History will appear in imagery. Thereafter, History will drag everything off to its nearby estuary. Mingling of fresh water and salt water, the Liffey in the Atlantic, piercing swoon: History abandons its wreckage to post-history. A perpetual dismissal, continually renewed.

Having passed the Barrière Saint-Martin, accompanied by a single cossack, Nesselrode made his way along "the boulevards crowded with people in their Sunday clothes. They seemed to have gathered for some festival, instead of the entrance of enemy troops." In that city which for a few hours was the focus of an absolute vacuum of power, he immediately looked for the one place that offered certain safety, the residence where power had always kept a room. There, behind the pale pilasters of the Hôtel de l'Infantado, Monsieur de Talleyrand was waiting. The white angel of the north, the czar, with his too-tight uniforms, his excessive politeness, and his eagerness to please everyone, though the steppes were howling behind him, had been warned by some unknown party (perhaps—some assumed, as always—by one of Talleyrand's agents) that the Elysée Palace, which he was planning to make his headquarters, was mined, a trap. Yet Talleyrand, who was a high official in the defeated government and who controlled policies which now had to be revoked, presented himself as inviolable. He enfolded Nesselrode (who had entered while he was being coiffed) in a cloud of powder—a protective cloud, the ultimate aura, which had emanated down from the throne and turned into vapor. But in fact, the point was to give the veneer of age-old custom to a scandalous scene: a conqueror comes to a defeated power like a guest, as if calling on an old friend, in order to feel safe. A few days later the stairways were abuzz with rumors at all hours. Talleyrand had reserved the mezzanine for himself; Nesselrode had taken the third floor; and the czar occupied the first, with his aides. In the courtyard, on bales of straw, the cossacks dozed.

Talleyrand was the first to understand that the new world—the one that had emerged from the Napoleonic age expecting to find a state of equilibrium—no longer expected or demanded a law, but wanted the semblance of a law. Any other solution would have been too harsh and would have quickly brought about its collapse. An untouchable law was something that people could not bear any-more—could hardly even think of, except perhaps in the case of a true eccentric like Joseph de Maistre, sitting on his terrace in St. Petersburg. An absence of law, a total subjection to force and to the temporary conventions among forces—that was precisely what the world could not bring itself to name, though it was enacted every day. Or rather: it could not name it, *precisely because* it enacted it. References to law still appeared necessary, therefore, but law itself was to prove almost empty, unable to sustain any examination. The law was thus coming to be a mere ornament for events, a flourish of pompous rhetoric, a useful word when you had to dedicate a monument, a springboard for the pharmacist holding forth in a café. The whole century was to abound, as no previous age had, in appeals to principles, though in the secrecy of its mind it retained a single principle regarding principles: the Napoleonic dictum *"Principes* est bien, cela n'engage point" (*"Principles* are fine—they don't commit you to anything"). As soon as Talleyrand throws the card of legitimacy down on the table, accompanying the gesture with a few forceful words, the sumptuous proliferation of *bêtise* begins. It will find its dazzled chroniclers in Baudelaire and Flaubert, later in Léon Bloy and Karl Kraus, and will arrange the celebration of its centenary for August 1914, replacing the fireworks of Versailles with rockets and the roar of mortars on the Belgian front. There was no further talk, then, of "legitimacy"—but there is always some abstraction, each one weaker than the last, that takes over the place where the law used to be. Now it was the turn of "neutrality." The sacred began to imbue not the coat of arms of a dynasty, but the paper of a treaty. At this point the only thing left to do was to remark, along with German statesman Bethmann-Hollweg, "All this for a word, 'neutrality.' All this for a scrap of paper." Henceforth an equivalence was established between "a scrap of paper" and a new kind of massacre, more extensive, more thorough, open to everyone, which would enable the ancient god of war to scorn once and for all the inept law that had dared try to yoke him.

"The legend of the origins of the Wahnungwe makes reference to a sovereign named Madsivoa. This name is thought to derive from *dsivoa* (lake, ford, pond)." Any Western theory of legitimacy is deficient in one respect: it knows nothing of the waters of origin. "Who made you king?" Aldebert, count of Périgord and ancestor of Charles-Maurice de Talleyrand, asks Hugh Capet, king of Ile-de-France and first in the line of French kings. But Capet cannot answer, "I come from Dsivoa, the pond of origins; I emerged from one of those bubbles that form spontaneously on its surface." Without those waters, *all* are usurpers. And the first usurpers can therefore appeal to only a single ally: time. When a sovereign power has existed *for a certain time,* the cruelty with which it first asserted its might is supposedly already cloaked and surrounded by the *douceur* of custom, by long acceptance—in short, by tradition. Thus, tradition no longer enables one to claim an origin, but now conceals it. All the great and terrible enlighteners, down to Nietzsche and Freud, have been fanatical seekers of origins and genealogies. Herein lay the Western world's peculiar *nefas,* which attracted and dazzled them. If one could fill the gap of that missing origin, they thought, one could at last make one's way without deception all the way to the present. Then they discovered origin as deception, thus choosing the form of deception into which *they* wanted to fall—and which would bedevil them to the last.

The notion of legitimacy blends the two fundamental operations of the mind: analogy and convention (that is, the process of establishing arbitrary equivalences). They are branches that fork from a single trunk, namely substitution. In the case of analogy, the only legitimacy is that of holy investiture, which through a play of resonances and sympathies descends through all the gradations of being. Where that resonance dies out, no legitimacy can be granted. In the case of convention, legitimacy is the prime example of the arbitrary agreement that makes possible the functioning of all sorts of mechanisms, ranging from language to society. As always, convention is concerned not with essences or substances, but with function—and it is ready to barter one form for another (for it is the very soul of substitution).

In 1956, when John Von Neumann used his Silliman Lectures to give a quick summary of recent and ongoing developments in machines that could calculate on their own, and when he began by distinguishing between digital computers and analogue computers, he gave new names to the two poles that secretly sustain us. The digital pole seems biologically secondary and dependent, for exchange always seems secondary to the object being exchanged. But then the digital pole takes command, revealing its ability to envelop the other pole, to absorb it—and, naturally, to exploit it. The digital pole confers great power, but it does not contain, within the machine, the physical reality of the varying values, which is a last palpable memory of the outside world. Digitality is pure sequence of signs: when its dominion is extended to everything, we no longer know what earth sustains us—or even if there still is an earth. We continue to experience the analogue pole, but we no longer know what to call it: it is mute emotion, which overwhelms and no longer flows into its old estuary. Digitality has given it a new bed made of indestructible silicon. Over it flows a silent stream, awaiting the Bateau Ivre.

"Monsieur de Talleyrand, descendant of one of the oldest families in France (sovereign counts, in fact), was the eldest of three surviving sons. Lame from childhood, he was considered unfit to appear in society and was destined for the Church, though he completely lacked any predisposition that might have made him tolerable to the Roman Catholic Church. Many times I have heard him say that, despised by his parents as a cripple who would never amount to anything, he had acquired in childhood a taciturn and grim disposition. He had never slept under the same roof as his father and mother, and they had forced him to renounce his right of primogeniture in favor of his younger brother." Etienne Dumont, biographer of Mirabeau, gives us a dry and detailed portrait of Talleyrand that immediately reveals a wound. Talleyrand's infirmity is acquired accidentally; it belongs to the randomness of history and luck. At the age of four, while in the care of a peasant woman, he injures his foot in a fall from a chest of drawers. And because of that accident, a chance event, Talleyrand is denied legitimacy. Talleyrand's lot is to *become* a foundling. From this point on, he will acknowledge a double lineage that originates from both the lowest and highest rungs on life's ladder. He will possess ancient blood, cursed by a stroke of ill-fortune; but he will also be the wild plant that grows in solitude. He who comes from the land richest in memories and he who has never shared his father's roof. The age-old root and the uprooted. He who has the power to give protection and he who is continually forced to seek it.

The nobility of the Talleyrand-Périgords is not a nobility of the spirit, nor is it attracted by the spirit. It is a biological nobility, which does not allow itself to be explained or justified. *Re que Diou*, their motto, means that the family will answer only to God. Will give answers, if any, that are invisible and unascertainable. For the rest, nobility is *"a name and a coat of arms."* It is an inheritance of which the individual is only a temporary bearer. And, as such, the individual merits no special attention, except when viewed as a means of considering the "family" ("For in the great houses it was the *family* that people loved, far more than its young members, about whom nothing was yet known"). This is the last form of sacrifice—by now hollow, reduced to its shell—perpetuated within the aristocracy, which can renounce the sacrifice only by renouncing itself. Hence Talleyrand will suffer horribly for the cruelty, the indifference, the capriciousness that surround him as an individual and sheath him in his youthful role of sacrificial victim (the lame firstborn who can only be discarded and abandoned to the Church, because he is incapable of achieving the one true glory, that of arms); but he will never explicitly deny the mechanism of sacrifice. On the contrary, his politics is founded on a respect for sacrificial heredity—the sole, even if intolerable, truth. But nothing is more intolerable than sacrifice that continues to function in an age that denies it, the age in which Talleyrand happens to live. The flowing, elusive quality of his politics mitigates that horror, glazes it for a while with the colors of its noble and bloody past.

The Primal Scene of politics-according-to-Talleyrand unfolded at the home of his grandmother Mortemart, "in a vast room of the château that we called 'the pharmacy.'" There, seated next to his grandmother's velvet armchair (where he was placed—as he stresses—by "birthright" at the age of five, just as he would later sit successively next to Napoleon, Louis XVIII, Charles X, Louis-Philippe), the young Talleyrand observed the primordial mystery of power: the ability to heal, which the thaumaturgic kings demonstrated on people afflicted with scrofula. (Louis XVI continued to exercise this power at Reims, and as a young chaplain Talleyrand saw him repeat to two thousand four hundred sufferers, who had come from the most distant provinces, the same words: "May God heal you; the king touches you.") Grandmother Mortemart used this power on ailing villagers, and in his boyhood Talleyrand devoutly took part in the ceremony. On those occasions, his grandmother "wore a silk dress trimmed with lace. She was adorned with a whole spectrum of ribbons and with bows on her sleeves that matched the hues of the seasons. The ruffles at her wrists were large and had three layers. A tippet, a bonnet with a butterfly bow, and a black cap that tied under her chin completed her Sunday outfit, which was more elaborate than the ones she wore on other days." Around her, a little court of Périgord nobles maintained order according to Rank, clearing a space for her, and flanking her as she sat in a velvet chair at a little black lacquer table, dispensing ointments, syrups, and other medicines to the peasants with ceremonial gestures.

His grandmother would indicate the ointment to be applied, and "one of the gentlemen who had accompanied her to Mass would go and fetch it. Another would present the chest that held the linen." Little Talleyrand would then take out a length of cloth, unfold it, and hold it while his grandmother cut it. Since the days of the Shang Dynasty in China, this has always been the duty of the Minister: to see that cloth to be used for bandages is cut with precision. In describing this solemn scene, Talleyrand (though he did not say as much) was presenting his lofty conception of politics, which would later follow designs no one can claim to have reconstructed. And in this same scene he perceived a reality that has remained unexplained and that would serve as his guide forever: "the heredity of feelings," the fundamentally nourishing, yet also destructive, relationship between time and any quality. Only time allows every reality to secrete its *douceur*. Otherwise, all is by nature harsh, insipid, arid. The old Périgord nobles, who paid homage to Madame de Mortemart and were prepared to leave no trace of their existence, heralded with their silent footsteps the arrival of the unheard-of, indicating to the child Talleyrand how he might bear it: "The habits of the Périgord nobility resembled their old châteaus: they had a grand and stable quality; the light entered them dimly, but softly. People proceeded with useful slowness toward a more enlightened civilization."

In all his actions, Talleyrand implied (but never mentioned and perhaps did not give much thought to) the sacred source of power. Herein lies the paradox of his art: he saw that this source was continuing to act in an age—the first age—in which the transmission of investiture had irreversibly ceased. Thus, sacredness had to become a fiction, and the challenge was to make it a powerful fiction:

to invent, along with Napoleon, a dynasty; to claim, along with the Congress of Vienna, that it was still possible to rely on a "principle"—specifically on that "legitimacy" only recently buried; to ensure, along with Louis-Philippe, that society would find even an uprising acceptable. Talleyrand believed less than anyone in the fictions he proposed. "Legitimacy" had become something akin to what the "ego" would be in the age of Mach: an unsteady but useful guidepost. He knew that each time the aim would be to maintain the fiction for a few years. After that, the simulation would approach its end: it would collide with the bedrock of simulated reality. But the transmission of power (as well as the transmission of thought) would still be—could not fail to be—a chain of those slippery, precarious fictions, which would manage briefly to capture the essence of power one more time, or at least momentarily remove the stopper from its bottle. Concerning the hidden difference between New and Ancient power, concerning the secret weakness of the New, which is linked specifically to its gaudy apparatus of power, Talleyrand has left us the parable of his grandmother Mortemart's pharmacy, accompanied by a curt but definitive comment: "There may be pharmacies that are better supplied and more scientific and that might perhaps be run by very famous physicians, even free of charge; but they could never attract as many poor people or, what is more important, do them as much good. Those pharmacies would lack certain powerful means of healing the common people: good will, respect, faith, and gratitude." With the greatest precision and a minimum of ostentation, Talleyrand meant to describe, here and only here, the charisma of power.

The Marquis de Lafayette is the Hero of Democracies. Always on horseback, his empty gaze sizing up the crowd, he eagerly seeks the "delicious feeling one gets from the smile of the multitude." He knows it is important to think little, but firmly. And above all, one must know how to seize the right moment for certain gestures that could serve as illustrations: an embrace at a window, while the throng outside roars; a white charger; a plume in the breeze. With his usual perfidy, which is this time almost stifled beneath the obligatory praise, Sainte-Beuve remarks that Lafayette transformed "the idol of honor into another idol: that of popularity." Further sarcasm: "La-fayette's primary motive is *opinion* in the honorable sense, glory in the ancient sense"—a reference to the way in which the *doxa* changed, from the ancient splendor of appearance to the mental sawdust of the contemporary.

The new rituals made Talleyrand laugh because they were so shrill and clumsy, as any new and secular rituals must be. But for Lafayette they are pure, fresh water that ceaselessly cleanses his uniform, which photographic plates are (and for some years yet will be) unable to record. This hero will be the model for many vulgarities, but it cannot be said that there's any touch of vulgarity about him. If anything, he's slightly ridiculous. He's still protected by a faint aura of ancien régime, the memory of the many beautiful women he won, even the difficult Madame de Simiane. His patriotic old age will be a venerated, somewhat faded banner. And from him emanate the Capital Letters that will reverberate in the halls of Parliaments, then in town squares, before they reappear, a bit surprised and reluctant, in the storms of steel of August 1914. Like everyone else, they "had not wanted it."

With Lafayette, an alliance is established between Good Causes and Stupidity. From this point on, whoever seeks the welfare of Man will cherish a grossly imprecise image of the man—kindly, obtuse, bombastic. Lafayette is escorted by the Unknown Soldier. For Good to regain the fascination of adventure, it must wait for Simone Weil. And this will be only because Weil gives close attention to the Good of Plato.

Lafayette is the true opposite of Talleyrand. They are born and die within a short time of each other; both have glorious ancestries; both take part in everything. Convinced from the beginning that he is *moving with the times,* Lafayette is above all intent on assuming the occasional historic pose and, meanwhile, on surviving. He has an infallible ability to avoid perceiving things. Talleyrand likewise *moves with the times,* takes on the current hue, changes shirts and oaths. But this is not the reason people will refuse to forgive him. On the contrary, it is because they have the impression that his amorality is coherent and faithful, that his perennially shifting and restless waters conceal solid, ancient stone that withstands the insults of time far better than does Lafayette's papier-mâché.

Talleyrand's revenge on Lafayette, after the many insults that were heaped on Talleyrand in Lafayette's name, comes from a judge who was equal to the task: Balzac's Vautrin. In the course of Rastignac's initiation, the ex-convict regales him with these words: "I have a friend for whom I have done much, a colonel in the army of the Loire who has just now been accepted into the royal guards. He has heeded my advice and has become an Ultra; he is not one of those fools who attach importance to their own opinions. If I must give you a piece of advice too, my angel, it is this: do not cherish your opinions any more than your words. When people ask you for them, sell them. A man who boasts of never changing his opinion is a man who forces himself to move always in a straight line, an idiot who believes in infallibility. There are no principles; there are only events. There are no laws; there are only circumstances. The superior man espouses events and circumstances in order to guide them. If there were principles and fixed laws, nations would not change them as we change our shirts. A man is not expected to be wiser than an entire country. The man who has served France less than anyone is venerated as a fetish because he has always seen red; at most he should be placed in the *Conservatoire,* among the automatons, under the label 'Lafayette,' while the prince at whom everyone casts his stone, and who despises mankind enough to spit in its face all the oaths it demands, prevented the division of France at the Congress of Vienna. They owe him a crown, but throw mud at him instead. Oh, I know a thing or two! I possess the secrets of many men! But enough of this."

(It is hard to vent one's fury on Lafayette. Apart from everything else, he's a likable ninny, who decides to become a Plutarchan hero the way others decide to become financiers. And he decides this also because it is a profession that one can pursue intermittently, that allows one to live in the intervals. When he enters the salon of the ideologue Destutt de Tracy, the lady of the house says *mon cher monsieur* "in an enchanting tone of voice," and everyone admires his tall figure, which is topped by "a cold, impassive face, a meaningless old family painting, a head covered by a short, badly made wig." But

Stendhal has no doubts: "I felt, without anyone's having to tell me, that Monsieur de Lafayette was simply a hero from Plutarch. He lived from day to day, without much wit, performing simply, like Epaminondas, the grand actions that came his way. Despite his age, he passed the time while he waited doing nothing but snatching at the skirts of pretty girls (*vulgo:* touching them on the ass), and he did this fairly often, without making a fuss over it." He was silly; but in the vague generalities of his speeches, there was a "basic elegance." And a basic indifference toward the elevated ideas he so fervently professed, somewhat like a libertine prepared to make any foolish declaration that might further a seduction. "Monsieur de Lafayette is extremely polite and even affectionate toward everyone, but *polite as a king.*" He knew in a "marvelous" way that "the essential thing is never to displease anyone and to remember everyone's name." While people speak to him of the political events of the day (and here he does not hesitate to encourage "all intriguers, all fools, all those who are swept away by their own bombast"), he has eyes only for a new visitor, a young girl from Portugal, glimpsed among the "fifteen or twenty little nieces of Monsieur de Lafayette, nearly all of them blond and with splendid complexions and ordinary faces," who were "lined up in battle array on the blue sofa.")

"Lucien had to endure from the good Gauthier what the young men of Paris call a *tartine* on the subject of America, democracy, the prefects who must be chosen by authority from the members of the general councils, and so forth.

"As he listened to these arguments, which can be found in print everywhere, Lucien thought: 'What a difference in spirit between Du Poirier and Gauthier! And yet Gauthier is probably as honest as the other is a scoundrel. In spite of my deep respect for him, I can hardly stay awake. How, after all this, can I call myself a Republican? This proves to me that I am not made to live under a republic; for me it would be the tyranny of all mediocrities, and I cannot reasonably tolerate even the most respectable ones. For me what is needed is a rascally and amusing prime minister, like Walpole or Monsieur de Tallyrand.'

"Meanwhile Gauthier was finishing his speech, with these words: '. . . but there are no Americans in France.'

"'Take a little tradesman from Rouen or Lyon, greedy and without imagination, and you will have an American!'

"'Ah, how you grieve me!' cried Gauthier, sadly rising to leave, as it was striking one."

⚜

Note for Lucien

Mon cher,

Nearly one hundred fifty years have passed since your meeting with the worthy Gauthier, and almost two hundred since the storming of the Bastille; I wish to give you some news. Followed by his companions—now no longer buried in the provinces but boldly penetrating all worlds that are in the process of being "liberated"—Gauthier has never stopped talking for a moment. Indeed, he invites any passerby to converse with him. Meanwhile, the *Ligue des Compagnons* has proved staunchly averse to being *déniaisée*. And when one of its allegorical female delegates allows herself to be debauched now and then, she soon returns shyly to office. We would like them all to be Ninotchkas, but even that physical type is difficult to find nowadays. The massacres committed for a worthy end were futile. And so were the fraternal slaughters. The wave of good intentions continues to ripple amid the currents of boredom. The cause of justice and of the people still fixes its gaze on little holy images, but it never attains their aesthetic delicacy. To this day, few people realize what adventures the Good entails; we have spent too many years being forced to feed off the Wicked, with their constant intrigues and fabrications. Around us there is an obstinate insistence on changing life, but without any specific notions of the facts of life. While you were using your kind of automatic writing to compose *Souvenirs d'égotisme* in Civitavecchia, you were hoping those pages would be published ten years after your death. Twenty years after would be too late, you feared: once all the *nuances de la vie* had changed, the reader would perceive only the masses. Then you asked yourself,

"But where are the *masses* in these games my pen is playing?" Well, think: Gauthier, that *nuance* of yours, has become a mass—or a multitude (as a woman professor said, not wanting to compromise herself too far with the catchwords of the day). I send my love, and expect you this evening for our game of whist.

—Talleyrand

The Prince of Wales was taking forever to get dressed, as always. To pass the time that morning, Laclos, with his distant manner and something vague and cold in his speech, fell into the trap that the Comte de Tilly—a shrewd man of the world—had set for him. "Monsieur de Laclos, who had no special skill at Court but who possessed all the gloomy impatience of a philosopher or a conspirator, preferred to chat rather than to keep pulling out his watch and sighing."

"How was *Les Liaisons dangereuses* born?" Tilly ventured, as soon as he saw the other man weakening. At last Laclos told him: it was a dream he'd had in the provinces, in Grenoble, a result of the tedium of garrison life. There had been a fellow soldier, now an illustrious scientist, who had had many affairs with women; he was a man born for women. One of them had been a lady of Grenoble, who appeared in the novel, considerably toned down, as the Marquise de Merteuil. Laclos and the soldier had talked together, and at times Laclos had advised him on how to proceed with his seductions. There had been many other affairs over the years—his chest of poisons; he had merely had to transpose them to a more suitable setting, namely Paris. That was how it had gone, more or less. Laclos broke off and abruptly concluded, "I took as much care as I could with the style, and after a few more months of work I cast my book before the public. Afterward I heard almost nothing of its fate, but I'm told it still lives."

At that time, just as Valmont had pulled Cécile Volanges' strings, Laclos was still pulling the strings of the Duc d'Orléans, whom many people thought of as a terrifying Valmont of politics. From London the duke sent strategic letters, which he had dutifully copied from drafts written by his adviser Laclos. What crystalline intoxication, to be the man who controls the man who presumably controls the plot of the Revolution! From the military solitude of the island of Ré, where *Les Liaisons* was composed, he had become as delirious as a spider that thinks it has the whole world in its web! A few months later, Laclos was trying to manipulate not only the Duc d'Orléans but also the Jacobin club. And he did, to a certain extent. Then the spider web was swept away by the torrent of events. In a box at La Scala, artillery general Laclos looked around, desolate: to him, nothing was as "boring as an Italian *opera buffa,* except perhaps *opera seria.*" A dragoon with ruddy cheeks, still a shy and curious boy, was ushered into the box reserved for army staff. Laclos' expression "softened" when he learned that this young fellow, Second-Lieutenant Beyle, was also from Grenoble. From the provinces to the provinces, he mused, thinking of Milan, a city which to him seemed utterly lacking in charm, consisting merely of streets and houses. Perhaps the moment had come to return to writing. One project, which he planned to pursue in his old age, was very dear to him: to write a work dedicated "to popularizing the idea *that the only happiness lies in the family.*" It would be no small undertaking. "It will be hard to arrange the events in the proper way, and the almost insurmountable difficulty will be that of arousing interest without falling back on any novelistic devices."

The mixture of styles and images that prevailed in 1790 would soon be reduced to a unity fearful of contamination. Any hybrid was bad. In the streets, the foolish variety in styles of dress disappeared and "men began wearing the uniform coat of the new world," first sign of the bourgeois who wishes to pass unnoticed. On the stage, as well, people rediscovered the unity found in the most tedious Golden Age that humankind has ever conceived. Chateaubriand, who in his American wanderings had just encountered the rustle of virgin forests, Creole eroticism, and the "sublime disorder" of Niagara Falls, also listened to the piping of the liberators: "While tragedy reddened the streets, pastoral poetry flourished in the theater. One saw nothing but innocent shepherds and virginal shepherdesses: fields, streams, meadows, rams, doves, golden ages beneath a thatched roof—all were revived, to the accompaniment of a flute, for cooing Thyrses and ingenuous knitters fresh from the spectacle of the guillotine. If Sanson had had time he would have played the part of Colin, and Théroigne de Méricourt that of Babet. The members of the Convention prided themselves on being the most benevolent of men. Good fathers, good sons, good husbands, they took their children out walking; they acted as nannies; they wept with tenderness at the sight of their children's simple games; they would lift those little lambs gently in their arms, to show them the horsies pulling the tumbrils that were taking the victims to execution. They sang of nature, peace, piety, charity, innocence, the domestic virtues. These bigots of philanthropy had their neighbors' heads cut off with extreme sensitivity, so that the happiness of the human race might be ever greater."

Air of Paris. Hegel roamed through Paris in amazement; and in that "Paris within Paris," the Palais-Royal, he obediently followed the instructions of the *Manuel des Etrangers,* even if Victor Cousin laughed at him. To Marie Helena, awaiting him in Berlin, he did not fail to mention the things he found most remarkable: "Today, for example, we went to an *abattoir*—a slaughterhouse, that is. In what other city in the world would I have visited a slaughterhouse? But this is one of the notable things—and there are a hundred others—that Paris owes to Napoleon . . . Before going there, we saw the Stock Exchange, also founded by Napoleon. What a temple!"

Let's try to remove Talleyrand from the portrait of his era, erase all trace of him. What is lacking then? Fluidity. The crudeness of the Revolution remains, as well as the crudeness of the legitimist years, the Directory, the Bonapartists, and the bourgeoisie. Like battering rams, they strike at the same wall. While every municipal partisan was finally discovering his metaphysics in the vision of the Party, Talleyrand maintained the indifference of sky, of water: mobile, elusive, intact among so many faiths.

Talleyrand did not like *bons mots.* To him, the only behavior that was in any degree perfect was that of a person he barely knew: his mother. And Talleyrand's mother avoided *bons mots* like the plague; she thought them the bane of all conversation. "When I visited my mother, I chose the hours when she was alone, so I could better appreciate the grace of her wit. In conversation, no one has ever seemed to me to have a charm comparable to hers. She had no pretentions whatsoever. She spoke only in nuances. She never uttered a *bon mot:* that would have been too outspoken. *Bons mots* are remembered, and she wanted only to be pleasing and to let her words be forgotten."

"The consistently light manner in which he dealt with the weightiest matters . . ." Talleyrand's *lightness*, and above all his lightness in dealing with the "weightiest matters," is the sign that reveals the hidden purpose he has chosen for himself. There no longer exists anything in the world that cannot be treated lightly: this is his premise. People are frightened to admit it, but Talleyrand accepts it and puts it to work in all his actions.

This is enough to create that incommensurable—many would say monstrous—distance between him and everyone else. Talleyrand knows he can use lightness because things no longer have a fixed weight. They fluctuate—immense, vaporous, poisonous bodies. They do not rest in themselves. Nothing stands firm. There is nothing less corporeal and more empty than the will, nor is it possible to find an immediately visible bond between that silent emptiness, pure compressed energy, and the rampant transformations that it provokes, often without granting any truce before the devastation.

⚜

To Live in the Stream

Talleyrand soon perceived that power struggles would no longer take place on a chessboard where one move followed the other with ceremonial slowness, but within a stream far stronger than everything it swept along. This was the "torrent" of which he spoke, referring to the years of the Revolution—the same torrent we encounter in the pages of so many of his contemporaries. "He could live only in the bustle and the torrent of *affaires*," Saint-Simon once wrote of the Regent. But that which this man who had been "born bored" had chosen as a stimulant was now carrying everyone and everything toward Amazonian cataracts. The torrential stream was not a miraculous accident that disturbed history and then disappeared; no, it was actually a manifestation of the new prevailing impetus—the fever for experimentation—that had become a part of history, transforming it forever. Talleyrand was to find it everywhere, under Napoleon but also under the Restoration, and finally under the bourgeois reign of Louis-Philippe. And he would have just enough time to savor the first fruits of the petty bourgeoisie, by encouraging the rise of Adolphe Thiers, an overeager journalist from the provinces. From an unsympathetic point of view, such as Talleyrand's, the Reaction and the White Terror were relay-runners coming on the heels of the Jacobin race: "I would also like to mention a decree of the Austrian army's Intendant General, Count Wurmser, to show the revolutionary spirit—I can call it nothing else—of those governments which claimed they were making war only against the Revolution, in the person of Bonaparte." As Talleyrand would point out in his note to the Allies dated July 31, 1815, the transition from the Revolution to Napoleon had been a transition from the *esprit d'égalité* to the *esprit de conquête*. And it could be said that with the bigotry of the Restoration, the *esprit de conquête* would achieve its goal of infiltrating all Europe.

Among the many illusions that Talleyrand did not harbor was that of order: he never recognized order around himself, even though he worked to establish it. For Talleyrand, from 1789 until his death, the Revolution never stopped. And he could see that it would not stop for a long time to come. On the eve of July 1830, he wrote to the Baron de Barante: "We are moving toward an unknown world without pilot or compass. Only one thing is sure, and it is that all this will end in shipwreck. The English Revolution lasted half a century. Ours is only forty years old, so there is no way I can hope to see its end. I doubt that even the present generation will witness that end; and unless events on which we cannot rely take place, those who will witness it will have nothing to celebrate. We are embarking on new adventures." For Talleyrand, what was revolutionary was an age in which actions and words, freed from any contingency and loosed like salvos, constantly invaded life, shaping it with rough fingers, forcing it to become a reaction. The intoxication of taking part in forward movement, as if a wave were not of the sea's making but a result of one's own will, was long considered a generous illusion; but in the end it nauseated lucid minds (Baudelaire and Flaubert, after 1848). Viewed from a distance of almost two centuries after that grand beginning, this illusion now merits nothing but contempt; yet it still nourishes the good conscience of the intelligentsia of the West (a West that binds the world like adhesive tape). One continually dreams of going "to the people," and finally shuts oneself up with them in a torture chamber.

For Tocqueville, too, the French Revolution was the start of a *"permanent* state," a new bonding of doctrine and violence that promised to last. Meanwhile a new species of man was ceaselessly at work, offering the world a unity that disintegrated everything around it, just as the monks in their cloisters had once stitched the world's invisible seams amid a civilization rent by invasions. This species is a "turbulent and destructive race, always ready to demolish and unable to build. It not only practices violence, scorns individual rights, and oppresses minorities but (and this is new) claims that this is what must be. It adheres to the doctrine that individual rights do not exist and that neither, so to speak, does the individual; there is only the mass, which is always allowed to do anything in order to achieve its ends." And even if Tocqueville wanted not to recount history but rather to think about it, his description already strays in the direction of the Russian novel: "For sixty years a great school of revolution has always been open to the public in some part of the world—a school where all restless, violent spirits, men laden with debts, . . . went to study and be trained." For example, the University of Berlin, where an uprooted nobleman, Bakunin, with money he borrowed from his friend Herzen, had gone to taste the "voluptuousness of destruction."

The murderous "torrent" of which Talleyrand spoke becomes a "tempest" in Metternich's "confession of faith" to Alexander I, written in Troppau on December 15, 1820—a reference text for all Reactionaries. The last two sentences of it read: "Any major state that is determined to survive the current tempest still has an excellent chance of being saved. A strong union of states based on the principles laid out here will overcome the tempest itself." The roaring whirlpools now gave way to dazzling ice. Reality threatened to freeze its devoted observer. A few days later, traveling to the Congress of Laibach, Metternich felt, like an inappropriate gift, the "first gusts from the south." They melted "the ice covering the windows of the carriage, which at some points was half an inch thick, in less than a quarter of an hour." For a moment he went back in time—no longer a prince but a household servant, and yet happy: "I breathed a new life, as domestics often breathe perfumes when they open a drawing-room door." That moment of suspended intoxication was extremely brief. Soon, the ice loomed up again: "Tomorrow we shall see the avalanche, the sorrowful avalanche of statesmen."

❧

Like a magician, Chateaubriand is continually playing shrewdly and mischievously with the exoteric and esoteric versions of his writing. In this way a meditative, visionary Chateaubriand emerges, embodying both his most laughable aspects and his most sublime, most celebrated, and most secret. On the one hand, we have the Chateaubriand who has tormented generations of students in the lycées of France—the man who always finds the right setting, cleverly arranges the props, adjusts the lights, and then "unburdens himself" in some meditation, with the same facility as the clerk who, during coffee break, tells his officemates about the problems he's been having with his car. Chateaubriand thus manages to keep a safe distance from Waterloo, to reflect calmly on that historic event, while in the background a cannon thunders far away. And so it is truly rare, as he himself admits, for him to cross "the silent and uninhabited halls of the Tuileries without some serious reflections." But his two styles of prose sometimes exist side by side. Abruptly, amid some dark, high-flown, vague inanities, a few wild, alarming lines will break out and then freeze—and immediately we hear the dignified murmur starting up again. In one of his many graveyard meditations (which are often as interchangeable as the discourses on moonlight he used to give before guests at the home of Madame de Villeparisis' father), we find these words: "Could it be that all is emptiness and absence in the realm of tombs? Will there be no lives made of nothingness, no thoughts made of dust? Mightn't these bones perhaps have some mode of life of which we are ignorant? Who knows anything about the passions, the pleasures, the embraces of these dead?"

In the "high politics" of literature, around 1830, an axis takes shape: Chateaubriand–George Sand–Victor Hugo. Worthy sentiments predominate, be they aristocratic and remote, as in Chateaubriand, or served up in brimming ladles from the thick soup of the people, as in George Sand, or hovering on visionary clouds, as in Victor Hugo. Ideals and Lofty Aspirations now become platoons of stern armed guards, stationed outside Art's sanctum. From a distance only their bustling activity can be seen, and now and then the rifles fire blanks, to remind us that the Guard may die but will not surrender, that the heart's realm is always the deepest of all, that an untamed spirit will never yield before the hostile world. Within the sanctum— hidden a bit from the Public's eye, among tents and rags, chests and trunks, caring nothing for Ideals or Audiences—lie the old, cruel lace fringes of Art.

Sainte-Beuve thought, regretfully and sardonically, that like certain wines, Chateaubriand would not travel well beyond the language and borders of France. Because he would lose his "magic, which is all in the syllables." And because he could not survive without his "frame, which is France—brilliant, vain, mad, sweet France." A stranger to ideas, yet indulgent when it comes to images, Chateaubriand is extremely sensitive to the play of sounds within every word; he is a master of the way in which the imperfect tense breathes, and is the inventor of the blue-green syllable. His characteristic orchestral color is found in every particle of his prose, just as Wagner's color inhabits every bar of the *Ring*. The destiny of these works lies as much in their timbre as in the events they recount.

◦❧◦

Exempla Voluptatis

Before devoting herself to fairy tales (like Madame d'Aulnoy before her), Mademoiselle de la Force danced at Ménilmontant with Monsieur de Briou, who knew whole pages of *L'Astrée* by heart. He was handsome, a minor aristocrat, and extremely wealthy. Monsieur de Briou's father was opposed to their passion and locked his son up in a room overlooking the palace courtyard. So Mademoiselle de la Force bribed a traveling showman to take his trained bears to Monsieur de Briou's courtyard and have them dance. Naked and perspiring, sewn into a bear's skin, Mademoiselle de la Force danced beneath her beloved's window. She managed to draw near him and arrange another meeting, while she beat time with her paws. Afterward, the showman handed out a basketful of figs to his bears and led them toward the Pont-Neuf.

"A neighbor who lived near the estate of Combourg had come to spend a few days at the château along with his wife, who was very attractive. Something happened in the village, I don't remember what; we ran to one of the windows of the drawing room to look out. I got there first, with the woman close behind me. I wanted to give her my place and I turned toward her. Involuntarily she blocked my path, and I felt myself pressed between her and the window. I no longer knew what was happening around me."

"A Negress of thirteen or fourteen, almost naked and of singular beauty, opened the gate of the enclosure for us like a young Goddess of the Night. We bought cornmeal cakes, chickens, eggs, and milk, and went home with our demijohns and baskets. I gave my silk handkerchief to the little African. Thus, it was a slave who welcomed me to the land of liberty."

.   .   .

"On those same pavements where dirty riffraff and men in frock coats are now seen strolling, young girls used to walk by in white tippets, wearing straw hats tied under their chins with ribbon, carrying baskets containing fruit or perhaps a book. They all kept their eyes down, and blushed when anyone looked at them. 'England,' says Shakespeare, 'is a nest of swans amid the waters.'"

UNE FEMME CURIEUSE: Voluptuousness is a state of the imagination that precedes, accompanies, and follows pleasure. It can be compared to certain things when they are bathed in moonlight—trees in a park, the steps of a staircase, the silhouette of a country house. A luminous glow brings out their true nature, and a wonderfully soft halo surrounds them.

At the "Bal des Victimes" in Abel Gance's film *Napoleon* (which is faithful to the *Légende* even in *Volupté*), Madame Tallien, Juliette Récamier, and Joséphine de Beauharnais seem like three *déesses* of the Folies-Bergère. They do not move in procession down a brilliantly lit walkway; they merely descend a few gray steps, emitting a "soft luminescence" (as one newspaper wrote), while from the background, through the bars of the prison, the distant light of the outside world haloes their shoulders and coiffures. The film is tinted mauve; the camera lingers on the open tunics of these flappers of the Directory. Bonaparte, a sullen voyeur, draws back into a corner. When the dancing resumes, the camera starts moving again. As the bodies mingle, growing ever softer, it becomes impossible to distinguish the curve behind a knee from the curve of a neck or arm. In this celluloid carnality, *la Gloire* blooms from the sackcloth of revolution.

cৎৡৄ

The Great Ball

With the Congress of Vienna, a new dimension of spectacle appeared in politics. At that prolonged social gathering, no one could believe that the object of the negotiations was the declared one: the restoration of monarchist sovereignty. There was, on the contrary, an eagerness to put to the test, amid lavish orchestration, the *language of concealment* that was to contribute so much to the political process in the decades to come. "The great pronouncements about 'reconstructing the social order,' 'regenerating the European political order,' 'establishing a lasting peace based on a division of power,' etc., etc., were intended to reassure the people and to give that solemn meeting an air of dignity and grandeur. But the true aim of the congress was *to divide among the victors the spoils taken from the defeated.*" Frédéric de Gentz made this observation in his memorandum of February 12 to the prince of Caradja, hospodar of Walachia. But a division of spoils among the victors is the aftermath of any war. If a discerning observer like Gentz felt the need to remark on this, it was precisely because he sensed that the pomp of the congress, far more than its final decisions, was its real novelty. A new aesthetics of politics was revealing itself. And Gentz sensed this so strongly that he wanted to record *in limine* the persistence, behind the mask of grand pronouncements and balls, of the ancient, indomitable object of politics: the "division of the spoils."

Metternich noted in the margin of Gentz's memorandum that this text was influenced by the "distinctive frivolity" of the author, though he nevertheless credited him with "the rarest of intellectual talents and a genuine treasure of positive knowledge." According to Metternich, Gentz had a bad habit of placing too much faith in his own impressions, "which were often formed on the basis of social conversation." But wasn't the congress precisely this—a constant stream of social conversation, in which spies and ladies played no less of a role than ministers and sovereigns? Metternich knew this better than most, and his final comment on the memorandum confirms it: *"All in all,* this report is correct."

At the Congress of Vienna, for the first time at a meeting of Western powers, there was a concern for popular consensus. Fear made this new precaution necessary, demanding innovation in language and manners. Talleyrand, as always the first to understand, could say calmly that at the congress he defended "the cause of the people." How could such a reversal have come about?

History, brilliantly, had made time rush backward. Those rulers of ancient dynasties turned up in Vienna just like parvenus, like primordial usurpers. The Napoleonic disease had infected them all. Napoleon's most perverse achievement was to erase that long period through which monarchs had lent *douceur* to their power. Now they all seemed lucky subversives, who nevertheless had to impose an invented patina of history on the cruelty of their rule. So they all fell into the trap of legitimacy, which Talleyrand had set. And they came out with "great pronouncements" meant to allay the fears of the people.

In their shortsightedness, they thought those pronouncements would suffice to keep them going for a long time. They did not take into consideration that those words were drugged: anyone who used them once would be driven to use them to an ever greater extent, and ever more frequently, until he was cocooned in them and had to require his subjects to use those same words, for in the meantime they would have become an essential instrument of power.

Yet a few months before the opening of the Congress of Vienna, this new trajectory of the word had been described from a perspective that gave a glimpse of the Stalinist trials. *On the Spirit of Conquest and Usurpation,* by Benjamin Constant, had been issued by the printers on January 30, 1814:

"Despotism banishes all forms of freedom. Usurpation, in order to justify overturning what it then replaces, needs those forms; but in seizing them, it profanes them."

.   .   .

"The despot forbids debate, and demands only obedience. The usurper prescribes a ludicrous test as a prelude to approval."

"There is no limit to tyranny when it seeks to obtain the signs of consensus."

"It was usurpation that invented those so-called popular sanctions, those speeches, those monotonous congratulations, the customary tribute that in every age the same men pay, with great prodigality and in almost the same words, to the most contradictory measures. In them, fear apes all the appearances of courage, to congratulate itself on its own shame and to express thanks for its own misfortunes. A peculiar stratagem that deceives no one! A game that impresses no one and that should have succumbed long ago to the arrows of ridicule! But ridicule attacks all and destroys nothing."

"In brief, despotism rules with silence and leaves man the right to remain silent; usurpation condemns him to speak, pursues him into the private sanctuary of his thoughts, and, forcing him to lie to his own conscience, robs him of the last consolation of the oppressed."

"Usurpation brutalizes a people while oppressing it—accustoms it to trample on what it respected, to court what it despises, to despise itself. And if usurpation manages to endure for any length of time, it actually makes impossible any freedom or improvement after its fall."

To be sure, these words describe the transition from Stalin to Brezhnev far more than the fall of Commodus or the effects of the Napoleonic empire, as Constant must have believed. But they also herald the reign of those paradoxical legitimist usurpers who, not long after, would mingle their whispers at the Congress of Vienna.

Constant mentions almost in passing one of the most bitter and incomprehensible truths for those contemporaries who, like Talleyrand, had been born in the age of *douceur*, when ridicule was still lethal: "But ridicule attacks all and destroys nothing." Here he was enunciating one of the *arcana imperii* of Sovietism. And one of the chief factors in the political strength of the Soviet leaders was precisely their understanding of this. If people use ridicule excessively—every day, relentlessly—its destructive power can be completely neutralized. Perfection is achieved when anti-Soviet jokes become part of the regime. And the results will be all the more fertile and lasting if this happens to the Russian psyche, which (as Gogol and Dostoyevski have demonstrated) is a virtuoso at "despising itself."

The theory of legitimacy, as it triumphs through Talleyrand at the Congress of Vienna, is based on two axioms of public law: "Sovereignty cannot be acquired by the simple fact of conquest; and it cannot pass to the conqueror if the sovereign does not cede it to him." The first point, however, prevented any tracing back to the source, because conquest casts its shadow so far into the past: one always finds some oppressed natives. The second point failed to offer a solution in cases where sovereignty is abandoned without being ceded: here there is a lacuna, a lack, as in the silent law of nature regarding the written conventions that sanction it. In political reality, too, there is need for a sanction—and it will be the "sanction of Europe." Here Europe presents itself for the first time as a *second nature,* a mystical body ("an almost mystical community of states," as Guglielmo Ferrero wrote) that has the power to confer sovereignty. In conclusion: it was recognized that nature's ordinances did not extend to all situations in life, but at times had to be supplemented and replaced by a second nature, identified as Europe. The insoluble problem for which the Congress of Vienna was trying to find a solution was not so much political as epistemological. The political solution was a shrewd pretense; as for epistemology, it could wait. But the scant plausibility of the whole thing was apparent, because the body of Europe was not "mystical"—or no more so than Madame de Krüdener, adventuress of regeneration, who traveled under the banner of the Holy Alliance. To cover this defect, after the Congress of Vienna a wave of rhetoric in favor of Order began to surge, and it has continued unceasingly ever since. Those roaring waters then became mixed with the increasingly angry enemy rhetoric, which was democratic and revolutionary. Baudelaire lifted his gaze from that dull swell to gather *les fleurs du mal* from the cliffs.

The right of conquest, which establishes its own law, takes us back to the arbitrariness of the linguistic sign. Legitimate sovereignty takes us back to the *lingua adamica,* to the sounds that express the secret names of things. Now, a grammar of Adamic language has never been reconstructed. And grammar is the action of language. The primacy of praxis sought to erase even the memory of Adamic language. But memory endures longer than action.

⁂

Treacherous Trifles

It was surely not reason, manipulated by unbelievers, that frightened Pascal. With a few fencing feints he could have run it through. What disturbed him, on the contrary, was the credulity of those unbelievers: their tendency to abandon themselves to precariousness while remaining fully aware of that precariousness, keeping their faith in momentary simulacra intact. A less modern believer, of that species which Pascal could not and did not want to belong to anymore, would never have become so irritated. He would have pointed at the world and the stars, would have suggested listening to the signs of the divine economy that echo there.

Pascal shared with the unbelievers a perception that the divine was absent from the visible world. For him, the world could serve only as a theological catapult for flinging us into something that disdained contact with the world. But proof by absence is the hardest. Observing men's rapt involvement in their amusements—their horrific gravity as they stalked their prey during a hunt, or rehearsed a dance step, or fingered fabric—he recognized in them the derided image of ancient worship, when the signs of the world were enough to fill the soul with awe.

.   .   .

Fénelon, in his implacable sweetness, could clearly see the enemy of his spiritual counsels: "Within, you must overcome your taste for the delicate life and your haughty and contemptuous spirit, together with your long habit of dissipation," he wrote to the Comtesse de Grammont. That new form of evil might appear bland, yet such an idiosyncratic whirlpool acted "like a torrent that sweeps all away, in spite of the best resolutions." The absolute rule of the nobility, hierarchic distance, detached now from any contact with the land, any exchange of feudal obligations, any immediate function, and abandoned only to the cruel game of Court favors, was rediscovered, revived—even to the point of tacit fanaticism—in the refinement of taste, in the pursuit of delicacies, in the gradual discovery of a unique style. And in the end, haughtiness came to play a major role in all this, as in some argument over a stool or a seat in a carriage. In each of those sudden, impassioned excesses of sensitivity, Fénelon recognized "the breaches the world has made." Thus, the pleasures of conversation could become lethal—could become virtually the most concrete and lasting image of ultimate Evil: "It will be impossible for you to abstain too strictly from the pleasures of social conversation."

Pascal intended his *Pensées,* which is read today as the breviary of inner restlessness, to be an arsenal of sharp, deadly weapons, to be unsheathed in the world. The vibrant urgency of the annotation is not aimed at likening writing to the throbbing of the soul (how futile that would be!). It is the impatience of someone who wishes to be an instant ahead of the enemy in delivering his blow.

The Modern is born when the eyes observing the world discern in it "this chaos, this monstrous confusion," but are not unduly alarmed. On the contrary, they are thrilled by the prospect of inventing some strategic move within that chaos, a new game that makes all the previous ones seem Ciceronian. It is a godless gaze of which only mystics are capable (Pascal was foremost among them).

☙

The History we are dealing with here is "synoptic and simultaneous." It is the immense carpet without borders, where "it is possible to juxtapose and knot tightly together, before your eyes, the most disparate or distant events," where events and comments on events and stories about events and the ghosts of events remain perpetually enmeshed on a bed of torture and pleasure, where forms and forces cannot disentangle themselves, where the gaze has always been exposed to the "terrible danger of touching symbols." Any judgment here is a thread lost in the tangle of the carpet, and its sole claim is that it has added its faint color to the texture of the whole.

Talleyrand: "There was something in Necker that kept him from foreseeing—and fearing—the consequences of the measures he himself was taking. He was convinced he would have complete power over the States General, and that the members of the Third Estate in particular would listen to him as to an oracle, would see things only through his eyes, would do nothing that was not approved by him, and would not use, against his advice, the weapons he was placing in their hands. This was a short-lived illusion. Thrown off that peak where his amour propre alone had set him and from which (he arrogantly thought) he was dominating events, he repaired to his refuge to weep over those ills he had never intended to cause, those crimes which horrified his rectitude but which, if he had been more skillful and less presumptuous, he could perhaps have spared France and the world.

"His presumption made him absolutely incapable of seeing that the movement then taking place in France was the product of a passion, or rather of the excesses of a passion, shared by all men: vanity. In almost all peoples it exists only in a subordinate form and represents merely a nuance of the national character, or else it is directed with intensity toward a sole object. But with the French, as with their ancestors the Gauls long ago, it is mingled in everything, and predominates in all things with an individual and collective energy that makes it capable of the greatest excesses.

"During the French Revolution, vanity was not the only passion that played a part: it stirred others, called them to its support. But these emotions remained subordinate, took on its colors and its spirit, acted under its direction and toward its ends. It provided the spark and led the movement, so that today we can say the French Revolution was born of vanity."

. . .

Benjamin Constant: "Almost all men are obsessed by the desire to prove that they are greater than they are; writers are obsessed by the desire to prove that they are statesmen. Consequently, throughout the centuries all great operations of extrajudiciary force, all recourse to illegal measures in situations of danger, have been recounted with respect, described with satisfaction. The author, seated tranquilly at his desk, casts opinions in all directions and tries to infuse his own style with the rapidity he advocates for decision making; he momentarily believes himself invested with power, as he preaches its abuses; and his speculative life is fired with all the demonstrations of force and power with which he embellishes his sentences. Thus, he endows himself with something of the pleasure of authority. He repeats at the top of his voice high-sounding words about the people's salvation, the supreme law, the public interest; he waxes ecstatic at his own profundity and is amazed at his own energy. Poor fool! He speaks to men who ask nothing better than to listen to him and who, at the earliest opportunity, will use him to test his theory.

"This vanity, which has distorted the judgment of so many writers, has created more difficulties than one would think during our civil conflicts. All the mediocre spirits who have won a share of authority were inflated with these maxims, which stupidity welcomed all the more readily since they served to cut the knots it could not disentangle. The fools dreamed of nothing but measures of public safety, great measures, *coups d'état.*"

The theory that vanity is a far from unimportant catalyst for great revolutionary events, which might seem a quip on Talleyrand's part, finds solid support in Constant. There is, in fact, a complicity between an emerging democratic foolishness and the megalomania of certain men of letters who are perhaps in a humble social position and now suddenly feel they can govern the world from their desks. All this reaches its climax and its downfall in Max Stirner. His predecessors were timid; they felt the need to camouflage Absolute Power behind some Good, and the first people they deceived were themselves. Stirner goes much farther—even so far as to infer the most radical antisociality (which he attributes to the "unique" and to the aphasic gang of unique individuals) from the presumption that was so widespread in his day: the ubiquitous tendency to tell society what the Good was and force it to adhere to the prescription.

᷒ℨᷮ

Sad Glory

While Napoleon's armies were advancing toward Russia, a cruel war broke out among the rebbes. The Rebbe of Lublin greatly preferred the oppressive decrees of Alexander I to the Enlightenment that Napoleon was thought to be spreading. It is said that one day the face of the Rebbe of Lublin appeared to Napoleon: in the front line among the Russians, he was pondering a strategy to annihilate the invaders. But Rebbe Rimanover saw Napoleon as heralding the last battles before the advent of the Messiah. Once again he allowed himself to imagine that it might be possible for time to accelerate. And he wanted to help bring about Napoleon's victory with cabalistic practices: he compared the baking of unleavened bread to the destruction of the Russian troops, turning a deaf ear to the pleas of many Jewish mothers whose sons had been conscripted. It is said that Napoleon called Rebbe Rimanover his strategist and gave him a mantle for the Torah. But the final sign of Napoleon's defeat came when, in the Sabbath prayer, the Rebbe of Kozhenitz once read Esther 6:13, *nafol tippol* ("thou shalt surely fall"), as *Napol tippol* ("Napoleon will surely fall").

Unmentionable because too often mentioned, washed away by the Legend, he is by now a funereal bibelot of glory on the mantelpiece. His victims are still standing on the "best organic laws," decreed at the Luxembourg, *imperatoria brevitas*, evocation of a spectral nature. "Fatigue, bivouacs, and loss of sleep have made me fat," he wrote Josephine, in his "ill-formed" handwriting and with his appalling spelling. "Horrible and grand" were a good pair of adjectives, which he used when recalling the sight of that "wretched city" (it was Mantua) in flames.

.   .   .

"A very astute usurper, very calm, despite his fits of rage, which are only means to an end; a man of some spirit, if we can call 'spirit' the knowledge of the heart's base side; indifferent to good and evil to such a degree that, unbiased as he was, he would perhaps have preferred the former to the latter, as safer. Moreover, he had studied all the theories of tyranny, and his amour propre would have been flattered to be able to display a kind of moderation as proof of his ability."

Napoleon's legacy: in the cult of the will and in the demand for control; a self-generated tension, a wind-up toy with a long spring. Control is illusory from the outset, but the majesty of the machine it moves nonetheless calls for veneration.

Talleyrand's legacy: in the finishing touches given to things, in the comma that determines meaning (precept of the Duc de Choiseul), in the sometimes almost imperceptible mark that style leaves behind, in the conviction that we are permitted, as a rule, to do *little,* and that this little is at most the result of ephemeral gifts like one's ear, one's sense of *kairòs* (the right moment), lightness, one's agility in breasting the waters of metamorphosis.

"His repugnance and contempt for those who call themselves philosophers are transparent at every moment. When he learned that things in Naples were going badly, that people were dying of starvation, that the new Court did not have a sou, he said coldly: 'That's their business. This is what happens when countries are governed by philosophers.' Nothing is more comical than the way he treats his former colleague in the Consulate, the famous Emmanuel-Joseph Sieyès. 'Well, Monsieur Sieyès, how's the metaphysics going?' 'What do the philosophers say about all this, Monsieur Sieyès?' This is the tone he adopts. Sieyès, for his part, closes himself off in an impenetrable silence." These gibes about metaphysics, reported by Gentz, were one of the finest pleasures that power afforded Napoleon. Yet there was one man who eluded this mockery: Talleyrand, a metaphysician incognito to everyone, even to himself.

.   .   .

We are always someone else's metaphysicians. The ideologue Sieyès was ridiculous in Napoleon's eyes, but Napoleon seemed clumsily archaic in the eyes of the financier Gabriel-Julien Ouvrard, because he failed to recognize the looming power that was to darken all empires: the power of credit.

"Napoleon knew of no sources of revenue besides taxation and conquest," Ouvrard wrote. "Credit was an abstraction for him; in it he saw only the dreams of ideology and the empty ideas of the economists." And once he was impudent enough to speak to Napoleon of what would one day take the emperor's place: "He rose from his chair and, drawing me over to the window, said, 'Monsieur Ouvrard, you have lowered royalty to the level of commerce.' 'Sire, commerce is the genius of states; it can easily do without royalty, but royalty could not do without it.'"

From the start, the figure of Napoleon casts us into difficulties, not only because of his Legend and his excessive fame, which is of a totally new character and no longer Plutarchan, but also because at a certain point we are forced to admit that, as the melodrama evolves, this figure is truly the historical incarnation of the principle of will, of the grand illusion that everything can be established from zero. The zero is the Revolution; the will is the Subject, which begins speaking after the Revolution. Talleyrand is the other pole: from the beginning he understood that the unprecedented history of which he was a part contained a mechanism that acted on its own. He camouflaged himself in it, content to tighten or loosen a screw here and there. Little "finishing touches," which he recognized as the only action still possible. Chateaubriand, who thought he was being cutting, wrote of Talleyrand: "He put his signature to events; he did not create them." This passion for "creating" events, part of the vainglorious legacy of the nineteenth century, linked Chateaubriand to his hated Napoleon. As for Talleyrand, it is certainly true that he insisted on "putting his signature to events" as far as possible, but he did not thereby feel inferior to anyone else who could be said to have "created them." Nor did he take on that role out of pride or calculation; he assumed it for reasons of ceremonial function, since by vocation he was unquestionably the Grand Chamberlain of history.

But that signature, which indeed was a tiny "finishing touch," had no less weight than other, far more influential enterprises, if we look at the haziness of events from a certain distance.

Napoleonic pomp, the imperial geometry that sought to divide the earth into administrative quadrangles, betrayed from the start an insidious weakness: it was corroded by emaciated ghosts. With the painter Girodet, the empty spaces of the sky began to fill with psychic substances that had the faces of the dead; henceforth, feet rested not on the ground but on the arms and fingers of disjointed souls. We see this in his *Apotheosis of the French Heroes Who Died for the Nation during the War of Liberty,* painted in 1802 and destined to embellish the *salon doré* of Malmaison at a cost of twelve thousand francs. Yet for the painter Gérard, the same milky, opalescent substances were evoked by Ossian's harp, which likewise ended up in the *salon doré* of Malmaison. And Jean-Pierre Franque's pyramids emitted vapors from which the wide eyes of deceased maidens emerged, scarcely able to bear their allegorical burdens.

Beginning with the battle of Marengo, Talleyrand saw Napoleon's politics in perspective. At that time he said to the financier Ouvrard: "Two paths are open before him. One is the federal system, under which each prince remains master in his own house after conquest, on terms favorable to the victor; thus, today the First Consul could reinstate the King of Sardinia, the Grand Duke of Tuscany, and so on. But what if, on the contrary, he wants to unite, to incorporate? Then he takes a path that has no end." Talleyrand, in his biological wisdom, possessed a gift: an understanding of limits. Yet he was well aware that the new brand of politics belonged to the unlimited. He also knew, however, that by now "all the levers of the old brand of politics are broken or at the breaking point." Still, Talleyrand could exist only in *les affaires,* the metaphysical name for politics. He would therefore unhesitatingly choose to follow the path of the unlimited, that detour spiced with novelty. The little courts of the émigrés did not attract him; already they were a stagnant mistake. Whereas it would be exciting, and grandly ephemeral, to make the limit coexist with the government of the man whose mission was to eradicate it. The relationship between Napoleon and Talleyrand was a fetish bristling with mirrors and nails. But one thing was clear in their bafflingly complex bond: the immense curiosity that attracted them to each other. For years they tried not to let this be seen, observing each other like two majestic beasts brought from remote and disparate climes and caged together in the same menagerie.

What was Napoleon afraid of after the battle of Austerlitz? On the eve of his most famous victory, he fortunately happened to be in the house of Prince Kaunitz, who had so humiliated the French ambassador during the Seven Years War and who used to clean his teeth at table (Metternich would never have done that). He had chosen Kaunitz's own room: there was a constant stream of "Austrian flags and Russian flags," as well as "messages from archdukes, messages from the emperor of Austria, prisoners who bore the names of all the great families of the empire." Then the courier arrived with the post, "an event which, in war, is greeted with the utmost pleasure." Napoleon asked Talleyrand to look through it in his presence. Letters in cipher from foreign ambassadors in Paris, decoded; police reports; bank matters. But there was also a long report from Madame de Genlis ("never has a woman been so decidedly *écriveuse*"), who reported some cutting comments heard "in the houses of what was then called the Faubourg Saint-Germain." Some implacable old woman had once again spoken disparagingly of him. When he read this, Napoleon was thrown "into a state of inconceivable violence. He cursed, raged against the Faubourg Saint-Germain. 'Ah! They believe themselves stronger than I,' he said. '*Messieurs of the Faubourg Saint-Germain, we shall see! We shall see!*'" Years of bivouacs were to pass before he would be avenged. And years of confinement in a cork-lined room, around a century later, for Proust.

The footsteps of the conqueror resounded in the Tuileries on the day he took possession of the place, accompanied by Count Pierre-Louis Roederer, then Counselor of State. To Josephine he had said, "Come, my little Creole, stretch out on the bed of your masters!" Roederer noted the "gloomy old tapestries and the darkness of the apartments." He said, "General, this is sad." And Bonaparte, knowing that the reply would promptly be transcribed among the counselor's papers, replied, "Yes, like glory."

Education is paradoxical in that it is largely composed of things that cannot be learned. Or of things that stand for what cannot be learned. Napoleon wanted to be surrounded by it, because he knew that nothing exists without it; but he wanted it to be present in *a single person,* on whom, at the right moment, it would be easy to concentrate his own hatred. To Napoleon, Talleyrand was education in that he was the past, the Rosetta Stone before the eyes of the conqueror. All the rest of the imperial train were engaged in a furious masquerade—stiff, virtuous, and pompous, because they were afraid of being ridiculed. Napoleon's secret bane was legitimacy; *therefore,* with the false logic of autocrats, he wanted to surround himself only with legitimate couples. He forced even Talleyrand, bishop and libertine, to marry. Thus ended the reckless, particolored years in which "husbands and wives in high society rarely saw each other and never quarreled. From the time of Napoleon, husbands became pretentious, their pride reawakened by the whim of a despot who decided that moral behavior should be practiced and who ordered women never to appear in public without their husbands." Stendhal explained the reasons for all this to the incredulous English: "In establishing a new court, this despot feared above all else the effects of ridicule, which in France is fatal and would surely have ensued if his freshly minted nobles had aped the follies and vices of the old nobility. Eager to avoid any irritation caused by the frivolities and scandals of a licentious court, and preoccupied with more important concerns, he thus commanded, with his iron will, that regularity and decency be the order of the day." But among those silenced ladies, among those adventurers whose feet were aching in their tight new dancing shoes, there was one person who moved fluidly, as if giving it no thought. Beside the heavy, dignified tread of the others, he made the light, mocking step of his lame foot heard. Talleyrand was the only one who could strike Napoleon with the weapon that left the great strategist helpless: *persiflage.* Until the end, when Talleyrand was in disgrace and many felt they could insult him with impunity, Napoleon knew that the Prince was still the same man who at the time of the Consulate had once invited him to the hunt at Auteuil. Stendhal, the chronicler who was most sympathetic to Napoleon, tells the story this way: "Talleyrand had a country house at Auteuil, a little village between the Seine and the Bois de Boulogne. 'I shall come to lunch at your house one of these days,' Napoleon said to him. 'I should be delighted, *mon général*,' Talleyrand answered, 'and since my house is very close to the Bois de Boulogne, you will be able to amuse yourself with a bit of shooting in the afternoon.' 'I do not like shooting,' Bonaparte replied, 'but I love hunting. Are there any boars in the Bois de Boulogne?' Bonaparte was a young man then, and having lived in Paris only a short time, he did not know that the Bois de Boulogne, like your Hyde Park, is simply a place to go strolling or riding. To find a boar there was obviously completely impossible. But a Frenchman can never resist the idea of playing a joke, even if it is at the expense of those to whom he pays the most servile court. Talleyrand, who takes great pride in his nobility, could not but feel displeasure at seeing a humble artillery lieutenant rise to popularity and power, not by reason of his high birth but by the vulgar means of intelligence and merit. His malicious nature thus prompted him to play a nasty joke on Napoleon, and when the latter asked him if there were boars in the Bois de Boulogne, he replied: 'Very few, *mon général*, but I dare say you will manage to find one.' The dinner and the hunt were fixed for the next day and it was arranged that Bonaparte would arrive in Auteuil at seven in the morning. Barely able to restrain himself from laughing to the point of tears, Talleyrand had two huge black pigs brought from the Paris market. They were transported at once to the Bois de Boulogne by two servants, who were ordered to set them free and make them run. Bonaparte arrived at Auteuil at the appointed time, accompanied by an aide-de-camp who already looked greatly amused, as the general kept talking about hunting in the oddest way. After breakfast, the company went off toward the Bois de Boulogne, taking along some hounds borrowed from neighboring peasants. Finally, one of the pigs was set free, and Bonaparte exclaimed, happily: 'I can see a boar!' Talleyrand, well aware that the animal would not flee at once before its pursuers, had given orders for a servant to chase it, mounted on a little Spanish horse and armed with a long whip. But Bonaparte was too intent on the hunt to notice this detail. So he set off galloping furiously on the trail of the supposed boar, which, after half an hour's chase, was finally taken by the hunters. The aide, who was beginning at this point to catch on and feared that the story would be exposed to public ridicule, decided to undeceive the general and, stopping him, said: 'Sir, you realize of course that this is not a boar but a pig.'

"Bonaparte flew into a violent rage. Immediately he galloped off toward Auteuil. He would no doubt have remonstrated bitterly with Talleyrand, and would probably have passed from words to deeds if he had not recalled the fact that Talleyrand was on intimate terms with all the highest society of Paris, and that this society would have mocked him if he were to take the whole affair too seriously. And so, when he reached Auteuil, he decided to make a joke of it all, but he could barely conceal his fury. Incredible as it may seem, Talleyrand, who was in excellent humor, immediately decided to make fun of him once again: Come now, General, it's true that the boar hunt was a disappointment for you. But it's not too late. Do not go back to Paris just yet. There are quite a few rabbits in the Bois du Boulogne. Louis XVI often used to hunt them. Door-locks and rabbits were the favorite amusements of that poor man! As you are aware, he was an excellent marksman. 'Yes, but I am a very indifferent marksman,' said Bonaparte, who still had not regained his good humor. 'Your ride must have given you an appetite,' Talleyrand continued. 'While you sit down at table and refresh youself, I will have my guns brought from Paris. They belonged to Louis XVI.'

"They remained at table for two hours, during which time Talleyrand went out of his way to cover the future emperor with the sort of elegant flattery he knew so well how to use. In the meanwhile some servants had been sent to Paris with the order to buy all the rabbits they could find. They acquired at least five or six hundred and brought them to the Bois de Boulogne, in a number of hired carriages. Bonaparte set off, armed with his rifle, and again accompanied by his aide. 'I'm not Louis XVI,' he said. 'I surely won't kill even one rabbit.' Nonetheless, he quickly killed quite a few. The aide, seeing the seriousness with which Napoleon slaughtered the poor animals, while talking constantly of Louis XVI, could not contain himself any longer and burst out laughing. When the fiftieth rabbit had been killed, Bonaparte at last seemed happy with his success. The aide could no longer restrain himself, and approaching his master, he murmured in his ear: 'To tell the truth, general, I am beginning to believe these are not wild rabbits. I suspect that rascal priest has played another joke on us.'

"Bonaparte, livid with fury, returned to Paris at a gallop. Six months went by before he made peace with Talleyrand, and he probably threatened to avenge himself if his host dared make any reference, in the drawing rooms of the Faubourg Saint-Germain, to shooting boars or hunting rabbits; and it is a fact that these two anecdotes have never gone the rounds in Paris." Even gazing on Moscow as it was being consumed by flames, Napoleon knew that there was one pair of eyes that viewed him as a ferocious hunter of rabbits.

The difference between Napoleon and Hitler was made plain by Léon Bloy, even before Hitler had invented Nazism (the year was 1912): "For those who see into the Absolute, war makes no sense unless it *exterminates,* and the very near future will demonstrate this to us. It is foolish or hypocritical to take prisoners. Napoleon was certainly neither a fool nor a hypocrite, but this supposed executioner was a *sentimentalist,* always ready to pardon, a magnanimous man who in spite of everything believed in the magnanimity of others, and we know what this incomprehensible illusion cost him . . . He was not, therefore, the monster that is required for total, apocalyptic war, with all its consequences—the abyss of war invoked by the abyss of turpitude. And it seems obvious that he will prove not to have been the precursor of this demon."

It is the Spanish war—rather than the Russian campaign, which displayed the recurrent ordeal among the powers—that holds the still only partly deciphered key to Napoleon and prefigures events which would devastate history. The war in Spain is the earliest successful vendetta of weakness over strength. The dour mountain people, the "proud and filthy beggars" who cruelly harried the French troops and were the first who "dared to fight as irregulars against the first modern regular armies," are not only the forebears of the Partisans (and later of the guerrillas and the terrorists), flouting all strategy and order, as Carl Schmitt has shown; they are also the precursors of a vast dark shape whose features are only now becoming clear: ethnic revolt, the rejection of the West as a soft epidermis superimposed on all lands, suffocating them. At ever shorter intervals the epidermis splits, as in Iran with the ousting of the Shah and with the murderous fury of the *mostazafin,* the disinherited paupers, which bring us back to the Partisan. Behind the Partisan is the Pauper. And it is the intertwining of these two figures which gives them their power to spread everywhere—as well as their capacity for self-deception. For the Partisan will tend (and always has tended, without knowing it) to serve an "interested third party," who in the end dispossesses the rebels more subtly, turning them into docile agents (but will it always be this way?); while the Pauper will tend (and always has tended) to seize the weapons of the Rich, in order to be even more harshly oppressed by other Paupers. This bitter revolt, this rejection of the West, which is achieved by exploiting all the flotsam of the West, all its words chopped into sharp fragments, is a belated, furious reply to the purpose which Léon Bloy in his theological sarcasm defined as "the lofty idea of general sacrifice of the poor." In its pure form, the Modern wants to eradicate the Pauper. Indeed, in the most arrogant instance it wants the Pauper to eradicate the Pauper. Thus, it seems fitting that the most widespread massacres have taken place in Soviet Russia, where the Pauper for many years has persecuted himself. But in history this phenomenon—whose rumblings we are only beginning to recognize today in every corner of the world and which will soon invade us from within and from without—first emerged during the war in Spain. Napoleon grasped the military significance of the Partisan (at least in the formula, "We must operate like partisans wherever there are partisans"), but he refused to recognize the new power that would result from the hybridization of Pauper and Partisan. And the disastrous course of the Spanish war was also a result of this. Napoleon did not want to understand and could not understand. He did not want to understand because he was under the illusion suffered by those who truly know human horror: the belief that horror is the same everywhere, and hence that the same cold stratagems that had worked with such success in Italy and elsewhere could also apply in Spain. As Madame de Rémusat observed, "One of the great faults of Bonaparte's mind . . . was that it saw all men as essentially the same, and did not see the differences that habits and customs produce in men's characters." He could not understand because he was himself the extension of something that, from then on, would never cease to spread its resilient gloss over the earth. The Pauper who wants to go on being poor, the Pauper who wants only to continue existing, who desires his land more than the development of his land, the "wretched ingrate" who spurns the offer of money: they are an outrage and an obstacle (for Napoleon and for the world that succeeded him). They are the most insolent expression of the resistance of matter (and then of "human material," which is now the object par excellence), of the opacity, the impenetrability, the signal of the fierce revolt of the land against its hasty, impatient surveyor. Only one charge can be laid against Napoleon, as was observed by Bloy, who did not fear risking the blasphemous mixing of the Legend with the Vulgate. He drew up "a famous code in which the nonexistence of the poor is taken for granted." Moreover, he dared to say, "I attribute great importance and glory to the elimination of begging." The bloody demonstration of this is still being acted out. "*Begging is forbidden.* He had abolished the Pauper, and that was his crime—which has been perpetuated."

Ↄ&ↄ

"The Mysterious Strength of Legitimacy"

A vicious circle: Legitimacy is the only force that guarantees the continuance of a government; but for a government to become legitimate, it must already have lasted a long time.

"The revolutionary spirit is right in maintaining that the principles of legitimacy are limited, conventional, fluctuating, easily undermined by reason; we, too, admit this. Nor is it mistaken when it states that those principles seem right and true only because men, in debating them, never exceed that point beyond which their weaknesses would be revealed. But it is mistaken, and shows its ignorance of the world it periodically ruins, when it confounds those principles with all the other fragile conventions of which social life is full. However fragile these principles may be, they differ from the others because they are endowed with a magical virtue: whenever men are tempted by Evil to violate them, they are seized with fear—the sacred fear of the violated rule."

"The secret nature of the principles of legitimacy is the power to exorcise fear."

On July 25, 1820, from Valençay (where the legitimate king, though he had been brought to the throne by Talleyrand, forced him "to avoid engaging in anything that he knows how to do"), Talleyrand wrote a letter to the duchess of Kurland with an esoteric postscript: "The mysterious strength of legitimacy is being lost because it has not been understood. All the men of revolution reduce it to a means of preserving the power of kings, whereas it is first and foremost a requisite for the peace and happiness of the people, as well as the most solid and even the only guarantee of the existence and continuance of nations. The legitimacy of kings, or rather the legitimacy of governments, is the safeguard of nations, and for this reason it is sacred . . ."

At the very moment Talleyrand uncovers the principle of legitimacy and measures all his actions against it, he nonchalantly neglects it in his acts. He signs the armistice of April 23, 1814, without any mandate: the king is not yet in Paris, and the intervention of the senate is, in everyone's view, a very flimsy stratagem. But Talleyrand wants to *precede* the king, who would make his negotiations more difficult. His secret thought is: *La légitimité, c'est moi.* There will always be time later for a feigned absentmindedness, as in his *Mémoires,* when he writes that he signed the armistice in his capacity as minister appointed by the king.

That secret thought was surely not aberrant, nor did it serve to flatter his ego—this would have been ludicrous to a man who had such a sense of style. Rather, once again, it foreshadowed a simple realization. Already at the Congress of Vienna, Talleyrand had seen that Wellington and Castlereagh were having some difficulty grasping the meaning of the word "legitimacy." As for the court of Louis XVIII, it could only come to resemble that of Ubu, as Bloy would have recognized. But the final confirmation was to come a few years later, with the revolution of the parvenus. Although an Orléans, Louis-Philippe waited nervously for the European courts to recognize him. He had sent Colonel Atthalin to St. Petersburg with a handwritten letter announcing his accession to the throne. Nicholas I allowed a fortnight to pass before answering. What was all this he had heard about barricades, alarm bells, and shooting? Then one day he read in the *Moniteur* that Talleyrand had been named ambassador to London. And to him this seemed enough. He said, "Since Monsieur de Talleyrand has aligned himself with the new French government, it must have a good chance of lasting." And so Colonel Atthalin finally received a reply. The Czar of all the Russias recognized the new King of the French. He had chanced upon legitimacy in a newspaper.

The captivating story of Western metamorphoses involves a whole series of "theological insurrections." How, after the priest Melchizedek, *auctoritas* and *potestas* become separate, how they are allied and how they clash, how one is subordinated to the other, how they exchange homages, how they are nourished and restrained by each other in relation to the many gods of the cosmos or to a single extracosmic god, how earth and heaven are divided, how finally *auctoritas* is absorbed into *potestas,* while injecting into it the spiritual venom that will henceforth render it demonic—all this is primarily a sequence of theological glosses.

The mechanics who perfected, oiled, and set in motion the bulky modern machine were theologians. After completing these tasks, they discreetly withdrew. All that remained was to initiate the least interesting aspect: the shift to action, a series of revolutions. All modern artificialism, which is by far the most efficient device for affecting the world and developing power, finds the seal of its tortuous history not in some secular empiricist but in Calvin. According to Louis Dumont's definition, this artificialism is the "systematic application of an extrinsic, imposed value on the things of this world." The act of operating on the world with such finely honed knives must originate in something outside the world; and it is precisely Calvin who finds that element in the will, insofar as it has the power of arbitrary decision, derived from God, who is "the archetype of the will." Something which is not of this world—and soon will choose to forget that this is its origin—is set in the center of the world and shakes it, claws it, searches it. The most devastating effects of such a will are destined to be felt when nobody remembers that the origin of its power is outside the world, because what is not of this world will no longer be mentioned; people will have to submit to it without acknowledging it. From theology we pass to a sort of black magic whose source cannot be discovered. For it is *in coelestibus.* Thus, in all his convulsions, in his claims to autonomy, in his imperious and groping gestures, "what we call the modern 'individual-in-the-world' has within himself, hidden in his inner constitution, an unperceived but essential element which is not of this world." Yet everything happens as if that dazzling crystal, that almond wedged in the psyche, did not exist. *Graecum est, non legitur;* but the language that is not read is the language that acts.

Talleyrand's ancestral line goes back to the legendary Aldebert. Around the year 1000, he supposedly made the following retort. Hugh Capet asked him, "Who made you a count?" and Aldebert replied, "Who made you a king?" A premature reference to the singular intimacy Talleyrand always enjoyed with the *arcana imperii.* The most dangerous point, for any sovereignty, is its origin. Aldebert touched on that point insolently, and thus proved himself a sovereign. As for the secret of sovereignty, the motto of the counts of Périgord alludes to it: "Re que Diou," "Nothing else but God" (a different but actually convergent interpretation is "No other king, save God"). Sovereignty may be attacked by referring to its origin, but the sovereign overcomes his ordeal when he refuses to be accountable to anyone except to something ("Diou") on whom no one can rely. This is the origin of that truth formulated by Disraeli, a truth that bears directly on initiation: "Never explain."

The elderly princess Isabella Czartoryska had already begun work on the *catalogue raisonné* of her treasures and curiosities, which included a little book containing plans that Vauban had sketched for fortifications, a braid of Agnès Sorel's hair, Madame de la Vallière's prayer book, and autographs of all the rulers of France from François I to Napoleon. In the evening, after her customary stroll on the grounds of her estate, she allowed herself to be questioned by the young Countess Potocka. Once she alluded to the time she had slipped into the study of Frederick the Great a few moments after he had left it: "Before a table covered with papers and maps was a dish of cherries with a note written in the king's hand: *I am leaving eighteen of them.* To one side, an old Hussar uniform spread out on a chair was waiting for someone to come along and mend it. Beside a letter from Voltaire, lying open, was a bill from a grocer, a Court purveyor. A music notebook had been tossed carelessly on a reading stand and, not far from this appeal to harmony, was a curule chair like the one in the Capitol, with the difference that one was of *rosso antico* whereas the other was of rough wood, and nothing concealed its base function." This was the last still-life of absolute power.

❧

Arcana Imperii

Originally power was scattered in one place, aura and miasma.
  Then it was joined in Melchizedek, priest and king.
  Then it was divided between a priest and a king.
  Then it was joined in a king.
  Then it was divided between a king and a law.
  Then it was joined in the law.
  Then the law was divided into many rules.
  Then the rules were scattered everywhere.

❧

The Origins of Sweetness

The fires of Beltane, described by Frazer: "After the cream is eaten, they divide the cake into portions, as similar as possible to one another in size and shape, equalling the number of persons in the company. They daub one of these portions all over with charcoal, until it is perfectly black. They put all the pieces of cake into a hat. Everyone, blindfolded, draws out a portion. The person holding the hat has the last piece. The one who takes the black piece is the person *devoted*, who must be sacrificed to Baal."

Wittgenstein notes, "The fact that cake is used for drawing the lots is also particularly terrible (almost like betrayal through a kiss)."

—When finally we began to wonder what a slice of cake smeared with charcoal tastes like . . .
—Philosophy has spoken of "qualities," but not of what the individual qualities are . . . What is sweetness?

The slice of cake in the Beltane rite is the *méros,* which is the *moīra,* the part that is fate. But it is important to note that the drawing of lots is still bound to a thing and not just to random numbers, which is fate without a body. In eating his own share of cake, the *carline* of Beltane eats himself, his own fate. What happens in his mouth will be repeated in the fire.

"Where you are, you can at least enjoy the sweetness of not hearing [public] affairs discussed." —Marie Antoinette, in a letter of April 1787.

While language in general became drier and duller, some words became charged with radiance; their meaning was multifaceted in a way never to be repeated. *Douceur:* from sweetness to delight to pleasure to slowness to softness to mildness to languor to tenderness to civility to smoothness. It is useless to try to circumscribe what, at different times, for different people, that word contained.

If fate is the indivisible part, sacrifice can be made only by feigning a whole. The "company" of Beltane pretends to represent a single being, and pretends that this being is a whole: the cake divided into so many equal parts. It can then give up *one* part, which is not its own part. To comply with divine sacrifice, which takes place within a whole, the human sacrificers pretend to possess a totality and omnipotence of their own. The only sign that betrays them: the black of the charcoal on the piece which falls to the Consecrated and Damned (the *Devoted* one).

"Thanks to such lasting peace and such perfect leisure, civilization had achieved an extreme sweetness." The history of progress is divided into two phases, separated by a sacrificial interval. In the first phase, for the more enlightened spirits the idea of progress was never separate from that of a constant sweetening process. From crude, harsh material, by polishing and soaking and gracefully smoothing, one would attain perfection without conflict or injury. But what is the subsequent phase? If perfection is the perfect baking of the Beltane cake, the next phase entails drawing lots for the sacrifice. The cake of the idle, which had exuded sweetness, is cut with blind equity by the guillotine. In the heart of progress the demon of the unlimited was stirring, whereas in the heart of *douceur* there was nausea. Once the equilibrium of *bon ton* was achieved, a headlong degradation was all that remained. The smoothest of languages also becomes the most inert; the sharpest arrow—the *bon mot*—becomes a tool of the trade in the vitiated air of newspaper offices. History after the French Revolution is the history of progress devoid of the patina of *douceur*.

After the Revolution, progress forgets sweetness. Its heart does not want it, since it is there that the demon of indefinite process dwells. Its reason does not want it, since reason now claims to be based on the Revolution, hence on the moment when sweetness was killed. And according to reason's immense fallacy, the sacrificial victim was to be seen as the Enemy. Even its legacy could be contagious. When the very memory of sweetness is eliminated, when all history becomes *son et lumière* and no longer cohabitation with protective shadows, then certain well-meaning, distressing expressions begin to appear ("leisure time," "quality of life"), just as people began to talk about "landscape" after nature had already been disfigured.

The nausea provoked by an excess of sweetness corresponds to the moment when the sacrifice should take place. One is nauseated because one feels guilty for having avoided the sacrifice.

The *state of sweetness* is not stable; it is occasional perfection, fleeting and insidious, the *dulcedo* of the mystics. When it becomes stable, sweetness demands to be devoured. Sweetness ends in the knife of sacrifice; sensual pleasure ends in spasms.

Douceur is the patina that is spread over life, that makes it livable—the dust on the butterfly's wings. Producing it requires slow, careful alchemy, long simmering, a gentle heat. But this is nonetheless a fire, which ultimately seeks to kill.

In the end *douceur* shrinks to a murmur, a voice wanting to "recueillir doucement l'esprit gentil des morts" ("gently gather up the kindly spirits of the dead"), as Céline says. Inadvertently it escapes the murderous heaviness of the world, "with its strained, insistent, wallowing characters, clinging to their desires, their passions, their vices, their virtues, their explanations." Ellipsis dots represent the gaps in a fretwork of shadows: ". . . pour parler après ça plus doucement aux choses . . ." (". . . to speak more softly to things afterward . . .").

༄

When the Duchesse de Saint-Simon was appointed lady-in-waiting to the Duchesse de Berry, she was assigned apartments at Versailles: an antechamber and five rooms. The only daylight came from the entrance. The Duc de Saint-Simon took the most secluded of those backstage rooms as his workspace. There he could not read or write without candles, even in the middle of the day. In the great empty idleness which had been forced on him, he heard the ranks come crashing down. Hunched in the stony bowels of the palace, he wondered, throughout the first five years when the *Mémoires* were laboriously taking shape, if what he was doing was not wicked. Thus, his first reader was a friend of his from Court—not at the end of another Versailles corridor, however, but at La Trappe: the priest Armand de Rancé. The Regent, who knew Saint-Simon as well as he himself was known by the diarist, considered him "as unchanging as God and fiercely tenacious." He was an excellent reader. He loved

Rabelais when everyone else found him gothic. So it fell to him unwittingly to set down those words, as if on an ornamental scroll, under the very last of all the delusions of omnipotence—that of the writer who has banished the world in order to possess it in his fantasy, with a rapacity exceeding that of any potentate. That feigned disorder was later to leave Versailles, but would continue to protect itself from the world behind Proust's cork-lined walls.

THE CHEVALIER DE B***: You must not think that Monsieur de Maistre was a harsh bigot haunted by darkening times. He was a lively conversationalist—and more than anything else he wanted the echo of his words to reach Paris, the big city, where he was to set foot too late. He wanted it to travel immediately round those salons that had nurtured *l'esprit* in everything that seemed most execrable to him, and were therefore the only fitting places for it.

His polestar was a belief that he did not belong to the rabble. He viewed his contemporaries as alien to all that was most noble, most tender, most sublime. At best, they might happen to be right. He would often wake up in a mood for revenge, with his sword drawn. Then fury would seize him and he would wish to destroy everything. From the moment I first saw him, behind a moonlit balustrade in St. Petersburg, where the whirlwind of the revolution in my country and a host of bizarre events had catapulted me, I found him the most exemplary and intelligent gentleman that life had ever presented to me.

I had spent my adolescent years under the rod of the Vendôme Fathers; but only the hum of the refectory, like that of an army of locusts, had remained in my ears, along with the solitary voice of a preacher who still used the mild unction of Massillon. I was not prepared to meet a man who combined religious spirit and military spirit with equal fervor. Scarcely had I met Monsieur de Maistre when he was urging me to make good use of my recollections of France, to observe tenderly all the guilty parties who were sacrificing one another with such extraordinary precision. For him, one deed alone was constant in the history of the universe: the shedding of human blood. Once I even thought him mad, when he asked, looking steadily into my eyes, "If we had records of massacres as we have meteorological records, don't you think we might discover their internal laws, after several centuries of observation?" But at once he perceived my bewilderment and apologized, with that immense amiability which counterbalanced some of his terrifying statements. "These things sometimes occur to me simply because, ever since I could think, I have thought of war."

Nothing embitters Joseph de Maistre more than the claim that something of value has been established through human agreement, convention, artifice. *Factice* ("artificial") is for him the worst of insults. When the Americans decide to build their capital city on the basis of a resolution, Maistre shudders as if this were sacrilege. And he immediately adds, "You can wager a thousand to one that the city will not be built, or will not be called Washington, or that Congress will not have its seat there." History then made sure that he lost his overwhelmingly uneven bet. Yet this is no indication of Maistre's blindness, but rather a confirmation of his fears. What most disturbed him was *improbability*, the apparent frailty of the evil that he saw spreading; whereas the truly satanic element was the fact that this very improbability threatened to become fixed, a stable situation, which in fact did happen. Even if Maistre refused to admit it, because it might have mitigated his damning fury, he foresaw that *man*—that aberration for whom the diligent republican legislators were working, that empty word ("Now, in the world, *man* simply does not exist")—could survive, and for a long time, without land, without roots, without any notion of unwritten laws, without any longing for "that indefinable quality which is called *dignity*." What is more, he foresaw that man could easily efface, like a blurred dream, the memory of all those things he had lost. And this would be the most alarming moment, for "if Providence *erases*, it surely does so in order to write."

Those new words would be written on a piece of flesh deprived of memory and would demand vastly increased bloodshed, to inaugurate a world which was no longer largely uninhabited and no longer contained vast wild areas, but which had been thoroughly sifted and trampled by the excesses of civilization.

Adalbert von Chamisso, poet and botanist, traveled around the world with the noble Count Rumanzov. One day their boat, the

Rurik, came to an island that did not appear on their maps. On landing, they soon guessed they were the first Western seafarers to set foot in those parts. The natives proved docile. They worshiped an idol. Chamisso was allowed to see it. A woman smiled from a framed etching. In that wonderful face, Chamisso recognized the features of Juliette Récamier as Isabey had painted them. The two men asked in vain how the etching had come to be washed up on the island. The natives would not tell, because they considered it blasphemy to talk about the origin of the gods.

∘჻∘

Eulogius

A gnostic history, which we lack, is largely made up of *"intersignes"* (as Massignon called them), unusual warnings, coincidences (as historians call them, to avoid them), erratic forms, buried relics, physiognomic marks, constellations latent in the sky of thought. Metternich and the poet Charles Nodier were educated at Strasbourg, a few years apart, in the shadow of Eulogius Schneider, an erudite and bloodthirsty Capuchin. Also in Strasbourg, Metternich took fencing lessons from the same master who had instructed Bonaparte. Nodier tells us that his father, "an enthusiast of classical studies, had determined to make a scholar of me"—with a method all his own. At the age of ten, the boy read Latin authors with an ease he was never to regain. But then he had to move on to Greek. So he was entrusted to Eulogius Schneider, with whom his father was corresponding because Schneider was "the highly learned editor of a German *Anacreon.*" Young Nodier, a bookish dreamer, discovered that his tutor was a despot, "driven to final conclusions by the logic of extermination." His revolutionary society, La Propagande, made a practice of destructive hatred, in the wake of that "long pink-footed pastorale which had been the eighteenth century." Dragged before the spectacle of the guillotine, Nodier listened to one of Schneider's Propagande followers speak "with a choice of expressions so attractively horrible, with such a despairing *anacreontism*, that I felt cold sweat run down my forehead and moisten my eyebrows."

Metternich had a tutor "whose name is associated with the curse of Alsace": he was to become a member of the revolutionary tribunal of Eulogius Schneider. And Metternich's professor of canon law, having become constitutional bishop of Strasbourg, was to appoint this same Eulogius Schneider his vicar general. Then the latter "abjured religion and his episcopate, burned the insignia of his position in public." Recalling those two wicked masters while writing a fragmentary memoir for his family archive more than fifty years later, Metternich wanted to make it clear that they had "never attempted to use violence against my opinions."

Coming down from the Jura, young Nodier arrived at night in Strasbourg and found lodging at "The Lamp" of Madame Tesch, who looked at him lovingly: the boy seemed to her a girl in disguise. His sleep was brief. "At break of day, tormented by an invincible restlessness, I was already walking through the deserted streets, amazed by everything and gripped above all by a kind of ecstasy before that magnificent cathedral, which the ancient world would have included among its marvels. I had never in my life seen anything like that choir of angels and saints which enfolded it with myriad figures and seemed to rise with it to the splendors of the heavenly Jerusalem, emerging from the rich tracery and transparent lace of its miraculous architecture. I was torn from my meditation by the blow of a hammer, and I saw the head of a saint roll to my feet. Another blow resounded, and this time the statue of the Virgin fell, with her child in her arms. I tried to find out where all this was coming from, and I discovered a man perched in the portal, dealing blows left and right, hurling frightful imprecations at those Gothic portrayals of the Lord's chosen. Little by little the populace had gathered in agitated groups, emitting bursts of laughter, grim shouts, and low murmurs. It took me a while to understand such frenzy, which had not yet reached the foothills of the Jura."

Madame Tesch immediately explained to her guest that the Abbé Schneider was now called Citizen Schneider and that his young pupil would absolutely have to address him with the familiar *tu*. This preamble in itself already displeased Nodier. The pupil was received by a grouchy maidservant. "Breakfast was served. It was a plate of oysters, *rara concha in terris*, a plate of anchovies, a bowl of olives, and a mug of beer. Citizen Schneider entered, laid his two pistols on the table, and sat down after greeting me curtly.

"I approached him and handed him my father's letter. Upon reading the first two lines he held out his hand to me, saying something, I do not recall what, in Greek, to which I replied by saying that I had not yet the good fortune to know a single word of Greek. Then he invited me to dinner and, when I declined, to supper. I had no pretext for not accepting. Still, I would rather have taken my supper at Madame Tesch's."

Citizen Schneider appears: "He was a man of thirty-five, ugly, burly, short and commonplace, with rounded limbs and a round head. The most remarkable thing about his livid gray face, blotched with red here and there, was the contrast between his black, close-cropped hair and his thick, dark eyebrows, beneath which sparkled two wild eyes shaded by tawny lashes. Endowed with an immense aptitude for learning and with a wit full of irony, which I found almost always coupled with cruelty, he had nothing about him that touched the feelings, nothing that moved a person, nothing that bound the heart." The first precept Nodier's professor of Greek imparted to him was that he should not mingle for any reason with the "society of the common people," dominated by Saint-Just, for it was "infected by the evil principles of the *moderatism* of the Convention."

As for Saint-Just, in his icy dandyism he did not approve of the learned, rapacious Capuchin. "The man in charge in Strasbourg was the former Capuchin Schneider—versed in ancient letters, strong in his German tongue, a fervent preacher, a spiritual adviser worshiped by women. Even today, in this city where a legend of execration has grown up around him, there are some women he loved (elderly now) who are still inconsolable.

"Schneider was a rabid democrat, in the fashion of the old Anabaptists or the tailor king of Leyden, who claimed to rival Solomon in the number of his women. This monk was insatiable: not content with those who, of their own volition, pursued him wherever he went, he requisitioned women.

"Nevertheless, he wanted to settle down and had just married a woman by means of force and intimidation. He returned to Strasbourg one evening with his conquest, his carriage-and-four making a great racket. It was late for a city at war; the gates were closed, but he had them opened. Saint-Just seized on this pretext, this aristocratic behavior with carriage and escort, and had him arrested that same night in his bride's bed. Next morning the city of Strasbourg, so surprised that its inhabitants couldn't believe their eyes, saw its tyrant tied to the guillotine. He remained there for three hours, in that pitiable position, and left it only to be sent to Paris, to his death.

"While he was thus exposed, Saint-Just was seen on the balcony overlooking the square, observing the suffering man with impassive hauteur. The Catholic populace, seeing the humiliation of that renegade, recognized the hand of God and covered God's and Robespierre's messenger with blessings."

Young Nodier was also there that day, in Strasbourg's main square, facing Saint-Just's balcony. His account clarifies the facts. Schneider had decided to marry in order to obliterate completely any memory of his past as a cleric, which was still held against him. He had chosen an Alsatian woman, beautiful and aristocratic, whose father he had had imprisoned and whom he had noticed in the swarm of petitioners. He set her father free, forcing the man to invite him to dinner. The daughter remained in her rooms. Schneider ordered that she attend the banquet and, in her presence, asked for her hand. Before an answer could be given him, he rose from the table and approached the open window; outside, the guillotine was being set up. The girl begged her father to accept the marriage request and, addressing her future husband, presented a request herself: she wanted to be married at once, but in Strasbourg, not in that little town of theirs, so that the marriage would be gloriously celebrated and everyone would forget the mistresses that, until now, Schneider had dragged in his train. The suitor agreed. The next day—preceded by his hussars of death, in a carriage drawn by six horses, seated beside his beautiful bride-to-be, followed by a squat red wagon on which his nomadic guillotine was set up, and finally by a little carriage in which sat the executioner, a pale, thin, serious-looking man who was the object of everyone's gaze—Schneider made his entrance into Strasbourg. It was half past three in the afternoon, a few minutes after the closing of the gates.

The procession was passing before the balcony of Saint-Just when the latter appeared. "There was a kind of solemn brusqueness in his manner. He did not encourage the cheering of the crowd; indeed he repressed it, with a sharp and peremptory gesture. His thick hair, powdered until it was snowy and contrasted with his straight black eyebrows, his head erect above his high, full cravat, the dignity of his tiny person, and the elegance of his simple attire never failed to have an effect on the multitude. He signaled the procession to stop, and everyone stopped."

His gaze, "shining and deep," already betrayed his wrath. But before he could speak, Schneider's betrothed flung herself to her knees on the ground. "Justice! Justice, citizen! I appeal to Saint-Just and to the Convention!" In a few sentences she told her story. The executioner confirmed it, adding that he had been ordered to remain ready in case the aristocrat refused to grant his daughter's hand. In the end, the betrothed even asked a reprieve for Schneider. At this Saint-Just became furious: "'Reprieve! Reprieve for the Capuchin of Cologne! To the guillotine!' he shouted, in an explosion that was unbelievable in such a methodical and controlled man. 'Have him taken to the guillotine!' 'Am I to cut off his head?' the thin man in the little carriage asked respectfully. 'I haven't that right,' said Saint-Just, quivering with rage. 'Let him go to the punishment that monster has invented! Bind him to the guillotine and await further orders!'"

A little later Nodier saw Schneider, with "his small eyes that seemed melted in their sockets," as he proceeded toward the guillotine, jabbed by the sabers of his hussars of death. Around them the outcries came in waves. Nodier was pressed harder and harder by the crowd and could not see over the heads of those in front of him. But he listened to the words of a volunteer from the Midi, who towered above everyone else and who felt obliged to offer his neighbors an account of what he was seeing.

❦

Metternich knows that, with the greatest efficiency and the greatest economy of materials, he must run a drafty old house afflicted with rusting window frames and clogged pipes. Talleyrand has never identified himself with any house; even when he wears his superb uniforms, a part of him is always on the high road, dressed in rags and playing in the fields, as his uncle once saw him doing as a child. He has never *set foot* in his father's house. There is something in him which is well hidden but brings him closer to the dispossessed and the uprooted—which allows him to understand the new, the barbaric, from within, and to invent shifting strategies so that in the violent course of events it may end up taking one direction rather than another.

Metternich was the great curator of the museum of Europe; like every lucid conservative, he knew that his work could last only a certain time. Talleyrand, on the contrary, aims at survival, moves from one temporary palace to another, regularly sees his books and precious objects sold at auction. He retains only his style, because he knows it is the only weapon for survival that can be trusted. Anyone who, in order to survive, succumbs to the moment and adopts its style will be killed by the moment that follows. Like a Taoist sage, Talleyrand is willing to admit that survival may be infinite. But if it is necessary to die, he knows he must accept this naturally. And even then he strives to hold on to his style, for the last time. "He died like someone who knows how to live," one lady remarked. It has always been a premise of Talleyrand's that the course of events is in itself murderous—and that the whole art of politics is henceforth the art of surviving the grip of circumstances. Thus, his work is more lasting than Metternich's: the legacy of the past is guaranteed not by its ability to be restored but by its capacity to evade a condemnation already laid down, postponing death moment by moment.

"What is history?" asked Jules Michelet. "Specification. The more history specifies, clarifies, characterizes, the more it is history, the more it is itself." The *Histoire de la Révolution française* accompanied him day and night, for almost ten years. He chose to write the last two volumes in complete solitude, near Nantes: "For my voluntary exile I chose the capital of our civil wars. I wanted to finish my book between Brittany and the Vendée." His decisive step had been to lock up his Paris library, taking with him "only the strictly necessary sources." Thus, Michelet retired to a place that could not be touched by the chronic contagion of *other* books, those "silent witnesses" which, by their mere presence, maintain complicity with divergent worlds and hinder the precise hallucination. Before leaving on a Sunday in May, toward ten in the morning, Michelet decided to visit the "principal museum of the *Terror.*"

"By this I do not mean Clamart, where Mirabeau is, as well as Madame Roland; nor do I mean the Madeleine, where along with the king lies the Girondist Charlotte Corday; nor do I mean Picpus, where André Chénier sleeps, with the nobility of France; nor Bourg-la-Reine, where Condorcet was laid to rest. I am speaking of the cemetery of Mousseaux.

"It is the resting place of Danton and Robespierre, of Camille Desmoulins, Saint-Just, Anacharsis Cloots, and Lavoisier.

"The weather contradicted those lugubrious memories: it was bright, mild, already bringing forth blossoms—the weather of a warm spring day caressed by breezes.

"Forgetful Nature! But France is even more forgetful. This place of death where the ground drank the blood of the fatherland, the very life of the Republic—what has it been turned into? 'A roadside tavern?' you ask. 'A place for drinkers?' No, a dubious dance hall! Thoughtless France here dances on her dead!

"This plot of ground, planted with young trees, is a detached corner of the old orchard that belonged to the Mousseaux estate. The grounds, once the property of the Duc d'Orléans, decorated in the Anglophile taste of the late eighteenth century and wretchedly adorned with fanciful architecture and fake ruins that have now become real, is pretty but very sad. It was the site of Marie Antoinette's last promenade (on June 20), and Robespierre on his gloomiest days, in Prairial and Messidor, supposedly often tried to soothe his frenzied agitation there. Afterward it became a place of festivity. In June 1848, Mousseaux was the center of the national workshops, whose abrupt suppression was to drown Paris in blood.

"The bit of orchard that I've mentioned, purchased in 1784 by the Farmers-General as land necessary for the new city walls of Paris, then acquired by the Municipality in February 1793, has been for some time an ordinary cemetery, divided into four sections.

"Eliminated as such, and cleaned out, it was sold. Subsequently it passed into the hands of the Marquis d'Aligre, one of the richest men in France, who in all likelihood knew nothing about any of this and rented out half the land for a dance hall. The rest, closer to the walls, is divided into little stony gardens, where the Parisians fancy they are growing flowers."

❧

L'Autrichienne

Marie Antoinette, her "terrible destiny sown throughout with *intersignes*," entered Strasbourg as a fourteen-year-old fiancée in a crystal coach, and thus drew near the threshold of the excess of meanings that would later overwhelm her. The crippled, the old, and the ill were hidden from her sight, just as they had been hidden from the young Buddha. On an island in the middle of the Rhine, the masters of ceremony had chosen the place where the archduchess was to be handed over, naked, to her husband's envoys. A special pavilion, its rooms decorated with tributes to the future queen, had been built to receive her. In the main hall one's gaze became lost among the vast tapestries, an inaugural gift from France.

Goethe, then a young law student, made several visits there shortly before Marie Antoinette's procession entered the city. Setting foot in the great hall, he saw something frightful. "The room had been hung with a great many brilliant, sumptuous tapestries, which were encircled by rich ornamentation and modeled on paintings by contemporary French artists. Now, I might perhaps have come to accept this style, since my feelings, like my judgment, did not readily reject anything entirely; but the subject was too revolting to me. Those images told the story of Jason, Medea, and Creusa—in other words, they portrayed an example of an utterly wretched marriage. To the left of the throne the bride was shown in the grip of the most appalling death, surrounded by people expressing sympathy and grief; to the right was the father, horrified by the sight of the murdered infants at his feet; meanwhile the Fury sped away into the air on her dragon-chariot. And just so this repellent, atrocious scene would not lack a crowning touch of absurdity, the white tail of that magic bull curled around from behind the right side of the gold-embroidered red velvet throne. The fire-spitting beast itself and Jason, locked in combat, were completely covered by a luxurious drapery . . . 'What!' I cried, paying no attention to the bystanders. 'Is it possible that a young queen, newly arrived in her dominions, could be so thoughtlessly allowed to gaze on images of what may have been the most horrible marriage ever consummated! Among the French architects, decorators, and upholsterers, isn't there a single person who understands that pictures represent something, that pictures work on the mind and feelings, make impressions, excite forebodings? Mightn't they just as well have sent the most ghastly specter to meet this beautiful and pleasure-loving lady at the border?'" But Goethe's young friends tried to calm him, assuring him that nowadays nobody bothered "to look for meaning in pictures; that to them, at least, nothing of the sort would have occurred; and that all the people of Strasbourg and the surrounding towns, who would gather there for the occasion, would no more entertain such fancies than the queen herself and her court."

The cruel recklessness that intoxicated France between the Regency and the Estates-General brought with it, among other things, an attitude of complete indifference toward images, a temporary obfuscation. As Madame Geoffrin said to someone who was boring her with an endless tale: "To be successful in France, one needs big knives and little stories." Big knives were being readied; little stories were being told. And everyone was moving on. But the image takes its revenge on those who do not look at it. The life of Marie Antoinette was becoming ever more smothered by symbols, even as people were taking less and less notice of them around her.

On an island washed by the currents of the Rhine, a wooden pavilion had been erected: "the house of the consignment." There, Maria Antonietta, as she was called in childhood, became forever Marie Antoinette. The consignment took place on the international border, which ran down the middle of the pavilion and through the great table in the center of the main hall. Marie Antoinette entered the pavilion from the Austrian side. In the last room before the border she was slowly undressed before the escort that had accompanied her from Vienna. Not even a ribbon or a hairpin was to remain in contact with her body. She was thus offered, naked, to fabrics woven in the new French land—to the silk shift, the stockings from Lyon, the little slippers fashioned by the Court's shoemaker. Her brief past, domestic and carefree, was to be forgotten. France was taking her as guest and hostage. The softness of the clothes that came to her from Versailles was the embrace of the new god. That pavilion, for Marie Antoinette, was an ephemeral *ghotul* without games, a house of cruel initiation, where the passage through ritual death was noted by the many eyes that were observing her and that would continue to observe her until her biological death. This act of sacrificial stripping effected her complete transfer to the land that was clothing her with her destiny. Protocol is the last power for protecting abandoned symbols. It ensures that symbols, even when they are not perceived as such, can continue to act, often with an added touch of sarcasm. Here an unwitting Psyche was entrusting herself to an Eros who was all too tangible in that silk and lace. The god for whom she was being initiated had a form too precise and too blasé; he no longer lived in a nourishing and protective cloud, could no longer withdraw into the invisible. It would be easy, one day, to strip him in turn. When she was imprisoned in the Conciergerie, Marie Antoinette still had fifteen shifts of fine linen edged with lace, a satin cloak, two dressing gowns, five bodices, and twenty-two batiste handkerchiefs. They were presented in court, those *corpora delicti:* locks of hair, skeins of silk, a little mirror, a woman's portrait, a piece of linen embroidered with a red heart pierced by an arrow. For the French, Marie Antoinette would conclude the Strasbourg ceremony only as the widow Capet, in a dress of white piqué, maliciously sketched by David as she was heading to the scaffold in the tumbril. At the end of the long ceremony in the house of the consignment, after she had crossed the imperceptible frontier in the center of the table, Marie Antoinette hid her head for a moment, sobbing in the arms of the Comtesse de Noailles, her new lady-in-waiting.

A prisoner in the Conciergerie, she asks only to read novels: she wants accounts of "the most frightful adventures."

Her story belongs entirely to the black century, to that metahistorical dimension of vendettas, expiations, blasphemies, and portents which is discernible even in the gossip of those days. Léon Bloy and Louis Massignon are the tutelary genii blazing at the door of the sepulcher. On one side, the execrator of grocers, agent provocateur of the Paraclete; on the other side, the grand vizier of Fatima and the Deuxième Bureau, of Lobachevsky and the Seven Sleepers. Both of them are chroniclers of the *mysterium iniquitatis*.

Inside the oval drawn with a single stroke, counterbalancing the too prominent and childish brow: the protruding, pensive lower lip of the Hapsburgs—that of Charles V bent over his clocks.

The *"Autrichienne"* (as she was immediately called by Mesdames, the three daughters of Louis XV) found implacable enemies *sine intermissione,* from the time she crossed the table in Strasbourg. But blood and the years have clouded people's memories; the faces overlap and blend with one another. Offended ladies of the palace, ministers, *tricoteuses,* sansculottes, favorites, purveyors—all come together in that hatred. Thus, one must go back to the Prince de Ligne, the playmate who conspired with Marie Antoinette to hide in another niche, behind the bust of Louis XIV which loomed over the groves of Versailles, the same bust that sometimes received the greeting of the young Comte d'Artois ("Bonjour, grandfather"). That evening Ligne gave up the idea: he was afraid they wouldn't give him a ladder to climb down from that uncomfortable position and would leave him all night behind the marble bust, perched up in the air.

An immense, enchanting "heedlessness" was the only crime Ligne felt he could attribute to Marie Antoinette. A crime chiefly of repeated "negligence toward boring men and women, who are always implacable." And in order to punish her, a pact was made among those Implacables, who from then on would produce boredom as exemplary English working women produced pins, with a wise division of labor among the dining alcoves of the Third Estate, the tribunals of the people, and the conceit of the nobility, united forever in their intolerance of every sign of frivolity and by their indulgence toward every yearning for mediocrity. Stendhal was to notice this, forced as he was into the vast "insipidness of good company," which moreover had claimed to resuscitate, between 1804 and 1830, the salons of 1780. But this time, surely, without heedlessness.

A baleful insight threatened: Would the ability to generate boredom perhaps make possible the recovery of the lost *bon ton?* The pact remained in effect, and there had been no lack of blood in which to bathe it. The trial of Marie Antoinette was the first, victorious insurrection of the Bores, the only moment when populace and nobility merged in a single mass.

⁕

The Woodsman and the Fisherman

When Talleyrand, romantic adventurer and faithless bishop, went riding through the American forests followed by Courtiade, the most impeccable of servants, he was trying with some difficulty to pass the time and to distract his mind from the dire news every ship was bringing from France. Amid the dense vegetation, far off the beaten path, a cry would sometimes ring out: "Courtiade, are you there?" Back would come the respectful and distant reply: "Heavens, yes, Monseigneur, I'm here." Talleyrand would smile at his own incongruity as a feudal remnant now on the other side of the frontier of *la société,* and he would look around. At such times he had the impression that he was moving against the stream of history, shifting both in time and in space as he gradually left behind him cities, villages, farms, and fields and ended up among the beaver hunters in Connecticut, wading through vast swamps and getting lost in the woods. In those images he seemed to see, decomposing before his eyes, the improbable amalgam of civilization which was returning little by little to its simple elements. "With every day that passes," he noted, "we lose sight of more of those inventions that our needs have made necessary as they proliferate. We seem to be traveling backward in the history of the progress of the human spirit." But that era of "progress" had many surprises in store. As he came up against the absolute basics, Talleyrand encountered two exemplary characters: the woodsman and the fisherman. He drew their portraits, which turned out to be not the profiles of two forms that had been abandoned by history in its earliest days but the foreshadowings of two faces that history was about to assume: the silhouettes of the first *new men,* who already awaited Tocqueville. In their native wilderness they were preparing to take the stage, as representatives of the masses. Indeed, they represented those who, in an age devoid of irony, would be called "mass men." The *odor specificus* of the masses came to Talleyrand not in the city but amid the desolation of untouched nature. It was a curious fact, one to be noted down. Talleyrand attached those two portraits, as instructive clinical cases, to his "Memoir on the Commercial Relations between the United States and England," which he was to read at the Institut de France on April 4, 1797.

The woodsman. "The American woodsman is interested in nothing. Any notion of sensitivity is foreign to him. Those boughs so elegantly sprouted by nature, the fine foliage, the bright color that enlivens a part of the forest, the deeper green that darkens another part—all this means nothing to him. He has no memories to call upon in any particular place. His only thought is for the number of ax-strokes required to chop down a tree. He has never planted anything; he does not know such pleasures. Any tree he might plant is worthless to him, because he will never see it when it has grown sufficiently large to be chopped down. Destruction is what keeps him alive. Destruction is everywhere; hence, every place suits him. He cares nothing for the field where he has done his work, because his work is only toil and no idea of sweetness is associated with it. What emerges from his hands does not pass through all the stages of growth that so touch the farmer's heart. He does not follow the destiny of his products. He does not know the pleasure of new ventures. And so long as he does not forget to take his ax with him, he has no regrets about leaving the spot he has dwelled in for years."

The fisherman. "The American fisherman acquires from his profession a spirit that is almost equally indifferent. His affections, his interest, his life lie on the margins of the society to which he thinks he belongs. We would be prejudiced if we believed that he is an especially useful member of it. For we must not compare these fishermen with those of Europe or believe that this is the way to train sailors—to create sturdy, skilled men of the sea. In America, except for the inhabitants of Nantucket, who hunt whales, fishing is a job for the lazy. The only courage these men show is to go two leagues offshore when there is no threat of bad weather, a mile when the weather is uncertain. And the hook is the only harpoon they know how to handle. Hence, their skill is no more than a little trick; and their activity, which consists in hanging one arm out of a boat, closely resembles idleness.

"They have no love for any particular place and know the land only by the ugly house where they live. It is the sea that feeds them. Thus, their homeland is determined by a few cod more or less. If these seem to decrease in one place, the fishermen move off at once and seek another homeland, where there are more cod.

"When certain political writers said that fishing was a form of agriculture, they made a statement that sounds witty but that contains no truth. All the qualities, all the virtues associated with agriculture are wanting in the man devoted to fishing. Agriculture produces patriots in the true sense of the word. Fishing can create only cosmopolitans."

It was not a La Bruyère of barbarity who spoke in these terms to the members of the Institut, but a sociologist of the age of inflation and of paramilitary gangs. Around him echo Rathenau and Hitler, and the hoboes clinging to freight cars, and the mounted police. We see not the trunks of majestic trees but waste paper fluttering over Wall Street in the Sunday silence. Removing Talleyrand's Woodsman from his frame of sylvan exoticism, we discover Jünger's *Arbeiter:* the uniforms of the soldier and the worker are already superimposed on him, without there being any need to unleash storms of steel. This man is a trigger of technical violence: his place can be any place, because his mind has lost the mnemotechnical *loci* from which it can hang images ("he has no memories to call upon in any particular place"). His shadow is that parasite the Fisherman, whom society absentmindedly counts among its members, though he does not belong to society. His inertia is malign and hostile; he is one of the migrant *Lumpen,* the proletarian starfish.

Woodsman and Fisherman will one day discover they are enemies; for the present, in the American wilderness, they are united in their hatred for the earth that still generously envelops them. It is a hatred for all that grows and that, in growing, becomes sweet and fades. Their pace is different from everyone else's: they strike blows, they pull and tug—gestures that are a metaphor for those of the gambler who rolls the dice. And in this devotion to the blow lies their cosmopolitan mission: the blow is the same everywhere ("destruction is everywhere; hence, every place suits him"); the plant has the flavor of a single place. The garrulous *citoyens* whom Talleyrand had left behind in Paris were still good, solid, agricultural patriots. But they already seemed archaic and out-of-date compared to these two new characters, who, beyond the frontier, were acting out the gestures of burgeoning history.

❧

Goethe in Venice

April, 1790

Gypsy girls like lizards
vanished into the tiny doorway.
Sarcophagi, urns, mold of gondolas,
little verses graze him
like the elbow of a child

as she runs past. Damp, dirty, futile movement,
murky hours in the nest of stone and water.
Foreigners cheated nonetheless.
The gazette tells of the National Assembly.
O Boredom, mother of the Muses!
A single talent remains:
to write the German language
following a tribe of jugglers.
But already the servant disinters among the dunes
a skull from the Jewish cemetery.
And in a ram's decayed muzzle,
sphenoid, ethmoid, shell of the ear,
shines the Original Bone.
From one vertebra
descends the All.

❧

"Thus ends the best day of our lives," wrote the *fédérés* of a French village, concluding their account of the holiday of July 14, 1790, first anniversary of the Bastille, day of the General Federation. "The wedding of France with France," wrote Michelet, and this was only one among the dozens of images that blossomed from his pen for the occasion. He did not allow himself to break the flow of the story with a single note of his own: "Even the smallest would have created an interruption, a discord, perhaps, in that sacred moment." An age beyond recovery, when the Revolution consisted of "innocence and credulity." Moments "prior to the fulfillment" (as was written on the tortoise shell of the *I Ching*), promise of an ultimate Deed, moments which then—in memory, as in lovesickness—become the Deed itself; afterward, "the little fox wets his tail" and the ultimate Deed becomes oppressive. Never push all the way to fulfilled happiness, with its touch of persecution. Stay with the *promesse de bonheur.*

Born of a cross between a bureaucratic innovation (the Departments proposed by Sieyès) and the capture of a prison (the Bastille consumed by erotic flames and cruel family spite), that day set in motion the primordial images which antedated the Temples and the

High Priests and which inhabited the Holy Places, the Altars of the Soil, and the Sacred scattered across the countryside and distributed between sun and shadows.

That this was truly a return to origins is guaranteed by the mark of kitsch, which here authenticates all the images: everything—from the anonymous reports of the provincial *fédérés* to Michelet, to Jaurès, even to the perennial quaver in the democratic Voice—is founded on the oath of that day. At noon on July 14, the town seems abandoned; only an occasional dog crosses the street. "No temple would have sufficed." There are no witnesses: all are participants. The Altar of the Soil is reestablished between sunshine and shade, in the center of the Holy Place; the ranks of the young are face to face, but memory does not suggest the verses of the *Shih Ching*, which respond to one another like the belling of stags. It is Liberty's sad lot to have to improvise. And if the mind, sleepwalking and sailing in the past, moves once more toward human sacrifice, the euphemism of the Enlightenment will produce this scene: "The newborn infant was placed, a living flower, among the flowers of the harvest. His mother offered him, set him on the altar. But his was not only the passive role of an offering; he was also active, he counted as a person, he made his civic vow through his mother's mouth, he claimed his dignity as a man and a Frenchman, he was already given possession of the Fatherland, he took part in hope."

Provincial France was celebrating the ritual in the open country, but Paris had to find a suitable place within its confines. The vast Champ de Mars was chosen, and an invisible architect adapted it sufficiently to give it the ceremonial hallmarks of the Holy Place: no longer a shapeless expanse, but a valley between two hills, leveled by thousands of hands. "By day, by night, men of all classes and all ages, even children, everyone, city folk, soldiers, abbés, monks, actors, sisters of Charity, beautiful ladies, women from the market— all carried a hoe, pushed a wheelbarrow or a cart. Children went before them, lighting their way; strolling orchestras enlivened the workers. And the workers themselves, as they leveled the ground, sang that leveling song: 'Ah! ça ira! Ça ira! He who is raised will be lowered.'" That job of leveling was also the social event of the week.

The Duchesse de Luynes had ordered a charming wheelbarrow of mahogany; she shifted gravel and soil with it, lending a hand in the effort.

On the day of the Celebration, amid vigorous gusts of rain and wind sent by the "good Lord," who is "an aristocrat" (it was said), one hundred sixty thousand people (or two hundred fifty thousand? or four hundred thousand?) watched from the artificial hills of the Champ de Mars, gazing down into the great central valley, where a broad pyramid rose: the altar of the Fatherland. According to one witness, "This altar was a huge construction, a hundred feet tall. It rested on four piers that occupied the corners of its vast square shape and supported some tripods of colossal size. These piers were linked by staircases so wide that an entire battalion could stand on each one. The staircases led to a platform from which rose, with a multitude of steps, a pyramid-shaped embankment crowned by the altar of the fatherland, which was shaded by a palm tree."

A few weeks before the Feast of the Federation, a rich and noble Prussian, Jean-Baptiste Cloots, turned up at the door of the Manège, heading a delegation that called itself the "Embassy of the Human Race." Just as the elusive "general will" spoken of by Rousseau was to be palpably manifested among the hoes and wheelbarrows of the Champ de Mars, so Humanity, this lady that the century had virtually invented, sent her representatives on ahead. "Who are you?" they were asked. "We come from Europe, we come from Asia, we come from America," they replied. "We are Mankind!" Georges Avenel, the inspired nineteenth-century biographer of Cloots, tells of that arrival with the thrill of a dash at the Vélodrome d'Hiver: "The excitement is mounting—the ecstasy is unanimous! Now it's the human race's turn! Between the nation and the human race is a mere finger's breadth. Yes, it's certain: the human race itself is at the door. It's waiting. Make room! All hear it, desire it. It's on its way. Here it is!" At last they appeared before the Assembly. There were thirty-six of them. There was Pio, the Neapolitan; Don Pablo Olivares, the Spanish victim of the Inquisition; Baron von Trench, who for ten years had worn sixty-eight pounds of chains in his Prussian prison. There were Dutch and English patriots. The Turk, the Arab, the Chaldaean were supernumeraries from the Opera, who had just been hired.

Some spectators also recognized, among the others, an interpreter of Oriental languages from the Collège de France and various domestic servants now out of work. Spurred on by the excitement aroused by the Embassy of the Human Race, the Assembly voted that evening to abolish hereditary nobility, with the consequent Fall of Names. The Cloots delegation, sent by the Kingdom of Operetta to announce the imminent infiltration of its subjects into Europe, gave the final impetus to the decapitation of these noble titles. The operetta would henceforth live on their fragrance.

The Feast of the Federation had just ended. Still quivering, Jean-Baptiste Cloots wanted to describe it to the "Sappho of the Gauls," Fanny de Beauharnais, his friend, a virulent writer and Josephine's aunt by marriage: "We won, we triumphed, and you weren't there! Hurry, Madame, hurry. Come and witness the gaiety of the free people who, in their happy enterprise, are taking their place among the Greeks and the Romans. Now we believe in the marvelous tales of the father of history and of his emulators Thucydides and Titus Livy. But I'll not describe to you a solemn ceremony that effaces the memory of all celebrations, ancient and modern. The picture that, for twelve hours, I had before my eyes could never be adequately rendered, with brush or with word. The place, prepared by our own hands, is stunning in its size, simplicity, and situation. Imagine the biggest coliseum in the world, crowned by the lovely slopes of Chaillot, Passy, Meudon, and Montmartre, while the lush boughs of eight rows of trees form a green cravat that envelops the arena and foregrounds three hundred thousand spectators in a charming frame. The arch of triumph, the bridge over the river, the tasteful altar, and the Roman-style palace presented an enchanting whole, with all the flags, all the banners, all the weapons, offensive and defensive, of the French Empire. The cannons, the music, the applause made heaven and earth tremble.

"I was at the head of the foreigners, in the gallery of the palace, in my capacity as ambassador of the human race, and the ministers of the tyrants looked at us with jealous, uncertain eyes. This national celebration takes us back two thousand years, thanks to some indefinable patina of antiquity that is all its own; and it carries us forward two thousand years, thanks to the rapid progress of reason, of which this federation is the early, delectable fruit. I cannot convey to you, Madame, everything I felt yesterday. My heart is sensitive, and my patriotism is ardent. Guess the rest and come as soon as you can."

Limping up to the altar of the Champ de Mars to celebrate the rite was the person considered most evil for the old religion and the new: Talleyrand, then bishop of Autun. It was not the clumsy king or the treasonous queen but the High Priest of the Celebration who was the blot on the affair—the person who guaranteed the presence of deceit at the center of the paradise improvised by the General Will. In addition to everything else, that Will, in its tumultuous vagueness, had needed a slight finishing touch—in fact applied by Talleyrand—in order for the Celebration to take place. To a certain extent, it is indebted to him for that day, which remains most radiant for those who dream of the masses' calm and spontaneous embraces. A month before, speaking in the Constituent Assembly, Talleyrand had been the one to claim that the "Feast of the Federation would never be sufficiently solemn" and had hinted then at the reasons for its usefulness: "Strengthening the ties of brotherhood among all citizens, making everyone aware of all the patriotism that animates the French, it will finally persuade the enemies of the Revolution, if there still are any, that any effort they might make to destroy it would be vain."

As bishop, Talleyrand had not said many Masses. The day before the Celebration, he rehearsed the ceremony at the Marquis de Sais-seval's home on the rue de Lille, together with his friend Mirabeau, who knew the liturgy better than he did; he had learned it in prison, to pass the time. For an altar they used the mantelpiece. The other guests, sitting in armchairs, laughed. Talleyrand's little dog was frightened and bit his episcopal cassock.

The immense procession set out from the Bastille at seven in the morning. The sky was lowering and gray. Repeated downpours. Delays. On all sides the crowd was pressing. The ranks were broken. People crossed the Seine on a bridge of boats. Then everyone, near and far, surrounded the blue and gold velvet tent of the royal tribune. On the steps were the king, the dauphin, and the queen, adorned with tricolor plumes. A throng of banners. Lafayette cantering on a white horse. Three hundred priests in surplices came forward, with acolytes in smocks and tricolor sashes. They were followed by Talleyrand, wearing his miter and leaning on his crook as he limped along. The orchestra rang out—all twelve hundred instruments. Passing in front of Lafayette, who had just dismounted from his steed, Talleyrand murmured to him, "Please don't make me laugh . . ."

At the end of this ceremony—the shrill idyll that inaugurated the age of mass politics—Talleyrand took off his episcopal vestments and had himself escorted at once to a gaming room. He won, and won enormously: he broke the bank. He took his leave. "I came away with more gold than I could carry in my pockets, to say nothing of the paper money." He went to the home of the Vicomtesse de Laval and, in the presence of his friends, poured those streams of gold onto a table. After supper he resumed gambling. He won again, enormously. "I returned to the Vicomtesse, to show her the gold and the banknotes. I was covered with them; even my hat was brimming. And bear in mind: it was the fourteenth of July."

The day after the Feast of the Federation, Talleyrand wrote to his mistress *en titre,* Madame de Flahaut: "If you were as pleased with your place at yesterday's ridiculous feast as I was pleased to see and admire you sitting there, you must have put up with the thunderstorm as philosophically as your friend Sieyès, who in the presence of sixteen people asked me, with that sardonic smile you well know, how I had managed to keep a straight face while so skillfully performing the farce of the Champ de Mars, and if I knew how many Christians among the one hundred thousand spectators had taken the national and Christian oath. I professed my ignorance in the matter. 'According to my calculations,' he said, 'they might come to five hundred, including the Duc [de Biron], you, me, and those of our party.' To tell you the truth, my dear friend, I fear that he overestimated the number of believers. And I will say this: although I am a philosopher, I deplore the people's increasing lack of faith. I share Voltaire's opinion: whether we ourselves believe in God or not, it would be dangerous for any society if the masses thought that no punishment was forthcoming in this world or the next and that they were free to steal, poison, and murder. We live in an age when doctrines contrary to morality have to be feared more than ever, because our laws have no force or support and because the majority of the people consider themselves superior to them. And what is most deplorable is the interest the Assembly takes in stirring up this spirit of *political and moral anarchy* among the populace. I am well aware that it is hardly gallant to beguile one's beloved with philosophical reveries. But to whom could I confide my most secret thoughts if not to you, who are above the suspicions and prejudices of your sex? . . .

"As for myself, let me say confidentially that I don't know who is more pitiable: the sovereign or the people, France or Europe. If the Prince relies on the affection of the people, he is lost. And if, for their part, the people do not maintain their guard against the character of the Prince, I foresee frightful events: I see streams of blood flowing for years, blotting out the enthusiasm of a few months; I see the innocent caught up in the same devastation as the guilty. Whatever may happen, either the cause of freedom is threatened, or the serenity of France is compromised.

"Far be it from me to suspect Louis XVI of being thirsty for blood, but a weak monarch, surrounded by bad advisers, easily becomes cruel, or (which amounts to the same thing) his weakness allows certain cruelties to be carried out under the authority of his name. However I view the consequences of yesterday's events, I tremble for the future . . .

"Burn this letter."

The unreliability of the historian. In the opinion of Louis Madelin, a distinguished Napoleonic historian, accounts of Talleyrand's remark to Lafayette during the Feast of the Federation are unreliable, because it "doesn't have the ring of truth." Chancellor Pasquier, who repeats the remark in his *Mémoires,* claims to have heard it from Lafayette himself. But Madelin insists that Talleyrand "was not a sacrilegious babbler; and Lafayette, an extremely serious character, was never capable of making anyone laugh."

Between the Fall of Names, indirectly provoked by Cloots's embassy, and the Feast of the Federation, Michelet is overcome by pathos; swept away by the eloquence of great moments, he bows before "the prophetic symbol." But in addition, bombast tactfully serves to protect the radiant nucleus of the Revolution: "In this system there is no handing down of antecedent merit, no caste of nobility. But there is likewise no handing down of prior guilt." The task of the Revolution is to efface original sin. Abolishing privileges that come with birth is only the exoteric aspect of a far more radical abolition: that of the guilt of the race, the guilt of Adam, the reprieve of original sin. Evil is henceforth reduced to an act that is consciously willed by an individual; it is not a legacy weighing on the fabric of life regardless of all will and consciousness, leaving its mark on everything. Here Michelet suddenly becomes a theologian. And from the shadows he evokes his adversary, Joseph de Maistre—the theologian who, in speaking of the Revolution, will always and regardless of circumstances speak of ineradicable original sin.

What is immediately striking about the Feast of the Federation is the nakedness of the symbol. When symbols rise again from sleep, from neglect, from mockery, nobody recognizes them—and then they demand to be transformed into Deed. The ghost that guides the Revolution is that of the *coniunctio,* of the Sacred Marriage. But the dawning act of union declines at once toward unity: "Alas! experience of the world teaches us the sad fact, strange but true, that union often dwindles into unity." So it happens that "yesterday, the Revolution was a religion; now it is becoming a policy." Yesterday, in Michelet's dream, the Feast of the Federation was celebrated; now it is the massacre that will be carried out, exactly a year later, in the same Holy Place.

Lafayette's white horse caracoled once again across the Champ de Mars on Sunday, July 17, 1791. The ceremony was still laughable, but this time it would recover the symbol missing the first time it was performed, the one that can stand for all symbols: the shedding of blood.

According to Michelet, "perhaps the fiercest royalists were not the nobles or the priests but the hairdressers." The slogan of the age— "Return to nature"—had pierced them to the heart. "Everything was moving toward a frightening simplicity." One of those hairdressers, unemployed and lustful, began roaming through the Champ de Mars on the night of July 16. He had a nasty little idea of his own. He wanted to hide under the planks of the altar of the Fatherland, to observe from below the ample flounces of the skirts of his lost customers, "the haughty republican women, the tribunes in bonnets, the orators of the clubs, the Roman matrons, the literary ladies," who soon "would climb up there so proudly."

The city was restless; the Assembly had just decreed, after some debate, the "inviolability" of the king. But opponents had drawn up a petition asking that "neither Louis XVI nor any other king" be recognized, and had brought it to the Champ de Mars. The people were to sign it that Sunday, on the altar of the Fatherland. The hairdresser chose as his accomplice an old, disabled veteran. They took some food and a cask of water. Hidden in the darkness, they began making holes in the planks with an auger. But early in the morning an itinerant peddler, a woman already waiting on the altar of the Fatherland, heard a strange noise under her feet: the two rogues were still at work with the auger. They were discovered. Soon a crowd had surrounded them. The fearsome laundresses of the Gros-Caillou came running. The rumor spread that the men had been caught with a keg of gunpowder and that they wanted "to blow up the people." A little later, their throats were cut. Toward nine in the morning the two heads were carried in procession to the Palais-Royal. Then began a sequence of orders, counter-orders, intrigues, murmurs, misunderstandings, rages. The crowd meanwhile was gathering on the Champ de Mars. Many signatures, many X's were added to the petition. A holiday atmosphere prevailed, and toward noon people wanted to organize some dancing. A witness saw the altar of the Fatherland as "an animated mountain, formed of myriad human beings one on top of the other." Then came Lafayette with his men. Somebody shot at him and was immediately arrested; Lafayette, magnanimous and vain, had him released. Later came more guards, the cavalry, the artillery, the mayor of Paris, and the astronomer Bailly, pale and overwhelmed by events. The crowd was also joined by a band of armed hairdressers, who wanted to avenge their colleague. There were shots, clouds of dust, cries. On the planks of the altar of the Fatherland lay the dead. No one knows the exact number;

many were thrown into the Seine. Since then, the history books have spoken of the "Massacre of the Champ de Mars."

On that hot afternoon, Gouverneur Morris, ever curious, tried to climb the hill toward Passy so that he could look down on the clashes of the Champ de Mars. But he failed to get there in time. Morris had arrived in Paris from Philadelphia just as the Estates-General were opening. In the United States he had revised the final draft of the Constitution, with a solid feeling for facts and possibilities. He had lost a leg in an accident. The French he stammered sounded like that of some remote province, unsuited to sustain the aphoristic sparkle of conversations. But in Paris, the American coat of arms was still enough to arouse a kindly curiosity. Soon he was being received as a faithful guest in many distinguished houses. He was assiduous and to some extent successful in his courting of Madame de Flahaut, who at the time had an apartment in the Louvre and was already the mistress of Talleyrand. Gouverneur called him "the bishop," and having made his acquaintance, pronounced him "sly, cool, cunning and ambitious."

Coming down from Passy on that Sunday, July 17, Morris spent the evening at Madame de Ségur's. Returning home, he had a contemplative moment, rare for him, as he looked at the Seine: "I think that one of the finest views I ever saw is that which presented itself this evening from the Pont-Royal. A fine moonshine, a dead silence, and the river descending gently through the various bridges between lofty houses, all illuminated (for the sake of the police), and on the other side the woods and distant hills. Not a breath of air stirring. The weather has this day been very hot."

§ᚷ

On Taste

"Le raisonner tristement s'accrédite." (*"Reasoning is sadly gaining credence."*)

—Voltaire to Madame du Deffand

Taste comes into being in order to inherit—what, exactly? Hard to say. But surely in all the civilizations that the reactionaries dreamed of, taste did not exist. *Meaning* was enough to suppress it. And meaning must sway on its foundations before taste can appear.

Perhaps someday a great anthropologist, a Mauss from some remote wilderness, will discover what *taste* was—as an object of study, definable on the basis of certain documents. For its appearance—and disappearance—certainly have an improbable quality in the history of societies. It is an efflorescence that gives no sign of ever recurring. It is short-lived and easily engulfed, but the effects of its appearance are irreversible. Its memory will not be effaced.

For a number of years after the fall of the "correspondences" (symbolic equivalences—the last canon), a tacit concordance among manners, gestures, and physiologies functioned as law. Although clearly precarious, this silent accord still made a show of being solid, set on an enduring foundation, and obviously more legitimate than every one of its barbarous predecessors.

In developing taste, French people of the eighteenth century imprison and diminish the meaning of literature. Their tragedies, which they find so satisfying, are laughably flimsy; but Napoleon will demand a *new* type of tragedy in vain. There's a flimsiness likewise to their verse—the insipid anacreontic. As for their opinions on Shakespeare: Voltaire sends *Julius Caesar* to the Cardinal de Bernis so that he can *laugh* at it. He is shocked because the Regent likes

Rabelais. Fontenelle finds the Sixth Eclogue of Virgil "bizarre." Madame du Deffand reads Saint-Simon with great amusement but disarms anyone who may criticize her for it: he has "an abominable style" and is not an *"homme d'esprit."*

What is taste, then, if it actually impedes a sure understanding of literature? Isn't this sure understanding of literature perhaps in its turn a subtle and belated accidental essence distilled from history, an essence that had not yet been officially analyzed, and would not be analyzed until much later, in the years of Baudelaire and Mallarmé? Taste, on the other hand, crystallizes earlier, and its origins are remote from the arts. Painting, literature, furniture: these are only a few of the many domains in which it is applied. But the source of taste lies elsewhere. Taste is now the hallmark of initiation; it is applied to everything and to nothing in particular. It is the seal on one's existence, the final replacement for a wisdom that one cannot even allude to without displaying bad taste.

Referring to Antoine Hamilton, Sainte-Beuve located the discovery of *netteté* (distinctness, clarity) between "the end of La Bruyère or Fénelon and the beginning of Jean-Jacques," a few decades in which something irreversible was crystallized—a form, a flavor of Occidental sobriety that would soon be corrupted, while nevertheless enduring as an indelible quality, a tacit accord hanging over everything. Anyone quick to complain of how the language of *netteté* has paved the way for the most pretentious insipidness (which is still rife) must nonetheless recall that the French language, "beginning with Pascal, became the language of the perfect *honnête homme*"—that is, the language of the perfectly civilized man. Shortly before being confined and almost strangled by the short sentences that Voltaire made so popular, the *honnête homme* had strolled around in the empty space between two chairs—and something still reminded him of a sinuous quiver, a reflection in clear water only slightly muddied.

Shame, which is the act of referring to the unnamed and which is called "taste" in its final phase, gave life beyond death to the language whose order was based on the axis of the world. This is why it was an act of extreme blasphemy when the axis of the world became the stratification of society. In such a society everything corresponds to something else, but like a mirror reflected in a mirror. What once upheld opposites without being visible becomes the only thing that vision can grasp. Opposites are illuminated momentarily to solidify the uniform background from which they rise. The disappearance of linear culture leaves the word and other sacrificial objects such as sound and image suspended in midair, without any rights or relationships, while the new tribe incessantly sacrifices to itself the empty and splendid remains of the tribe that has been buried. The final liberation takes place in a state of total blindness. If nothing can refer to an axis, words become constellations of the thing itself. They are delicate filaments, and easily broken, but are the only ones to have come into being without the ready assistance of an arbitrary decision. Such fragility restores the difference that has been effaced. Now only that which can be effaced is faithful.

༄

A visitor to the Salon of 1828 happened to encounter Talleyrand: "Advancing toward us, or rather dragging himself forward, between two valets dressed in black, was a kind of immobile figure, who with his halting gait made his way past daubs and masterpieces, past Coudert's paintings and Picot's czarina. He looked like one of Curtius' figures in which the wax has turned out a bit too yellow, or an automaton traversing the Louvre in order to take its place in the exhibit on French industry." During those last years, Talleyrand's physical image signaled that all history, under his guidance, was preparing to enter the Musée Grévin. The bourgeois age was sick with history, and this was responsible for its occasional display of arrogant euphoria. But no one dared note that this sickness was the consequence of an impalpable fact—namely, that the familial knot connecting the present to the past had been severed. In Saint-Simon all the generations of peers and bastards are entangled in this knot; the dead go on living at Versailles, a few suites down the hall. But with Michelet everything is already hallucination: the present is only an irritatingly faithful hallucination. History, in the sense of *family history*, has been buried forever. Infected by the bombast of the emancipated, bourgeois Frenchmen under Louis-Philippe had always "taken pride in understanding all history," as Sainte-Beuve sarcastically remarked. But they were merely preparing to lay it to rest in the illustrations of the *Magasin Pittoresque*. The automaton and the wax statue are the new Guardians of the Threshold. Now people must pay tribute to them both, in order to gain access to the future and the past.

Throughout his life, from the time of his first public appearances, Talleyrand was stung by accusations and insults of every kind. From the anonymous gazetteers to the monarchs, from the new emperor to the democratic shopkeepers, all tasted the pleasure of inveighing against him. The themes that recurred, with endless variations, were corruption, treachery, falsehood, crime. In an age in which Good Feeling flourished, he had the privilege of being the shining example of Evil. After his death the historians chimed in, and they have not yet exhausted the topic. The dossier of his misdeeds is thick; condemnations overlap, and at times echo one another. At the age of seventy-three he was slapped and kicked in public by an aggressor. When Charles X asked him for details concerning this incident, he replied: "I was punched, Sire." In the life of a politician, insults do not matter; only humiliations matter. For Talleyrand, through all the reversals of fortune and political upheavals, the moments of true embarrassment were rare, and rarer still the moments of humiliation. Among the latter, the worst were not the famous scenes in which Napoleon abused and threatened him, but rather two encounters with Louis XVIII—King Ubu, old gamekeeper accustomed to shooting at poachers—whom Talleyrand beyond any doubt had restored to the throne. And in his eyes Talleyrand would always remain a poacher, even though the king was indebted to him for making his return to France possible. As Chateaubriand observed, Louis XVIII, "though not cruel, was not human." Late one night at Mons, as the king was departing in his carriage, Talleyrand ran limping after him, though he had not wished to pay homage to him during the day; "I'm in no hurry," he had remarked. One of his favorite sayings was, "There are few political transactions whose nature will not admit of some postponement." Yet that night he was abruptly wakened, was forced to forgo his long toilette, and had to rush out into the road, leaning on the arm of Monsieur de Ricé, only to hear those few mocking words addressed to him: "Prince of Benevento, are you

leaving us? The waters will do you good. Be sure to write to us."
The other meeting took place during the second Restoration, when
Talleyrand was prime minister and asked his king for a pledge of
greater trust. According to the Baron de Vitrolles, "Monsieur de
Talleyrand, usually so skilled at gentle insinuation, this time had
doubtless calculated that he must use more peremptory language.
The king, unaccustomed to such a tone, was shaken and remained
silent for a moment, staring at the ceiling. 'Very well,' he replied at
last, with a serene expression, 'I shall choose a new ministry.'" Writing
to the Duchess of Kurland the next day, Talleyrand acknowledged
(to the extent that his style allowed) the injury he had sustained:
"His ingratitude is not sufficiently veiled." None of the many new
men with whom Talleyrand had dealt, beginning with Napoleon,
would have been capable of wounding him so coldly. It took this
obese, insensitive creature who cared only for his own tranquillity,
it took a Bourbon, to bring down on the Prince, almost unawares, a
vendetta that was born from the depths of his blood.

As literature proceeds along its tortuous course to become absolute, it encounters satanism. The two come together in their shared
passion, a sin that only the greatest theologians have thought to
include among the mortal ones: curiosity. The image of the writer
then becomes Milton's Satan when, "reaching the earthly paradise,
he flew immediately to the Tree of Life, the tallest tree in the garden,
and perched there, like a cormorant, without trying in the least to
recover his life, but rather using the tree only to see farther on, *for
prospect.*" This could well serve as the motto for the fever of experimentation that since Sainte-Beuve's time has never ceased to throw
forms into disarray: *for prospect.* Didn't the theologians, after all,
condemn the new science for this same basic sin of empty curiosity?

"The disease of literature and of *art,* as it is said, is very common
in our time . . . Perhaps never before, I dare say, have phrase and
color, the falseness of the literary word, so predominated over content and truth as in recent years. The reign of the pen has replaced,
literally, the reign of the sword." Just as Marx would relentlessly
chronicle, through its smallest stages, the emancipation of exchange
value, so Sainte-Beuve minutely observed the emancipation of the

word. It was a process in which he saw himself as an accomplice, though at the same time it repelled him. The sinuous verbosity of the new writers, who circulated among the pressrooms and unwittingly discovered the industrial uses of the word, their intoxication when they realized that the word was willing to do anything and could cover everything, seemed to him to have descended secretly from the same origins as the imposing prose of Chateaubriand. And these were also the origins of Hugo, who continued to write with his "vulgar soul of a barbarian, energetic and shrewd." But the ultimate poison in the matter still lay elsewhere. Out of that same odious proliferation would arise the *new*, which Sainte-Beuve, in the timid reaches of his mind, was not prepared to follow, even if his clairvoyance kept him from being unaware of it: the new of Baudelaire, then of Flaubert, both carried away by absolute literature. The degraded word and the perfect word were preparing to mingle their waters, as in certain gnostic rituals. Sainte-Beuve, who always refused to go one step beyond good and evil, now realized with dismay that in the world around him there existed no "basis" or "truth" on which he could lean. And he spoke to himself in his secret tone, that of the delicate cynic: "I was a petty thief as a youth; as an old man I shall be a pirate. Oh, how I would have preferred to be a good literary gentleman, living on his estate as a poet!"

❧

Metamorphoses of Style

Guez de Balzac once boasted he had "found something that many were seeking—namely, a certain little art of combining words and putting them in the right place." Remove the "little art" and there is nothing left but "the secret force that animates words and that comes from Heaven, whence come, as well, greatness and majesty."

Sainte-Beuve introduced Guez de Balzac with these words: "Nobody represents more naïvely than he the *man of letters* seen as a species, with his primitive solemnity, his flawless state of preservation and provincial gentlemanliness, his absolute respect for all the trappings and pomp of language, his perfect ineptitude in everything else."

". . . like Guez de Balzac, who, when Saint-Cyran spoke to him of salvation and grace, could find nothing to say but, 'How beautiful!' To which the exasperated Saint-Cyran once replied, 'You seem to me, Monsieur de Balzac, like a man who, seeing a spot on his face in the mirror, can find nothing to say except that the mirror is fine and beautiful.' And Balzac, struck by the precision of the analogy and the appropriateness of the image, could not help exclaiming, 'Ah! What you've said is so beautiful!' At this point, Saint-Cyran despaired of him and of all those wits who care for nothing but imagery and turns of phrase."

Guez de Balzac, gaudy cocotte of the word, liked to admire from a distance the austerities of Port-Royal. And Saint-Cyran, the fiercest and most austere of fathers, made him shudder voluptuously when he lashed him with contempt and scorn. Once Balzac spent three months composing and polishing a letter to Saint-Cyran. From the start he combined hyperbole and metaphor, but in addition to an unshakable vanity he displayed the sufferings of an anxious lover: "I am well aware that my language will not please you and that you will frown upon this letter." At once, however, he takes wing again: "It must be stated, Monsieur, that you are the greatest tyrant in the world today; that everyone will soon fear your authority; and that when you speak, one finds it impossible to retain one's own opinion if it does not conform to yours . . . Of course, there is a certain pleasure in letting oneself be forced to embrace happiness and in yielding to a man who never uses violence unless it benefits those subjected to it."

Saint-Cyran set that long letter on the mantelpiece, without opening it. Writing to Monsieur d'Andilly, he mentioned a "letter from Monsieur de Balzac that I intend to read three days from now." A month later, distressed at not having received any reply, Balzac begged a friend to approach Saint-Cyran and ask him if he had ever received the letter. Saint-Cyran answered that of course he had received it; indeed, he apologized for the delay and said he would make up for it then and there. In the presence of Balzac's friend he wrote a brief response, which was greatly admired.

"The famous writer thus spent about thirty years without interruption on his estate, completely taken up with the contemplation of himself and his literary work, which had been precocious and brilliant but which had never matured. His enemies called him *Narcissus;* he gazed at himself all day long, in fact, in the canal of the Charente, or in that *Mirror* of rhetoric that seemed so beautiful to him. He never refreshed his wit in the outside world or in relations with people. In the end, he inflated himself in a vacuum. Solitude spoiled his wit, just as the world spoils it for others."

"Three days before his death, he was still revising his manuscripts. He had fair copies made before sending them to the printer, for he attached as much importance to these details and to the most trifling flourishes in his books as he did to anything else. He died in this manner, on February 18, 1654, thinking confusedly of his flowery witticisms and his conscience—sincere no doubt, since he had solemnly converted, but converted in accordance with his defect and weakness, which always reappeared."

"Nature, history, geography—the universe—existed only to furnish him with his sole and favorite booty: the metaphor. Let's look at ourselves carefully; let's delve into our literary conscience. I suspect that more than one eminent modern writer is not as far from Guez de Balzac as he thinks." Looking at himself carefully, Sainte-Beuve suspected that he himself was one of those "wits who care for nothing but imagery and turns of phrase."

Like a malicious genealogist who insinuates venomous comments into a family history, Sainte-Beuve established Guez de Balzac as the forefather of the style-obsessed writers of French prose. So fatuous and ridiculous at its birth, this cult, whose origins are beyond all conjecture and will remain forever obscure, had a long and adventurous life. It no longer gazed on itself in the waters of the Charente, but sailed everywhere, even to the ancient Ocean, to the point of losing its way on the Bateau Ivre. In the writing of Rousseau, over and above his "thought and basic genius," Sainte-Beuve's ear perceived "the movement, the cadences, the pauses, the articulations, and in a certain sense the skeletal structure" of Guez de Balzac's prose. But there were other feats as well: with Chateaubriand, style became sumptuous plunder and subjected all to its dominion. The *esprit de conquête* was no longer the sole property of politics. "Chateaubriand is a great writer, a great conqueror and invader in matters of style. (This is basically his only unity of passion and feeling: the unity of the artist of style.) He is not a realist, or a Christian, or a republican, or a socialist, but all of these things—and more—simultaneously or in succession, according to what can be harvested from all fields of ideas in the way of images, of more or less beautiful and seductive metaphors. He cannot resist them; he flings himself on them. He is a marauder in the grand manner, a collector of brilliant and flowered tithes—royal lilies, red carnations, and even violets hidden among the grass and bluebottles of the cornfields of Beauce. Wandering across the fields, he is drawn to everything that is lovely and available for the plucking. Although he has sown nothing there, he takes his booty, the multicolored flora of all harvests."

Proust referred to style as the "sign of the transformation that the writer's mind imposes on reality." Once the academic distinction between "form" and "content" is abolished, a distinction respected by Sainte-Beuve, thought manifests itself in what was long considered mere decoration. After Chateaubriand's resonant plunder, the scattered and fragmented materials merge in Flaubert: "All the elements of reality are rendered down into one uniform substance, with wide, unvaryingly polished surfaces. No flaw remains. It has been rubbed to looking-glass smoothness. Everything is shown there, but only by reflection, and without affecting the consistency of the whole. Everything at variance with it has been made over and absorbed."

"Style," René Daumal has observed, "is the imprint of what we are on what we do."

. . .

Proust descends upon Sainte-Beuve with flaming sword. Here the absolute literature of Baudelaire, of Flaubert, of Proust himself takes its revenge on the man who preferred to bow before any member of the Noailles family or before ministerial power, rather than devote an extra word to Baudelaire. As avenging angel, Proust is free of doubt; but justice suddenly blinds him. Just as Sainte-Beuve looked with acid suspicion on all of literature's claims to be absolute, as if this violated the rules of the game, so Proust ultimately accused Sainte-Beuve of having an idea that, by tortuous paths, brought him close to the central idea of the *Recherche:* "Never in his life did Sainte-Beuve seem to conceive of literature in a really profound way. He placed it on the same level as conversation." In fact, his books "seem like a series of connected drawing rooms to which the author has invited various conversationalists. They're questioned about the distinguished people they have known, and their evidence is doomed to conflict with evidence given by others, thus showing that in the case of men whom we habitually praise there is much to be said on both sides, or that those who don't agree must represent a different school of thought." Here, precisely where Proust wanted to offer a devasting description of Sainte-Beuve's "method," he revealed its secret, which was in fact very close to his own. Sainte-Beuve's *Causeries,* accumulated Monday after Monday, but also his *Chateaubriand* and even his ponderous *Port-Royal,* if looked at from a distance and in sequence, prove to be, thanks above all to the artifice of conversation, an immense hallucinatory novel in installments, crammed with rumors, allusions, interrupted recollections, gossip, fleeting images, echoes, reappearances. Everything flows in a single, slow, inexorable current that disappears into Sainte-Beuve himself, into his somewhat timid life in the shadows, as the last of the delicate souls. His "method," which "consists of not separating the man and his work," surely did not claim to have any theoretical substance. But it was an excellent pretext that allowed him to describe with impunity—while saving appearances, at times even excessively—the hundreds of lives, rooms, landscapes, encounters, elegiac pleasures, piercing barbs that he continually daydreamed about in his study. This underhanded sort of literary criticism is "virtually incompatible with practicing Christianity," Sainte-Beuve admitted to himself in his

Cahiers, which were for him "the lowest drawer of the writing desk, a piece of furniture in one of the inner rooms that other people are not allowed to see." This was not so much because it constantly obliged him, against evangelical precept, to "judge, always judge others" (here the slight hypocrisy he often adopted follows him even into his secret room), but rather because he found it a continual, irresistible temptation to "reproduce the other, to transform oneself into him, as I often do—a procedure that is in essence thoroughly pagan, an Ovidian metamorphosis." But at least once we encounter an explicit confession: "Some people take my essays on authors for literary criticism and complain because my subjects absorb me so. They fail to perceive that in those pieces the criticism is a secondary element: for me, each essay is first of all a portrait, a painting, the expression of a feeling. They do not realize that, forced as I am to write for *periodicals,* I have found and as it were invented a way to continue there, in a somewhat disguised form, the novel and the elegy. But three-fourths of all readers, the common run of intellectuals, do not even notice this."

There is an experiment, a test, for verifying these observations. Any reader of the *Iliad* who is unwilling to linger over the list of ships' names is unlikely to be a good reader. In the same way, as a preliminary approach to Sainte-Beuve, one can try opening the *Table générale et analytique,* which is a four-hundred-page list of the names mentioned in the fifteen volumes of the *Causeries.* There we find unknown people and classical heroes, kings and men of letters, grand ladies and politicians, the worldly and the cloistered. It is an endless tapestry of voices, judgments, events, reports, and words once lost and here recaptured. Wasting his talent week after week on books that the vicissitudes of publishing deposited on his desk, Sainte-Beuve after many years had constructed, with toothpicks and moss, that grandiose, excessive, maniacal edifice which was much like a novel but which he would never have dared present as such. By virtue not only of its size but also of a profound affinity in its conception, the *Table générale et analytique* of the *Causeries* takes its place alongside three other great indexes of names: that of Saint-Simon's *Mémoires,* that of Balzac's *Comédie humaine,* and that of Proust's *Recherche.*

❧

Long before the time of Goethe and Napoleon (who met, hardly by accident, to exchange unforgettable banalities, as if preordained to figure in *Reader's Digest*), the Anthropos of the new age, the universal man whose feet were planted in the fatherland of the sky and whose mind for the first time combined all the planetary variants without exception, was Gottfried Wilhelm Leibniz. For him, the infinitesimal calculus was the prelude to an expansion—from Kamchatka to America—of the realm of the enlightened and brutal Czar Peter, as the provincial disagreements of the churches converged in a *prima materia* of revelation, just as in China the Jesuits merely had to persuade Emperor K'ang-hsi of the benefits of assiduous use of optical instruments in order to cleanse Confucian learning of its excessively Asiatic impurities. This all-knowing man was buried at Hanover "like a highwayman," his friend Ker de Kersland noted. The only mourner following the bier of this first cosmic secretary and secret counselor of the divine was his undistinguished private secretary, Eckhart.

The physiocrat François Quesnay, a brusque man with a certain "monkey-like air," was Madame de Pompadour's physician. He lived in cramped quarters on a mezzanine above the apartments of the favorite, where every day the policies of France were decided. At supper he often received Diderot, d'Alembert, Duclos, Helvétius, Turgot, Buffon. Madame de Pompadour, who could not entertain the same guests for reasons of protocol and propriety, sometimes went to her physician's rooms to greet them and stayed on to take part in the conversation.

Louis XV ennobled Quesnay in Madame de Pompadour's apartments. He took three pansies from a vase made at the Sèvres factory (which had been founded at Madame de Pompadour's behest, for France up to that time had been unskilled in the new art of porcelain and had imported 500,000 livres' worth every year from Saxony and Japan), and he said: "Here, Quesnay, I ennoble you, and I give you a coat of arms that speaks." At that moment, political economy was born.

.   .   .

One of the events of global importance that took place in the years just before the Revolution was the definitive sanctioning of the alliance between snobbery and the Left. At the time, people did not use the terms "snobbery" or "the Left," but suddenly the most imitated and often the most elegant ladies began to discuss customs duties and Virginia tobaccos, spinning mills and credit, and they even ventured to make a few references to net income. The general interest (alas, though it was an interest all the same) became the center of conversation, concealing the dissipation that usually ensues when *esprit* is abandoned to itself. From that moment on, the higher snobbery, which always needs some discreet disguise, would know what cloak to cover itself with: the worthy Cause. Such causes were social and musical, humanitarian and progressive, erotic and Asiatic. But the star of the Just shone on the brow of the ladies as they received the guests at their dinners, their parties, their languid picnics.

Equality is an initiatory idea. Only through a highly artificial process such as initiation can one succeed in evoking "the equal"—an entity that does not exist in nature. After 1789, when Masonic emblems become the basis and tacit premise of civic life, though their character as emblems and their initiatory ancestry have been forgotten, the world of inversions defines its territory. Double movement: all are initiates, but initiation itself vanishes definitively from immediate reference. It remains only in the perennial shadow of conspiracy and will emerge again in libraries, with the great academic ethnographers.

At the beginning of the Revolution, and later in each of the canonical stages (except the Terror, and not by accident: history, from now on, will have to choose between two main paths—that of Talleyrand and that of the Terror), each new event already requires an ultimate guardian, a malign preceptor who will seize its wrist and help it write the new pacts: Talleyrand. Each time, he helps chaos assume an acceptable form. In every act that has an excessive and hence paralyzing symbolic potency, we glimpse that pale hand of his in the shadows, supporting the hands of others, of many others, a long line of friends and enemies. To him we owe the final draft of

Article 6 of the Declaration of the Rights of Man: "The law is the expression of the general will. All citizens have the right to participate personally, or through their representatives, in its formation. It must be equal for all, whether it protects or punishes. All citizens, being equal in its eyes, are equally eligible for all positions, honors, and public employments, in accordance with their capacities."

⚜

Belated Nostalgia for Sorrow

Talleyrand and Madame de Staël had been lovers, in the days when she used to explain to Monsieur de Surgère, between one *contredanse* and the next, what the "domain of the Occident" meant. Though unable to forget the ungainliness of her body, Talleyrand had written her from America asking for help, and she had offered him so much that he was able to return. Later she made six visits to Barras to urge Talleyrand's case. Once she burst into the Luxembourg palace in a state of dishevelment, and in a choked voice explained to Barras that Talleyrand was on the point of throwing himself into the Seine if he did not become minister of foreign affairs; he had only ten louis left. If politics, in its metaphysical sense, demands a knowledge of "how to make women carry out orders" (as Talleyrand insolently explained), Madame de Staël carried out orders with proud impetuosity and generally arrived at her goal.

They respected each other as supreme potentates of conversation, but Talleyrand developed a sort of coldness and intolerance toward her. In 1812 he said to Madame de Kielmannsegge, "Madame de Staël may think me a fierce individual, but this at least is sure: intellectually she is repugnant to me." The Marquise de Beaulaincourt told Edmond de Goncourt that she had dined twice in her life with Talleyrand, and both times she heard him tell the story of how the Neckers had had to order a *tourne-cuisses* for their daugher, to correct her feet and legs. For a long time Madame de Staël tried not to forgive Talleyrand his betrayals, abandonments, and nastiness, but she never succeeded. In her novel *Delphine* she felt compelled to introduce a character, Madame de Vernon, who is a shrewd portrayal of Talleyrand's coldness: "No one knows better than I how to exploit indolence: I use it to thwart, as naturally as possible, the activity of others . . . Except for three or four times in my life, I have never taken the trouble to want something; but when I make up my mind to undertake such an effort, nothing can deflect me from my aim, and you can be sure that I achieve it." Once, in a letter written in 1809 from Geneva, Madame de Staël managed to address Talleyrand with the only words that could pierce his invisible armor: "Adieu. Are you happy? With such a superior spirit, don't you ever arrive at the bottom of everything—at sorrow, that is?"

But Talleyrand had already indirectly answered Madame de Staël, whom he so scorned. The words of that letter touched a spot that his energetic band of detractors did not even perceive. What were treachery, corruption, venality, and ferocity compared to that accusation which admitted of no appeal and which nailed him to the ignorance of sorrow? It was with another woman friend—Madame de Rémusat, likewise an excellent conversationalist but not as imperious and aggressive as Madame de Staël—that Talleyrand one day in 1808, thanks perhaps to her ability to "stir his soul, so often dozing out of habit, intention, and indifference," allowed this reply to slip out: "Il eût peut-être mieux valu souffrir" ("Perhaps it would have been better to suffer"). In Talleyrand's system this sentence, perhaps the only sublime *bon mot* among the many, is the equivalent of Flaubert's phrase, "Ils sont dans le vrai" ("They're doing the right thing"). A jealous, despotic vocation had seized each of them. Writing, for Flaubert, implied killing life; living out *les grandes affaires,* for Talleyrand, implied killing pain. The mask of the artificer had become glued to their faces—and it could never be removed, even for a moment, without leaving them deformed, sincere. They carried on to the very end, without trembling. One had folders bulging with quotations for *Bouvard et Pécuchet;* the other had something analogous—the negotiations of 1831 on the Belgian question, and most of all his long, impeccable death agony, cadenced by the various phases of the pardon of the Church, mother of sorrows. Sketching a volute of funereal rococo, Franz Blei remarked: "Over this belated nostalgia for pain extends the mask, as well as the legend that is also called Talleyrand."

⊱✢⊰

The Languor of a Park in Berry

Having once again quieted Europe by resolving the Belgian issue, the Prince is living quietly as lord of the castle at Valençay, protected by his beloved granddaughter Dorothée, Duchess of Dino. Now in his eighties, he takes to jotting down liquid, ordinary words, which appear behind his last shield: the monotony of his existence. "I arrange my life in such a way as to be monotonous, wishing to seal myself within the walls of domestic habit. I am neither happy nor unhappy; my health is neither good nor bad; I live without pain or illness. I am gently growing weaker, and if this state of languor does not cease, I well know how it all might end. But this neither distresses nor frightens me. My work is over. I have planted some trees; I have built a house; I have done many other foolish things as well. Hasn't the time come to make an end of it?" Yet almost without his being aware of it, little paralyzing phrases occasionally slip out, flinging open the past, the secret: "Nothing causes me anguish, because I am prepared for everything"; "I do not struggle against necessity."

A guest at Valençay, the Duc d'Orléans, son of Louis-Philippe, had the opportunity to see the plaster casts of the legs of Talleyrand's women friends. The name of the model was incised on each. Over the course of decades, the Prince had thus been able to have a great many delicate stockings woven for these women. Now almost all of them were dead.

The curs of history flung themselves snarling on Talleyrand because (it was said) he would never believe in anything, not even history itself, *ultima dea.* But to the aristocratic Madame de Dino, the creature he loved most, the aristocratic Talleyrand once said, "There is nothing less aristocratic than incredulity."

Between the cyclical and ceremonial (though no longer ritual) age into which he'd been born and the experimental age that surrounded him at eighty—and that still expected him, at the least, to solve the Belgian problem—the difference, as Talleyrand clearly saw, lay not only in what was being produced but in what was being depleted. The Princesse de Vaudémont died on New Year's Eve, 1832. In her last years she filled her household with animals. She generously assisted the poor. Talleyrand had met her fifty years before, with his mistress and protector the Comtesse de Brionne; from that time on, they had considered themselves friends. At her house Talleyrand had become reconciled with Fouché and had listened with impassive benevolence to the intrigues of Aimée de Coigny. Her teas were "the locus of greatest danger for the unsteady government. One could plot there in perfect safety. The chairs were so comfortable, the life so pleasant and inane, that the spies fell asleep." In the interim, Napoleon had fallen from power and died; and so, once again, had the Bourbons. Montrond, a corrupt libertine and gambler suited to every kind of shady venture, and the man whom many identified as Talleyrand's evil genius because they wanted to attribute an evil genius even to the Devil, saw the Prince weep only once: when the news of his old friend's death reached London. On that occasion Talleyrand wrote, "Our times are characterized by the fact that, within what we call 'society,' certain things are coming to a definitive end. There was a time when a famous salon, or a person influential because of his wit or judgment, could be replaced. Today we see clearly only what we have lost. What will be born is still hidden. Thus, despite all the bravado of the young, the present time seems to me the golden age of the old; and this proves it is society itself that is ending." The old man was no longer the mediator of an experience, because that experience ended with him each time. But in this way he became something still more mysterious and impressive: a stone abandoned in a field, cut by an unknown hand, according to unknown rules. Such survivors, deprived of descendants, have faces that are striking in their isolation. Their uselessness is majestic, and the wisdom they perhaps do not possess and surely do not wish to hand on gazes at us in silence, like every memory that agrees to destroy itself.

❧

"Little triangular brackets finished in Chinese lacquer adorned the four corners of the drawing room and supported four plaster busts. The busts were covered with black crêpe to protect them from dust or as a sign of mourning, for these were the busts of Louis XVI, Marie Antoinette, Madame Elisabeth, and the Dauphin." That most terrible of acids, a stagnant virginity (as the Catholic roué Barbey d'Aurevilly once observed), corrodes the lines of profiles. Members of the provincial nobility wander amid mourning and dust, through vast rooms whose smoke-blackened walls separate them from the thick Norman darkness. But the Restoration is likewise a memory, the evocation of a strength that will continually be denied the revolutionaries, who are always too true to themselves: "The Jacobins of France were as grumpy, solemn, and pedantic as the Puritans of England." Their fierce enemy in the region between Valognes and Coutances, the Chouan knight Des Touches, made them think of other things. "La belle Hélène," they called him, because of his ephebic good looks; and "the Wasp," because of his stinging raids, and because he knew how to vanish into thin air, even into the waves, in his primitive dugouts, amid the mists of the Channel. There is an erotic quality to feudal homage, to feudal loyalty, that eludes all democratic devotion: from the Chevalier Des Touches to Clark Gable—all "gone with the wind." Guerrilla warfare is an abstract game in which ultimately you cannot recall even for whom you are fighting. The difference is in the eye that looks at a naked body. Aimée de Spens undresses at the window, doubly spied upon: by the revolutionary Blues, who have been led to think she is alone, and by the Chouan Des Touches, who, concealed in her room, looks at her body from the other side of the light. Years later, feudal eros still makes Aimée blush. And when Barbey d'Aurevilly, like an indiscreet chronicler, goes to visit Des Touches at the hospice in Caen, he finds him seated on a stone: "With those eyes that had once peered through fog, immense spaces, the sea, enemy ranks, and the smoke of battle, he looked only at some red flowers to which he had just compared Aimée and which, in the abstraction of his madness, perhaps he did not even see."

In the first days of the Revolution, whenever blood was shed, a cook named Desnot would be somewhere on the scene. After Bernard-René de Launey, governor of the Bastille, was run through by dozens of bayonets, a voice came from the crowd: "The Nation wants his head, to display to the people." And thus Desnot, who had shortly before received a kick in the groin from the struggling governor, was assigned a task: "Since you have been wounded, cut off his head." But Desnot refused the saber that was offered him: he wanted to hack at Launey's neck with a little black-handled knife that he always carried in his pocket and used for neatly cutting meat in his kitchen. Eight days later, a similar scene took place. A multitude of bayonets pierced the body of Louis Berthier. But this time it was the dead man's heart the people wished to display. The cook Desnot, who was going about sporting a magnificent dragoon's helmet which he had picked up at the Tuileries, claimed that this time he did not act on his own initiative; he simply obeyed a soldier who, after opening Berthier's torso with a saber, cut out the heart and handed it to Desnot with these words: "Dragoon, justice is done. Take them this heart." Followed by the little group of executioners, Desnot decided to show it also to Lafayette, who shuddered. Then they roamed about the Palais-Royal, still carrying the heart. At last they paused at a tavern to have supper. They set the heart on a table and began drinking. But meanwhile, beneath the windows, a throng of curious people had gathered, demanding Berthier's heart. According to his own account, Desnot threw the heart to the crowd, which then carried it all around the garden of the Palais-Royal on a bed of white carnations. That was all he knew.

The theologian Yeshuotl raised his eyes and said to Monsieur Godeau: "If you really want to regulate your life and judge history, you should at least know how God spends his days. He has set aside for himself a certain place in heaven, four cubits by four, and there he studies the Talmud for the first three hours of the day. From the fourth to the seventh hour, God sits and judges the world. But since he sees that the world is guilty, he rises from the seat of Judgment and goes to sit on the throne of Mercy. During the third part of the day, he sits there and feeds all the creatures of the world, from the rhinoceros to the flea. During the fourth part of the day, God sits and plays with the Leviathan."

❧

Around Port-Royal

A great, gloomy sky; a deep, revolving, unknown universe, where now and then, in certain places and at certain times, life is collected, produced, renewed. Man molders briefly and dies, along with the myriad insects, on this island of grass that ripples in the swamp. Gazing up at this sky was the abbey of Port-Royal, risen from a ditch full of brambles, where water sleeps. There, three leagues from Versailles, one was already in the desert.

This impoverished cloister, covered with weeds even in its early days, its rows of arches extending in the mirrors with the passing of the years—this cloister, which was at once school and Cour des Miracles, where spiteful Ossianic foundlings, shuddering harvesters of tears, haughty executioners of the Reaction and their twins, prompters of the Revolution, were raised—this cloister . . . How is it that, from the reforming of a convent for girls, near which intractable hermits used to gather (they surveyed the desert with a spyglass)—how is it that ungovernable events could unwind from this domestic skein, this fine string produced by the retting of lace, hair shirts, jute, and palm leaves?

The first dangerous Moderns were not atheists and libertines, timid offshoots of *Freigeisterei,* protected by erudite comments as they grew. "In general," as Joseph de Maistre was to say definitively, "the atheist is quiet. Having abandoned the moral life, he rots in silence and hardly ever attacks authority." To threaten the world's order, to raise heads from perpetual submission, it would take "a theological club, a gathering place—*four walls,* in short, and nothing more." The "four walls" were those of Port-Royal; and in that same desolate spot, which was never far enough away from the bonds of passion, in that Thebaïd a few leagues from Versailles, lay the infected gauze that would bandage the world. That solitude did not deceive Maistre. It was a minuscule vortex that called up the dead, the unborn, because "every sect . . . needs the crowd and especially women." A frantic chatter formed the halo of that false calm. In the mad virgins of Port-Royal, in those unshakable snobs of the spirit, Maistre recognized the great array of *tricoteuses* greedy for the guillotine, saw the pale women nihilists with suitcases full of explosives, saw the wretched of the earth, the women who would incarnate the eros of destruction. There was no point in dwelling on the usual foolish Jacobins, always tethered to facts, stifled by words still incognito. We must go further back, to the devout solitude, the torments, the self-abasing gestures before an absent Grace. That was where "the eternal crime of our unhappy nature" really surfaced—in the realization, amid the silence and the weeds, that "the human heart is naturally in revolt." For those who look back to this moment, it seems perfectly obvious that the Revolution of 1789 must be laid first of all at the feet of those stubborn few: "Nothing is more alive than that sect. Certainly, during the Revolution it showed so many clear signs of life that there seems no justification for considering it dead." An invisible Jansenism was scourging the world. Alien to every royal court, rugged and meditative, those learned clerics became winds of fire. They were "far guiltier than the ignoble workers who completed the job [of the Revolution], for it was Jansenism that struck the first blows at the cornerstone of the edifice." Reading these words of exasperation, we see Joseph de Maistre, that "toy soldier of the Holy Spirit," waving his arms in the void. And here one might think, as so many mediocrities have, that his visionary sarcasm detaches him irreparably from reality. But a celestial friendship comes to our aid. The term "Jansenist," for Napoleon, was the worst possible insult (he was once heard raging against someone, using an ascending series of epithets: "He's an *ideologue,* a MEMBER OF THE ASSEMBLY, a JANSENIST . . ."). Reacting just as the legitimate king Louis XIV had reacted, the usurper recognized that such people were the Enemy. And so both of them "in their spontaneous hatred, denounced him [the Enemy] to all the authorities of the universe." Napoleon read Maistre's *Considérations sur la France* in 1797 in Milan. Cioran has remarked, impassively, that that book "revealed Bonaparte to himself." In fact, if there is an ultimate truth in the paradox that says "The principal dogma of Jansenism belongs entirely to Hobbes," Joseph de Maistre can, in the same way, be seen as corroborating the usurper whom he had always abhorred and as finding him a favorable witness. Celestial affinities tend to invert relations. In heaven, atheists are often accused of credulity. Meanwhile Joseph de Maistre and Bonaparte converse amiably as they gaze at an immobile sunset from the terrace in St. Petersburg.

Jansenius

"Monseigneur étudie" ("The Monsignor is studying") were the only words that could ever be heard outside Jansenius' door.

He died of a plague that claimed him as its only victim in the town, and that he had contracted in various archives (his enemies whispered) by touching infected papers.

At the Frankfurt Fair of September 1640, people talked about nothing but the *Augustinus* of Jansenius.

The Superintendent of Gardens

He sent sealed baskets filled with fruit, which hid the fragrance of certain pears. These had been chosen with patient deliberation from hundreds of trees and packed in such a way that it was impossible for them to bruise each other.

Hamon

Orans, legens, latens, silens.

At Port-Royal, he was the physician par excellence. He was recognized as one of the most ingenious specimens of the Christian in decline who retains a calm, sad beauty—a man who contemplates and meditates on the irrevocable harmonies of nature, but who all the same devours the heart of charity with childish abnegation. His expression and manner generally expressed a smiling humility, an austerity blended with elegance. He was suspected of speaking about Grace through riddles, using medical terms.

Early on the night of his death, he was heard to repeat, at intervals, the word "silence." And, at times, "Jesus, Maria, sponsus et sponsa."

In his last years he was seen going from village to village on a donkey, with a book open before him, on a lectern fixed to the saddle. Little slips of red paper inserted among the pages marked the passages that had most struck him. Even if the landscape around him was bare and unremarkable, in his imagination he was always in an enchanted forest where every object concealed another, and truer, entity behind it.

He had been the tutor of Racine, who asked, in his will, to be buried beside him.

Pascal

One encountered him mostly in the fortress of the mind: a logical, geometric spirit who scrutinized all causes. Diaphanous, torrid, eloquent, he used new procedures to measure the wilderness of the sky. People had no difficulty seeing him as the perfected human intellect at its most distinct, at its most self-contained, at its most detached with respect to the universe. It was separated from the latter by a grim moat that did not allow the mind to perceive any analogy between the automatic existence of nature and the incursions of Grace.

Madame de Genlis used to tell this story with great relish: Around 1789, the Duc d'Orléans, who was laboring over his alchemical experiments, needed a skeleton, and no one could find anything better to offer him than the bones of the *pauvre Pascal,* buried at Saint-Etienne-du-Mont.

·   ·   ·

—I did not hesitate to employ my shrewdest fencing skills, and covered my arm with the curé's cassock. What did I care about circumstances and camouflage, so long as it was a duel to the death?

—If he perceived the incommensurable in such a seditious way, no form of harmonic mediation would be able to penetrate it. Yet there is one such form which, in its proportions, adapts finite terms to the infinite and which, although it does not thereby construct an impossible bridge between them, establishes communication, allowing the world to be pierced by that occasional void through which the breath of the supernatural flows.

—Because man carries on an endless inner conversation that it would be best to regulate, if not to exterminate . . .

—Now I see the time approaching when the libertines of the mind will cease to be esteemed and emulated, and will be judged to be as insistent and tedious as our curés are today. This will not be because their ideas are viewed as abhorrent, but because everything will be regarded with indifference, except pleasure and business.

—But there is a special complicity between the mystic and the libertine. Both are creatures contrary to nature, who take the void for granted and draw from it the bitterness and brutality that characterize their pronouncements. If Calvary enlightens them, they superimpose it not on a terraced landscape but on a vast field furrowed by chance, devastated by force, or made sterile by the customs of society.

—Thought emerges into the light, tattooed with emotions and memories, like certain enigmatic beings in classical myth who emerge from the waves covered with seaweed. But we are surrounded by an opaque surface which seems to make such an apparition exotic. We are mistrustful. We have long minced words and have been gripped by subtle sensations, but still we cannot say that we have had any thoughts . . .

.   .   .

—You ask my opinion of the Solitaries? Well, as a saint who is dear to me once said, I often view them as bloated with pride and conceit, stuck in their cramped cells like a dragon swollen with venom in his cave.

—*Fascinatio nugacitatis* ("charmed by trifles").

Saint-Cyran

Thus, the question was how to divide up the body of Monsieur de Saint-Cyran, frozen majestically in the position in which death had come to him, and with so solemn an expression on his face that it seemed even his fiercest enemy could not have endured his blind gaze. His heart was assigned to Monsieur d'Andilly, according to an old agreement between him and Monsieur de Saint-Cyran that said he would retire from the world once he had received the desired heart. The entrails, however, were reserved for the devotions of Mother Angélique. Lancelot had the task of severing Monsieur de Saint-Cyran's hands, but his right to them was contested by Monsieur Le Maître, who, arriving late, was not satisfied with the "paltry riches" that had been allotted him from Monsieur de Saint-Cyran's body—riches that were afterward buried within the walls of Saint-Jacques-du-Haut-Pas.

Jenkins

He was known as Monsieur François, gardener of Port-Royal. He came from far away. An English gentleman and a disciple of Monsieur Le Maître, he had come to consult him about a lawsuit. And Monsieur Le Maître had converted him to the spirit.

When the twelve rebel nuns were evacuated from the cloister, the archbishop, accompanied by a procession of about fifteen officials, wanted to visit the garden. There they found Monsieur Jenkins, hoeing. The archbishop approached him and enjoined him to leave the place immediately. Then he continued, in a sociable tone, "You are more suited to wielding a sword than a hoe." Jenkins raised his face; it was prematurely wrinkled, with high color and prominent cheekbones. With that sweet irony that saints sometimes display, he replied: "For twenty years I have worked in this garden and have never asked for money, because I thought I would end my days here. But if you wish to send me away, you must pay me for all my past work." These words were too subtle for the archbishop, who muttered in embarrassment, "Better the sword, better the sword."

He died, after forty years of service to the nuns. On his grave, obscured by rank weeds that are alive with long snakes, the epitaph Monsieur Dodart wrote for him can still be read: "Always at work in the open air, always silent, always solitary before God, toward whom he directed his soul with frequent prayers. Never idle, except during church services; never in a hurry, except to be among the first at Mass. Gentle with all, smiling and serene; and familiar only with God."

Flavie Passart

As a novice, she kept some fleas she had found on the body of Mother Geneviève Le Tardif, cherishing them as holy relics because they had sucked the nun's blood. She had grown up among visions, spirits, and necromancy, which she sometimes mentioned to the girls in her charge. She applied the Holy Thorn to the tear duct of little Margot, who was cured after a few hours. This miracle created a sensation and brought a halt to the impending persecution. When confronted by the Formulary of the Five Propositions, no one was initially more fervent in opposing all capitulation. For three years, divine apparitions repeatedly ordered her not to sign. Meanwhile she was humiliated by some of the other nuns for what they perceived as her lack of seriousness and steadiness. Finally she signed—and it was she who handed Monsieur Chamillard the list of nuns who were to be forcibly removed from the convent.

Angélique de Saint-Jean d'Arnauld d'Andilly

To the officers of justice and the soldiers who had come to take her away, she said her name with the pride of one who sees every battle as a skirmish in the grand conflict between the Arnauld family,

God's ambassadors, and the world, represented by the Jesuits. She pursued an ideal of serene heroism and arrogant austerity, but she was obsessed with the irrepressible fear that her lamp might go out. In an all-too-vivid dream the detested Flavie Passart, greedy for relics, appeared to her, taking the place of the Mother Superior and dismissing the sisters. Where was she sending them? She herself was confined in a dark little room with the Sisters of the Annunciation. Behind her she had three locked doors, which were opened three times a day. She felt as though she were in a strange land, in a place from which there was no avenue of escape that was shorter than her remaining life. To avoid having to listen to the Jesuits' preaching, she celebrated the church service alone in her prison, singing and marching about the room. She sprinkled the bed with holy water, to drive out the spirit of sloth; the table where she ate, to protect herself from fastidiousness; the space between bed and wall, which served as her oratory, to ward off distraction; the place where she worked, to arm herself against curiosity and attachment to her work, which consisted of decorating reliquaries; and above all the door of her room, to prevent the spirit of seduction from entering. Her happiest hours were at night: "I wish I could convey how beautiful and devout all this was—to be alone thus, in the heart of the night, to bless God in a prison, singing his praises for no one's ears but His, and hearing nothing but a deep silence in the midst of this great city, whose noise never ceases except at that hour, for carriages continue to pass by until eleven and even later. Words cannot express how lovely and captivating all this is." In the face of such passages, Sainte-Beuve had to reveal what he had been seeking in Port-Royal for many long years: "If—as a profane man and a former poet who seeks poetry in all things, and even (needless to say) in religion—I occasionally find poetry in Port-Royal, it is certainly here. It is what we have just seen and nothing else, a poetry without sunlight or flowers that exists only within: pure fragrance."

Mother Angélique suddenly abandoned the Sisters of the Annunciation in the archbishop's carriage. That journey in the darkness of a July night, through deserted city squares, had evoked verses in her mind. She, too, believed that "this poetry was indistinguishable from religion itself." Here, Sainte-Beuve paused again briefly to whisper his secret, which, as always, went unheard: "A girl of Smyrna or Chios, traveling at night, would have found passages from Homer running through her mind; a modern one would have thought of lines by Byron or Lamartine. But Mother Angélique thinks only of verses from Scripture, which at every moment testify to God's presence—the God of the Jews and that of the Gospels. There is no time for the flower to bloom and to be plucked in the face of these realities, which are too immediate and too serious not to be daunting. To believe too much, *to believe too sincerely,* is not conducive to the play of the imagination. Alas, even feeling too much is perhaps a mistake. Might one say that the best way to pluck this flower and this golden fruit is simply to separate them gently from their background?" Modern man cannot believe too steadfastly, but not because he does not wish to believe. Another firm devotion demands that he adhere to a certain falsity, just enough to give breathing room to the imagination, which otherwise would remain oppressed and nearly suffocated in a dense substance. All the Modern lies in that *gentle separation from the background,* in that tiny disjunction, in that imperceptible aperture that allows the void to circulate, in that unreal knife-edge that now separates every faith, every passion from itself.

CHRISTINE BRIQUET: I was infatuated with a certain aristocracy of devotion, and it seemed to me that the people at Port-Royal knew, better than anyone else in the world, what Grace is. Thus, I joined that sect of refined and kindred spirits, contemptuous of all who did not speak their language. It was said we were as pure as angels and as proud as devils.

During our periods of seclusion, we sometimes strolled in the garden, among the plants trained by Monsieur Jenkins and surrounded by the gentle glow of the fireflies' sexual organs. Sometimes, on clear frosty nights, we even approached the outer wall. Immediately beyond it, among the boughs of a rain-splashed tree, we could glimpse the black form of Monsieur de Sainte-Marthe, who murmured devotional discourses to us.

As our sterner Sisters well know, we long tried to discover what exactly is meant by le Vernis des Maîtres ("the finish of the Old Masters"). We sat in a circle on the ring of stones at the edge of our luxuriant garden. We agreed finally on the solution offered by little Marceline, who saw in that concept first of all a transparent unity, a sort of fusion in which all things, losing their original appearance as things, are arrayed side by side in a particular order, penetrated by the same light, reflected in one another, without the omission of a single word that is inimical to this blending. Until we heard her impart those stringent definitions in her high-pitched voice, we had been wandering for a long time in search of a Rule to which we ourselves would have to subscribe. And we did not know that right in our Augustine, in the methods of that machine of his which exterminated the Pelagians despite all their disguises, quiet indications were occasionally concealed which could bring us closer to that place at once abhorred and desired—the place known as *le Vernis des Maîtres*. Undivided light! Patina of Grace! We found you where we least wished to: in the artful play of forms and in the play of appearances. For us, it was a far-reaching discovery; and one might say that at this moment the first silent crack appeared in the abbey of Port-Royal-des-Champs.

THE ABBÉ DE SAINT-PIERRE: It was, I believe, the autumn of 1687, in Paris, when nature was divesting itself of all its colors and letting them soak for a few days before engulfing them in the mire of the carriage tracks. I was tirelessly pasting together the brief memoranda and *obiter dicta* of the famous men to whom I had succeeded in gaining access. Monsieur Pascal attracted me more than any of the other pale stars of the abbey did, and I was determined to search the peculiarities of his conduct for a clue that would guide me toward certain disordered impulses in the *Pensées*. In those days I used to pay occasional visits to Monsieur Nicole in the Place du Puits-l'Hermite; his conversation was divided between memories of the likable Monsieur de Tréville, always in the company of ladies, and memories of Monsieur Pascal, which were far more important to me. Monsieur Nicole, however, became aware of this greedy interest of mine, and deepening still further the multitude of wrinkles around his eyes, to accentuate his expression without changing his voice, he said, "My dear Abbé de Saint-Pierre, your eagerness betrays you, it seems to me, in your search for recollections of our glorious men. You think of the Spirit the way you dreamed of being received at Court as a child. Nothing has ever seemed so regal to you as the harshness of Monsieur Pascal. But you never knew him, so it's useless for you to take such pleasure in contemplating his image. One thing, at least, you don't know: that he collected seashells."

✣

The Ruin of Kasch

Four *melek* (kings) ruled the great realm of Kasch: the first in Nubia, the second in Habesch, the third in Kordofan, the fourth in For.

The richest among them was the Nap of Naphta in Kordofan. His capital lay in the direction of Hophraten-Nahas. This king possessed all the gold and copper in the country. The gold and copper were transported to Nubia, where the great monarchs of the West sent for it. From the East ambassadors came across the sea, and in the South the king ruled over many peoples, who forged him weapons of iron and sent him slaves. Thousands of these slaves lived at the court of the Nap.

The Nap of Naphta was the richest man on earth. But he led the shortest and saddest life of anyone who ever existed. For each Nap of Naphta could rule his land for only a certain number of years. Every night during his reign, the priests studied the stars, offered sacrifices, and built fires. They could not miss a single evening of their prayers and sacrifices; otherwise they would lose sight of the celestial trajectories and would not know when, according to the stars' dictates, the king was to be killed. And so it went for a long time. Day after day, year after year, the priests studied the stars and recognized the day on which the king had to be killed.

Once again the day of the king's death arrived. They broke the hind legs of the bulls. All the fires in the kingdom were extinguished. The priests lit a new fire and summoned the new king. The new king was the son of the sister of the king who had just been killed. The new king was called Akaf. It was during his reign that the ancient institutions of the kingdom were irrevocably changed. And the people say that this change was the cause of the ruin of Naphta.

The first task of the new Nap was to decide who would join him in death when the appropriate time came. The Nap chose these companions from among his nearest and dearest. Now, some time before, a king from the distant East had sent a man across the sea to Naphta, a man famous for his skill in telling stories. This man's name was Far-li-mas. And so Far-li-mas arrived among the slaves at the Court of the Nap. King Akaf had seen him. And Far-li-mas had pleased King Akaf. King Akaf said, "He will be the first of my companions. For all the time left me before my end, he will entertain me with his stories. And he will cheer me after my death as well."

When Far-li-mas heard the king's decision, he was not frightened. "It is God's will," he said to himself.

In those days it was the custom in Naphta to keep a fire perpetually burning, as people still do in the remote areas of For. The priests always chose a boy and a girl to maintain the fire; these two had to guard the fire and lead a chaste life. And they likewise were killed, not along with the king but when the new fire was started. The moment the priests lit the new fire for King Akaf, they selected the king's youngest sister to be the keeper of the fire. Her name was Sali (at least, that was what they called her; her full name was Sali-fu-Hamr). When Sali heard that the choice had fallen on her, she was afraid. She felt a great fear of death.

For a time the king lived in happiness and contentment; for he enjoyed the riches and splendors of his land, and spent his evenings with friends and foreigners who had come as ambassadors to the land of Naphta. But one evening God sent him the thought that each of those delightful days brought him one day closer to certain death. The king was frightened. He tried to dispel the thought, but did not succeed. King Akaf became very sad. Then God sent him a second thought: that he should send for Far-li-mas and have him tell a story.

Far-li-mas was summoned and came to the Court. The king said, "Far-li-mas, today is the day you must make me happy. Tell me a story." "No sooner said than done," Far-li-mas replied, and began telling a story. The king listened. The guests listened. The king and the guests forgot to drink. They forgot to breathe. The slaves forgot to serve. Far-li-mas' story was like hashish. When he finished, all were immersed in pleasant oblivion. King Akaf had forgotten his thoughts of death. None of those present had noticed that Far-li-mas had been talking straight through the night. By the time the guests took their leave, the sun was already high.

The next day King Akaf and his guests were impatient for evening to come, so that Far-li-mas could begin his story. Now Far-li-mas had to tell a story every night. The news of the fables of Far-li-mas spread throughout the Court, the capital, and the country. And each time, Far-li-mas told a better story. Every day the king gave him a beautiful garment, and the guests and the ambassadors gave him gold and precious stones. When he walked through the city, a swarm of slaves followed him. The people loved him. The people began to bare their breasts before him.

The news of the wondrous tales of Far-li-mas reached far and wide. Sali, too, found out about them. She sent a message to her brother the king: "Let me listen once to the tales of Far-li-mas." The king replied, "Your wish is my command." And Sali came. She wanted to listen to the story. Far-li-mas saw Sali; he lost his head for a moment. Far-li-mas saw only Sali. Sali saw only Far-li-mas. King Akaf said, "Why aren't you telling a story? Don't you know any more?" Far-li-mas tore his gaze from Sali and began his tale. At first the story of Far-li-mas was like hashish when it induces a slight daze; then it was like the hashish that brings on sleep and leads to unconsciousness. After a short while, King Akaf and the guests dozed off. But they went on listening to the story in their dreams, and were soon in a state of utter ecstasy. Only Sali kept her eyes open. Her eyes were glued to Far-li-mas. Her eyes drank in all of Far-li-mas. Sali was brimming with Far-li-mas.

When Far-li-mas had finished, he stood up. Sali stood up. Far-li-mas went toward Sali. Sali went toward Far-li-mas. Far-li-mas embraced Sali. Sali embraced Far-li-mas and said, "We do not want to die." Far-li-mas laughed into Sali's eyes and said, "The will is in you. Show me the way." Sali said, "Leave me now. I will seek the way. When I have found it, I will send word to you." Sali and Far-li-mas separated. The king and his guests slept on.

The next day Sali went to the high priest and said, "Who decides the day when the old fire must be extinguished and the new one lit?" The priest said, "God decides." Sali said, "How does God communicate his decision?" The priest said, "Every night we study the stars. We never lose sight of them. Every night we look at the moon; every day we know which stars are approaching her and which stars are moving away. This is how we know the hour." Sali said, "Must you do it every night? What happens if one night you do not look?" The priest said, "If one night we do not look, we must offer a sacrifice. If for many nights we did not look, we would no longer know our way." Sali said, "And you would not know at what moment you should put out the fire?" The priest said, "No, we would no longer be able to do our duty." Sali said, "Great are the works of God. But the greatest is not his writing in the sky. The greatest is life on earth. I realized that last night." The priest said, "What do you mean?" Sali said, "God has given Far-li-mas the gift of storytelling, as no one has ever possessed it before. This is greater than the writing in the sky." The high priest said, "You are wrong." Sali said, "You know the moon and the stars. Have you ever heard the stories of Far-li-mas?" The high priest said, "No, I have never heard them." Sali said, "Then how can you judge? Believe me—all of you, when you listen, will forget to look at the stars." The high priest said, "You allege this, sister of the king?" Sali said, "Prove to me that I am wrong, then—that the writing in the sky is stronger and greater than life on earth." The priest said, "I will prove it."

The high priest sent a message to King Akaf: "Allow the priests to come to your palace this evening, to listen to the stories of Far-li-mas from sunset till moonrise." King Akaf replied, "I consent." Sali sent a message to Far-li-mas: "Today you must tell your story as you did yesterday. This is the way."

When evening came, King Akaf gathered his guests and the ambassadors. Sali arrived and took her place beside him. All the priests came. They bared their breasts and flung themselves on the ground. The high priest said, "The stories of this Far-li-mas must be the most splendid of God's works." King Akaf said, "Decide that for yourselves." The high priest said, "Forgive us, O King, if we leave your house at moonrise to perform our duties." King Akaf said, "Do as God wills." The priests sat down. All the guests and the ambassadors sat down. The hall was full. Far-li-mas came forward. King Akaf said, "Begin, my companion in death."

Far-li-mas looked at Sali. Sali looked at Far-li-mas. King Akaf said,

"Why don't you tell a story? Are there no more to tell?" Far-li-mas turned his gaze away from Sali. Far-li-mas began to tell his tale, at sunset. His story was like the hashish that clouds and captivates. His story became like the hashish that produces oblivion. By the time the moon rose, King Akaf and his guests and the ambassadors had dozed off, and all the priests lay in a deep sleep. Only Sali remained awake and absorbed with her gaze the ever sweeter words falling from the lips of Far-li-mas.

Far-li-mas brought his tale to an end. He stood up. Far-li-mas went toward Sali. Sali went toward Far-li-mas. Sali said, "Let me kiss these lips from which such sweet words come." They sucked hard on each other's lips. Far-li-mas said, "Let me embrace this form, the mere sight of which gives me strength." And they embraced, entwining their arms and legs; and they lay amid all the sleepers and were happy to the point of heartbreak. But Sali rejoiced and said, "Do you see the way?" Far-li-mas said, "I see it." They departed. In the palace only the sleepers remained.

The next day Sali went to the high priest and said, "Now tell me: Were you right to scoff at my words?" The priest said, "I will not give you an answer today. We will go once more to listen to this Far-li-mas, for yesterday we were not suitably prepared." Sali said, "Very well." The priests performed their sacrifices and recited their prayers. They broke the fetlocks of many oxen. Throughout the day the prayers in the temple were never interrupted. That evening all the priests returned to the palace of King Akaf. That evening Sali again sat by the side of her brother, King Akaf. That evening Far-li-mas resumed his story. And before dawn broke, everyone had fallen asleep in the ecstasy of listening. But amid the sleepers lay Sali and Far-li-mas, and they sucked happiness from each other's lips and entwined their arms and legs. And so it went, night after night.

Among the people, the news of Far-li-mas' stories spread first. Then the rumor circulated that at night the priests neglected their sacrifices and prayers. A great uneasiness seized everyone. One day an important man of the city met the high priest. The important man said to the priest, "When will we celebrate the next feast of this year? I would like to make a journey and return in time for the feast. How long is it until the day of the feast?" The priest was embarrassed. It had been several days since he had looked at the moon and the stars.

He had learned nothing more about their course. The priest said, "Wait one more day and I will be able to tell you." The important man said, "Thank you. Tomorrow I will come to see you again."

The high priest gathered his priests together and asked, "Which of you has lately observed the course of the stars?" None of the priests answered, because all had stayed to listen to the stories of Far-li-mas. The high priest asked again, "Hasn't even one of you observed the course of the stars and the position of the moon?" All the priests were silent, until one of them, a very old man, stood up and said, "We were all in ecstasy, reclining before Far-li-mas. Nobody can tell you on which day the feasts must be celebrated, when the fire must be extinguished, and when a new one must be lit." The high priest shuddered and said, "How could all this happen? What shall I tell the people?" The old priest said, "It is the will of God. But if this Far-li-mas has not been sent by God, put him to death; for if he lives and continues to speak, everyone will listen to him." The high priest said, "What must I say to the people?" Everyone remained silent. Then they parted.

The high priest went to Sali. He asked, "What were the words you said that first day?" Sali replied, "I said, 'Great are the works of God. But the greatest is not his writing in the sky. It is life on earth.' You reproached me for my words and said they were wrong. Tell me now, today, whether I lied." The priest said, "Far-li-mas is against God. Far-li-mas must die." Sali said, "Far-li-mas is the companion in death of King Akaf." The priest said, "I shall speak with King Akaf." Sali said, "God is in my brother, King Akaf. Ask him what his thoughts are." The high priest went to King Akaf, whose sister Sali was beside him. The priest uncovered himself before King Akaf, bowed down, and said, "Forgive me, King Akaf." The king said, "Tell me what troubles your heart." The priest replied, "Speak to me of your companion in death, this Far-li-mas." The king said: "In the beginning, God sent me thoughts of my death. I knew that it was growing nearer, and I was terrified. Then God made me remember this Far-li-mas, who had been sent to me as a gift from the Orient, beyond the sea. With the first thought, God darkened my intellect. With the second, he comforted my soul and made me and others happy! For this I have given Far-li-mas many garments. My friends have given him gold and precious stones. He has made generous donations to the people. Now he is rich, as befits him, and the people love both him and me." The high priest said, "Far-li-mas must die. Far-li-mas destroys order." King Akaf said, "I will die before Far-li-mas." The high priest said, "God will decide the matter." King Akaf said, "So be it. All the people shall see." The high priest left. Sali said, "King Akaf, my brother, the way is nearing its end. The companion of your death will be he who reawakens you to life; but I demand that he be the happiness of my existence." King Akaf replied, "Then take him, Sali, my sister."

Messengers ran throughout the city announcing that Far-li-mas would speak that evening to the populace, in the great square. In the great square, between the king's palace and the houses of the priests, a veiled seat had been erected for the king. When evening fell, people collected from all sides and formed a circle. Thousands and thousands of people gathered. The priests came and took their places. The guests and the ambassadors came and took their places. Sali sat beside the veiled King Akaf. Far-li-mas was called.

Far-li-mas came. All the servants of Far-li-mas followed him. They were dressed in splendid garments. The servants of Far-li-mas sat beside the priests. Far-li-mas bowed down before King Akaf. Then he took his place.

The high priest stood up and said, "Far-li-mas has destroyed order in Naphta. Tonight he will demonstrate whether or not his was the will of God." The priest sat down. Far-li-mas stood up. He looked into Sali's eyes. Far-li-mas tore his gaze from Sali and turned it on the crowd. Far-li-mas looked at the priests. He said, "I am a servant of God and I believe that the evil in men's hearts is abhorrent to him. On this night God will decide." Far-li-mas began his story. The words that came from the mouth of Far-li-mas were sweet as honey. As the first summer rain soaks into the parched earth, so his voice penetrated his listeners. The mouth of Far-li-mas gave off a scent more subtle than musk and incense. The head of Far-li-mas shone like a torch in the black of night.

At first the story of Far-li-mas was like hashish when it makes wakefulness happy. Then the story was like hashish when it makes dreams delirious. Toward morning Far-li-mas raised his voice. As the Nile rises in the hearts of men, so his words swelled. To some, his words brought serenity; to others, they were as terrifying as the appearance of Azrael, the angel of death. Happiness filled the spirits of some, horror the hearts of the others. The closer morning came, the mightier that voice grew and the more it resounded within the people. The hearts of men rose up against one another, as in battle. They raged one against one another like clouds in the sky on a stormy night. Flashes of wrath met thunderbolts of fury. When the sun rose, the tale of Far-li-mas reached its end. Ineffable wonder filled the confused minds of the people. For when the living looked around, their gaze fell upon the priests. The priests were stretched out on the ground, dead.

Sali stood up. Sali bowed down before the king. Sali said, "King Akaf, my brother, cast aside the veil; show yourself to your people and perform the sacrifice yourself. For these men have been cut down by Azrael, by God's command." The servants removed the veils from the throne. King Akaf stood up. He was the first king the people of Naptha had ever seen. And King Akaf was handsome as the rising sun.

The populace rejoiced. A white horse was led forward, and the king sprang onto its back. To his left was his sister, Sali-fu-Hamr; to his right, Far-li-mas. The king rode to the temple. Inside the temple the king took a spade and dug three holes in the sacred earth. He threw three seeds into them. The king dug two holes in the sacred earth. Sali threw two seeds into them. And immediately the five seeds sprouted and grew before the eyes of the people. At noon the ears of the five plants were ripe. In all the courtyards of the city, fathers broke the fetlocks of great bulls. The king extinguished the fire. All the fathers of the city extinguished the fires on the hearths. Sali lit a new fire and all the virgins came to take some of it.

From that day on, no one else was ever killed in Naphta. King Akaf was the first king of Naphta to live until it pleased God to take him, at an advanced age, to his bosom. When King Akaf died, Far-li-mas was his successor. Under him Naphta reached the peak of its happiness, and its end.

For the fame of King Akaf as a wise and well-advised king spread quickly through all countries. All the princes sent him gifts and sent their clever men to learn from him. All the great merchants settled in the city of Naphta. King Akaf, on the eastern sea, had many great ships which carried the products of Naphta to every part of the world. The mines of Naphta could not supply enough gold and copper to keep the shops full. When Far-li-mas succeeded King Akaf, the country's happiness reached its peak. His fame had reached all countries, from the eastern sea to the western. But as his fame grew, envy took root in men's hearts. When Far-li-mas died, the neighboring countries violated their treaties and made war on Naphta. Naphta was defeated. Naphta was destroyed, and with it the most magnificent palace of the kingdom. The great realm fell to pieces. It was overrun by savage peoples. Men forgot the mines of gold and silver. The cities disappeared. Of Naphta's glory years, nothing remained but the tales of Far-li-mas, which he had brought with him from the land beyond the eastern sea.

This is the story of the ruin of the land of Kasch. Its last remaining sons live in the land of For.

⚜

Among the Ruins of Kasch

Early in 1912, Leo Frobenius set out on his fifth African expedition. He had just returned from Africa. "I needed only three days to embrace my little daughter in the Tyrol, my wife, and my brother; then it was off at once to Africa, but this time to the eastern part.

"Suez—Port Sudan—Khartoum—El Obeid . . .

"And here we are. Once again we are swimming in happiness." He was seeking the way to the lost mines of Hophrat-en-Nahas. He arrived at El Obeid during preparations for a solemn celebration in honor of Lord Kitchener and Sir Reginald Wingate. Frobenius was not expecting this; he had quite different matters on his mind. But the "great man of For" had sent "ambassadors and presents and various other things" to El Obeid for the festivities. "'Various' indeed! For example, a very old camel driver by the name of Arach ben Hassul, who carries in his heart the most splendid legend of the past: the legend of Kasch, or Napata. Now you, too, are pricking up your ears, my friend, aren't you? It's quite mad! Served on a tray, in little more than half an hour, the wisdom of millennia! After all our discussions on these matters, you will of course understand immediately what this means to me, if this old bearer of myths can say how it happened that a king of the East sent a messenger to the Court of Napata, and this messenger told splendid tales and then changed the form of the State. The king of the distant East, beyond the sea! This must be some place in the Indian Ocean. Is it possible that in the future we shall be right in calling the Indian Ocean the Kaschitic Ocean?"

And so it happened that the camel driver Arach ben Hassul told the story of the ruin of Kasch. "Ambassadors and envoys of nations came from all over to pay homage. Among them were inhabitants of For. They stood out from all the others because of their splendid camels, and a camel race was even planned. One old man, very skilled, had come to Obeid to take care of these racing camels; this was Arach ben Hassul, a descendant of the ancient copper guild in Kordofan. Long extinct in that land, its last descendants live in the Dar For . . . No less extraordinary than the man himself was his way of imparting his learning. For seven days he remained seated with the others, among the tellers of tales who had gathered around me. For seven days he sipped his coffee with the others. For seven days he said no word beyond a greeting when he arrived and a goodbye when he left. To any question about ancient matters he would answer, 'I do not know.' For seven days he sat and listened with profound attention to the tales recorded in this volume [the fourth volume of Frobenius' *Atlantis*, where the story of the ruin of Kasch was published for the first time], never making his presence known except by lending an ear.

"But when the eighth day came, he rose to his feet, ran his hand over his face from his eyes to his chin, and said, 'I speak.'

"After which he came down from the *angareb,* sat on the ground, and asked the storytellers of Kordofan, 'Do you know what you are telling to the *taleb?* You do not know. It is difficult to know.' Then he drew a line in the sand and said, 'This is For.' He drew another line and said, 'This is Napht. For was the son of Napht.' He drew another line and said, 'This is Habesch. Napht was the son of Habesch.' He drew a fourth line and said, 'This is Kasch. Habesch and his brother Masr were the sons of Kasch. Kasch was the *mahdi* of Kordofan. He came from far away, from beyond the sea. The stories you tell are stories of the time of Kasch, and among these there is another story, but you would not understand it, for in those days everything was different from the way it is now. Now in Kordofan there are trees here and there, but then there were many, many trees. Now in Kordofan the fields are unproductive; then they were fertile. Now in Kordofan there is little rain; then there was much. Now in Kordofan there are few villages, and they are small; then there were big cities, bigger than in Egypt. Now in Kordofan there is no longer anyone who can work copper and gold and iron and brass; then all the copper, all the gold, all the brass in the world came from Kordofan. At that time great *meleks,* great kings, governed Kordofan, and all the nations brought gifts to the *meleks.* From that period your stories have come down, and there is one story that tells how those tales were told. But you would not understand it.'"

Years later, Frobenius reflected on what Arach ben Hassul had said: "The storyteller began by remarking that For (the first lord of the Dar For) was the son of Napht and that the latter was the son of Habesch (Abyssinia), but that he and his brother Masr (Egypt) were the sons of Kasch. It is not hard to recognize in Napht or Napata the first lord of what today is Nubia (which reached its apex long ago, with Meroe). Nevertheless it is quite curious that Kasch (which inevitably brings to mind the Kushites of the Egyptians and of the Torah) is explicitly defined as the lord of Kordofan, hence of a region that today is a land deserted by civilization and that has become the homeland of nomadic marauders who retain some traces of a chivalric tradition." El Obeid, the largest city of Kordofan, was where Frobenius had heard the story of the ruin of Kasch. There the men sit for hours in coffeehouses and talk about prices and crops. Nothing else seems to exist for them; nothing seems to have preceded their monotonous conversations. "I have never been in a region of Africa where the landscape is so uniform and speaks so little of the past as in this central region of the lands of the Nile. And I have never met a people so unable to see into the depths of things—a people so universally impassive and indifferent to the questions about where we come from and where we are going." But one day that desolation, separated from ancient times by an opaque veil, was visited by the breath of tales. That breath came from "the Kasch of the East," from *Arabia felix,* and perhaps from even farther off: from the western shores of India. One day it brought the doctrine of the ritual murder of the king, and one day it brought the story of the ruin of Kasch and the scent of the *Thousand and One Nights.*

Years later, Frobenius reflected on the paideumatic stage to which the story of the ruin of Kasch belongs: "The legend of the ruin of Kasch can only be late, very late. It is a recollection of a state of things long vanished—a memory of the days when men with complete self-abnegation, which sometimes reached the point of self-immolation, 'enacted' the destiny of the stars. It does not belong, however, to the period when that attitude flourished; rather, it belongs to the period in which that attitude was fading—when emotion had weakened in the people and they were beginning to give in to the need to form concepts, at the expense of their vitality. Taken as a whole, this legend already entails a representation. The idea of *what is historical* has come into being here. This creation represents in a certain way the process through which decisive parts of the field of civilization have dissociated themselves from the rest and have entered the profane. It is quite a singular creation, and I could not cite another one like it anywhere in world literature."

This is the story of the passage from one world to another, from one order to another—and of the ruin of both. It is the story of the precariousness of order, the ancient order and the new. The story of their perpetual ruin.

Scheherazade and Far-li-mas: their stories postpone death, but do not suspend it. What they suspend is the death sentence.

Joseph de Maistre is one of the priests of Naphta.

When men played the part of the stars, they were strangled with a black thong.

. . .

The law can be observed by a single subject. Sacrifice demands a dual subject. For this reason, in the law we recognize the exoteric side of sacrifice. Esoteric in its nature, sacrifice can only give way to storytelling, which vanquishes it in an ordeal involving both. Storytelling is the esoteric of the esoteric, the secret of the secret: it teaches us how to live outside the cycle, in the hashish-like suspension of the word. It is the way of life that comes to light after the defeat of sacrifice, yet it retains the gesture of sacrifice diluted in all gestures. But it is not enough to save Kasch; indeed, it hastens its ruin. For many generations the priests had strangled the king after observing the stars; for a few years the inhabitants of Naphta lived in the memory of the words of Far-li-mas, before Naphta was destroyed. "Of Naphta's glory years, nothing remained but the tales of Far-li-mas, which he had brought with him from the land beyond the eastern sea."

From afar, Far-li-mas and Sali appear to be the heroes of a new order, based on revolt against sacrifice. Seen close up, Far-li-mas and Sali are elements of the sacrifice that defeat other elements of the sacrifice. They shift the weights and the accents. They untangle in an unprecedented way the mixture of communion and expulsion, of hierogamy and assassination. In order for story to succeed in replacing bloody sacrifice, it must contain in itself something no less powerful than the *soma,* the mysterious substance of the Vedic sacrifice. And the word of Far-li-mas is the *soma.* Hierogamy is represented by the joining of Sali and Far-li-mas, "entwining their arms and legs amid the sleepers." Sacrificial expulsion is represented by the death of the priests, who are struck down by the word of Far-li-mas in the ordeal. To escape the enforcement of the bloody sacrifice, Far-li-mas and Sali become variants of the characters in the ancient sacrificial story of Mo-ye and Kan-tsiang:

"Kan-tsiang and Mo-ye, male and female, were two swords. They were also husband and wife, and both were smiths.

"Kan-tsiang, the husband, having received an order to forge *two* swords, set to work; but despite three months of effort, he was unable to make the metal melt. When his wife, Mo-ye, asked him the reason for his failure, he at first gave her an evasive answer. She insisted, reminding him of the principle according to which the transformation of the *holy material* (which is metal) demands (the sacrifice of) a person for its fulfillment. Kan-tsiang then told how his master had succeeded in melting the metal only by throwing himself, *with his wife,* into the forge. Mo-ye declared herself ready to give her body, if her husband would have his own melted.

"Mo-ye was a good wife. She, no less than her husband, deserved to give her name to one of the two swords. Her devotion was absolute. But it did not extend to having her body consumed instantly. Like Yu the Great, T'ang, and the Duke of Cheou, husband and wife cut off their hair and trimmed their nails. *Together,* they threw the parings and hair into the forge. They gave the part to give the whole.

"As the couple carried out their act of devotion, the Yin and the Yang *mingled their breaths* to assist the melting: the bellows were operated by three hundred *maidens* AND *youths,* all VIRGINS.

"Another author gives the same number: three hundred. According to him, *only* VIRGIN *maidens* were summoned to create the flow of air.

"Mo-ye, according to one version, fulfilled the act of devotion ALONE. She threw herself into the forge. It was a story of sacred union, a *marriage* with the god of the Oven."

The Chinese irony of the nail parings and hair in the forge does not conceal the original form of the sacrifice: hierogamy and suicide. Sali and Far-li-mas, clever melters, separate the elements of the sacrifice. They couple among the sleepers, protected by the veil of the word. And they let the priests be slaughtered, let them be struck down in the ordeal by the word, as if by the sword that the sacrifice helps to forge. The lifeless bodies of the priests replace those of the hierogamic couple in the forge, as if they were the nail parings and hair of Mo-ye and Kan-tsiang.

Sali and Far-li-mas defeat the priests because the two of them remain awake, he narrating, she listening. Everything is displaced into the pure act of awareness. In the ancient order of the sacrifice, the stake to which the victim was bound existed in the mind and in the world; and distinctions between them were inadmissible. Now everything goes back to being invisible: the sacrificial offering is the story. The conflict with the previous order remains visible, since the last victims are the priests. The sacrifice is absorbed into perfect wakefulness.

In Naphta a struggle occurs between the order of bloody sacrifice, which depends on the stars in the sky, and the order of a life without attachments, which speaks in the stories of Far-li-mas and will be disguised in history. Far-li-mas wins the struggle—and history begins. But it is a victory that lasts only a short time, the victory of a single dual subject: Far-li-mas and Sali. In fact, both orders are condemned to ruin.

Far-li-mas is not opposed to sacrifice: when Akaf announces that he has chosen the storyteller as "companion in death," Far-li-mas is not frightened. The one who is frightened is Sali—victorious Antigone and African Eurydice. And in her, Far-li-mas recognizes a "will" that seeks a new "way." Far-li-mas' "gift of telling," which rises like the waves and carries the listener only to a state of intoxication, replaces the "writing in the sky," which governs growth in nature and the recurrence of regicide. As Sali said to the priest, "life on earth"—oscillating, changeable, without preestablished order, like Far-li-mas' stories—has revealed itself to be a "greater" work than the "writing in the sky." Sali's "way" is an ineradicable statement: "From that day on, no one else was ever killed in Naphta."

"If one night we do not look, we must offer a sacrifice," say the priests of Naphta. The priests look at the sky, to read there the sign of the sacrifice. And they perform a sacrifice when they are unable to read the sky. Sacrifice is the end and sacrifice is the means. Sacrifice is what is read and what allows reading. This is the vibrant circle of the old order.

The subject who escapes death in the sacrifice is a dual subject, just as the subject who had constituted the sacrifice was dual. Akaf is saved only through the work of Far-li-mas, his "companion in death," the bird of the *Upanishads* that contemplates and here tells stories. And Far-li-mas is saved only through the help of Sali, who finds the "way." Hierogamy is the seal of the dual subject.

.   .   .

It is not during the day but at night that one can see the current position of the world, by observing the positions of the stars. And Far-li-mas tells his stories at night. The priests, whose task is to remain awake and devote their vigil to contemplating the sky, sink into sleep, under the sway of the words that Far-li-mas utters, as his gaze joins that of Sali in perfect wakefulness. In this double trajectory, from sleep to vigil and from vigil to sleep, we see the breathing of history.

The death of the priests in the ordeal is as grand as the ruin of Naphta is harsh and swift after Far-li-mas. Envious neighbors overpower and destroy Naphta, which has meanwhile become a rich center of trade. There is nothing more to be said. The old order has ended, amid visions that cause men's hearts to swell like the Nile.

After the priests have become victims, at the center of the sacrificial circle formed by many thousands of people, the veil before the king is raised. The fruits of this last sacrifice are the plants that Akaf and Sali sow after the priests' death and that sprout at once. The veil drawn aside by the king is the sign that they have now entered the order of manifest esotericism; they are not protected, but abandoned to the raging flux of events.

The ruin of Kasch comes *after* the death of King Akaf. And until the very end Akaf upholds sacrifice, though without sacrificing himself. Far-li-mas, on the other hand, cannot perform the sacrifice. He is neither priest nor king; he is only *the other side* of the last king. The kings die out with Akaf, and the priests must succumb in the conflict. The king who is not sacrificed is the last king; he cannot hand on his life to a successor. The situation is the reverse of the modern one: Louis XVI, the first king who is sacrificed (Charles I had not attained the status of pure exemplar), marks the end of royal sovereignty.

With Far-li-mas another sort of power is introduced: the reign of the word, which follows that of blood. It is a reign that does not kill according to ritual, but causes death through a disorder that arrives rapidly, invincibly. The words of Far-li-mas replace the sacrifice; like sacrifice, they have the power to command obedience, but they do not have the power to determine the length of the cycle. Time now is only the pendular swing between an empty flow, without attachments, and suspension in the drug of the word. The words of Far-li-mas live by their own strength, but they cannot reflect the position of the stars.

Far-li-mas manages to postpone death. When it comes, it is no longer a bloody sacrifice but the obscure and intricate ruin of Kasch. Yet something survives that destruction: his words. Under the reign of the priests, nothing would have escaped. The hand of God would have annihilated the kingdom in silence. But a voice continues to tell the story of the ruin of Kasch.

The legend of Kasch teaches us that sacrifice is the cause of ruin, but that the absence of sacrifice is also the cause of ruin. This pair of simultaneous and contradictory truths hints at a singular and more obscure truth, which lies in tranquillity: society is ruin. And from this obscurity a sign points us to something further, something on the bedrock: society is ruin because in it reverberates the sound of the world—its incessant, consuming drone.

In storytelling there is an element that is deeply opposed to mortal judgment, that skirts its coercive side, eludes the descending knife. Storytelling is a going forward and a turning back, a wave-like movement in the voice, a continual canceling of borders, a dodging of sharp spears.

The ruin of Kasch is the origin of literature. The *soma* is the origin of sweetness.

The Ruin of Kasch is one of the stories of Far-li-mas.

The stories of Far-li-mas have the effect of the *soma:* they act like the honey of sacrifice, its fruit. Spreading the honey of sacrifice, Far-li-mas defeats the bloody sacrifice. But that honey ends with him: since the cycle of the stars has been abandoned, the certitude of the *soma* is no more. It is now an erratic gift. After the death of Far-li-mas, Naphta will end in ruin. Only its stories will remain to nourish the arid, avid body of history. Nothing is said about any successor to Far-li-mas. That would be getting into literature.

"The King of Chou was seated with the Prince of Fan. At a certain point the courtiers of the King of Chou declared that the principality of Fan had been utterly lost. The Prince of Fan said to the King of Chou, 'The ruin of my principality is not enough to destroy its existence.' If the ruin of Fan was not enough to destroy its existence, then the existence of Chou would not be enough to preserve Chou. Looking at things from this perspective, we clearly see that the principality of Fan could not declare that it had been ruined, any more than the kingdom of Chou could call itself safe."

❧

Elements of Sacrifice

Sacrifice does not serve to expiate guilt, as the textbooks say. Sacrifice *is* guilt—the only one.

Sacrifice is self-elaborating guilt. It transforms murder into suicide. It enables us to see murder from a perspective in which the vanishing point is suicide—a point that is so far away we find ourselves gazing at the origin of all things. Where we encounter divine suicide: the Creation.

The basis of sacrifice lies in the fact that each one of us is two, not one. We are not a dense and uniform brick. Each of us consists of the two birds of the *Upanishads,* on the same branch of the cosmic tree: one eats, and the other watches the one that is eating. The revelation of the sacrificial stratagem—that sacrificer and victim are two persons, not one—is the dazzling, ultimate revelation concerning our selves, concerning our double eye.

History is also summed up in the fact that for a long time men killed other beings and dedicated them to an invisible power, but that after a certain point they killed without dedicating the victims to anyone. Did they forget? Did they consider that act of homage futile? Did they condemn it as repugnant? All these reasons had some sort of bearing on the matter. Afterward, nothing remained but pure killing.

The Creation is the body of the first victim. In the Creation the divinity amputates and forsakes a part of itself. Thereafter the divinity can only observe the amputated limb, in the hands of necessity.

Quechcotona, in Nahuatl, means both "to cut off someone's head" and "to pick an ear of grain with one's hand." The perception which lies at the origin of sacrifice is, in fact, that every act of *picking* is also a *killing*—that any uprooting, any detaching of something from what it is connected to (and if we go from one link to the next, this is nothing but the All), is a killing. But life, if it is to be perpetuated, demands that something be picked. Sacrifice enshrouds the first uprooting, the first detachment, the original *decisio* (from the verb *caedo,* meaning to kill a sacrificial victim with spilling of blood), in a vast, delicate, extremely fine network, which links the cavity of the wound to the All at the moment it is opened. It is possible to pick merely an ear of grain, but the highest accretion of power occurs when "picking" means killing a person. Not uprooting a stem but using the "obsidian butterfly" (as they used to say in ancient Mexico) to cut a still-throbbing heart from the torso of a supine victim. When one tears away the network that links the heart to the whole of the body, one is inundated with six or seven liters of blood. This is life's abundance, which is vouchsafed forever only in that blood.

The Vedic seers (ṛṣi), like the Aztec priests, had a keen sense of the precarious. Every moment of time had to be torn away by force—with the violence, the steadfastness, the precision of sacrifice—before the sun could stop, before everything could once again be dispersed in Ahi Budhnya, "the serpent that dwells in the depths of the sky," formless immensity, darkness upon darkness.

. . .

The Aztecs were perpetually at war, but not out of desire for conquest. For them, war was mainly a device by which they procured prisoners, who then became sacrificial victims. Twenty thousand a year, according to the calculations of some scholars. In relation to sacrifice, war was a by-product. When sacrifice ceased to be an institution, it withdrew into its subordinate power: war. In August 1914, the entire liturgical apparatus of sacrifice was once again unpacked from the trunks. The bloody images were dusted off and made the center of attention in homes and newspapers. During the Second World War, in contrast, it was enough to focus on a single word: "holocaust."

Experimentation is sacrifice from which all guilt has been expunged. The sacrificial pyramid, where blood has soaked into the hot stones of the altar, becomes a vast slaughterhouse, spreading horizontally through some nondescript urban neighborhood.

The slaughterhouses of Chicago, our university laboratories with their corridors reeking of dismembered frogs, and our camouflaged power plants in the desert are the sites of a single cult. They distribute power through violent intervention, through decisions whereby all is concentrated on procedures, so that their capacity for control is always being perfected. Hadn't the Vedic seers already said that "precision, reality is the sacrifice"? The more perfect the control, the richer the material to be developed, the more intense the power released, the more uncontrollable its outcome.

In technology, the *accursed part,* the *fire's part,* has become experiment's boundless waste, dedicated to the unknown god, who is the god of the unknown. And, as in sacrifice, it is the irreversibly destroyed part which guarantees future life. Only research that is conducted in the dark, that ventures into the unknown, can give sufficient nourishment to the process. Nothing is more laughable than disputes over the *limits* of experimental research. As if that which is based on the abolition of limits could be contained within a boundary narrower than that of the All, without negating itself. Such disputes are fomented by foolish and incredulous priests against the stern masters of the cult, as if a brahman had dared cast doubt on the tenet that the gods demand sacrifice.

A sacrificial act is any act in which the actor contemplates himself as he acts. The victim, the offering, is he who acts. The sacrificer is the eye that contemplates him. Thus, any act can be a sacrifice. Indeed, archaic society can be considered, in its functioning, as a "perpetual sacrifice"—a phrase that René Guénon coined, and used as if its meaning were transparently obvious: "Since sacrifice is the ritual act par excellence, all other acts share its nature and are somehow integrated with it, so that it necessarily determines the general structure of a traditional society. For this reason, we can say that everything in such a society truly constitutes a perpetual sacrifice."

The magnificent edifice of the Vedic sacrifice—that temple of temples where every brick is a Borobudur, with hidden galleries adorned with bas-reliefs invisible from the outside—is not enough to cover, behind all its obsessive affirmations, the place of doubt, a tiny wound on the intact skin of the horse that is to be sacrificed. This locus of doubt is the existence of a victim who replaces the *yajamāna,* the sacrificer. The only reply to the divine sacrifice of Prajāpati would be the suicide of the sacrificer. Instead, the killing of a victim becomes the reply. "The victorious Horse went to his immolation addressing his thoughts to the divinity," and someone reassured him that "the axe will not cause lasting harm to your body." This concern for the victim's assent is revealing, because it assumes that such assent might be lacking. But here it is not a matter of uncovering an ancient deception, of the sort that would appease all the agents of the Enlightenment, who are capable of perceiving only the smallest evil (and the smallest good). If at the scene of sacrifice at least two beings are present—the victim and the man who strangles him with a thong—it is because the substitution has already taken place in the mind. The very act of naming, the arbitrary decision that enables a thing to be annulled and replaced with a sound, contains the same primordial murder that the sacrifice at once exposes and tries to heal. The continually renewed fabric of correspondences, the meanings each time attributed to the single syllable, to the single meter: it is all a vast attempt to mend the woof around that minuscule rent produced by the word, by the mental image that annuls a presence to evoke an absence, by the sign, by all that replaces something else and that *stands for* something else. Over this gap another magnificent edifice has been built, the opposite of that of the Vedic sacrifice, which in its incessant expansion seems both to foreshadow it and to want to conceal it, until the cycle rouses it in its present form, within us, around us.

The fact that nature is cadenced by recurrences, by time's breathing, shows that it is a sacrificial object. The world is a part of divinity that divinity has detached from itself, allowing it to live according to its own rules and no longer according to divine whim. But the invisible cord between divinity and creation is not entirely severed. The divinity can also take back its world and intervene in it brutally: it can obliterate order, prevent the stars from returning. Hence the sacrifice performed by men: along that same cord, which becomes the column of smoke rising from the sacred pipe, rises the human offering—that part of life which is not allowed to live unless it is reabsorbed by the sky from which it descended. In surrendering part of the world to the divinity, the sacrificer wants the divinity to surrender the rest of the world to him, and to cease intervening in its arbitrary, uncontrollable way. The sacrificer also wants the divinity's permission to use the world. Thus, the first consequence of the eclipse of sacrifice will be that the world will be used without restraint, without limit, without any part being devoted to something else. But here, too, the end overlaps with the origin, like a reflection and hence reversed: once sacrifice is dissolved, the whole world reverts, unawares, to a great sacrificial workshop. There is only one statement that, amid universal uncertainty, no one would dare cast doubt upon, since it has become assimilated and obvious: namely, that the world lives insofar as it produces. This is the same obvious truth that the *Rig Veda* recognizes when it says that the world lives insofar as it sacrifices. Just as originally the divinity could sacrifice only itself, since nothing else existed, so now the world sacrifices, under other names, itself to itself, for the divinity has vanished. The unwitting sacrificers now resemble the Sadhya, those obscure "gods before the gods" who later fell "because they considered themselves above sacrifice." But a power can also fall because it believes that sacrifice has been enclosed in a room at the Musée de l'Homme.

If industry is a sacrificial workshop, the prestigious value of the New implies that any innovative object is redolent of the ashes of immolation. An unknown quantity of material has been burned to produce it. The New is that part of the victim which the gods have not touched at their banquet. The gods devour the precious proto-type and leave men the endless copies. Thus, industry is founded on reproducibility. But every movie star is a constellation, incorpo-rated into the heavens after being devoured by the gods.

Seen from the outside, the actions of the unenlightened, though obeying the ritual order, cannot be distinguished in any way from those of the enlightened. They eat, they fight, they sacrifice, they embrace—using the same gestures. The only difference, and an invisible one at that, is that the enlightened are *detached* from the fruit of their actions. According to the *Bhagavad Gītā,* action must be performed by all, enlightened and unenlightened alike. This is because, first of all, action is taking place within us at every moment ("Never, not even for a single instant, do we cease to perform some action; for even without willing it, we are compelled to act because of the qualities [*guṇa*] that constitute nature"). Even when we are completely immobile, we continue to breathe; in breathing, we offer up a sacrifice; in offering up a sacrifice, we offer up the world. Second, we are obliged to act because, if our actions obey the *ṛta,* the order (like the sacrificial action), they help turn the wheel of cosmic articulation ("Thus turns the wheel"). Even if we act without being aware of our actions, we still help turn the wheel—but in the direction that leads it back to the undifferentiated: "The worlds would collapse if I did not perform my action. I myself would bring about universal confusion and would cause the worlds' creatures to perish." With lucid terror, the Hindu seer perceived the threat of the return to the undifferentiated, which comprises every other threat. At the same time he knew that necessary action, even if conscious, cannot lead to liberation if it contains none of that mysterious element—detachment. The *ṛṣi* gave the highest meaning to action, asserting that without its constant support the world could dissolve any moment. Yet they also asserted that one must separate oneself from action—through *detachment*.

There is always a *path of action* and a *path of awareness* of action. The latter, which is the Esoteric, presupposes—as its illustrated sheath—the path of action, which is the Exoteric. All gnosis is an emphasis on the path of awareness of acts—the path of thought, of knowledge. The formula for the access to this path appears again and again in the *Upanishads:* "He who knows thus." In this way a vast, imperceptible distance is established between he who acts thus and he who acts in the same manner but "who knows thus." Today we are in a situation of forced esotericism, because the path of action has been obliterated, because there is no longer a particular action required at any particular moment: all actions are performed at every moment, and any articulation of them is perceived only in their simultaneous accumulation or in their indefinite juxtaposition. The Esoteric here encounters its greatest risk: now nothing can be known except esoterically, and many people think esoterically *without being aware of it*. This is the supreme evil, the challenge and the taunt of Inversion, the parody within which all gnosis is obliged to move, sometimes even disguising itself as unawareness in order to escape capture. But at the same time the Esoteric is now lured by a most extraordinary challenge, always latent, now surfacing: to take *everything* as support (illustrated sheath) of knowledge, and no longer just those actions that belonged to the order of the sacrifice, the calendar, the cycle. To take as support the total dispersion, the fragmentation. This delicate, dizzying transition evokes the Doctrine of the Forest, the boldest part of the Vedic texts, in which it is hinted that, since sacrifice is all, we could actually dispense with performing it in society. Instead we could simply lie in wait in the forest and see it performed there at every moment, in our very physiology, in our very breathing, just as today everything can be described as a moment in the cycle of production and consumption.

It is said that sacrifice is the origin of exchange; but exchange is a set of which sacrifice is a subset. And exchange, in turn, is incorporated into another category, which alone makes it possible: sub-stitution. This *stands for* that; he who *gives* this *takes* that.

The origin of substitution does not even lie in the ability to give names (and thus replace things with them). It lies in the ultimate and all-encompassing ability to shape mental images: invisible, fleet-ing, sporadic entities, states of awareness that overlap with what is perceived—or that even replace it, delete it. Here we witness the original bifurcation of the psyche; here the two birds of the *Upan-ishads* descend from the sky to cling to the same bough. The bird that eats is the one that is constantly *obliged* to perceive (to feed himself), by receiving stimuli. The other, the bird that watches, constantly superimposes his gaze on the gaze that the other bird trains on the world.

Every act can be viewed as a form of sacrifice if the process of giving and taking, the metabolism inscribed in every gesture, is discernible in it. Sacrifice thus comprises every act leading to the awareness of this process.

THE SENATOR FROM ST. PETERSBURG: Arrogant orphans of rituals and ceremonies, haven't you noticed that you are in a most dangerous place—too close to the point of origin? Mental sacrifice, the only one you could know, was the esoteric aspect of that slaughterhouse once concentrated on the altar at which offerings were made. You have no further need for Prajāpati, who used to be dismembered and emptied in all corners of the world; or for the nameless man whose sole heart used to be torn from his breast; or for the animal that looks at you with humanlike eyes as it awaits the knife; or even for the plant that is liquid fire. Silent, motion-less, immersed in thought, you can proceed to the invisible act from which every other act stems: the offer of the self to the Self—the only gesture that can still temper the harshness of the turning wheel. And from there nothing prevents you from con-tinuing in society, like the Neva, which is flowing behind us even as we speak. To be sure, you know that the upper waters do not respond to sacrificial fire; you have renounced the Vedic arithmetic which allowed you to follow the course of the cosmic game. Yet if you do not continue to sacrifice (though no one, not even yourselves, is aware of it), your thought will become that of a meek rabble ceaselessly telling the rosary of opinion. An even more obscure constraint will clutch at your throat and drive you to identify yourselves with things that are, after all, unimportant— such as yourselves. Even in solitude you will be persecuted by a horde of voices, as at the Café du Commerce. And very few among you will even rise to the insolence of the libertine accustomed to exchanging his thoughts for a lacy cravat. Obeying a despot you have never seen, you will end up realizing that living is too costly.

The most shameless metaphors are those that once upon a time established the poles of the world order. "Woman-cow" and "man-bull" bear witness to this, as well as to a pervasive contempt for the civilization of the goddess. Industry does not strive to annihilate tradition, as a reactionary thesis would claim; on the contrary, it brings it to completion—as traffic in archetypes. To this end it conceals the foundation of tradition, the sense of a continual violation of order, which rituals meant to heal through an interrupted exchange in which what had just been shamefully and inevitably appropriated was given away. The sacrificial exchange is contradictory because it denies the very basis of exchange and trade—namely, the unit of measure, which is not common to human language and the world of nature. Myth established the impossible symbolic system that would make exchange possible. Thanks to this impossibility, exchange was rescued from the transgression that marked its origin. For kitsch reveals not only the annulment of natural relations but also the curse that transforms the moment of original violation (when relations were given a name) into an unending nightmare. The forgetting of this transgression is the foundation of industry. Thus, what exists is a chain of messages, equal in validity, convergent in meaning, disparate in form. What is missing are the conscious agents that interchange them and the thing that proposes them. All this could be an image of the Word. Industry, therefore, deserves our thanks: knowledge can come only *per speculum in aenigmate*—"through a glass, darkly."

.　　.　　.

THE CHEVALIER DE B***: As an adolescent I went through what were called the "storms of revolution" in my country, and I think I learned one thing above all. I now know that our greatest enemy (in any case the shrewdest) is society, the very concept of society. Once upon a time it was content to portray itself as a great body, a giant racked by occasional spasms. Today it has swallowed the seas underground and in the heavens, from the Yellow Springs to Eridanus; it has incorporated stars and magma; it has subsumed into itself everything that exists. The primordial giant, the Great Animal that Plato had long ago hallucinated, will seem like a mass of tiny Sèvres pitchers compared to the immense glass bubble in which society has enclosed the world: everything is a seedling in its greenhouse.

The foundation of inversion: society manages to absorb into itself all the images of the divine, as well as those of nature. It incorporates everything that once stood *opposite* society, everything from which society detached itself, with which it negotiated its life at every moment: the triple hub that links the wheel of the articulate to the triple *pada,* the hidden region of the inarticulate, from which the articulate descends, on which it depends, to which it returns. Connections: Durkheim's formula—"The religious is the social"—is a sign that this enveloping society already exists; indeed, it is clearly perceivable, to such an extent that it can be introduced as a scientific hypothesis. In Simone Weil we have the first revolt against this secular form of religion, a revulsion parallel to that which Lucretius felt when he saw the "blood of four-footed creatures spilled copiously over the altars." Weil was the first to recognize the most insidious peculiarity of the social: the "mystery" through which there exists "an apparent kinship between the social and the supernatural." She was the first to affirm that, because of this kinship, the *only* idolatry is that which bows before society and the only enslavement is "enslavement to society."

Thus greeting Buddha: "Shell? Milk? Moon? Jasmine? Crystal? Snowflake? Linen cloth? Pale cloud? Oh, whiteness! Oh, burst of laughter! A row of parasols rises to the heavens! The adorable parasols illuminate the world; three-times-ten gods, wondrous birds, and blessed singers of paradise are delighted with them. Bow in ceaseless worship of Buddha, kinsman of the Sun!" When Buddha convinced the five monks, his first disciples, that he was the Awakened, he immediately compared himself to "a stag that lives in the forest and runs over its slopes. In complete security he advances, rises, or lies down; in complete security he rests. He cannot be reached by those who prepare traps." The first image of liberation that occurs to Buddha is that of the victim who has eluded the sacrifice, the prey that has eluded the hunter.

The passage from the Vedic world to Buddha is a passage from hunger to thirst. For the ṛṣi, "in the beginning all was wrapped in death, in hunger, because hunger is death." For Buddha, according to his speech in Benares, all that must be avoided is "thirst." Hunger belongs to the metaphysics of sacrifice; it is the hub around which it revolves. Thirst belongs to the metaphysics of the forest, which has escaped sacrifice but discovers that this is not enough to escape desire. Buddha discovers that desire is not necessarily linked to killing—or rather, that killing continues even in the most innocuous act. His discovery goes further along the same line as that followed by the brahman turned *sannyāsin* (renouncer). And almost in an almost impious way it reveals how they converge and how the renouncers hadn't gone far enough. Withdrawn into the forest, far from the site of sacrifice, the *sannyāsin* had discovered that it was not enough to be freed from the sacrificial act: every instant of life is an act, and behind each act there is a desire, just as behind each sacrifice there is a desire for the fruit of the sacrifice. Now, with the coming of Buddha, the *karma* (any act) is no longer primarily a sacrificial act; it is naked action, any action. The All, which resonates in universal interdependence, the Vedic rosary of identifications— this is that, which is that, which is this—is suddenly silent. Now the names of the various interwoven threads seem unimportant, occasional, momentary. The only thing that matters is their unchanging nature: to be threads, woven, imprisoning. This is the *pratītyasamutpāda:* the all-enveloping net of the sacrifice. But it no longer resonates with harmonics. When touched, it emits a hollow sound, which once signaled the sympathy among its parts but now testifies only to its own immense existence. For the ṛṣi, the interdependence of everything was won and built by sacrifice; for Buddha, interdependence had always existed and was insignificant. Why celebrate it, why help it continue to weave itself, if one only had to unravel it carefully, thread by thread, with the same precision the Vedic seers used in the reverse action, in order to slip through the mesh of the net?

The relationship between science and the unknown parallels and varies the relationship between the Vedic brahmans and their multiple gods. The existence of the unknown demands a vast and continuous expenditure of energy, of life. And the fruit of this sacrificial work, from which every *opus* derives, is an occasional discovery, a gift granted by the unknown to its priests. And just as the Vedic gods feared that, through sacrifice, the priests might succeed in becoming truly immortal (following the path of the gods themselves, who originally had become immortal through sacrifice), so the unknown might fear that this profusion of offerings is not a repeated gesture of homage but a prelude to conquest. Yet science, besides being clever and greedy, is also modest and nearsighted—and this reassures the gods, who now hide behind the unknown as if it were the logo of some association. Science wants only one kind of gift: it wants verifiable facts, which can be tested in controlled settings, replicated. In their long history, the gods, hidden in the darkness, always knew that the most precious gifts do not belong in such a category. What cannot be verified, controlled, or replicated is, first of all, happiness. The fatal trick of Prometheus is thus reenacted. Men make sure they obtain the fat part of the offering, that nucleus of energy which nevertheless presupposes hunger and death. And with a faint note of sarcasm, the gods agree to be deceived: they will take only the fumes of the sacrifice, those uncontrollable scents that disperse through the air, but that are pure pleasure and do not presuppose hunger and death.

The renouncer (the *sannyāsin*) seeks liberation (*mokṣa*) from the world; the gnostic condemns the elements of the world (*stoicheîa toû kósmou*); the libertine nonchalantly uses the world; anonymous technology exploits the world as its raw material. The renouncer is orthodox; the gnostic is a heretic; the libertine is an atheist; anonymous technology believes in itself. An illegitimate line of descent that rules the world.

The whole history of modern philosophy is deeply troubled by sacrifice, by its terrible truth. In Hegel, the dialectic is a transcription, an adulterated translation of sacrifice; Schopenhauer is the *sannyāsin* of the West, the renouncer, and as such is always connected with sacrifice; Abraham is the sacrifice around which Kierkegaard's thought revolves; and Dionysus (and the Crucified, who signs two "letters of madness" on January 4, 1889, in Turin) is Nietzsche's sacrifice. In contrast, sacrifice is absent from the epistemological line running from Kant to the Vienna circle by way of the formalization of systems. But here the premise is that knowledge is an artificial limb, to be offered to science. It is left unsaid that this artificial limb will later be offered by science to technology, so that the latter can carry out the sacrifice under the name of experiment, and so that finally the sacrifice can be multiplied through the methods of production.

There is the wisdom of the officiant and there is the wisdom of the victim, and these increasingly diverge in history. From the wisdom of the officiant derives the sovereignty of the subject, who constructs from himself the edifice of knowledge. From the wisdom of the victim derive the three words of Aeschylus, *"tō páthei máthos"* ("from suffering, knowledge"), which refer to the passion of initiatory knowledge. The scandal of Christ is that he is at once priest and victim, as in the beginning; the two paths converge in him.

When Descartes speaks of the *negligible,* we know that he means the *victim,* the part cut away from order and thereafter condemned to nonexistence—killed without being offered as a gift. Simone Weil wrote, "The notion of the negligible marks the passage from the finite to the infinite."

The din of applause drowns out the victim's cries. When the movie star or the politician is killed for being "too famous," it is said that the murderer is mad. But his madness reveals the origin of the applause.

. . .

The thorn of sacrifice is the choice of victim. The Vedic network of correspondences envelops all and connects everything with everything else; countless texts repeat that the officiant *is* the victim, just as the bricks of the altar are intense thought. But at the conclusion of the ceremony the officiant goes home, while the victim remains lifeless on the altar. What is killed in the victim is the irreplaceable element, the unique essence, the evanescent singularity that eludes the mesh of correspondences—the little wrinkles around the eyes of Tollund Man, who died by hanging and who was preserved intact for millennia in the blue clay of Denmark. Iphigenia, offered as a sacrifice in Aulis (a Pompeian fresco shows her being dragged to the altar, her breasts bared and her arms raised to heaven, with the sacrificial knife poised above her), later became a priestess in Tauris. In the myth, the victim who has a name is enveloped by the divinity in a euphemizing cloud, so that the incurable laceration will be healed. In this, too, the profound matter-of-factness of myth is clear: it reveals that no theology, no *connexio,* can ever remedy the killing. In the victims who become stars in the sky or whom the gods snatch up to heaven or rescue at the last minute, myth gives way to fairy tale, as it does at its beginning and at its end. All of a sudden, we have proof that "And they lived happily ever after" preceded "Once upon a time." What remains unmentioned but assumed and perceptible in the crystal-clear air of exemplary actions is that unique body slaughtered on the altar, so long as no god steals it away in his cloud.

The theory of sacrifice makes all repeatable and reversible acts—breathing, lovemaking, playing music—revolve around the two irreversible acts: eating and killing. These are the two acts in which the arrow of time wounds with a wound beyond healing. Around that wound now rises the cosmic tent, the great fabric that connects everything with everything, repeats everything in everything. But its secret is that little rent in the middle: the open wound in the victim, the life without palpable return. It is the esoteric of the esoteric, the secret of the secret, the ultimate *tremendum* in the archaic world and the most banal and widespread of perceptions in the new world: the irreversibility of time. Once again the godless world proves to be the world of compulsory esotericism.

❦

Law and Order

It is significant that we say "law and order"—that it is not enough to say only "law" or only "order." In fact, the word "order" does not repeat, does not *echo,* the meaning of "law." Order is what law, on its own, cannot achieve. Order is law plus sacrifice, the perpetual supplement, the perpetual extra that must be destroyed so that order may exist. The world cannot live by law alone, because it needs an order that law alone is unable to provide. The world needs to destroy something to make order; and it must destroy it outside the law, with pleasure, with hatred, with indifference.

The modern age is founded on the misguided assumption that the words "law" and "order" are synonyms, that we say "law and order" because if we use an emphatic pleonasm we will command more respect. Destruction, precisely because it no longer has an acknowledged existence, takes shape in darkness, gathers together, adapting its dimensions to the law that would claim to deny it. The more vast and ramified the law, the more devastating the destruction that eludes it. Every war arises for the purpose of creating the order which the law is always powerless to provide. The Marxist idea of revolution acknowledges this impotence of the law and at the same time appropriates the whole apparatus of sacrifice, exploiting it to establish an order that denies the metaphysical foundations of sacrifice.

The impotence of the law stems from its inability to deal with surplus. The law presupposes an undivided subject. Sacrifice presupposes a dual subject: the sacrificer and the victim. And the surplus is, in fact, the victim. Therefore, the law is always the exoteric of sacrifice.

"Surplus value," the modern term for the "accursed part" and the starting point of the Marxist attack on capital, becomes the object of a dispute that can be resolved only by revolutionary violence, once we have recognized the law's impotence in dealing with surplus. Surplus value is the object of the sacrifice, which a new priestly sect wants to conduct in a different way. But like the haruspices of ancient Rome, the Marxist priests agree with their enemies when they claim that the dispute is not about the object of sacrifice (that is, what is destroyed in sacrifice). Marxists speak of private property, public property, fair distribution of resources. They deny that the surplus, instead of belonging to the oppressor class or the oppressed class, belongs to nature—the modern name for the Other.

Surplus is the excess of nature with respect to culture, the part of nature that culture is obliged to gamble with, consume, destroy, consecrate. In the process of dealing with that excess, every culture draws its own portrait. Law tends toward monotony; its variations are paltry compared to the rich diversity of forms. And the variety of forms determines the range of the sacrificial games.

Sacrifice is inscribed in our physiology. Any order, biological or social, is founded on an expulsion, on a quantity of consumed energy, because order must be smaller than the matter it orders. The only order without visible expulsion would be analogous to the metabolism of plant life. It would be a culture that managed to exist without being founded on difference, hence without any foundation at all—a culture indistinguishable from the rustling of a tree.

Every sacrifice is the recognition of an Other. After all emancipations have been achieved, the West will be unable to recognize anything but itself. Its paralysis, which is hidden behind the turmoil of praxis, results from the fact that it no longer knows to whom it should give itself. But although the gods fell, the hypostases did not. Thus, the world ultimately gives itself to the clumsy, sinister procession that Max Stirner described—to Reason, Liberty, Humanity, the Cause. But awakening from those hypostases is bitter, more so than awakening from any other superstition.

The *Upanishads* demand that destruction take place at the moment of maximum awareness. In the *Bhagavad Gītā,* Arjuna receives the revelation from Krishna just as he is preparing to kill his relatives on the field of battle. The secularized world turns its eyes away from destruction. It also turns destruction away from its eyes, just as it turns the bombarded city away from the eyes of the pilot who has dropped the bomb—and who is already flying far away.

Porphyry is the perfect Western *sannyāsin*. He knows sacrifice, knows its secrets, its unspeakable aspect. But a sort of nausea grips him in the face of "the impurity that comes from flesh and from blood," the fumes of the immolated souls. The world, for him, is "sorcery" (*goéteuma*), a potion that dulls the mind. He has only one desire: to wake and to remain wakeful, to undo the bonds of the sorceress, to become an apostate from the world, and thus to detach himself from it, because "detachment" is *apóstasis*.

"Detachment can be achieved through violence . . . But—as we see in perceivable things, for example—something that is violently torn away takes with it a part or trace of that from which it has been detached." In contrast, a clean detachment, without residue, is accomplished by constantly averting the mind from impure objects, a process reminiscent of uninterrupted prayer. Here Porphyry is speaking as an observer of the psyche, in terms that communicate by affinity (as in the exchanges of letters that used to take place among seventeenth-century scientists) with the great Buddhist masters and with the hermits of the Thebaïd. But he chooses a remarkably urban path to detachment, a little lake of silence in the metropolis, an existence unrecognizable from the outside by any sign other than sobriety and clarity. He performs only a "sacrifice of thought" (*noerà thusía*), presenting himself to the god "in a white garment and with a completely calm soul and a light body, free from any oppressive fluids or passions of the soul taken from other beings." In the pagan twilight, Porphyry is a man weary of rituals, incense, and spells, not because he doubts their power but precisely because he is familiar with that power—and knows that it would bind him even more to the demons of the world. Like the *sannyāsin* in the forest, Porphyry hides in the imperial city. "We who every day train ourselves to die to others," he writes, using the verb *apothnéskein* with the dative—a construction unknown to his masters, though we find it again in the writings of Paul ("dead to the law," "dead to sin"), the most philosophical of the Jews, in whom Porphyry recognized a "race of philosophers."

The gods to whom Porphyry is devoted pay more attention to the "behavior of the sacrificers than to the abundance of the things sacrificed." Regarding the object of sacrifice, for them "the best consecration is a pure intellect and an impassive soul." Here, as earlier in India, the sacrifice tends to withdraw into the invisible. Nothing on the outside allows us to know what is happening within the sacrificer, aside from a small gesture that Porphyry likens to those dictated by good manners: "The honors we reserve for the gods should be like those that we accord good men when we rise to allow them to sit in the best places. They should not be like the payment of taxes." This reference to good manners toward the gods is the sublime last message of the pagan world.

Sacrifice creates the most tenacious of bonds between society and what is external to it. But the sacred margin of contact with the external—the geometric locus of sacrificial acts—also allows the existence of an inner zone, profane *in pectore,* which now can expand without being constantly threatened by the sacred. In the act of destruction—even if what is destroyed is nothing more than grass— the guilt that gives rise to culture is affirmed: its detachment, its self-isolation from everything else, deriving from the way it isolates a thing-victim and expels it. In dedicating the victim to something other than itself, society recognizes its own dependence on that from which it has been detached. At the same time, it keeps the external at a distance, offering it the victim instead of itself. This is reverence. This is also the cunning of enlightenment. At the outset, the two were inseparable. Cunning enveloped in reverence, slowly corrosive, like the poison (German: *Gift*) in the gift.

In Guénon's formula, sacrifice reflects (and thus inverts) the *solve et coagula* of origins: what was divided in creation is now united again. "The essential function of sacrifice is to 'reunite what has been separated,' and thus—so far as man is concerned—to reunite the 'I' with the 'Self.'" Hence the *coniunctio,* the hierogamy, which is inter- woven with the acts of sacrifice: the ritual foundation of the inter- weaving of Eros and Thanatos. Hence the smell of slaughter that is the aura of sex. Yet how can an act of violent expulsion and destruc- tion be an act of joining, of restoration? In killing the victim, culture violently detaches itself from the thing, severs a tie that binds it to the whole. But in dedicating the victim to the divinity, culture reunites the destroyed thing (which stands for culture itself) with the whole. In this pendular movement lies the double nature of sacrifice. And the difference is determined by the point at which the movement stops, a point that could be either at society's internal center or at a center external to it. In the Vedic texts the answer is obvious: the center into which the sacrifice flows lies outside society. The sacrificial dugout sets off from the formless and profane existence of the *yajamāna,* the "sacrificer," patron and beneficiary of the ceremony; in the course of the ritual, it crosses the treacherous and tugging waters of the sacred, which is *made* there; last, it delivers the victim to the divine ocean, which reabsorbs him, as the *ātman* absorbs the *jīvātman,* as the Self absorbs the I. Then the sacrificer returns to his life. A lethal Eros, a loving murder, the archetype of every journey.

In his *De Abstinentia,* Porphyry debates whether or not the *nómos,* the law, extends to animals. He points out that in fact the *nómos* does not extend to all of nature; rather, it is based on the separation between an area in which it reigns (society) and an area abandoned to whim (animals, and nature with them). Law therefore cannot sustain universal interdependence: its intervention implies the severing of bonds which the law itself does not specify. Where the law does not speak, chaos—which stands for anything—reigns. Where the law does not speak, anything can reign.

Law becomes dumb when it reaches society's extravagant margins, its superabundance; this is the zone in which animals are killed, silently, unmentioned by the law. It is the belt of sacrifice that girds society, its infula.

From the *Laws of Manu:* "A householder has five slaughterhouses, [as it were—namely,] the hearth, the grindstone, the broom, the pestle and mortar, and the water vessel, by using which he is bound [with the fetters of sin]. In order to successively expiate [the offenses committed by means] of all these [five], the great sages have prescribed for householders the daily [performance of the five] great sacrifices. Teaching [and studying] is the sacrifice [offered] to Brahman, the [offerings of water and food called] Tarpana the sacrifice to the manes, the burnt oblation the sacrifice offered to the gods, the Bali offering that offered to the Bhûtas, and the hospitable reception of guests the offering to men. He who neglects not these five great sacrifices while he is able [to perform them] is not tainted by the sins [committed] in the five places of slaughter, though he constantly lives in the [order of] house[-holders]." Delicacy on the part of the Vedic seers: the five murder weapons are domestic objects (broom, water vessel), to show that murder penetrates the simplest, the most commonplace, the most unconscious of acts. A room is swept, a victim is strangled: the *connexio* makes one act resonate with the other.

The fact that we are composed of *ātman* and *jīvātman*, of a "Self" and an "I" (as Guénon translated the terms), coexistent and subordinated, was a truth already perceived in the West in the hermetic tradition (every alchemical *operari* implies it) and later in German Romanticism, in the intertwining of Doubles. But the official course of philosophy, the Locke-Hume-Kant sequence we find in textbooks, had always striven to erase any duality from the mind and tended to reduce the subject to the command center, whose reliability remained to be tested. The task of patiently checking the joints, a task undertaken by Kant, led finally to the shattering of the joints, which Nietzsche accomplished with his hammer. In the subject's place an empty cavity now yawned. Obscure beings passed through it, like dolphins' backs, momentary impulses. Meanwhile, science agreed to transform itself once and for all into a prosthesis, an apparatus fastened during laboratory hours to a subject, who conducted himself like a good citizen of the realm of Public Opinion. Yet within that very rigorous epistemological project, devoted to Ockham and to the elimination of all superfluity, the original duality of the subject would emerge once more. In the last years of the nineteenth century, when people began to talk about the paradoxes of set theory, another line began to emerge, one that would lead to Gödel and then spread in every direction: the sign of a definitive disruption, of the now recognized inadequacy of all language which would not include self-reference. And here, in the duality between a language that has a referent and that which has itself as referent, the two birds of the

Upanishads, ātman and *jīvātman,* reappeared. At the very core of science, as at the core of Vedic ritual, the two birds once again exchange gazes, clinging to the same bough on the immense tree of life.

The eternal return shifts the cycle beyond the Zodiac—a vision stirred by anguish, perceiving the gigantic numbers now invading the empty spaces between the stars. Auguste Blanqui in prison at Clairvaux: "At night, clinging to the bars of his cell, he conversed with the stars." It is impossible to experience pure, unrelated fragmentation. The ring, which was adorned with the animals of the Zodiac, is now expanding beyond measure and becoming encrusted with cosmic dust.

"Nodding the head." The last gesture remaining in the face of life's blows was the gesture that, according to the oracle, the sheep should make before being sacrificed: "Descendant of Theopropos, the gods forbid you to slay the sturdy race of sheep. But if, after a libation, an animal willingly nods its head toward the purifying water, I say that you may appropriately sacrifice it."

Ahnungslos, "omenless": this wonderful German word describes the condition in which the West now finds itself, after millennia of tortuous history. To be born "omenless," unshadowed by guilt or grace, is our original modern *status,* the unexpected demand that we rid ourselves of the world—a demand lurking behind every shop counter, laboratory table, professor's desk, cash register. At the core of this condition, as always, is a sacrificial action. "If one consecrates, it is in order to desecrate better," said our Ancestors. In those days, the world weighed horribly on everyone; everything had too much meaning; every twig contained too much power. An ineffable dream began to take shape: that the most beautiful thing was to lighten one's load, to cast off the world. To do this, one had to concentrate the sacred into one victim—and kill it. Afterward, there was nothing to do but return to intoxicating banality, which was at last profane. For the pure Westerner, the possibility of letting his thoughts become empty, arbitrary, and meandering was the only Siren worth obeying. He has deceived all the others—and without much effort.

. . .

From the tangled skein of sacrifice, the West chose a single thread, which it wanted to separate from all the others: the expulsion of the sacred through the killing of the sacrificial victim. Without any great regret, it renounced eating the sacred, gave up absorbing a tolerable part of the source of all power, of the inexhaustible *soma*. Henceforth, domestic cooking was enough—or at most a banquet among friends, with perhaps a few courtesans chattering away. But there remained something murky and shocking in those sacrificial practices: the impurity (before it became focused entirely in the victim) was in the subject himself, in the sacrificer—and it oppressed his life, which he now wanted to be simply transparent and cruel. At the end of a long, obscure process, sacrifice became trial by law. With the advent of the law, guilt, which belongs to the sacrifice and above all to the sacrificer, is immediately displaced onto the victim. He is no longer called the "victim" but the "guilty party." When life is brought to trial ("life being guilty," as Joseph de Maistre will one day remark), the law severs the connection between guilt and the process of life. In a trial by law, guilt is outside the law; all it expects of the law is to be stabbed through by it. Between *Oedipus the King* and the Gospels, sacrifice has completed its transformation into trial. Henceforth the law will choose the victim. Yet a fully effective trial—inasmuch as it liberates us from the sacred—is a trial in which the innocent is condemned. This fact reveals that the law has always been and will forever be overwhelmed by something prior to it, stronger than it. Pilate washes his hands because he feels that the law is powerless to absolve. Christ is condemned not by the law but by the impotence of the law. He is condemned by the crowd and its priests.

The sacred is concentrated in the victim, is suppressed in the victim, and emanates from the victim. In any case, the sacred must be killed, because it inspires terror: its perpetual contagion makes life impossible. The only other alternative is a modern invention: keep the sacred from being seen. Thus, it is either terrifying or unperceived. But the situation in which the sacred is not perceived for what it is reproduces, in reverse, the situation in which original terror prevails. It is something widespread, omnipresent, which inspires people to kill almost without reason and which drives them to inflict fierce tortures—on themselves, on anyone at all.

The specifically modern sacrifice is an immense industrial undertaking which rejects the name and memory of sacrifice. One speaks of entire classes as subjects for elimination, or of the inevitable "dropouts" who are ejected from the machinery of society every day. But all this is something society owes to itself. Thus, divine beings are still anointed, still recline on furs, still adorn themselves with flowers and snow-white draperies before an invisible knife descends on them. Astral archons in the form of young women, arrested for shoplifting in department stores or killed by Veronal.

For Vedic India, "I" and "Self," *jīvātman* and *ātman,* were like the sacrificial stake (*yūpa*) that the victim was tied to. "Closer to you than your jugular vein," says the god to the mystic, because it is the knife that has severed that vein.

> *"Nature is a haunted house—but Art*
> *—a House that tries to be haunted."*
>
> —Emily Dickinson

"Art is magic delivered from the lie of being truth," said Theodor Adorno. Constitutionally incapable of being grasped, art can be given only a genetic definition—and Adorno's is perhaps the most beautiful. Eluding the constraints of magic, such as the ones that sacrifice demands, is not only a shrewd act of reason, which rejects those powers. It is also a gesture that opens up an unheard-of dimension: that of playing with sacrificial objects, with relics and relicts that the shipwreck of the world of magic has left on the shores of the psyche. All the characteristics of art—from its pervasive ambiguity to its cathartic function as revealed by the naturalist Aristotle, to its "disinterestedness" as formulated by Kant—are vestiges of sacrifice. In Beckett's "Faire cela, sans savoir quoi," we hear once more the *operari* of the origins, which was sacrifice itself; while the "sans savoir quoi" recalls the nullified powers that act anonymously, in darkness. The peculiarity of the West lies not in the fact that it discovered the Beautiful, but in the fact that it allowed the Beautiful to hover in a suspended state, that it slackened the victim's noose. To elude the "lie of being truth" is also to elude truth itself, to avoid suffocation. Hence art's unwavering hostility toward all social order, which in every case embodies a claim to truth. In art speaks the voice of the victim who, in extremis and forever after, has escaped being killed, when ritual had already channeled all sacrality back into that killing. Art has a light step because it wanders in the forest. The altar is now bare.

Only in a completely secular society like late nineteenth-century France, with its *instituteurs* bloated with free thinking and eager to demolish Gothic chapels and found a secular morality, could Durkheim have made his brilliant discovery: that the religious is the social. Never before, and nowhere else, could anyone have formulated, with such Ecole Normale zest, an axiom that implies the divine cloud has been totally reabsorbed in the Great Animal referred to by Plato and by Simone Weil. Durkheim, descendant of a family of rabbis, is a dry Jew, one who never went back into the water after crossing the Red Sea. For him the sea does not exist: society has absorbed it. The brightest anthropologists of his school, Mauss and Granet, were, on the contrary, wonderfully damp. The "total social facts" they described, sometimes with a seer's precision, were the first adequate depictions of the archaic societies as places in which cosmic transactions were performed. "Alors que tout est en nuances . . ." ("Everything being a question of nuances . . .") was the secret motto of Mauss—and of Granet. While in another *cabinet,* across the Channel, Frazer was clothing our origins in a grand series of "ready-made suits" (Dumézil), Mauss pondered every detail of the behavior of peoples he would never see with the same maniacal and implacable gaze that Saint-Simon had used to scrutinize court protocol.

The conclusions of Mauss and Granet are, in the end, diametrically opposed to the ones reached by Durkheim. But Durkheim's axiom— "The religious is the social"—is one of those false principles that reveal a looming truth. Only another sort of genius, René Girard's, would manage to drive analysis to the fierce end that Durkheim had not foreseen in his statement. Girard is one of the last surviving "hedgehogs," to use the typology that Isaiah Berlin craftily derived from Archilochus' dictum, "The fox knows many things, but the hedgehog knows one big thing." The "one big thing" that Girard knows has a name: scapegoat. For Girard, all theological speculations on sacrifice, the vast sacrificial tangle (which leads to more than just the scapegoat), are priestly attempts to conceal the horrible truth. He thus accepts, though with heroic intelligence, the West's most petty game: "demystification," "demythification," and "unmasking," before one is initiated into the mystery of the mask. But although his fury and sarcasm leave the Vedic seers unscathed, he takes aim at modern anthropologists with exuberant zeal. What is unmasked here is not the Veda but the euphemistic, professional circumlocutions with which science has covered the uninterrupted killing, the perennial shedding of blood. Devoted to social functionality, anthropologists display an increasingly clear resemblance to those Victorian prudes who went to great lengths to avoid any mention of feet and legs. In their presence Girard incessantly repeats "Molière's inexhaustible comment, 'Ah! qu'en termes galants ces choses-là sont mises!' ['How elegantly those things are phrased!']."

So Girard is inspired not by the sociological laboratory but directly by the evangelical text. His entire life's work can be read as a dazzling commentary on the words of Caiaphas: "Expedit vobis ut unus moriatur homo pro populo, et non tota gens pereat" ("It is in your interest that one only should die and not the whole people"). Caiaphas here stands for the politician: "No one has done better than he has in politics." And his lucidity suggests the tacit foundation of every society: "This is the terrible paradox of men's desires. They can never agree on the preservation of their object, but they can always agree on its destruction. They are never in accord except at the expense of a victim." This mechanism is, for Girard, *the* mechanism of sacrifice: but, curiously, it is never so obvious as in modern society, which has proudly moved away from sacrifice. To find a perfect "text of persecution," Girard has to fall back on a passage against the Jews in Guillaume de Machaut's *Jugement du Roi de Navarre*. This would be explained, according to Girard, through the progressively antisacrificial action of evangelical truth, which first allows the horrible reality of the scapegoat to emerge; and ultimately, over the course of time, causes it to be generally condemned, as today anti-Semitism is condemned. In this tortuous application of the Enlightenment, however, Girard's chief weaknesses emerge: persecution, in fact, has never been so widespread as in the modern West, which knows nothing of sacrifice and considers it a superstition. The expulsion of the sacred, which is a part of sacrifice, now becomes housecleaning, physiological evacuation. The Jews are filthy insects that have to be swept out of all healthy Germanic dining alcoves. We speak of Stalin's "purges": millions of alleged opponents were evacuated to the camps. The fact that *communis opinio* condemns anti-Semitism and persecution in general is a derisive corollary of the fact that persecution itself—for every kind of motive: racial, political, religious, terrorist—has become the lingua franca of our planet's politics. If the truth about sacrifice is affirmed when we use the word "holocaust" to denote the extermination of the Jews, without even recognizing that the word is a technical term of sacrifice, then this truth resembles Antichristic parody more than it does the word of Christ. Still, Girard's hypothesis touches on a truth which no anthropologist had ever approached. It grazes the open wound of sacrifice, posing the most serious yet always evaded question, "Who will immolate whom?" We know from Sahagún, from the oracle of Delphi, and from Baudelaire that, in a proper sacrifice, "there must be consent and joy on the part of the victim." But we cannot tear our gaze from the sacrifice of Polyxena, as depicted on a Tyrrhenian amphora: The girl is held like a rolled-up rug by three warriors, who grasp her under their arms at her ankles, knees, and bosom. Decked in helmets and greaves, all three men display sharp profiles. Neoptolemus, also wearing helmet and greaves, plunges a large blade into Polyxena's throat with his right hand, while with his left hand he clutches her hair, the better to raise her head and bare her throat. Blood spurts onto the altar. Behind Neoptolemus, Diomedes looks on, a spear in his hand. And another character averts his eyes.

No theological speculation can efface this vision. And this vision cannot efface theological speculation, as Girard would like. As is often the case with ultimate things, the most that has been said on this matter was said in a story by Chuang Tzu: "The officiant of sacrifices, in ceremonial dress, approached the pigs' pen and spoke to them in these words: 'Why does it repel you to be led to your death? I shall fatten you for three months. As for myself, for ten days I shall mortify myself and for three days I shall fast. Mats of white straw will then be laid down for you, and your limbs will be placed on engraved vessels. What more do you want?' Then he thought about what the pigs might prefer, and he said, 'They would prefer to be fed husks and bran and to stay in their pen.'"

Girard projects backward to the beginning the delirium which Western man first unleashed and then, with a shudder of credulity, took for reality: the autonomy of society, along with society's claim to refer only to itself, to explain everything in relation to itself—and therefore to consider the victims sacrificed to the stars as so many propitiatory offerings to group stability. For Girard, it is as though the sun, the moon, fire, plague, and wind existed only as cover for some social tension. This incongruous claim is much like one that Marx made: the water of a waterfall "has no value" because it is not produced by labor. Such statements betray the clumsy, imperious *Setzen* of the mind—the "setting" which presupposes that nothing existed before being *set* by the movements of human thought. Fortunately, the world is not like this. And Girard performs a violent extrapolation to arrive at the heart of violence: his victim is silent nonhuman reality. Yet there *is* a sense in which the world was like this: society's claim to sovereign isolation was latent from the outset, and was not openly declared until several millennia later. Girard presupposes that at the origin we find not death but killing—a lynching, to be precise. But before the lynching, there is hunger: "Death is hunger." In hunger, death and murder are joined. In order to survive one must eat, and therefore must kill, because harvesting a plant also means killing. This is the condition to which Zeus condemns humankind after he has discovered the sacrificial deceit of Prometheus: the gods, after being deceived, will henceforth have only the smoke from burning meat and the remaining "white bones," but men, who *choose* rich meats, will also inherit hunger, and hence death. This primordial event is the foundation of sacrifice, the indissoluble ṛta. In offering the sacrifice, we accept—even behind the stratagem of substitution, which temporarily keeps us alive—the fact that we ourselves will one day be devoured, if not by men, then by those gods who are invisible guests at the banquet: "killing always means killing oneself." This perfect overlapping of sacrifice with a cosmic physiology is, in Girard's eyes, a mere trick, because he refuses to turn his gaze from social physiology even for a moment—

and therefore does not grasp that the latter's power is overwhelming precisely because it gradually appropriates cosmic physiology until it absorbs it completely. But Girard's biased perspective is invaluable: it reminds us that sacrifice, from its inception, has helped society cast off the sacred that would otherwise have paralyzed it. Following this single thread, we move easily from prehistory to the present—which might give the impression that we have found the key to the enigma, the stone discarded by the builders. Whereas in fact this only explains the cunning of sacrifice, the shiny little stone set in the throat of the *t'ao t'ieh,* the composite beast of the origins. From that point, in a coherent sequence, we quickly arrive at the day when people believed that the danger of the sacred was not so serious after all—when the consul Paulus Aemilius, with calm Roman cynicism, said that sacrifice should no longer be used to further the prosperity of the Republic. By then it was enough to leave that prosperity just as it was; the Romans themselves would take care to increase it. After this, the only thing left was to forget sacrifice. In time, all became superstition—and, as such, "the repository of all truth," according to Baudelaire.

Girard is perhaps the first to make strict application of Durkheim's axiom, which he calls "the greatest anthropological intuition of our time." In fact, the cloud of the religious envelops the entire social nexus down to its smallest details; for Girard, however, it is as if it were released by those details. Thus, some elementary facts are still untouched by that violent, diffuse interpenetration of the social and the religious: time's irreversibility, death, hunger, desirability. These are ultimate things; Girard would transform them into products of the mimetic conflict that results in the violence of sacrifice. Yet even in a society rescued from the deception of sacrifice, they would remain intact. With his hypothesis, Girard can explain the cyclical nature of time, but not its irreversibility; he can explain killing, but not death; he can explain the conflict of mimetic desires, but not the existence of desire. Let us turn the axiom upside down, then, and say that *the social is the religious.* Every detail of the social nexus thus corresponds to an area in the cloud of the religious where we find the powers that the social nexus had proposed to deal with somehow: the art of compromise, of giving and taking, of sacrifice. Here again, as always, the question is whether or not to recognize those powers. Where the thousands and thousands of Vedic gods dwell, Ockham's razor has severed every name. But although the gods and their names have disappeared, the cloud remains. The cloud is the unknown god.

The *negligible* in Descartes is the sacred—the accursed, rejected, uncontrollable part. By the time he comes up with this formulation, society has established a safety zone in which one can act without interference: sacrificial procedures have been replaced by laboratory conditions. But the meaning of ritual behavior has been completely altered: sacrificial gestures strove to manage the sacred, to maneuver it with caution; laboratory procedures tend to suppress it. Inside the glass cage move sterile, artificial hands; under the clinical light, they pick up an animal's stiffened body and carry it toward the rubbish bin. When a laboratory explodes, the memory of sacrifice is revived. Today, people's expectation that accidents will occur at a nuclear plant is pure ritual expectation: all eyes are fixed on the moment when the contagion will begin once more to spread.

Sacrifice ensured that one could find an area in which to live and act without fear of blows or destruction—an area that was designated outside the sacrificial circle. Only in the other zone, the zone of the sacred, within the circle, could one be struck down or destroyed.

What we customarily call magic is the little that remains of magic once it has been deprived of its basis in action: sacrifice.

Magic is resonant thought. Sacrifice presupposes this universal resonance. Thus, the outcome of sacrifice is always uncertain; it is a perpetual ordeal in which forces clash like sounds. And no one can confine a force, because its ramifications are endless. Nobody knows where a force ends, just as nobody can trace all the harmonics of a sound.

Law presupposes itself. Therefore the law strives, but never actually manages, to speak unambiguously at all times. Lacking this definitive clarity, the law asks, more modestly, that we not doubt its pronouncements too often. It is right, then, that the word "law" itself should denote social rule and natural rule. It makes no difference whether these rules refer to a divine commandment or to a statistical frequency; they are rules to which the world in general adheres. With these rules we can, *almost* always, live together. Nowadays, the law makes no claim to offer us any more than this.

The *isolation* that knowledge performs on the given is a repetition of the act of *sampling* that society performs on nature in order to establish itself. It represents a passage from the continuous to the discontinuous which is necessary to establish difference—in particular, *the* difference, namely that from nature itself. The sacrificial offering is the surplus which must be severed, expelled, celebrated, burned, because otherwise society would once again coincide with nature. That surplus is the disorder and the sequence of killings that precede the law, but it is also everything that exists prior to society and that secretly feeds it: the "hidden ocean" of Varuṇa, without which the social order would dry up and crumble to dust.

We always face the problem of how to use the excess part, the part that, if added to society, would result in nature—but a multiple nature, an Inferno or an Eden.

Sacrifice is also a long-term strategy for arriving at the expulsion of the sacred. Living without the sacred seemed at one time a perfect, light, desirable condition.

To become divine or to expel the sacred: this is the oscillation, the weft, of sacrifice: communion, expulsion.

In the realm of experiment, we occupy the position of inverse deities. Like the gods during sacrifices, we inhale the fumes, allowing bodies to be destroyed. Today the smoke of sacrifice consists of the numbers, the experimental procedures.

There are two modes of effecting substitution: by convention (murder) and by substantive correspondence (sacrifice). Correspondence kills that which replaces; convention kills that which is replaced. Correspondence presupposes that the replacement will go on living in the replaced, since both are fragments of the "resonant substance" from which the world was born, of which it is made. And their positions are reversible: anyone can someday replace another as victim of the sacrifice, because natural death does not exist. Every death is a sacrifice.

Convention cancels the given. It transposes into signs those properties of the given, and only those, that it wants to represent. Birth of the formal system.

At times, sacrifice involves the killing of an individual being. Convention leaves apparently intact the given it represents, but killing is implicit in its rule. The time will come when whole communities will be part of the discarded reality, killed by convention.

The zone between the opaque tranquillity of the profane and the limpid calm of the divine is sacred. It is the zone of blood, of danger—a magnet for violence. When Diomedes hurls the javelin at Aphrodite, what spurts from the wound above the goddess's wrist is not blood but the mysterious *ichór* etymology unknown: lymph. The gods, Homer says, "eat no food, nor do they drink of the dark wine, / and therefore they have no blood and are called immortal." Plutarch glosses: "By this he means that food is not only a means to live, but also a means to die." Food, blood, and death are confined within the same circle.

The *Upanishads* persist in attributing sacrifice to everything: to breathing, nourishment, lovemaking, words, action. Because sacrifice is the only form that responds, in the veins, to life—that pursues it in its movements, whether involuntary or arbitrary, without pause. The form of sacrifice is latent in the existence of blood: life that is renewed, *but only for a time,* as an uninterrupted and ephemeral construct. It is life, but can never achieve the endless duration of the transparent lymph that circulates in the gods. Just as blood is fed every day by obscure victims, so life as a rule demands the murderous construct which is renewed daily at the sacrificial stake.

The maiden with the swollen, protruding lips sank into a peat bog in Schleswig-Holstein. And there she was dug up, intact. The taut skin, like old leather, made her look Hamitic. Her shaved head lay in profile; her eyes were covered with a blindfold; and between the index and the middle finger of her right hand she held a birch twig.

Thus was she drowned in the bog, about two thousand years ago. Was she blindfolded like Eros because love is superior to the intellect?

Two ultimate questions, Job's and Arjuna's, are addressed to the divinity: the first concerns being killed, the second concerns killing. The divine reply, in both cases, is overwhelming and elusive. In each case it is not an explanation but a majestic, cosmic epiphany. There is no precise answer. They are two definitive questions which will not accept anything less than a total answer. Leviathan, which "maketh the deep to boil like a pot"; and Krishna, who resembles "a mass of fire darting flames on all sides."

Sacrifice gives a canonical, repeatable form to a pair of actions: giving and taking. All the meanings of these actions—without which communication, and hence society, cannot exist—are enclosed in sacrifice. And what could be possible if these actions did not take place simultaneously? Survival—if survival could depend only on taking. But here the primordial connection appears: taking is inadmissible without some giving, for it is promised that every giving will lead also to taking. The far that dominates the near and the mediate that dominates the immediate are the premises of every culture. He who takes and does not give destroys something that will perhaps never return again. He who kills the stag during the hunt will perhaps never see the stag appear again. He who gathers the fruits of the earth will perhaps never see them grow again. The first pact, the first give-and-take, is with nature, with animals, with plants—and, behind them, with the powers they embody. What is offered to us for the taking demands to be given back to what has offered it; the acceptance of this nexus is the basis of the sacrificial life, the ceremonial attitude toward existence. The pathos of this action lies in acknowledging that at the center of every give-and-take there is a killing. What we take, we kill or uproot. What we give cannot be less; it would then imply that we should kill ourselves. But this would interrupt the flow of exchanges. And here we see the great cunning of sacrifice: substitution. Sacrificing something that *stands for* something else sets in motion the very machinery of language and of algebra, the conquering digitality. The deception by which one can, on the altar, slit the throat of a substitute victim and not of the designated victim expands power immeasurably, and this expansion will completely erase from consciousness the need for sacrificial giving. Pure exchange, which systematizes substitution, gradually expels uniqueness, the vestige of the primordial victim. In the end, the world will be inhabited only by substitutes, hence by victims unaware that they are victims, because the irreplaceable priest who raises the knife over them has no name and no shape.

With the exception of clearheaded believers, who form a hardened minority, the world's inhabitants consist of believers who have acquired their faith through family custom, and utter nonbelievers—the moderns, those who for some reason feel obliged to deny the existence of anything supernatural. The latter include the most extreme bigots, but also the contemporary world's most characteristic citizens. These are the people who do not subscribe to any faith or engage in any secular idolatry (belief in science, in socialism, in the individual, in the free market, in the proletariat, in progress). What do they believe, then? Here we once again encounter a fundamental difference: between the person who uses sacrificial categories and the person who rejects them. From the beginning Nietzsche speaks in sacrificial terms, following the wishes of Dionysus, his god; Carnap speaks like all those who consider sacrifice a superstition, since it is eminently unverifiable; Freud wants to reveal the sacrifice at our origin; Jung wants the sacrifice to be performed. Literature does not even need to talk about sacrifice. In one of its forms—absolute literature (genealogy of *décadence*: Baudelaire, Mallarmé, Benn; or Flaubert, Proust)—writing takes on the features of a sacrificial offering, which implies that the author has in some sense been destroyed.

Romanticism marked the great reawakening of sacrifice. It valued the dark, the impure, the uncontrolled, the landscape, the incongruous, the somnambulistic, the sentimental, the foreboding, the passionate. Everything that, however awkwardly, speculation could define as the Negative was its terrain: new sacrificial terrain, where we once again encounter the intoxication of doubled things, which is always invigorating and destructive, as it had been long ago only around the sacrificial stake. But nobody now can assume the role of officiant, or of sacrificer. In the absence of a ritual, of an order, there is only the role of victim—a victim roaming the forest, prey of Rudra, waiting for his deadly arrows. This is the disease, the consumption, that afflicts Novalis and Keats. For Hölderlin, Rudra is Apollo, who smites him in Bordeaux. When the writer becomes officially *maudit,* with the advent of Rimbaud, it is already time to change: it is time to sell arms in Harar. The victim discovers, sadly, that the world has already prepared an archaic niche for him. He must return to the forest. In the city you can be anonymous, scarcely visible; you can write business letters in English; you can sit in a café after office hours. The forest is Pessoa's trunk, crammed with names.

The experimental society surely did not have to wait for Lenin, much less for Hitler, to make itself heard. These two were epigones who simply found they had suitable means for implementing the visions of general improvement that so many of their predecessors had harbored. The cold and inventive face of the experimental society, its technological face, is scornfully silent, anonymous; this society is concerned above all with establishing new procedures in factories, offices, banks, rural areas. In its other aspect, spouting words and always full of plans, the experimental society finds its original tone in the voices of the provincial Jacobins. Here is a certain Monsieur Leclerc speaking on May 12, 1793, as a delegate from the Lyons committee to the Jacobins of Paris: "We must establish a Machiavellianism of the people; we must wipe all that is impure from the surface of France." And here is Monsieur Baudot speaking before the Jacobins of Strasbourg, on 19 Frimaire, Year II: "The egoists, the thoughtless, the enemies of liberty, the enemies of all nature, must not be counted among her children. Aren't they perhaps just like all those who oppose the public good, or who simply play no part in creating it? Let us destroy them completely . . . Even if there were a million of them, shouldn't one perhaps sacrifice the twenty-fourth part of oneself to destroy a cancer that could infect the rest of the body?" But these voices still tremble with indignation. They do not have the purity of one who is concerned solely with the future of the nation, like Monsieur d'Antonelle, who held that "to construct the republic it was necessary to establish approximate equality and, to this end, to exterminate one-third of the population." With this sober suppression of "one-third of the population," so that finally money and property would not be so unevenly distributed but would be judiciously uniform, the aim was to eradicate all possibilities for insolent luxury—courtesans, games of chance, vast empty spaces— just as the profligate use of wit was likewise condemned as essentially contrary to republican virtue. In its clear phrasing and its eagerness for mediocrity, this obscure proposal expresses the idea that later would merely add, for variety and spice, specific designations of Jews or kulaks or class enemies in general as the prime candidates for membership in that "third of the population." In the proposals of the provincial Jacobins, Burckhardt saw "the innermost nucleus of the Revolution," and he noted: "Here the new France can clearly be discerned. It does not aim at socialism or at communism, through which its proponents would achieve only a mediocre universal wretch- edness and the equality of enjoyments (whereas they wanted equality of rights, with the secret qualification that later the others would be overpowered). Rather, they want new private property, distributed in a more or less uniform fashion, but in abundant measure. And in order for those chosen few to be *well off,* a great mass of people must die. The goal is the modern *well-being* of the French." From his observatory in Basle, enlightened by hatred, Burckhardt recognized the numbing well-being of capital and the punitive wretchedness of socialism as stars in the same constellation.

Primordial faith, the faith to which all others lead us back, is the affirmation of the *"nusquam interrupta connexio"*—of universal inter- dependence. We can choose to acknowledge this interdependence, though we cannot necessarily claim to have precise knowledge of it. The other possibility, that of denying it, allows us to believe only in what we choose, in what we agree to choose. Here there is no consistent meaning: the meaning is given each time. And as it is given, so is it taken.

The powers of the universe find many images—tree, rose, lotus, pomegranate, all the forms of nature—in which to show themselves. In contrast, the *connexio,* in order to show itself, needs an act, a process: sacrifice. This is the only act suited to so great a thing, because it contains death; and in that death there is killing, violence, and life that circulates. Sacrifice is the act in which the process of the whole is summed up.

"Orate sine intermissione" ("Pray uninterruptedly"): this dictum from Saint Paul lies at the threshold of linear time—a boundary where chasms yawn, the chasms hinted at by real numbers as these are set out in a straight line. Nothing is less homogeneous than linear time: it is marked by varying rhythms over dense periods and voids, momentary and unrelated spurts, clashes of incompatibles, the double life of the discrete and the continuous. But in the new state of things, this is not what defines it; rather, it is defined by its inability to retrace its path, by its lack of periodicity. This leads us to think of an act that takes place *sine intermissione:* uninterrupted prayer. In ancient times, prayer always had a moment of its own. Now the writing in the sky no longer specifies the right moment, prior to which the act would be sacrilege. Now the moment is always right and always wrong. The only way out is a continuous act: *Orate sine intermissione.*

The ritual of sacrifice is introduced and accompanied by songs, formulas, meticulously established gestures. But as a whole, it proceeds toward a center that is close to silence, an inarticulate murmur *(anirukta),* grains of sand of the inexhaustible life, around the moment of immolation. The participants then avert their eyes and whisper the last formulas. Only the neutral, sober voice of the priest stands out, as he indicates to the sacrificer the actions of the killing. *"Agone?"*—"Shall I act?" asks the *victimarius* or *popa* (executioner). In that question, that blunt Roman expression, lies the memory of an ancient perception: that every act is a killing. At the priest's sign of assent, the *victimarius* brought down the knife. In India, people preferred not to see the blood: a noose was used to strangle the victim.

The extinction of sacrifice. The victim gradually loses its power. We become detached from the animal—it is no longer considered so close to us that it can be substituted for us. Humans, now protected by the law, are rejected as victims. Thus, the last victim will be a god condemned by the law.

. . .

The pre-Christian past is one long process of euphemization, edulcoration of sacrifice. With Christ, sacrifice suddenly finds its cruelty again, is again revealed as lynching. At the same time, the cycle of sacrifice is sealed, because no sacrifice can come after Christ's, except a continuous commemoration of the sacrifice: the Mass, which avoids the shedding of blood *(incruente immolatur)*. The act of conflating a piece of bread and a sip of wine with the body of the god-victim marks an irrevocable break with precedent. But even more of a break is the fact that from now on, animals will no longer be killed on altars: there will be no further attempt to expel evil *"sanguine taurorum et hircorum"* ("with the blood of bulls and goats"). With the Christian era, bloodshed disappears from the ritual, and this becomes a premise for doing away with the ritual itself. The next step demands a secular version of sacrifice: regicide. Charles I, then Louis XVI: a double seal. And here again one irreversible deed, the killing of *that* victim, inaugurates a new age: society will no longer have to cut the throats of sheep on altars, but neither will it commemorate beheaded kings. Yet in August 1914 the word "sacrifice" returns and triumphs. Now the ritual involves more than a single wretched being: an entire generation of anonymous men is exalted to the status of noble victim and lowered into the pits, which have been transformed into trenches.

∞℘∽

The Doctrine of the Forest

The Vedic seers considered birth first of all as killing. The world of origins was stifling, oppressively dense, slimy—the bed of the cosmic swamp. It was an immense curled-up animal, incubating life in its entrails. Until the jaws of the animal were propped open; then Dawn was released from the darkness, and things fell into an interconnected, articulated order. Spaced and breathing, they receive the gift of the *ṛta*. The prop that forces the jaws to remain open is the axis of the world; it is the separation between heaven and earth; it is the king with his arms upraised as he is consecrated in the ceremony of *rājasūya*. Around this axis every wheel revolves, divided by spokes, whereas originally the wheel was one, immobile, full. Varuṇa is the god who ensures that "the path of the *ṛta* is opened, so that one may arrive happy at the other shore. The road of heaven has become visible." Varuṇa is he who "raised the prop in bottomless space," who "prepared a vast road for the sun to follow." But Varuṇa is also the locus of origins. He has "measured the first creation" with the power that is exclusively his: *māyā,* the "measuring magic" (as Lilian Silburn phrases it in her illuminating version). The noose with which he will punish his victims unites the two aspects of his nature forever: Varuṇa is both the undifferentiated waters and the *ṛta*—the differentiating order.

The fabric of the articulated has lacunae. It eludes matricial narrowness, anguish (root: *angh*); it allows the membranes of the embryo to be abandoned; it introduces birth, since birth always involves a violent separation of the self from everything else, the severing of the last noose of Varuṇa: the umbilical cord. This metaphysical process became a novel and initiated human history, at the point when Indra wanted to repeat Varuṇa's enterprise and thus appropriate it, when he wanted "to send the sky and the earth still farther away." Then Indra "struck a great blow at the serpent Vṛtra, who concealed the waters within himself, enshrouding them in darkness." Indra also seized the *soma*. This is the archetype of every dragon-slaying. T'ao T'ieh, Tiamat, the Minotaur, Marduk, Theseus, Saint George—all these figures appear on the scene. Indra's violent undertaking inaugurates a new regime of sovereignty. Indra usurps it from Varuṇa, but Varuṇa remains the source of all sovereignty: that which has nothing to conquer but which nurtures every conquest. The consecrated king will sit on a throne that is "the navel and the womb of kingship . . . practically equivalent to Varuṇa's watery residence." But Indra, as he kills Vṛtra, is also being born as the king; he abandons the remains of his placenta on an anthill, which here stands for the matrix. He now sees these remains as evil (*pāpman*), for they would suffocate him in the life between sky and earth. Wanting to be born, the murderer-hero moves through the viscera of the monster, through the composite coils of the *t'ao t'ieh*, before reaching its mouth, which will spit him out into the light. He is Theseus, who must move through the entire labyrinth before he can see and confront the Minotaur. The most basic characteristic of the labyrinth is that it is a continuous thread, a great noose coiled around itself. In this it is like Varuṇa, who is articulation itself but who is linked by an indissoluble nexus to an unarticulated origin. It is also like the *sūtra*, the "thread" which "from both the macrocosmic and the microcosmic point of view links all states of existence with one another and with their Principle"; people say that "he who knows this thread, this internal agent, knows *brahman*, knows the worlds, knows the gods, knows the *ātman*, knows all." To see the labyrinth from the outside, and to kill it in the figure of the Minotaur, you must have moved through it to its center, which is the mouth from which you emerge into the space of isolated things, things separated and arranged in a precarious articulation: the space where the sacrifice must incessantly weave an airy connection between void and void. The danger for the hero who simultaneously kills and is born is that he may lose contact with his cosmic victim, his enemy who is nevertheless the source of all power: the waters. Goethe's Mothers are versions of Varuṇa. That is why a child is baptized after birth, and why the heir to the throne is anointed in the ceremony in which he is consecrated king. That is why the young calf is licked by its mother immediately after birth: so that it will not dry up, so that it will recall the water of its origin, the "hidden ocean" of Varuṇa.

The law is always double: law as rule of the world, law as rule of people among themselves. The first belongs to Varuṇa; the second to Mitra. Each has its prescriptions, its crimes, its punishments. Their actions can be concordant—and then the two gods approach each other as perfect complements in a unitary duality: Mitra-Varuṇa. The civilizing sweetness of Mitra, "everyone's friend," can exist only insofar as it stands out against the dark and remote background of the sovereignty of Varuṇa. "Mitra is this world; Varuṇa is the other world," the *Śatapatha Brāhmaṇa* clearly states. Mitra is the world of men; Varuṇa is the rest, perennially surrounding it, capable of squeezing it like a noose. Gradually sloughing off the world and its terrors, the beings united by social contract are led to recognize only Mitra, who is first and foremost the god of contract. Thus, that single law—which was the "meek law" of Stifter, so long as it coexisted with Varuṇa's order—grew darker, because the unrecognized shadow of the companion deity fell upon it more and more. Meanwhile Varuṇa's nooses continued to tighten around their victims, who no longer knew anything about the unfathomable depths from which the nooses were cast, and who did not even know that these were the results of so many sentencings under a law that no one could decipher anymore.

One must ultimately ask the most ingenuous and the most important question: Are the Vedic connections (*bandhu*) true? In studying them, we gradually reconstruct their marvelously intricate web, which spreads over everything. And from the moment we enter the world, we are forced to look at them as at an immense cathedral of matchsticks, perfect and superfluous. We know that life reproduces itself anyway, even without their help. Yet we are also irresistibly attracted to that all-enveloping layer of resonances. And whatever we think, at a certain point we realize that we are unwittingly using a corner of that submerged cloak. The only form of life that succeeds in totally rejecting the Vedic connections is that of Bentham, our Pharaoh, today a mummy in London. An unknowing life. The Vedic connections are grandly superfluous, and Bentham is grandly inadequate. We are in the middle, wavering.

Nothing is so repugnant—or so pathetic—as the language of sacrifice on the lips of someone who does not know its premises. Nothing is so devastating as the act of sacrifice in the hands of someone who does not know its premises. Nothing is so irrepressible as the return of the words and gestures of sacrifice in someone who does not know its premises.

Varuṇa is the origin that prevents living and without which living is impossible. To begin to live, the nooses of Varuṇa must be severed; to continue living we must be joined, moistened by his primordial liquid.

.   .   .

After years of research, two great scholars have this to say about the Vedic seers:

Lilian Silburn

"In the eyes of the Vedic ṛṣi, the immediate, the primitive, has an amorphous, multiform, precarious aspect. The succession of days is not guaranteed, and the stability of the cosmos must continually be reestablished. The Vedic cosmos is, in effect, a painful cosmos of anguish, contraction, pressure (aṃhas), which takes the form of darkness (tamas) and fluidity (salila), in the image of the dark sea of the origins, the limitless, immeasurable, formless arṇava forever threatening to swallow all . . .

"To the ṛṣi of the Vedas, nothing seems certain: not human life, or sunrise, or the fall of water. Thus, most of the hymns of the Rig Veda follow a single plan: the invoked God is told again of the helpful deed he once performed long ago on behalf of some cosmic or sacrificial personage, and, in the final verses, he is implored to reenact this same deed at the next sunrise, for people usually want protection from the anguish that comes from having no support during the night."

J. C. Heesterman

"To the Vedic thinker, the whole universe was constantly moving between the two poles—of birth and death, integration and disintegration, ascension and descent—which by their interaction occasion the cyclical rhythm of the cosmos. In this world of floating forms, there are no hard and fast lines; conceptually different entities and notions interchange with bewildering ease. All things, entities, notions, powers are connected with each other. Nevertheless, this world is not the chaos it seems to be at first sight. The point at issue for the Vedic thinker is not to disentangle and differentiate conceptually different entities and notions but to realize, to know, their connections (bandhu-). In the course of this process, the connections converged more and more; and in the end, as is shown in the Upanishad texts, the intrinsic coherence of the universe was formulated in the ultimate connection tat tvam asi. In principle, this identification of man with the cosmos is present in ritualistic thought. The place of sacrifice is by virtue of the code of connections identical with the cosmos: the three fires are the three divisions of space, the course of the sacrifice represents the year. On the place of sacrifice the cosmic drama of death and rebirth, integration and disintegration, ascension and descent, is enacted and, reversely, through the same code of connections brought to bear upon the macrocosmos. In the centre of this sacrificial world stands the sacrificer for whose benefit the cosmic processes are set in motion by the ritualists, who know the connections. Thus the whole world is centred upon the sacrificer, who 'becomes all this' and represents in his person the cosmic drama."

In a memorable essay written in 1959, Louis Dumont saw in the *sannyāsin,* the Hindu "renouncer," the first exemplar of the individual in a form that, after many adventures, has reached the contemporary West. Perhaps through excessive devotion to the Weberian theory of ideal types, however, Dumont strongly emphasized in his essay the opposition between *sannyāsin* and brahman, and was actually pleased to see this confirmed in their latter-day canonical images: on the one hand, the emaciated figure of the *sannyāsin* with his bowl, his staff, and his orange robes; on the other, the "brahman, whom we can portray as he is already seen on the north portal of Sanchi (Vessantara Jataka): a potbellied fellow displaying an inimitable blend of arrogance and greed." What contrast could be more obvious, more radical? But how much does that image of the brahman owe to the wicked priests of Cecil B. De Mille, and how much to the oppression of the *kaliyuga,* the age of obscurity? If we place ourselves once more inside the tangled evolution of the Vedic sacrifice, everything is again called into question; the passage and the contrast no longer seem so clear-cut. Finally, the *sannyāsin* might seem to us the ultimate fruit of the Vedic sacrifice, permeated by all its lymphs, premise of unheard-of vicissitudes (Buddhism first of all). But he is comprehensible only if one penetrates, and once more loses oneself in, "the wilds and ravines of sacrifice."

Through what one might call the "cracks" in classical sacrifice, Heesterman managed to glimpse the outlines of a preclassical stage of the Vedic sacrifice, in a compelling analysis *à la* Mauss (and Granet). His stereoscopic view makes it possible to isolate and arrange on different planes the traces of the development of Vedic sacrifice, a marvelously complex and articulated form which is itself the archetype of all articulation. The liturgical hinge of classical sacrifice is the relation between the *yajamāna*—the "sacrificer," who procures the offering, gives the tribute to the officiants (*dakṣiṇā*), and collects the fruits of the sacrifice—and the brahman, supreme authority in the ceremony. The relationship is one of delicate and tortuous complementarity, indissoluble complicity, concealed opposition, such that it merits a place all its own among the hundred and one values of the genitive case listed by the grammarian Patañjali: it is the *srauva* (liturgical) relationship, which reminds us that "the sacrifice is unquestionably a relationship between mortals and immortals, between mortals and the dead; but it is also an interpersonal and social relationship of mortals among themselves." Behind this relationship we perceive certain features that Heesterman had linked to another, more ancient image: that of a mortal rivalry, mortal because death is the outcome of the dispute. In sacrificial giving there is a double act: a giving by the *yajamāna* to the Invisible and a giving by the *yajamāna* to the visible brahman, who assists him in the ceremony. And from the *yajamāna* the brahman receives two gifts: "what is injured in the sacrifice—what belongs to Rudra," the particle of the victim's body that has received the mortal injury, small as a berry; and the *dakṣiṇā*, which Maurice Bloomfield (who always subscribed to the image of wicked and greedy priests) suggested translating as "baksheesh." The sacrificial gift of the *yajamāna* to the brahman is the prototype of the poisoned gift. What is given is what is most dangerous—that which contains danger itself: death. And this applies not only to the "injured part" but also to the *dakṣiṇā*, which is equated with the dismembered body of Prajāpati. The generosity of the sacrificial patron is thus primarily a liberation from the fearsome excess of life, whose weight falls on the brahman. This gift is a challenge and a trap. Behind this act Heesterman reconstructs a different drama, in which the sacrificial site is at once the scene of a violent clash and the table at which the guest is welcomed. Every sacrifice is an ordeal, an uncertain clash of forces, exposed to gusts from the heavens and arranged according to a cycle that has two points of dramatic reversal: the two equinoxes. He who sacrifices demonstrates how long he can remain in contact with "Rudra's part" (a variant of the "accursed part") and how he is able to rid himself of it. As Mauss was the first to realize, the important thing is to know how to enter the sacrifice; but it is equally important to know how to leave it. The *dakṣiṇā,* the holy wage, "is the price that must be paid so that the profane body of the sacrificer can return to its owner," so that the *yajamāna* can return intact to community life. In it we recognize the traces of preclassical sacrifice, which is like a cruel game in which the loser is the one who, at the end, is left holding the ball. By reconstructing the scenario of that phase of sacrifice, Heesterman radically modifies our view of the brahman. That purest of pure beings was originally the opposite: he absorbed into himself every impurity, accepting it in the gift that the impure *yajamāna* passed onto him. The brahman is "the *bhiṣaj,* the healer of the ritual, but this must originally have referred to the healing of death. Since the classical ritual does not admit of impurity but only of infractions against a correct execution of the ritual, the brahman's function was transformed into that of redressing ritual faults. In the preclassical system, then, his role was that of taking over death and impurity."

Much of what would later be seen elsewhere, diluted over the centuries, is contained in the evolution of the Vedic sacrifice as if that evolution were a sphere of maximum density. The brahman, who originally bore the full weight of impurity, becomes the immaculate specialist in silence, who intervenes only to correct the mistakes of the officiants. This is the transition that will be presented in the West, amid much philosophical ferment, as the passage from the tribal world of sacrifice to the world of law in the polis. For the Hindus, who are less overweening and less casual about sloughing off the world, it was merely a shift in ritual procedures. Yet this transition laid the foundation from which would arise the figure of the *sannyāsin,* the renouncer who abandons, first and foremost, the scene of the rite.

For Dumont, this creature at the edge of society, this first "individual-outside-the-world," is the supreme innovator in Indian thought, the one actually "responsible for all the innovations that India has known." He is the eccentric figure who will finally shatter from within every holistic framework and will eventually become the "individual-in-the-world," hence the very avatar of man in the modern Western world. Complex routes and ironies. But as Heesterman has shown, the *sannyāsin* is certainly not a figure sharply detached from and opposed to the world of sacrifice. On the contrary, the *sannyāsin* is the perfect result of the long, subtle, lacerating evolution of that world.

If the Vedic sacrifice is the grandest, most coherent, most detailed attempt to affirm the All of the world, the very consistency of this undertaking causes an insurmountable anguish. The Vedic sacrifice asserts itself in thousands of prescriptions, in thousands of connections, in thousands of mythological details. But the more the texts accumulate and the more ramified the ordering of the acts becomes, the more we are afflicted by impotence and exhaustion. Sacrifice, which aims at constructing the world so that it will be possible to live in it, tends to invade every moment of time the world grants us. The basis of sacrifice is desire, the desire for a fruit that is the world itself; but analysis reveals that desire inevitably imprisons and smothers us like the three membranes that threaten the infant, like the excessive fullness of the undifferentiated, from which sacrifice is supposed to free us. In those three membranes abandoned in the ceremony, sacred sacrificial remnants that contain the germ of the world in a future cycle, the brahman comes to see the world itself. And then a further, dizzying possibility emerges: that we need no longer construct the world, but only free ourselves from it. This is the origin of renunciation. Hidden in the forest, the brahman-turned-*sannyāsin* will no longer try to affirm the world, but will aspire to *mokṣa,* to "liberation from the world." The obscure birth of Buddhism then emerges as the last act in the evolution of the Vedic sacrifice.

The decisive step is the renouncer's refusal to eat animal flesh. The majesty of sacrifice survives only so long as creatures are killed on the altar. When such gestures cease, sacrifice is ready to be transformed into moral law. But the peculiarity of the *sannyāsin* lies in his renunciation of something that he nevertheless recognizes as the basis of order—namely, killing. In his choice there is no trace of the Enlightenment's rejection of the malign *religio,* as in Lucretius, but rather a decision to remain on this side of life, which in the end can be transformed into a Beyond.

For the Vedic seers, sacrifice corresponded to the uninterrupted construction of the world. Its foundation was desire; its aim, the fruit of the world. Actions were linked in a cosmic game of giving and taking. The Roman *Do ut des*—crudely juridical—here had its counterpart in the *Dadami te, dehi me* ("I give you, give me") noted by Mauss. Yet what was always at stake was not the individual's destiny but the fate of all existence, which is forever in danger. The Vedic seers had thrown themselves into this vast enlargement of desire and its fruits; and this is why the later reflection of the *Upanishads,* ultimately sealed in the *Bhagavad Gītā,* could arrive at the discovery that is the indelible sign of India: detachment, the metaphysical name for renouncing the fruit of sacrifice.

Sacrifice as action (*sacra facere*) is initially confined to the single act of the brahman: eating the dangerous part of the victim, the "wounded part." In the end it is annulled as a visible act by the renouncer, who completely forswears any contact with the killing. But from the renouncer, from the individual-outside-the-world still obedient to the sacrificial attitude, we trace a series of circuitous routes (which Dumont has barely begun to reconstruct), to arrive at the individual-outside-the-world of Christianity, and then at the individual-in-the-world definitively outlined by Calvin, who contains "in himself, concealed in his inner constitution, an unperceived element of otherworldliness." This paradoxical heir of the Indian renouncer is none other than the modern Western individual. Once he reenters the world, he will exploit it with unprecedented contempt and lack of restraint.

From the sacrifice, through the brahman, to the renouncer. From the renouncer, through the individual, to technology. The process, which began as an attempt at maximum affirmation of the world (and devout dominion of the world) in the doctrine of the Vedic seers and shrank to the analytic negation of the world (with Buddha), begins expanding again with the renouncer, the individual-outside-the-world. It culminates in the emancipated and enlightened individual-in-the-world and, through him, in the anonymous subject of technology, an enterprise of dominion, control, affirmation— though it is no longer clear of what, since the quanta have meanwhile dissolved the world beyond any possible localization.

Henceforth the name of the new sacrifice will be *experiment*. The sacrificial attitude continues to operate in it, but it operates invisibly, unwittingly. Wherever it surfaces it is rejected, rightly, as a relict.

In the Western world, governments and newspapers often speak of "sacrifices" when the state of the economy demands drastic measures. The word nowadays appears only slightly less frequently than technical terms like "inflation." It is another of the many signs of the presence of the archaic. In present-day usage, "sacrifice" connotes a series of economic interventions implying that individuals renounce certain goods. But in this usage the word loses its most basic meaning: destruction. Here nothing must be destroyed. It is assumed that the goods to be renounced will be much more useful and much better employed in other ways. Part of the money that would have been spent on consumer goods, on images of play and pleasure, will serve to augment the funds of the State. The word "sacrifice" would be out of place, therefore, if it did not reaffirm that in the realm of the divine the counterpart of the individual is society itself—because it knows how to utilize what the individual gives up, how to make it productive in the realm of the invisible. In contrast, there is a true sacrifice, one that implies destruction, taking place at every moment on the planet; this sacrifice is known as experiment. It is premised on the cancellation of every metaphysical memory of sacrifice—a cancellation so extreme that, as a result of a sinister misnomer, researchers speaking laboratory jargon talk of "sacrificing" animals when they get rid of them after experiments. Yet the scientist who uses this term will be unable to assign a meaning to it once he has left the laboratory: he regards it as a remnant of superstitious beliefs. Economists, on the contrary, feel no embarrassment about using it. On one side, an actual sacrifice that cannot be named; on the other, a fictitious sacrifice that is always named— these two prongs silently hold the world in their vise, until the day the contrasts and contradictions in the use of the word "sacrifice" are annulled: with war, the richest of experiments. In wartime, the word "sacrifice" occupies the front pages of the papers even more than during economic crises, and everyone knows that it involves blood, destruction, and death. Uniformed soldiers are interviewed and declare that they are prepared to make the "supreme sacrifice."

The entire nation declares itself ready for "sacrifice" every day. In the end, monuments to the fallen are all that remains.

ↂↈↂ

Archives and Will-o'-the-Wisps

There is no essential reason for history to be distinguished from literature. *Carmen solutum*—so Quintilian once termed history. Like "poetry without meter," and thus lacking a preordained formal framework, historical research is the gradual construction of an artificial memory, the successive undoing of the strings of an endless series of cardboard boxes in the archives. Each box, like a mnemotechnical locus, encloses a psychic essence, which history releases. History finds itself when it decides to let the sources alone speak—and understands that these sources can be *anything at all,* can be whatever there is. Burckhardt, in his *Griechische Kulturgeschichte,* was the first to highlight this necromantic aspect of history. The historiography of recent decades—in its preoccupation with the most irrelevant trivia, in its capacity to absorb whole shelves of documents on the verge of crumbling, investigations never read by anyone, not even by the clerk who transcribed them—has proceeded along this path, even if it has tended to delude itself about its motives. Myriad researchers thought they were coming closer to certainty as they waded through oceans of paper; or actually believed, as they compiled numbers and charts, that their methods resembled those of science. Yet the greater the accumulation of raw data, the more it became clear that every historical trail was a mute puzzle. Behind those names, those notarial acts, those judicial files, stretched the immense aphasia of life, closed in upon itself, lacking all contact with a before and an after. History itself provides official descriptive data only in order to disappear. The true historian, then, is the one who crosses the garrulous wasteland of archives to arrive, with a bit of luck, at the right dust-covered folder, at those rare points where deafening names begin to resonate among themselves against the background of silence and take on a unique outline—like someone who lives in our neighborhood and whom we have occasionally met in the street, and who now gives us a glimpse into his disastrous private life.

Richard Cobb recalls his "favorite uncle," a country doctor who often took his nephew with him on his rounds: "He was a tremendous gossip, and endlessly inquisitive about people; indeed, I think he only practiced medicine in order to get into other people's houses. I would sit waiting in his car while he did his rounds, and, after each visit, he would come to the car triumphantly with some new item of malice, rather like a researcher after a good day in the Archives Nationales." Just as his doctor uncle liked to enter other people's houses, so young Cobb enjoyed his family's frequent moves: "On the whole, I rather enjoyed them, because in this manner I was able to see the inside of a very wide range of houses; and, all my life, it has been an almost obsessive urge with me to get my foot in the door, to get behind the façade, to get inside. That, after all, is what being, or becoming, a historian is all about—the desire to read other people's letters, to breach privacy, to penetrate into the inner room." But that "almost obsessive urge" was diametrically opposed to the impulse to collect anecdotes as tokens of familiarity with the Great. The true historian is the prime enemy of every hunter for the Memorable. His desired prey is primarily what has eluded memory and what has had every reason to elude it. After lengthy training in this struggle with the opaque, he will be able to test himself against Plutarchan figures, who are, in contrast, obscured by an excess of testimony—that thick carapace which history secretes to keep them remote from us. At the end of his arrogant rise, the historian wants to meet Napoleon as if the latter were a stranger. At this point he becomes part visionary, and can muster the insolence to begin a book as Léon Bloy did: "The history of Napoleon is surely the most unknown of all histories."

A fragmented, quantic history. Expansion of phosphorescent traces. Vast protective darkness. Electric flashes. Verifiability of the single scene, even of the dust lying on the furniture. Absolute uncertainty of the sequence. Rambling discourse of forms. Nocturnal sleep of a greenhouse.

On July 22, 1809, near the village of Notendaal, which has vanished from all maps, three bogus sailors appeared. Many people saw them, since the flat landscape made it impossible to hide. They had come to kill and rob the elderly van Aarts, an innkeeper and his wife. One of them cut the throat of Elisabeth van Aart with a jackknife while she was showing him the bed where he and his mates were to sleep. They found a few florins and some jewels. They also stole food and wine, of which they drank a bottle while sitting by the edge of a little stream. The next morning they sang a requiem for the souls of the murdered couple in the village church of Essen, on the border. They did the same in Antwerp a few days later. People saw them in various squalid taverns, where they played cards, boasted, slept three in a bed. In Antwerp they drank with three prostitutes at the La Vigne inn, and were arrested as they were returning to their own inn, Le Cygne. On February 28, 1810, the three false sailors were hanged in the square in front of the town hall of Steenbergen and remained hanging there until sunset. Over the head of each was a piece of wood bearing the words, "Murderer of two people."

Cobb studied the records of this sordid, stupid crime. There is nothing in the story to arouse one's curiosity. Every detail bespeaks the normality of its sordidness, and everything seems to stem from a clouded mind. The actors in the drama knew few words; even fewer manage to filter through the questioning and survive the transition from Flemish to French. But Cobb the historian wants to go further than the judge, who is satisfied with sentencing the men to death. The historian wants to sentence people to life. Through his intrusive investigation, he wants to wrest from the unknown even the thoughts and words that never took shape. During their months in prison, the three bogus sailors were forced to recall every detail of the week of *life* they had spent squandering the mediocre spoils of their murder: "A week, in such very young lives, is a very long time indeed. And most of the time that remained to them to live was used to find out all that there was to be found out about that week, all at least that could be expressed, put into words, by people who had few words. We have tried to go one better than the judges, whose curiosity did not go beyond the point of obtaining a conviction and of wresting from the three poor wretches a plea of absolution, and to attempt to reconstruct thoughts and sensations that could not be put into words. The historian has much the same assignment as Proust, but he does not have the advantage of Proust's own memory; he has to construct, then to pillage, other people's." This is history.

After years of research, Cobb realized that the archives tracing the counterrevolutionary Terror were ultimately even more fascinating than those concerning the Jacobin Terror. After all, "the Revolutionary government bureaucratized death in the pursuit of a program of virtue"—and this is sufficient to ensure not only horror but boredom. The only limit to the program's absolutism concerned the age of the victims: it was decided that a person had to be at least fourteen to die on the guillotine, except in certain areas where the civil war was particularly bloody. But that was the most that could be said. The Jacobin persecutors, with a few exceptions (such as the violent, troublesome, bestial Claude Javogues), later proved to be the earliest bureaucrats, sitting primly among their papers and unexceptionable above all in their mediocrity, which enfolded them like the tricolor sash.

The perfect exemplar of this species was a certain administrative official named Cochon, who was quick to offer his services as prefect during the Restoration even though he had voted for the condemnation of Louis XVI. He typifies the bureaucrat we find in the shadow of all regimes, who acts with limpid impartiality, sentences to death those who are powerless today, and does favors for those who might be powerful tomorrow. And pure, uncontaminated Terror has a disadvantage in that it generally lasts only briefly—a few months— whereas the White Terror continued, with peaks and remissions, from 1790 to the Consulate; and some of its protagonists even had the good fortune to live through the second White Terror as well, in the summer of 1815, almost repeating their own cycle in the space of a few years. "On pouvait s'installer dans la Contre-Révolution" ("One could find a comfortable place in the Counter-Revolution") was a prevalent feeling. Cobb himself, blending sarcasm with matter-of-factness in a general statement at the beginning of his book

Reactions to the French Revolution, felt compelled to declare that "historians of individuality, not to say of crankiness and of the extremes of eccentricity, will be much better off with the Counter-Terror than with the bureaucratic Terror of the summer of 1794." The archives, for them, will be generous. They will no longer yield monotonous accusations against various "enemies of the people" guilty of having raised their eyebrows like pre-Revolutionary aristo-crats (this was one of the charges punishable by death, in accordance with the law of 22 Prairial). Instead, they will regale historians with cruel exploits, strict vendettas, elaborate tortures—each incident wor-thy of being savored, and each embellished with myriad novelistic details concerning women instigators and tribal hatreds. The bandits' caves were stuffed with sumptuous clothing, since the celebration of luxury—which, along with the ancient fodder of revenge, was the soul's ultimate food—had withdrawn into that bloody nomadism.

❧

Postcards from the Quaternary

I

In the deep dust of the earth,
a little Magdalenian whistle.
No longer a piece of chipped flint
in a toilsome struggle for life.
But tiny notches on the three faces
of an eagle bone
marked off a year of moons.
The scholars described it as
"decorative" or "insignificant":
it was the first book.
Not so much *faber* but contemplator
of the sky, absentmindedly
he blew on the whistle.

II

The first woman's face
is five centimeters high.
A delicate coiffure
rises above a slightly
rounded forehead.
Wear has not clouded
the oblique, pensive gaze.
Carved in mammoth ivory,
it was abandoned
at Dolní Věstonice.

III

In the cave at Sterkfontein (Transvaal),
when men first appeared,
acknowledged as such by science,
they settled in the same chamber
where their ancestors
had been devoured in turn
by hyenas and great cats,
the previous inhabitants.

⁂

The Demon of Repetition

The repetition that abounds in history presupposes the whole history
of repetition. The further back we go, the more repetition becomes
shrouded in majesty. The rarer written traces become, the more
imposing is the part repetition plays in them. It seems that signs are
drawn chiefly to indicate how something must be repeated. Protocol
is the first literary genre. For something to have meaning, it must
be repeated—and if one thing is to be repeated, everything must be
repeated. The coronation of a king, or even a hunting expedition,

demands a recapitulation of history from its origins, until from all this sprouts the tiny bud which is the next deed, protected and sustained by all the previous ones, the last stitch in the center of the enormous net. Racing toward us in time, the powers of repetition are gradually abrogated, as with the goddess in the Underworld: at every threshold a cloak and diadem are torn from her by the Invisible Hand. In the end, we see not a dazzling nakedness but an empty carcass, an animal legacy that the coldness of the mind would like to dissolve. Paul Valéry, the authentic New Man as he has been chemically distilled in the solitude of the algebraic Ego, views that carcass as the most tiresome of diseases: he calls it "cyclosis," "the cyclomania of our being." "I was born," he tells us, "at twenty, exasperated by repetition—that is to say, by life. Rising, dressing, eating, excreting, sleeping—and always these seasons, these stars— and history!

"Everything known by heart—

"to the point of madness . . . This table repeats itself before my eyes, and has done so for thirty-nine years!—This is why I cannot bear the countryside, the tilling of the soil, the furrows, the expectation of harvests—All this passes for 'poetic.'

"But for me the *poetic* is the opposite of this sad drudgery, which is as mortally circular as the diurnal rotation and the other—"

Below the Acheron, which Freud had resolved to stir up in the epigraph to *The Interpretation of Dreams,* lies the region of blind germinations, the vast inorganic silence that is sometimes wounded by improbable life. Freud came to this abyssal region, well "beyond the pleasure principle," just after the end of the war. But what was it that drove him to question "twenty-five years of intense work," especially as he did so on the basis of theories that could easily be considered "mystical" and even confused with the libidinal heresies of the traitorous son C. G. Jung? What was it that had once again so deeply troubled the psyche of the man Sigmund Freud, who had the strange characteristic of recapitulating, in all his anxieties, the entire history of the West? It was repetition. With the perfect candor that, along with his "impartiality of intellect" in describing "ultimate things," made him the only analyst who managed throughout his work to raise himself to the sacrificial status of Patient, Freud tells us: "Once, as I was roaming the unfamiliar and deserted streets of a small Italian town on a sunny afternoon, I found myself in a district whose nature could scarcely be in doubt. At the windows of the little houses, only painted women were visible, and I quickly turned around and quit the street as soon as possible. But after wandering aimlessly for a while, I suddenly found myself on the same street again, where my presence began to attract attention. My rapid retreat had only one result: after several other vicious circles I found myself in the same place, for the third time. At this point I was seized by a feeling that I can only describe as disturbing, and I was happy when—having given up any further attempts at exploration—I found myself back in the square I had left just a short while earlier."

Then Freud moves on to a second example, where the mischievousness of "involuntary repetition" seems even more insinuating, because it takes the form of pure chance—the coincidence that arises from the world without even asking the subject for the ambiguous collaboration of wandering aimlessly in a foreign country. And Freud here, as on so many other occasions, conceals from us the fact that he is talking about a personal experience: "Nobody pays much attention if, when depositing one's overcoat in the cloakroom, one is handed a claim check with a number on it—let's say 62—or if the cabin one has been assigned on board a ship bears the same number. But the impression changes if these two circumstances, which are insignificant in and of themselves, follow each other in close succession, and one happens across the number 62 several times on the same day; all the more so if one were actually to observe that in everything bearing a number—addresses, hotel rooms, train seats, and so on—the number that appears is always the same, in whole or in part. We find this sort of thing 'disturbing,' and anyone unarmed against the lures of superstition would feel inclined to impute a mysterious significance to this obstinate recurrence of the same number, to see in it perhaps a sign of the age up to which he will be permitted to live."

The person "unarmed against the lures of superstition" was Freud himself, when faced with the repeated appearance of the number 62 in the course of his travels in 1909 in Greece, where he was obsessed by the thought that he was to die at the age of sixty-two. And as he was writing those lines of his essay "The Uncanny," hiding the fact that they concerned him directly, Freud was only several months past his sixty-second birthday. Immediately after describing these two examples, Freud introduces for the first time in articulated fashion (and already with references to *Beyond the Pleasure Principle,* which would soon be published) the compulsion to repeat—the last and supreme divinity in his mythology: "Predominant in the psyche's unconscious is the *compulsion to repeat,* which probably derives from the innermost nature of the drives themselves, and which, being strong enough to impose itself in spite of the pleasure principle, confers on specific aspects of the life of the psyche a demonic character, which is rather clearly expressed in the impulses of the child even in his earliest years and dominates a part of what occurs during the analytic treatment of neurotics." Here Freud was trying to ge beyond psychical reality, forcing his way toward metapsychology and striving to deal once more with the demonic power of nature. The same repetition that nature incessantly offers us in the array of its forms appears everywhere in the life of the psyche: not only in the *fort-da* ("away-here") repeated by the child, who makes the spool vanish and reappear so that he can master his anxiety at his mother's absence; not only in the dreams of those suffering from traumatic neurosis, who encounter their trauma in them again and again; not only in the behavior of the patient who, impelled by the neurosis of transference, enacts the suppressed elements themselves instead of remembering them; not only in the story of the embryo that is "obliged in the course of its development to recapitulate . . . the structures of all the forms from which it has sprung, instead of proceeding quickly by the shortest path to its final shape" (all of which are cases discussed in *Beyond the Pleasure Principle*). There is yet another repetition, even more menacing and insinuating—one that Freud refers to in his examples in "The Uncanny" as a way of introducing the repetition compulsion and that he does not deal with in *Beyond the Pleasure Principle*. It is an errant, indomitable repetition: that of random signs that accumulate, that hint at a connection, a "mysterious significance." Here the repetition is hybrid, at once part of the changing scene of the outside world and part of the psychical scene, where it claims a place. The repetition of a sign in the outside world transforms that sign into an omen—an allusion to the presence of a meaning whose origin we do not know and of which we cannot rid ourselves. Every meaning that we have not established or produced ourselves is disturbing. Coincidences are disturbing, because they hint at fate, at a network of meanings that precede us, accompany us, trick us. The compulsion to repeat is addressed to someone in us (the Double, heir to the Self of the *Upanishads*) who is enveloped in that network of meanings and who sometimes appears there, replicating our own image. There are "normal people . . . who give the impression of being pursued by a malignant fate or possessed by some 'demonic' power," but what is disturbing about them is not so much their psyche's willingness to be ensnared by repetition as the elastic promptness with which reality comes toward them, unfailingly offering its services so that the compulsive repetition will be fulfilled. The most intolerable suspicion, for Freud, is that there might be a complicity between the outside world and the psyche; yet he actually encountered this complicity, in the estuary where the waters of the unconscious mingle with those of the world. Unable to admit that this conspiracy involved an excess of meaning, since this would have unhinged his whole construction, he admitted only that it indicated a convergence of nature and the psyche toward the same point: the origin as the locus of the undifferentiated, of insignificant repetition, where meaning—like every other tension—is annulled.

This was the unacknowledged threat conveyed by those tremors in the foundations of everyday life—and Freud, lying to himself, took care to state in "The Uncanny" that it had been many years since he had felt any such tremors: "The author of this essay must confess to a certain deafness in this matter, when in fact a particularly sharp receptivity is needed. For a long time he has not directly experienced or become familiar with anything that might arouse in him a sense of the disturbing." Once the door is opened to the world outside us, two opposing possibilities are offered: either we accept a nature that speaks through capricious oracles and extends into the psyche, engaging it in dialogue; or we consider nature as a still-life, which protects the life that has grown up over it and which is eager to lead it back to inanimate calm. The latter is the path Freud *was forced* to take. The unnamed Thanatos appears, in the most radical passages of *Beyond the Pleasure Principle,* as a supreme power who does not so much clash with Eros as use Eros for his own ends ("the pleasure principle actually seems to serve the death instincts"). The welter of erotic urges masks the ongoing action of the death instincts, which "seem to do their work unobtrusively." The relationship is a cruel harmony, more than a conflict. It displays a convergence, in two different styles, toward a single end: the punishment of the guilt which is life itself, its enforced return to inorganic calm, from which it has been drawn by an obscure and unnatural tension—"a force that has not hitherto been clearly recognized," as Freud says. And he clarifies: "The tension which then arose in what had hitherto been an inanimate substance endeavored to cancel itself out. In this way the first instinct came into being: the instinct to return to the inanimate state." In the tangled construction of *Beyond the Pleasure Principle,* Freud outlines the insurmountable cosmogony of the Modern. Valéry's impatience with repetition and Freud's dark view of the compulsion to repeat spring from a single source: terror in the face of the nonhuman origins of meaning, which are manifested in the demonic arbitrariness of coincidence as well as in the implacable monotony of nature. *Beyond the Pleasure Principle* has yet to be read as the record of a lonely patient named Sigmund Freud, who had the strength to recapitulate in the most sober and precise way the syndrome of Western history: the need to "wrest" an order from nature but at the same time agree that this order, as a variant of the compulsion to repeat, should be only a large vicious circle that ultimately leads to the annulment of itself. Gazing at the landscape of civilization, Freud wrote: "Whereas cleanliness is not to be expected in nature, all ideas of order have been inspired by her. Man's observation of the great astronomical regularities not only furnished him with a model for introducing order into his life, but gave him the first points of departure for doing so. Order is a kind of compulsion to repeat which, when a regulatory rule has been laid down once and for all, decides when, where, and how a thing shall be done, so that in every similar circumstance one is spared hesitation and indecision." Coincidences, too, are "similar circumstances," but their function is to remind us of the meaninglessness of everything. For Freud, coincidences can refer only to death. "It was still easy at that time for the living substance to die," Freud writes in his hallucinatory vision of primordial times. Civilization, on the other hand, makes death difficult. It is chiefly a question of style, of choosing "ever more circuitous detours" and making sure that the organism succeeds in achieving what it most wishes: "to die only in its own fashion." As Goethe said to Eckermann on the subject of entelechy, "The fact that man shakes off what does not relate to him is for me proof that something of the sort exists." According to Freud's theory, that grand concept diminishes in the ultimate demand that both civilization and the individual make: to die in one's own fashion—to trace an unrepeatable arabesque, before the mute calm that knows no meaning begins once more to prevail.

The phenomenon whereby the world's disparate signs are repeated until they condense into so many omens has a precise opposite—namely, the forced repetition of a word, which soon makes it lose all meaning and leaves it at our feet like an opaque shell of sound. In these two experiences we find, in the private and secret space of our mind, the original schism. This was the schism that appeared when the world became too charged with meanings: even as those meanings took on a life of their own, uncontrollable, looming, overwhelming, so that their excessive power finally made them converge toward a single meaning (death), another world was forming, the precinct of culture, where humans imposed their will, used their ability to give names, to establish meanings through the artifice of convention. If we fear repetition in the signs that come to us from the world, it is because in that repetition we discover that the world's powers are always there, dozing perhaps, and surely somewhat removed, but still present and ready to swallow us as if we were a word in their language. If we feel strangely uneasy when we note that a word, automatically repeated, seems to lose all connection with its meaning, it is because at that very moment we sense the weakness, the precarious nature of the act on which all culture is based. To think is to set out hesitantly toward the site of that twofold uneasiness, in an effort to escape simultaneously from nature and from culture. This is why thought is an intermittent and improbable activity.

Sacrifice: to repeat the irreversible.

· · ·

Coincidence is the appearance of a constellation in an individual's life. In big cities, we cannot see the night sky; so it takes shape again in us through these fleeting apparitions.

Myth, if not repeated, wastes away and finally dies like the gods—dies many deaths. But the world, which has forgotten even to bury it and which has immediately plunged into the statistical cloud of the New, suddenly realizes that its actions cannot be arbitrary, even if it would like them to be. How else do we explain involuntary repetition—that dull murmur of familiar words and of sights already seen—and the compulsive movements that accompany it? Nowadays everything is a prayer mill. Tibet cannot be seen; no one prays; no authority can demand ritual homage. Yet everything continues to travel in a circle, past a series of obscure stations. When Talleyrand was alive, those stations had names that were redolent with associations and ready to be disseminated in lecture halls: Ancien Régime, Revolution, Terror, Directory, Empire, Restoration, Citizen-King. Never again would we encounter those sharp profiles; they were stamped on the last coins, which were immediately withdrawn from circulation and replaced by the more practical, more powerful paper money. Even nature was wrapped in old newspaper. But one thing did not allow itself to be wrapped—indeed, it wrapped things more than ever—and this was repetition itself. Marx once felt the treacherous vertigo of repetition when a new 18 Brumaire, led by a new Bonaparte, passed before his eyes in the newspapers. But he immediately dispelled the ghost because he believed that he himself was the ghost, the one who would assign the parts in the Répétition Finale (last rehearsal). The repetition had no end; and soon, horribly, it would repeat him as well.

"The tradition of all past generations weighs on the minds of the living like a nightmare. And just when they are working to change things and transform themselves—to create, that is, what has never before existed—at times such as those of revolutionary crisis they anxiously summon the spirits of the past in order to take them into their service. They borrow from them their names, their battle cries, their costumes, and appear on the new historical scene in this old and venerable disguise and using this borrowed language. Thus, Luther disguised himself as Paul the apostle; the revolution of 1789–1814 donned first the clothing of the Roman republic and then of the Roman empire; and the revolution of 1848 could do no better than parody first 1789, then the revolutionary tradition of 1793–1795." So wrote Marx in December 1851 (though he was looting images and formulas from a letter that Engels had written him on December third). Earlier, between November 1850 and March 1851, in Sorrento, Alexis de Tocqueville had written passages in his *Souvenirs* concerning the revolution of 1848 ("There have surely been revolutionaries more wicked than those of 1848, but I do not think there have been any more stupid"), noting, on the subject of that May, "It was a parody of February 24, as February 24 itself had been a parody of other revolutionary scenes." Recalling the invasion of the Chamber of Deputies, he had already written: "Frenchmen, especially in Paris, freely blend memories of literature and the theater with their most serious demonstrations, and this often suggests that the sentiments they display are false, whereas in fact they are only clumsily decorated. In this case, the imitation was so obvious that the terrible originality of the deeds remained hidden. In those days everyone's imagination used the garish colors with which Lamartine had painted his *Girondins*. The men of the first revolution were alive in everyone's mind; their actions and words were present in everyone's memory. Everything I saw that day bore the visible stamp of those memories; and still it seemed to me that everyone was more concerned with staging the French Revolution than with continuing it . . . Though I could see the end of the performance would be terrible, I was never really able to take the actors seriously; and the whole thing seemed to me a poor tragedy performed by provincial amateurs."

Thus, both Marx and Tocqueville realized that they lived in an era dazzled by the New, though the age continued to practice the cult of bloodthirsty repetition. The sequence tended to be the following:

the New inevitably takes over (since the principle of "eternal revision," as Burckhardt dryly phrased it, is anointed and granted sovereignty);

the New tends irresistibly to repeat some fragment of the Canonical
Phases, which themselves repeat other ghosts;

technology disrupts everything, initiating a process in which proportions and weights are constantly modified, distorting acts in continual anamorphosis, which invades time;

repetition releases its unforeseen novelty, and the New is faithfully
repeated through an alliance among the grotesque, the atrocious,
and the portentous, which transmits the shock of the Modern as
if from a trembling séance-table.

"Compulsion to verify" is what one might call this disease that
has infected us forever. But where did the disease originate? In what
desire, in what perception? If the West feels such a violent need to
affirm, to impose repetition, this is precisely because the West, as
never before, feels the absolute unrepeatability of every element, the
precarious but irreducible life of every detail. Without the compulsion to verify, without the empty repetition, we would not have been
able to bear the surfacing of disconnected appearance, wavering,
without offspring, without correspondences—a vision that had never
before been evoked *on its own*. The unique flavor, the anguished but
triumphantly hovering meaning, of every pure form in the West is
present in this precariousness, even in its most intense manifesta-
tions, as an imminent destruction. Hence our need for stone, for
solidity. But no civilization has been so unsolid, so exposed, as the
West. The West abandons mythological repetition only to impose on
itself a repetition diffused through matter, because it doubts not only
that everything may be repeated in a certain way, but also that the
world itself, as deed, manages to reproduce itself. This extreme
feeling of imminence, of something held in suspension, requires an
equally vast counterbalance—and at the point of equilibrium we find
a first response, stubborn and bold. It emerges from the piano: it is
the *moment musical*, a paralyzing power, dissolving yet affirming (and
this time there is no need for magic, which is always too charged
with meaning), even though that sound inevitably returns only to a
phrase, to a limpid and predestined quaver—wanting that which is

fleeting because it is fleeting. "Nothing, and over it the enamel," whispered Benn.

THE CHEVALIER DE B***: Whether history repeats itself is a foolish question, but the effects of the idea that it does so are devastating. The act of repetition is like a faded scrap of Oriental fabric: in it survives the mythic heritage, the ability to see a certain gesture as an exemplar, the sense of a destiny linked to a form. Louis XVI incessantly reread, with fear and horror, the story of Charles I, until Louis himself ended up on the scaffold. The Duc d'Orléans tried to recreate the Fronde of the Cardinal de Retz, but found himself on the same scaffold shortly afterward. Circumstances can be superimposed—or even mockingly opposed; what counts is that every action contains the ghost of another action. Just as no book exists that is not a reprise of or a reply to or a consequence of another book, so in every act an invisible hand is placed on the hand that moves, guiding it, pressing it, or restraining it. Regarding every event, we must ask ourselves: What was trying to repeat itself here? Sometimes it is difficult even to find the clues to a connection, because events have been so disfigured by the randomness that composes history itself. In the idea of repetition lies our entire relationship with the past: figures detach themselves from time as if from an immense lapse of memory, in eager anticipation of reappearing. Some are wretched and clumsy— and at times this is precisely when they achieve their maximum, most murderous force.

Repetition is the invisible step backward that accompanies every act. Historians distinguish themselves above all by their ability to combine that step with their account of actions, of visible acts. But in order to do this, they must throw caution to the wind and mingle with the shadows, emerging from the past as if from Avernus. Michelet, Burckhardt, Warburg, Tocqueville . . .

Chateaubriand viewed life in Paris during the Revolution as a "collection of ruins and gravestones from all centuries, piled pell-mell in the cloisters of the Petits-Augustins; except that the debris I speak of was alive and constantly changing." Repetition is characteristic not only of order but of chaos, of the moment when orders mix, Greek and Gothic, blood and enamel. The Revolution was also the first total spectacle, the *Gesamtkunstwerk* that emerged from the salons and sewers and appeared on a stage which comprised an entire city. The great tragedian Talma made his debut shortly after seeing the Marquis de Favras hanged. Chateaubriand assures us that "the paths of the Tuileries gardens were thronged with giggling women," while the footsteps of the crowd resounded in the recently deserted convents "as in the abandoned halls of the Alhambra."

Like all great mythologists, Freud bases everything on a phenomenon that remains almost unknown: the return to the inorganic. In their migrations over thousands of kilometers, birds and fish are thought to be seeking the land of their origin, which is the inertia of matter, the state that exists prior to the emergence of life. This is the inescapable consequence of a principle that, under various names, had always guided him. At the time he wrote "Project for a Scientific Psychology," he called it the "principle of neuronic *inertia*," whereas in *Beyond the Pleasure Principle* he termed it the "principle of constancy," defining it as a "tendency operating in the service of a function that is designed to free the mental apparatus entirely from excitation, or to keep the amount of excitation in it constant or as low as possible." If, therefore, the pleasure principle also involves a return to a previous state (and here the myth of Eros in Plato's *Symposium* was a help to Freud, since he was puzzled as to what event copulation could possibly repeat), then this implies, when translated into phylogenesis, a return to the inorganic, which is the state that *precedes* life. Freud's construction is founded on no more than this; but the premises of that unremarkable act are precisely what remains to be said and what Freud does not want to say. It is difficult to pass off that "principle of constancy" as a calm experimental observation. Rather, for Freud it is the invisible Hermes that allows him to build what is most indispensable to him: a caesura, a defensive barrier that will prevent the subject (that is, Sigmund Freud) from falling into the unspeakable swamp inhabited by the Ouroboros. And Freud chooses the least verifiable caesura, the one marked by the emergence of life, because he needs to identify all the life that precedes *our* life (and hence all nature) with death. Thus, he is not talking about the inorganic—a clever device that allows his discourse to refer to the framework of some scientific publication. What he is anxious to establish is the equation between all nature (organic and inorganic) and death. Why, in fact, should the compulsion to repeat be the expression of a death instinct? Didn't Freud himself admirably explain, in reference to the child's *fort-da* game, the function of such repetition in controlling, dominating, and hence exalting the power of life? We have to roam at some length through the tortuous prose of *Beyond the Pleasure Principle* before we find the radiant *peradam,* the sentence from which all else derives: "The elementary living entity would from its very beginning have had no wish to change; if conditions had remained the same, it would have done no more than constantly repeat the same course of life." But that original "course of life," inasmuch as it is opposed to the "tension" which establishes the emergence of real life (ours), becomes for Freud equivalent to death itself. Primordial nature's tolerance toward life extends merely to the point of allowing it to appear (life is *octroyée*—granted by an unknown authority), but only so as to be able to repeat it immediately, and thus absorb it into its own death-knell. Repetition is exemplified not only by the rotation of the stars but also by physiology: breathing, sleeping, hunger. The mark of death, in Freud's view, is stamped on everything—like the number on the ticket given to him in the cloakroom. It is not only chance but nature in its entirety that we must keep at bay. The final connection: nature is death primarily because it kills. Nature is always an excess that threatens us. Freud wanted to trace back the psyche to a scientistic delirium, to translate its "figurative" language into the language of physiology or chemistry—which are themselves, after all, only "figurative languages," as Freud himself observes with cruel self-irony. In this delirium, one sign insistently recurs: the excessiveness of nature's dominance over perception, which survives only because it takes "small specimens of the external world," because it confines itself to "sampling it in small quantities." Indeed, to escape nature's overflow, the psychical apparatus actually kills a part of itself in order to build around itself an insensitive "protective shield," a last defense against the murderous fury of external nature. This "protective shield" is the "outer layer" of the apparatus itself, a layer that agrees to die, becoming "to some degree inorganic" in order to save "all the deeper ones from a similar fate." This visionary glimpse has nothing to do with any physiological process, but everything to do with the archaic theory of sacrifice, which is here rewritten in the "figurative language" of an imaginary physiology in which—if we wish to understand what is going on—we have only to replace the phrase "protective shield" with the unspeakable words *sacrificial victim*. This, Freud observes, is true for the stimuli which come from outside; but the cerebral cortex is a cork plank between wind and waves. We defend ourselves against the wind of the world, perceiving as little of it as possible, raising up against it the part of ourselves that we have killed in the sacrifice; but the waves come from the darkness within the body, and against them there is no defense— unless we resort to "projection," which catapults into the outside world the battering rams that assail us from within. Moving swiftly and attracting no attention, Freud here arrives at the deduction that paranoia is a normal, constant experience of the psyche.

The discoverer of historical laws will always have about him something of the mad inventor of useless patents. His scheme is to trap his interlocutor in a corner and explain how, at home, he has created perpetual motion. Would we like to have a look at the machine? It's right here . . . Ever since Polybius wrote his elementary considerations on the cyclical nature of the forms of government— first monarchy, then aristocracy, then democracy, then again monarchy, ad infinitum—history has continued to prove him right, as it has proved many other and far more complex cyclical theories. But it has done so with mocking magnanimity, because in the end Polybius' law (if it can really be called a law) pompously confirmed history's senselessness, which appears even greater once its hidden mechanism is revealed. If history is to have an unassailable surface it needs a telos, which would annul history. Otherwise, every secularized cyclical pattern of forms will lead history back to dreaded morphology, reaffirming its subjection to nature. Then Spengler looms up; in his opinion, "'mankind' has no purpose, no idea, no plan, any more than a species such as the butterflies or the orchids has." Freud—with his characteristic style of thought and his austere masters—could not allow a telos, but neither could he abdicate in favor of nature. So he bowed to mute origins, admitting their hegemony.

Yet he would never grant them the character of unnamed life. They had to be the articulation of death, from which life decided—provisionally—to detach itself. Civilization is a curved line of seashells on the sand, but it encloses the ciphers of its form. The sea that washes it away will never possess it.

"But lift thou up thy rod, and stretch out thine hand over the sea, and divide it; and the children of Israel shall go on dry ground through the midst of the sea," says Yahweh to Moses, who is being pursued by the Egyptians. "The cloud was seen to cover the field with its shadow, / the dry land to emerge from the water that had been there before, / a path without barrier through the Red Sea / and a green meadow through the stormy waves / where they passed, like one people, those protected by thine hand." Thus says the Wisdom of Solomon. To pass through the Red Sea with dry feet—act of salvation, glimmer of the chosen—is also to repeat the Creation. The Red Sea dries up just as in the beginning the earth, the ground on which walk the feet protected by the Lord, was parted from the lower waters: "Elohim called the dry land Earth; and the gathering together of the waters he called the Seas." The "green meadow" that replaces the "stormy waves" is now a momentary excess of divine love. If it implied a progressive drying up of nature, it would turn into a ruinous condemnation. But that image, as promise of a total civilization of nature, will continue to guide successive generations: those of the dry priests of Judaism, who prefer to set their feet on the tilled plain rather than abandon themselves to the ocean's fluidity, and who regard the sea as the grave of the Enemy. Later, when Yahweh's presence is obscured, the divine gift will become the vision of an immense reclamation, no longer a wonder come down from the sky but the laborious conquest of the subject.

"Wo Es war, soll Ich werden" ("Where It was, there shall I be"), Freud's heraldic motto, presupposes a draining of the Zuider Zee—once again in connection with a "salvation," though secularized, anguished, uncertain: "We may legitimately doubt whether it is possible to gain supreme wisdom by this path. Nevertheless, we must admit that the therapeutic efforts of psychoanalysis follow a similar approach. Their aim is essentially to reinforce the Ego, to make it more independent of the Superego, to widen its field of perception and enlarge its organization, so that it can appropriate new areas of the Id. Where the Id was, the Ego must take over. It is a process of civilization, such as the draining of the Zuider Zee."

We find another dry priest in Lévi-Strauss. Having reached the Finale of his Tetralogy, he feels compelled to define himself as "someone never touched by any religious uneasiness." What firmness of intellect in one who, like a new Linnaeus, spent years drawing up a taxonomic table of the myths in which tribes of *la pensée sauvage* ("savage thought") had evoked their gods! Yet so long as he remains in the vegetable and mineral purity of myth, a passion free of reservations and doubts drives Lévi-Strauss to reconstruct those stunning architectures, which unawareness protects from the warm comminglings of life. If, in fact, some errant trace of the "affective life" were to surface too insistently in the myth, Lévi-Strauss would not concern himself with it but would leave that task to the attentions of another, more disreputable kind of priest: "Every manifestation of the affective life that did not reflect, at the level of consciousness, some notable incident blocking or accelerating the work of the intellect would no longer belong to the human sciences. It would come under the heading of biology, and it would be up to others, not us, to deal with it." There is, however, something in those concluding pages of *Mythologiques* that still upsets him—and that continually reappears in the experience of his "savage" thinkers, as well as in the spiteful observations of some of his academic colleagues. This something is ritual. Driven by a painful compulsion, those who develop myths have always had a tendency to celebrate rituals. Lévi-Strauss observes them with sympathetic embarrassment, and sees in their ceremonial acts "that very characteristic mixture, composed of both obstinacy and impotence, which explains why ritual always has a maniacal and desperate side." Here we find a tone close to that of Freud's observations on obsessive behavior, on neurotic "ceremony" as descendant (and progenitor) of "religious practices": "Any activity can become 'obsessive' behavior in the broad sense of the term when it is complicated by the addition of little gestures and cadenced by pauses and repetitions." This single sentence contains the two peculiarities of ritual which ultimately proved fundamental for Lévi-Strauss: "fragmentation" (in Freud, the use of "little gestures") and "repetition." But what is the function of these two elements? Confronted by the glory of the Discontinuous, the majestic procession of binary oppositions that constitute civilization like algebraic bricks, ritual continues to bear witness to the unhappiness, the obscure nostalgia, that finds no satisfaction in the Discontinuous. With a theatrical skill worthy of one of Wagner's dramatic climaxes, Lévi-Strauss here unveils an idea that has been accompanying him like a troublesome companion: not only does ritual not duplicate myth in action (that would be a horrible *contaminatio*), but it actually chooses to move away from myth. Ritual wants to recover the "fluidity of lived experience" (this is how the Red Sea is referred to, after centuries of intellectual austerity). Ritual wants to plunge us back into the mobile element which "constantly strives to escape through the mesh of the net that mythic thought has cast over it and that holds only its most sharply delineated aspects." It's a hopeless undertaking. It forces Lévi-Strauss to resort to the terms of the "affective life" (here again, an age-old abrasion has ultimately produced this formula), which now develops threateningly and in the very way that Freud had already described: "In dividing and subdividing the operations that it details ad infinitum and repeats unrelentingly, ritual devotes itself to a meticulous task of piecing together: it plugs the interstices, and thereby fosters the illusion that it is possible to retrace myth backward, to make something continuous from something discontinuous. Its maniacal concern for marking the smallest units of lived experience by means of division, and for multiplying the same by means of repetition, reflects a painful need for guarantees against any rupture or possible interruption that might compromise the development of such experience . . . All things considered, the opposition between ritual and myth is the same as that between living and thinking, and ritual represents a degeneration of thought which is granted to life's servitudes . . . Forever doomed to failure, this desperate attempt to reestablish the continuity of lived experience, dismantled by the schematization with which mythical speculation has replaced it, constitutes the essence of ritual." It is a vision of sadness and desolation, which is set against the transparent *harmonia plantarum* that Lévi-Strauss loves to contemplate: that between the genetic code, "savage" thought, and (crash of cymbals) the scientific intellect that deciphers both the genetic code and "savage" thought, all united by the indissoluble and flashing nexus of binary oppositions. With these stones, and only these stones, can we build the House of the Discontinuous—the only true Temple of Solomon, which will rise on the newly drained land.

The revelations about the world and about himself that Lévi-Strauss placed at the end of his Tetralogy help us understand why he has always devoted so little attention to the dirtiest of rituals: sacrifice. But this unwelcome guest in his anthropology could not help appearing, however briefly, in his final orchestration of themes. This happens just as Lévi-Strauss is trying to claim, in opposition to Victor Turner, that ritual creates nothing at all. Indeed, one can say that compared to "categories, laws, and axioms," the adamant agents of the Discontinuous, ritual "is used, if not to deny them, then at least to obliterate temporarily the distinctions and oppositions they promulgate, accentuating every kind of ambiguity, compromise, and exchange among them." In the rectilinear city of the intellect, sacrifice is the harbor area: narrow alleyways, illegal transactions, smell of the sea. And here Lévi-Strauss sends us back to a quick analysis of *La Pensée Sauvage,* where he attempted to establish a permanent division between totemism and sacrifice, so that the tireless Australian classifiers would finally be freed from all suspicion of that stain. The opening is already extreme: "The fact that the history of religions could view totemism as the origin of sacrifice remains, even after so many years, a source of amazement." But the reason for this shock is immediately obvious. The totemistic system is based on a series of parallel classifications, developed with subtlety and rigor, according to the sound rules of the discontinuous. Sacrifice, in contrast, is based on continuity, on retracing again and again a path from the profane to the sacred, and from the sacred to the profane. The principle of substitution, which dominates it, mingles in the shadows with the imperative of connection, and the latter implies a sequence of links that traverse nature and society in every direction. Thus, "sacrifice lies in the realm of continuity." And this is the realm that Lévi-Strauss will never legitimize, the place of "ambiguities," of "compromises," of contaminating "exchanges." In sacrifice, Lévi-Strauss glimpses the greatest possible crime against culture: "sacrifice relies on comparison as a means of abolishing difference." Here he summons as mute witnesses, without ever uttering their names, the supreme enemies of his thought: the Vedic seers. No form of thought is as abhorrent to him as their tireless march through the three worlds, saying "This *is* that," respecting no taxonomic boundaries, rejecting the caesuras that alone should ensure meaning and that are here inevitably concealed with wild orchids, or worse. Meanwhile, behind everything looms the hateful category "interdependence"— now referring not to relationships but to substances, a mystical network that enfolds all logical networks. This is the real Enemy; and here pathos finally betrays the scholar. The confrontation between totemism and sacrifice gradually turns bitter, until it is transformed into a kind of heartfelt condemnation: "Totemism, or what we claim to be such, limits itself to conceiving a homology of structure between the two series (the natural species and the social segments)—a perfectly legitimate hypothesis, since the social segments are institutionally established, and since it is within the power of every society to make the hypothesis plausible, to make its rules and representations conform to it. The system of sacrifice, on the other hand, introduces a nonexistent term: divinity. And it adopts an objectively false conception of the natural series, for (as we have seen) it represents this as continuous." Here we suddenly come upon the great anthropologist accusing religious ceremony of speaking of something "nonexistent," namely "divinity." Why such intolerance? Perhaps we are close to the threshold where "savage" thought becomes, for Lévi-Strauss, too "savage" and no longer deserves to be called "thought." His analysis is paralyzed by a *horror continui*. And suddenly his language is no longer that of impassioned description but of rejection—one might almost say for moral reasons. This thought *must not* be thought. In the end his only alternative is to approach insult, with the shrug of a taxpaying *citoyen:* "Thus, to define the difference between totem and sacrifice, we cannot merely say that the former is a series of references and the latter a system of operations; that one develops a system of interpretations while the other proposes (or believes it is proposing) a technique for achieving certain results: one is true, the other is false. More precisely, systems of classification are situated at the level of language. They are codes, made well or less well, but always aiming at the expression of meanings, whereas the system of sacrifice represents a special discourse—one devoid of common sense, though it is often used." The conclusion of anthropological science, then, would be that sacrifice is a discourse "devoid of common sense."

છ્જ

Goethe's Birthday

In Karlsbad, where he had come to take the waters, he listened "with tears in his eyes" to Catalani singing "Kennst du das Land" at the home of Prince Joseph Schwarzenberg, until a fit of jealousy made her voice crack. To his son August he wrote that the inhabitants of the place now behaved like pirates in their dealings with the foreigners. "In any case everything is very expensive, and becomes even more so with each passing day because of the exchange rate." As his sixty-ninth birthday approached, he felt that the forces of his entelechy were driving him toward "repeated puberty," a long Indian summer. He wanted to celebrate in solitude. According to Eduard Genast, "On the morning of August 27, Goethe ordered Karl, his faithful manservant, to bring up two bottles of red wine and to set them on two facing windowsills. Then Goethe began pacing up and down the room, pausing at regular intervals first at one window, then at the other, and drinking a glass at each pause, still on his feet. After a while Rehbein, who had accompanied him to Karlsbad, entered the room.

GOETHE: Dear friend! What day is this, and what is the date?
REHBEIN: It's August twenty-seventh, Excellency.
GOETHE: No, it's the twenty-eighth, and it's my birthday.
REHBEIN: No, no, I would never forget that; it's the twenty-seventh.
GOETHE: That's not so. It's the twenty-eighth.
REHBEIN (firmly): The twenty-seventh.

GOETHE *(rings; enter Karl):* What's the date?
KARL: The twenty-seventh, Excellency.
GOETHE: Go to—! Bring me the calendar!
(Karl brings the calendar.)
GOETHE *(after a long pause):* Damn! Then I got drunk for nothing.

⚜

Sacrificial Crumbs

After Golgotha, sacrificial victims were untied from the stake. Christianity's concern for living creatures would demand an immolation only *per figuras.* But the miasma of the sacrificial victim had to be removed; such a concretion of nature, of power, vulnerability, malediction, and healing virtue, was no longer admissible. It had to migrate far away, abandon the cities, wander over the oceans, through nameless lands, among beasts and composite beings. From time to time, in the towns, it reappeared as the Wild Man. He can be seen in the background of one of Pieter Brueghel's paintings, with his hesitant paws and green fur, advancing toward a deceitful woman, who offers him a ring. Behind his back, an anonymous man prepares to kill him with a crossbow—and the emperor holds an upraised sword. Subsequently, in a scene never depicted by Brueghel or by anyone else, the Wild Man is mortally struck by the crossbow, amid a circle of villagers. According to a story told by Boccaccio, "in St. Mark's square in Venice a hunt takes place" in which the prey is "the Wild Man." He appears "all smeared with honey and covered with madman's feathers," with "a chain around his neck and a mask over his head," while flies and wasps swarm around him, attracted by the honey. Thus, sacrifice, rejected by society unless distilled in metaphors, found its way back to its origin: the hunt. Henceforth it would be evoked only by the hissing sound of a deadly stab-wound in the middle of the ocean. It was left to wave-tossed vessels to encounter the contagion of sacrifice. Generally it was necessary to cross the Equator and sail to the inverted world of the southern hemisphere.

An albatross flew up from the whiteness and emerald gleam of the ice, messenger of the dazzling place that was receiving and enclosing the Ancient Mariner ("The ice was here, the ice was there, / The ice was all around"). The powers of sacrifice have become concentrated in the mass of ice; they send the albatross on ahead, to be received on the ship according to the laws of hospitality, the last vestige of sacrifice. But the Ancient Mariner kills the albatross for no apparent reason, and with this one shot of the crossbow a reverse sacrifice is performed. Iphigenia had to be sacrificed to raise the wind; but the killing of the albatross brings the air to a standstill. The ship stops and becomes ghostly, captured by the immutability of literature, "As idle as a painted ship / Upon a painted ocean." The sea itself, from its depths, begins to rot. The Ancient Mariner's act derives a certain majesty from its utter arbitrariness. It obeys no ritual, not even some crude folk custom destined to become a footnote for some local scholar. Even the sanction of the other seamen, who approve because the albatross is considered a herald of fog, is invented ex post facto. The Ancient Mariner's act is a sudden, murderous reply to the albatross, to the way it beats its vast wings. His act, in its automatism, erases every past—and the past will in turn fall upon this act, first as a curse, then as a gradual assimilation of the Ancient Mariner with the albatross, which he now wears hung around his neck. Here reminiscence arrives at the origin, at the image of sacrifice as self-sacrifice, and hence of the killer as his own victim. The shot from the Ancient Mariner's crossbow, unexpected, unexplained, is the first distinct image of the evil that will accompany a century of satanism for ladies.

Coleridge wrote "The Ancient Mariner" in response to general advice that had been proffered by Thomas Burnet in the seventeenth century and that became the poem's epigraph: "Ne mens assuefacta hodiernae vitae minutiis se contrahat nimis, et tota subsidat in pusillas cogitationes" ("So that the mind, too used to the life of today, may avoid becoming constricted and concentrating exclusively on petty thoughts"). Civilization had already reached its peak in that fluid and narrow century in which Coleridge had been born, and now it was beginning to feel the clutter of its own minutiae, the mental shards forever prattling around it, while the Whole had been expelled because of its lack of taste and measure. Like the Vedic gods of ancient times, the Transcendental Subjects felt themselves constrained by lack of space. Coleridge's albatross convinced them that whenever the Whole reappeared, an obscure impulse would drive them to kill it. But the albatross was still too much like a sign on paper. It heralded only the reemergence of the Whole. The Whole: the Whale! Then the whiteness of those wings expanded into the immense wrinkled brow of Moby-Dick.

Once history's Equator has been crossed, what was formerly silent must be proclaimed vigorously in all its detail; indeed, that is the *only* thing which must be stated. Now it makes its appearance on the scene, isolated, radiant. Just as the loquacious Sadean protocol takes the place of the hierogamic cloud, so the slaughter of the whale replaces the brahman's silence before the suffocated victim. Pornography has less to do with Eros than with a theological duty: everything that was hidden must be revealed. The secret languages must again be made illegible, no longer because they are hidden but because they are offered to the eyes of all. *The 120 Days of Sodom* establishes a serial order, which is the closest one can come, in the combinatorial sky of thought, to the periodicity of the Zodiac. And the search for Moby-Dick passes through the cycle of the constellations, until Ahab prepares for the last act of his hunt, angrily trampling on the quadrant, that lingering sign of mankind's dependence on the sky. In the center of these two wicked circles is the epiphany of killing. In Sade the maidens wounded by libertine excesses are thrown by Minski, the Muscovite ogre, into a courtyard full of wild beasts, "where they are devoured in less than three minutes." And Juliette, who watches, assures us: "Je n'ai de ma vie perdu de foutre plus lubriquement" ("I've never had such a voluptuous orgasm"). Melville goes further. Whereas Sade refers only briefly to the wounded flesh and straightway returns to his prolix and evil chatter, which is even more *échauffé* by the spectacle, Melville raises literature to butchery, pushes it beyond an unheard-of threshold, imposes on the page what we always knew was happening, but happening offstage and outside the word. "The ivory Pequod was turned into what seemed a shambles; every sailor a butcher." Literature had blossomed out of sacrifice, but it had never before described the act of butchering; rather, it had been the labyrinthine garland around that void. With Melville, butchery becomes the actual center of the book. The Taylorist factory, which Sade had already evoked in the fierce rhythms of the *120 Days,* now reappears in the slaughtering of the whale, described with a meticulousness as greedy as that of Marcel describing the Guermantes' ball, but here carried out under the southern sun and accompanied by the stench and dizzying perfumes of the immense cadaver. Now, amid the indifference of sea and heavens, surrounded by a limitless space, butchering (which in the city is concealed behind cement walls) has once again become a delicate severing of the cosmic elements. Even the Arché—the Principle underlying everything—becomes palpable, at the point in the novel when the wild Indian Tashtego nearly dies, "smothered in the very whitest and daintiest of fragrant spermaceti; coffined, hearsed, and tombed in the secret inner chamber and sanctum sanctorum of the whale." It is an image of the sweetest death, this fall into "Plato's honey head." Thus, at the end of the dissection, when all usable material has been extracted from the slain animal and its decapitated body is again consigned to the waters, what finally reappears is something inexhaustible, ineradicable—a "white phantom" that need never fear harm from any human knives, or from the beaks of birds or the teeth of sharks, those creatures that rival man in the eternal "vulturism of earth." The headless white carcass floats away on the water. Soon we shall encounter it again under the name of Moby-Dick: "The vast tackles have now done their duty. The peeled white body of the beheaded whale flashes like a marble sepulchre; though changed in hue, it has not perceptibly lost anything in bulk. It is still colossal. Slowly it floats more and more away, the water round it torn and splashed by the insatiate sharks, and the air above vexed with rapacious flights of screaming fowls, whose beaks are like so many insulting poniards in the whale. The vast white headless phantom floats further and further from the ship, and every rod that it so floats, what seem square roods of sharks and cubic roods of fowls augment the murderous din. Beneath the unclouded and mild azure sky, upon the fair face of the pleasant sea, wafted by the joyous breezes, that great mass of death floats on and on, till lost in infinite perspectives."

.　　.　　.

Giorgio de Santillana wrote: "Marcel Griaule, who brought unknown cultures in the western Sudan to our attention, often asked the local authorities to tell him something about the inhabited lands and what they knew about distant countries. He was surprised that they always pointed to the sky. Then he finally understood: for them, 'inhabited lands' meant the zone of the Ecliptic." That wonderful "finally understood" refers also to Santillana himself. Like a footloose Western gentleman, he had traveled the victorious pathways of science for decades, had seen them culminate between Galileo and Leibniz. And now, looking at the Animals of the Zodiac, an oblique band on the horizon, he realized that *pondus, numerus, mensura* had already enlightened and dominated another world, in quite a different sense, beginning at a Time Zero that he thought was approximately when the equinoctial sun had risen in Gemini, around 5000 B.C. He then began to travel the celestial paths of that other science, lovingly collecting odd bits of text from mythographers and ancient singers. One day he went back to Ernst Cassirer's writings on "symbolic forms," the most articulate work of that great scholar who had long been a guide for him. He realized that almost nothing in those pages was still valid.

Frances Yates told a similar story. Just prior to the Second World War, she had begun studying Giordano Bruno, above all because he belonged to the Italian Renaissance, and she, like so many young Anglo-Saxons devoted to culture, found the very sound of that phrase exciting. At first she intended to translate *La cena de le ceneri*, "with an introduction emphasizing the boldness with which this advanced philosopher of the Renaissance accepted Copernican theory." But something about that intrepid knight of the Modern was unconvincing: "Was Copernican theory really the subject of the debate, or was there something else implied in it?" For a long time she pondered Bruno's mnemotechnical writings without being able to say what they were about. When she finally had the key in her hand, she immediately saw the Animals of the Zodiac rise and conceal themselves in the wheels of memory. The oblique band of the Ecliptic was again telling the stories that the Dogon people had read there: "Wanting to explore their geographic horizon, [Griaule] tried to discuss the inhabited lands, what these tribesmen knew about the world surrounding them. But soon he saw them once again pointing upward, to indicate boundaries in the sky. And he realized that for them the phrase 'inhabited lands' referred to the celestial zone between the two Tropics: a band comprising 47 degrees in the sky, lying on both sides of the Equator. Those are the true and only 'inhabitants.'"

As we move backward in history, we see that guilt and evil recede ever further from the wicked intentions of the subject and assume the majestic reality of number. Original sin becomes a mathematical and divine fact, an event *in coelestibus,* like all events that merit discussion. Articulated in time, the evil, the guilt, the fundamental disorder that accompanies us is manifested in three forms. I list them in the probable order of their discovery.

The obliquity of the Ecliptic. In the *chi* (χ) drawn by the Demiurge in Plato's *Timaeus,* the Ecliptic is the axis of the Other with respect to the Equator, which is the axis of the Self. From the obliquity of the Ecliptic descends the drama of the seasons, taken away from the perennial, symmetrical equilibrium of the equinoxes, which we would have if the angles were right angles. That drama will be the basis of every rise and fall, of every adventure, every journey; it is the original disorder of the world.

The Precession of the Equinoxes. Abandoned to itself, this retrograde movement—which reveals evil in an even clearer way—exploits the divine weariness, as Plato forcefully explained in the *Politicus:* "Listen. At certain times, the god draws the entire thing along its circular path. At other times, when the assigned periods have elapsed, he lets it go, and then it all begins to rotate on its own in the opposite direction, for it is an animate being and has received intelligence from the one who composed it originally. Now this tendency to retrograde movement is innate in it" because "the being that we call heaven and world," however hard it may try, cannot be granted immunity from change, and so it has been accorded a "circular retrograde movement that separates it as little as possible from its own proper movement." A consequence of these two opposing cosmic movements is the fact that time is divided into eras, because of the continuous slow shifting of the celestial references. Hence the passage from the era of Gemini to that of Taurus, then Aries; hence the succession of worlds that collapse in flames or sink beneath the waters.

The incommensurability of $\sqrt{2}$. Simone Weil speaks of this as "the drama of the incommensurables." But she goes on to say that the scandal of this discovery, "far from being a defeat for the Pythagoreans, as is naïvely thought, is their most marvelous triumph." She uses the image of a scale that has on one dish two cubes of side 1 and on the other a cube whose side is equal to the diagonal of the other two cubes. Under these conditions, equilibrium can never be attained: *no* amount of weight added or removed will ever make it possible.

Sacrifice recognizes the noncorrespondence between the discontinuous and the continuous, yet it also recognizes the necessary bond between them. This bond is embodied in the sacrificial victim. The victim fills the gap between the discontinuous and the continuous. But precisely because he fills it, he must be destroyed. And the world then reverts to its earlier state, in which distinctions are made according to the parallel series of the discontinuous and the continuous. The wheel divided into 360 segments, gods, days, and degrees continues to turn above the solid wheel of Vṛtra.

Guilt and, ultimately, Christian sin descend from ritual imprecision, like the cadet branch of an ancient family. Ritual is the *kairòs,* the "right moment," that extends over every segment of time. This exalted precision, this trenchant perception of order—outside of which every delay, every uncertainty of action is guilt, the evil to which all evil is reduced—was born from a long, desolate exploration of experience. Nothing that was perfectly regular and symmetrical had ever appeared in any of its parts. There were only some minuscule points in the sky, moving along inflexible paths. *That* was order. It was all the more overwhelming to discover that even there, something was not right—or rather everything was as it should be, but slightly shifted, because of Precession. Or else it was the calendar calculations that at the end left a residue, a clot of surplus time: an excess here as well, which had somehow to be eliminated. The accursed part was nesting amid the celestial spheres.

There are two kinds of substitution. One says *a stands for b*, and implies that *a* annuls *b*, kills it, sometimes to discover how it works. The other likewise says *a stands for b*, but in the way that a chip of granite stands for the mountain from which it has been detached. Between these two kinds of substitution there is a bifurcation, a Y that long roamed the cosmos but is now concentrated in the mind's core. The symbol—not the one that linguists speak of, but the one we find in the Eleusinian Mysteries—belongs to the second kind of substitution. The symbol keeps superimposing itself on an invisible mountain. The fact that it is a discontinuous wrinkle always turned toward the continuous is revealed in the origin of its name. *Symbolon* means the broken halves of a piece of wood or pottery which come together to reconstitute a smooth and solid surface, barely incised by a transverse wound. More than teaching substitution, to which it must still pay homage, the symbol teaches interpenetration, the inevitable layering of things. The symbol is a ghost that enters another ghost, mingles, dissolves there, escapes. It drags behind itself, in a golden chain, everything it has passed through.

All things change, whether or not one accepts the "sacrificial interpretation of life," a formula that appeared in *Etudes traditionnelles,* tucked away in a review that Guénon wrote concerning an article by Coomaraswamy. According to Guénon's interpretation, "actions, having an essentially symbolic character, must be treated as the supports for contemplation (*dhiyālamba*); and this presupposes that every practice implies and includes a corresponding theory." Every practice, every act, voluntary or involuntary. What, in fact, is more sacrificial than breathing? An invisible vise now squeezes every instant, forces it to constant oblation. But if nothing is offered, if sacrifice is pigeonholed with superstition, what will happen? "Revolution, through sacrifice, confirms superstition," Baudelaire warns. Unmentioned, sacrifice continues to demand its victims; it once again becomes nomadic, moving the sites of its cult everywhere. Why? Is reason, which has prohibited sacrifice, perhaps not strong enough to extirpate it? Or is it perhaps true, as Baudelaire claimed, that "superstition is the reservoir of all truths" and that truths eventually assert themselves, like traces of crimes?

The triple deception of sacrifice. Humans deceive the gods, through substitution of the victim. The officiants deceive the victim, hiding the knife among the ears of grain because up to the end they fear he will rebel. And humans are deceived by the gods, who demand sacrifice in order to guarantee life—but then, through that act, allow death to be confirmed.

The rice thrown at newlyweds originated in the grains of barley that were once scattered over the sacrificial victim. The grains evoke the ancient practice of stoning the victim—the surest method of killing, because it permits one to kill the victim without even touching him.

Transition from sacrifice to experiment. In sacrifice, everything is based on the premise of an other, of many others, invisible, who respond to the *right action*. By making an irrevocable offering, man indicates that he is ready to listen and that he anticipates a reply— and he must repeat this sign of receptiveness over and over again. Experiment is based on the premise that the *right action* grows out of accumulation. The researcher tests a thousand acts in uncertainty and darkness; only one of them will be the *right action*. All the others, which entail a dissipation of energy, are lost, tributes to an unknown. The application of the *right action* to the world, and the possibility of repeating it forever, will lead to an increase of power corresponding to the life exalted by sacrifice.

Critics reproached Guénon for writing about metaphysics like an accountant, without trembling, without soul. They found him uninspired. But Guénon was simply obeying the "initiatory and specifically Rosicrucian precept according to which it is proper to speak to each individual in his own language."

Let us erase the names of the gods, the founding myths, the ritual precepts. What, then, is left of sacrifice? The discrepancy between the discontinuous and the continuous, between rational numbers and real numbers—and the realization that continuous and discontinuous must remain linked.

The cycle is the perception on which every mythology is based. And the cycle is written in the sky, in the recurrence of the constellations. The terror of killing is, above all, the terror that the cycle may not exist, that the animal may not return, that the star may not reappear. The slight disorder we observe in the sky (the obliquity of the Ecliptic, the Precession of the Equinoxes) corresponds to the immense disorder that prevails on earth (death).

Technology takes the place not of magic but of sacrifice. Like sacrifice, it is chiefly a way to control danger, which not only means violent conflict within society but also the destructive and self-destructive power within life itself. The plague stands for the conflict among men, just as the conflict among men stands for the plague. Sacrifice requires a perfect awareness of destruction; if this clear-sighted perception is missing, there is no sacrifice. Technology is content to justify itself with claims of its practical utility.

In Kafka, bureaucratic procedures illuminate not some degenerate state of the law but its rise, its dawn, its first emergence from swampy waters, when the abstract and the arbitrary shone in all their extraneousness to nature. It was precisely then that nature became the Village and agreed to work at the inn, serving the weary Lords who occasionally came down from the Castle.

The "force field between the Torah and the Tao," which for Walter Benjamin defined Kafka's place, was also Benjamin's own place. But it was surely not a psychological or philosophical one. It was the saturnine dwelling, the celestial zone where the *ṛta* and the "hidden ocean" live together, where Law is immersed in the fluidity of the Waters. On the bottom lies the *xvarnah*, the radiance of Glory— which Benjamin, as the *xvarnah* roamed the world in exile, found in the *aura*.

·   ·   ·

In a letter to Robert Klopstock, Kafka proposes two variations on the story of Abraham: "I can imagine another Abraham, who surely would never manage to become a patriarch, or even a ragman. This Abraham would be immediately willing to comply with the request for the sacrifice, prompt as a waiter, but he would be unable to carry out the sacrifice, because he cannot leave home. He is indispensable; the running of the house requires his presence, and there is always something to be tidied up—but if the house is not tidy, he cannot leave it. The Bible confirms this, saying: 'He set his house in order.' And Abraham already had an abundance of everything. If he had not had a house, where would he have brought up his son, and on what beam would he have placed the knife? . . .

"Then there is another Abraham. A man who sincerely wants to perform the sacrifice in the right way and has rightly grasped the meaning of the whole thing, but who is unwilling to believe that the responsibility has actually fallen on him, on this repugnant old man, and on that dirty youth his son. He does not lack the true faith. He has that faith, and would make sacrifice in the proper spirit, if only he could believe it was his lot. He is afraid that, riding out as Abraham with his son, he might be transformed along the way into Don Quixote. Everyone would then be horrified at the sight of Abraham, but this Abraham fears that people would die of laughter if they saw him. Yet it is not the ridiculous in itself that he fears—or rather, he fears this, too, especially if everybody were to laugh all at once. More than anything else, he fears that this ridicule will make him even older and more repugnant, and his son even dirtier, and both of them even more unworthy of being called. An Abraham who comes without being called! It's a bit as if the best student is solemnly receiving a prize at the end of the year, and amid the expectant, anxious silence the worst student comes forward from his seat at the dirty last desk, because he mistakenly thinks he has heard his name, and then the whole class bursts out laughing. And perhaps he has not really made a mistake—perhaps his name has actually been called. The teacher may intend that the awarding of a prize to the best student be at the same time a punishment for the worst.

"Terrible things . . . Enough."

.   .   .

A few months before his death, Benjamin wrote a letter to Gershom Scholem in which he spoke of his latest discovery concerning Kafka: "I think the key to Kafka's work is likely to fall into the hands of the person who *is able to identify the comic elements in Jewish theology.* Has there been such a man? Or would you be man enough to be that man?"

In his letters, Rancé remarked with his characteristic harshness that we must all consider ourselves sheep at the slaughter, *tanquam oves occisionis.* As Victor Hugo said, "The gospel makes God a shepherd. The Trappists make him a butcher." But shepherds, who protect their flocks, also slaughter them little by little. The secular practice of euphemism, of which Hugo here gives an example, allows us to perceive only the idyllic image of the shepherd. If we place ourselves (as Hugo did) outside sacrifice, no criticism of sacrifice can assail the compulsion to kill. So the compulsion will remain powerful, though tacit. Only certain Altaic peoples, shepherds and herdsmen who once practiced sacrifice, managed to develop, in the form of a ceremony, the most radical criticism of sacrifice. "The Tatars of the Minussink region used to sacrifice a *living* white horse to the god of thunder. After praying on the sacrificial spot, they would remove the horse's bridle and let the animal run away. From that moment on, the horse was free and untouchable. The Buriats also put a bowl of milk on the back of the animal consecrated to thunder. The priest who officiates at the sacrifice sprinkles milk on the animal's back and at the same time toward the four cardinal points of the compass. Then he envelops the horse in fumes, burning some herbs and the bark of a resinous tree. Then he ties some ribbons to its mane, and finally the horse is sent out into freedom. At the place where the bowl of milk falls from the horse's back, all pray for health and prosperity. An animal thus consecrated is never again used to serve humankind. When the animal dies, its mane and tail are cut off and tied to another horse, which replaces the previous one." This undoing of the knot of life, which takes place with the killing of the adorned sacrificial victim, can be opposed with equal strength by only one other undoing: that of the bridle of the captive horse, which releases life in life. But this gesture, which is the only fitting opposition to sacrifice, is born from within the sacrifice itself; it treads the same ground, wears the same ribbons, repeats its actions to the end. Then the hands that were about to come together for the sake of strangling are joined in the act of undoing the bridle. The horse disappears into the taiga or continues to follow the herd; but the animal is treated as if it were invisible, since no one can touch it, much less use it. Nobody can sell it, and nobody can buy it. That white horse is the Double of all horses, which by the power of grace we are allowed to glimpse next to all the others. But the Double cannot be used—it can only be released. At the place where the bridle was undone, everything remains as if the lifeless body of the victim were present. The fumes of the Oriental spruce linger in the air, for we are at the point where "no smoke without god" is the rule. The bowl of milk has fallen to the ground, and according to the way it lies, divine favor or disfavor is communicated. Even the ribbons in the mane are an element of mimicry, another point of similarity between the freed horse and the sacrificial victim. But there is one last dizzying gesture in which the ceremony of the consecrated horse corresponds to the metaphysics of sacrifice: when the liberated horse dies, its mane and tail are cut off and are attached to the horse that *replaces* it. Here we reach the heart of sacrifice: substitution. And this deadly machinery is reversed in a pledge of perennial life. As the white horses replace one another in sequence throughout the generations, they become like a single horse that never dies. This is the extreme point of the reversal of sacrifice—achieved in a remote age, in an area of central Asia still retaining vestiges of shamanism, where white horses are consecrated to thunder. The next step has never been taken. No man has ever felt another man's hand undoing the invisible bridle that is around his neck. Nobody has ever been totally freed from being *used* by other men. And the practice of being "used to serve humankind" is steeped in the venom of exchange, which slowly—or sometimes abruptly—kills.

&

The Anti-Romantic Child

Some fools endowed with genius are the voices of fate. Almost unwittingly, they give a metaphysical resonance to their every utterance. A whole civilization charges them with the responsibility for speaking certain decisive, regulative sentences that no one else wants to say in their full harshness. For us such a man was Bentham, a genuine hero of *Ahnungslosigkeit*—the inability to perceive the Powers.

"Directly or indirectly, *well-being,* in one shape or another, or in several shapes, or all shapes taken together, is the subject of every thought, and the object of every action, on the part of every known *Being,* who is, at the same time, a sensitive and thinking being."

"Money is the instrument of measuring the quantity of pain or pleasure. Those who are not satisfied with the accuracy of this instrument must find out some other that shall be more accurate, or bid adieu to politics and morals.

"Let no man therefore be either surprised or scandalized if he find me in the course of this work valuing everything in money. 'Tis in this way only can we get aliquot parts to measure by. If we must not say of a pain or a pleasure that it is worth so much money, it is in vain, in point of quantity, to say anything at all about it, and there is neither proportion nor disproportion between Punishments and Crimes."

"The only common measure the nature of things affords is money."

"I beg a truce here of our man of sentiment and feeling while from necessity, and it is only from necessity, I speak and prompt mankind to speak a mercenary language."

. . .

"Now then, money being the current instrument of pleasure, it is plain by uncontrovertible experience, that the quantity of actual pleasure follows in every instance in some proportion or other the quantity of money." Bentham asserts this proportionality between money and pleasure only to say immediately afterward that it cannot be determined precisely: "In large sums the ratio of pleasure is in this way less than a ratio of money to money. There is no limit beyond which the quantity of money cannot go; but there are limits, and those comparatively narrow, beyond which pleasure cannot go."

Bentham thus asserts with complete confidence the paradox of a unit of measure that exists but that does not actually apply in every case, because variations in circumstances also cause continual variations in the proportionality between the two series (money and pleasure). And if a law can be established in this correspondence, it must be a law that will affirm a different *ratio* in the progression between the two series.

The decisive steps:

1. establish the need for a unit of measurement;
2. identify the unit as money;
3. lead the limited back to the unlimited.

Bentham destroys the correspondence, observing the different *ratio* between the two series, but reasserts it immediately afterward. In this way he excludes all the areas in which the problem of limits arises (*great* pleasures and *great* sums), only to insinuate that the *normal,* regular, and legal orbit is precisely that where proportion is still respected, and hence is the ambit of *little* pleasures and *little* sums: "For all this, it is true enough for practice with respect to such proportions as ordinarily occur [*variant reading:* small quantities] that *ceteris paribus* the proportion between pleasure and pleasure is the same as between sum and sum." For society to be well ordered, it must consider *great* pleasures hostile and disturbing in relation to the whole. But not because they conceal the power of the unlimited. On the contrary: it is because they would compel us to recognize that the power of the unlimited is concealed in money itself.

John Stuart Mill—the first guinea pig to receive a strictly Benthamite education, one based entirely on the criterion of usefulness—did not react with sumptuous delirium, as Judge Schreber would in an analogous situation. On the contrary, he managed to write a magnanimous essay on Bentham. A genuine respect and lucidity guide Mill's words, which involuntarily reveal more than what they say on the surface. First, he offers us the most fitting definition of the Master, presenting him as "the great *subversive*" and, in particular, as "the chief subversive thinker of an age which has long lost all that they could subvert." Bentham was the first living *tabula rasa,* a stolid and insolent child who could have no doubts because he had no experience—and would never acquire any. "He had neither internal experience, nor external; the quiet, even tenor of his life, and his healthiness of mind, conspired to exclude him from both. He never knew prosperity and adversity, passion nor satiety. He never had even the experience which sickness gives; he lived from childhood to the age of eighty-five in boyish health. He knew no dejection, no heaviness of heart. He never felt life a sore and a weary burthen. He was a boy to the last. Self-consciousness, that daemon of the men of genius of our time, from Wordsworth to Byron, from Goethe to Chateaubriand, and to which this age owes so much of both its cheerful and its mournful wisdom, never was awakened in him. How much of human nature slumbered in him he knew not, neither can we know. He had never been made alive to the unseen influences which were acting on himself, nor consequently on his fellow creatures." With Bentham, the anti-Romantic child, a genuine *new man* was born: he who knows nothing, calculates everything, and in the end resolves everything.

Bentham is the happy autodidact. The calculation of pleasure erases the incalculable past, with its sackful of ghosts that obscure additions and subtractions. But we rarely find cases like his, watertight and sealed off. More often the autodidact is afflicted by a dark uneasiness, like that of Auguste Blanqui in the prison of Fort du Taureau, who projects the cosmos in his mind, sees that "the forms are innumerable, yet the elements the same," and realizes that the cosmos is therefore a jumble of duplicates.

Wherever there is no initiation, we find the autodidact. Wherever knowledge is not wisdom transmitted through experience, everyone is enrolled in correspondence courses.

E***: Our fate is governed by two mummies: that of Lenin in his tomb, and that of Bentham at University College, London.

∽❧∽

Limits

The history of the Enlightenment serenely denies limits. Since its god is convention and since everything is raw material for convention's handiwork, at most the point will be to change convention every time resistance is encountered. But all conventions have one thing in common, namely *faith* in convention—and the raw material may one day rebel against this faith. Then the limit reappears, an exotic figure that was first revealed in Greece and that the Greeks venerated at a time when they were perfecting the first methods for erasing it. Today we have it before us again; it is the most disturbing of figures, the most ambiguous of memories. Simone Weil was the only one clear-headed enough to recognize it by its proper name. Those who do not recognize it in thought are forced to see it rise again from deeds, translated into and camouflaged by the jargon of systems, complexity, control. Or else they are forced to see the limit reappear in the anxiety over some material that falls short, over energies irreversibly consumed, over some insurmountable lack. And each time the ancient exorcism resounds: we will find new conventions, we will proceed with severe revisions of method. The circle is repeated but becomes ever narrower, until it tightens into a noose.

The society of exchange is based on the transgression of limits, but it does not accept the state of natural fragmentation in which it finds itself more and more often. It does not accept it because such a society takes totality as its point of reference. The image may change at every moment, but it must always have a frame, and the frame must remain constant for as long as possible. Otherwise the images would overflow into the corridors. From the achieved and imperfectible totality of the canon, we thus pass to a totality that frames every fragment as its telos. Every fragment is supposed to be temporary, awaiting a promised whole, which will redeem it. Progress would be a weak idea, innocuous in its helplessness, if the totality did not loom up behind it yet again, imposing an indomitable bond, greedy and narrow, on a reality that operates through a continual severing of bonds.

The passage from the world of canon to that of convention is achieved by substituting the "barrier" for the "sacred limit," as Marx made clear in his *Grundrisse der Kritik der politischen Ökonomie (Foundations of the Critique of Political Economy)*. Changing a canon means changing a world. Changing a convention means that different results will occur within the same world. The results are compared on the basis of the development they have achieved. Violating the "sacred limit" means abandoning an order that is the order of society because at the same time it is the order of the world. Breaking down a "barrier" means proposing a new procedure.

Monsieur le Capital creates an artificial nature, which is imposed as even more natural than nature. By instituting credit, capital creates the illusion that it can be a continual self-creation, instead of an interrupted, periodic self-creation, like nature. The crisis that besets capital is, in fact, *cyclical*. Madame la Terre reminds us of her existence, and tears to pieces the façade of artificial nature. Here again, we see capitalism's declared esotericism. Continual self-creation is what appears at the end of initiation; but *inversion* demands that it be viewed as concrete reality and that it be immediately perceivable.

Marx defines "capital" as the incessant knocking down of barriers: "The only premise is that there is movement beyond the point of departure." At the same time he crouches in ambush, waiting for the (approaching) moment when capital will reach its own limit. But what is the *limit* of that which is perpetually exceeding limits? Despite all his vituperation, Marx could barely conceal his most insidious fear: that such a limit did not exist. The same fear surfaced (though much more innocently) in Rosa Luxemburg's indignation against Tugan-Baranovsky: "It is clear that once one has granted the unlimited accumulation of capital, one has also demonstrated the unlimited vitality of capital." In fact, in Marx's speculative apparatus, the *péras* (or any other strict notion of "limit") was completely absent. "Development," by definition, was undefined. Indeed, it was this same assumption of ceaseless movement that inspired sudden flights of lyricism. And once again it was Luxemburg who displayed them in their most exposed and transparent form: "It should be clear that the capitalist mode of production, which claims to stimulate technology to its highest level, actually erects a high social barrier to technological progress because it places utmost importance on profit. Once this barrier is demolished, technological progress will advance with such power that the technological wonders of capitalist production will seem mere child's play in comparison." There is thus a *harmful* destruction of limits that has, as its counterpart, an inevitable and *beneficial* destruction of limits. Like quarrelsome but inseparable children, capitalism and socialism play the same game, though with bitter conflicts of style—"twin and rival forms of a single identical faith."

♱

Process

The word "process" comprises what Adorno and Horkheimer called *Aufklärung,* what Nietzsche called *Nihilismus,* what Heidegger called *Nihilismus* and *Metaphysik,* what Marx called *Kapitalismus,* what Monsieur Homais called *progrès,* what Guénon called *le règne de la quantité,* what Freud called *das Unbehagen in der Kultur,* what Spengler (and also Wittgenstein) called *Zivilisation.* It also implies the slow movement of the *absolutes Wissen* described by Hegel ("for the self must penetrate and digest all the richness of its substance"). This entails clipping from the interior of global history a shape of Western history within which a sequence of events and transformations un-folds under laboratory conditions. Nobody really knows what gives rise to the sequence, or where it ultimately leads. But there is con-siderable agreement (though each time expressed in different terms and according to different values) on the various transitions that occur within the sequence, in a chain reaction. Transitions that can be verified in every area. Chopin and the merchant bank.

What still remains to be conceived: a process that has an unques-tionable direction, a direction with a sign. But this sign is no longer a plus or a minus, as (respectively) Condorcet and Joseph de Maistre would have it; rather, it might be a sign resembling one of the animals depicted in the Shang bronzes—an animal that comprises many other animals, including the plus of Condorcet and the minus of de Maistre, but connected, entwined, enlarged with many other signs that are less easy to read. This composite sign challenges us to attempt a decoding—one that will conflict with the decoding of each of its parts.

What is the first negation of the whole? A negation that negates not a detail but a characteristic of the whole—namely, its interde-pendence. From this step follow all subsequent steps. Once the interdependence of the whole is negated, the world is left divided into aggregate segments, varying in size and stability, from which individual elements occasionally break free and become autono-mous.

This process of *becoming autonomous,* in which constitutive ele-ments escape the authority and looming presence of the context, was for many decades known as "nihilism." It functions much like the progressive release of discrete substances from a compound that includes them all. And once released, those substances have an effect on the compound. Above all, they contribute to its further breakdown.

❧

Glosses on Marx

Marx's perpetual ambivalence toward the Modern becomes clear whenever his argument focuses on the ancient world. Since we are accustomed to the fury of Marx's moralizing thunderbolts against the perversity that surrounded him, we might expect to find him more serene and at peace when dwelling on ages past, but this is not the case. Indeed, it is here that he reveals his greatest unease: "Thus, the old view, according to which human beings are the aim of production regardless of their specific national, religious, and political character, seems very lofty when compared to that of the modern world, in which production is the aim of mankind and wealth the aim of production." But the old view only "seems" more noble and elevated; the phrasing reveals how little Marx thinks of it. Again, his intolerance certainly does not derive from reasons of the heart (from, say, the fact that the ancient world was based on slavery). Rather, he believed that the ancient world was not sufficiently powerful. Above all, it was not constructed so that its functioning could necessarily and automatically exalt power, independently of the direction in which it was applied. "Wealth," in fact, if judged according to the way it functions, is far *richer* (and much more *interesting!*) than the devoted service of man to man that obtained in the ancient world, where "the question is always [one of establishing] which mode of property creates the best citizens." The bourgeois world of wealth, of course, is not much concerned with creating virtuous citizens; if anything, it broadens the *comédie humaine* to include every species of monstrosity. But in compensation, "if wealth is stripped [Marx, in officer's uniform, visits a cocotte's dressing room and glimpses, behind the delicate screen, her ancient—more than ancient, actually modern!—sweetly blurred nakedness] of its limited bourgeois form, what is it if not the universality of individual needs, abilities, pleasures, productive strength, and so on, created through universal exchange? What is it if not man's complete dominion over the forces of nature, both that of so-called nature and that of his own nature?" Here, casting off his shyness, Marx at last expresses his innermost feelings. Antiquity, yes—lovely statues, beautiful and quotable poetry, heroes, tombs, columns. But how narrow and passive the ancient world was, if we compare it with majestic bourgeois wealth—the precipitous abstractions from which it is born, its endless warehouses, which are only apparently filled with things. To the penetrating gaze, they contain the phantoms of ever-greater needs, pleasures, qualities, powers, collected within a pulsating, expanding nebula. Marx, we must remember, is above all greedy: he wants *more* of everything. He distrusts quality, when it is not simply the seal of greater quantity. Even if quality existed on its own, it would always be less admirable than a quantity that continually threatens to increase. At this point, we hear Marx's secret heart beating. But it is not the Schillerian heart that dreams of belonging to a worthy community, of overcoming malign schisms, of rediscovering blades of grass. No: it is the pride of total "dominion," first over "so-called nature" and then over man's "own nature." This is a promise of power. This is intoxication from the Nothing that drives the machine—inexhaustible fuel, release of forces! And even the idea of a process that is an end in itself, which Marx branded as infamy in hundreds of pages of analysis, calling it the sovereign perversion of the world of goods—well, even this now appears to us as something far more exciting than the "childish" and limited world of antiquity, however well-meaning it may have been.

After his reference to "man's dominion over the forces of nature," Marx continues in these terms: "What is it [wealth] if not the absolute realization of his [man's] creative gifts, with no presupposition other than prior historical development, which makes this totality of development—that is, the development of all human powers as such—an end in itself, and not one measured by a predetermined criterion? A totality of development in which man does not reproduce himself in a single specificity, but produces his totality?" Here we witness the reappearance of an old obsession: the unit of measurement. But once again, the situation is reversed. The ancient world had, as a frame of reference, an actual *canon* of man, which seems to have been a utopian state of society that in itself possessed the criterion of perfection. The modern world, on the contrary, has no real use for perfection. Its only unit of measurement is work time—meaning abstract work, an empty unit, without any special features. But it is precisely this empty unit that allows man to *produce* (note: not *reproduce!*) himself to a degree unheard of in any other world. At this point it becomes obvious what part, what party, Marx chooses; what is speaking here, in almost brutal fashion, is his love for the Modern, for its ability to multiply and glorify itself without any plan, in every direction. For its only end is the *whole,* the immediate possession of everything, and not just a canon that *corresponds* to the whole. To achieve totality, elements can be accumulated anywhere—in attics, in basements, in drawing rooms. Vices, virtues—everything is of use, provided it comes in large quantities. Humankind becomes an immense port, where spices and exotic fruits pour in. No order is necessary. All that is required is a constant multiplication of the whole, to the point of saturation.

And when the whole has been achieved? Then humanistic concerns and considerations will reappear: man fishing in the morning and playing the flute in the evening—"all-sided" man, proudly refusing to be deprived of any of his countless tentacles. But here, too, a surprise is in store, ready to spoil any *image d'Epinal.* Far more than the virtuous worker educated in technical schools and in the factory, this total man tends to blossom into a total monstrosity, celestial and infernal, a cross between Juliette's Minski and Dostoyevski's Myshkin (Stirner realized this truth at once). All the rest is humanitarian kitsch, closer to Homais than to Fourier—and the two, in fact, are not so far apart.

Elsewhere, however, throbs the passion of Marx: we see him filled with lucid fervor before the demonic nature of *process.* To be sure, it is process that fascinates, not its result. The constructing of the power of the void. Here, too, the fundamental opposition between the two worlds reappears. Reread the last sentence of the passage quoted above: "A totality of development in which man does not reproduce himself in a single specificity, but produces his totality." The ultimate opposition, then, is between *reproducing* and *producing.* "To reproduce" is the verb of the world of the canon, dominated by rituals which strive each time to bring process back into order, to *reproduce* an order, that of the *r̥ta,* which sustains the cosmos as well as society. "To produce" is the verb of the world of hegemonic exchange, where it is essential to be able to use a functional artifice that will enable process, as it unfolds, to bring with it—despite everything!—an increase of power. This happens precisely because the direction of production is *not* determinable, and is actually neglected, whereas research is focused chiefly on intensifying and expanding the means of production. It is, in fact, only in their evolution that we see any consistency.

The world of production knows no models and sets itself no limits; its limit can only be the whole. From maximum fragmentation, engendered by the absence of models, it wants to converge toward maximum unity, which is that of a whole immediately possessed. And this demand for totality hovers like a ghost over every part of the process, since the absence of totality causes keen anguish. That hovering ghost, a temporary healer, is kitsch.

("In bourgeois political economics—and in the age of production that corresponds to it—this complete working-out of the human content appears as a complete emptying-out; this universal objectification appears as total alienation; and the tearing down of all limited, one-sided aims appears as sacrifice of the human end-in-itself to an entirely external end. On the one hand, this is why the childish world of antiquity seems a loftier world. On the other hand, it really is loftier, in all areas in which one seeks closed shapes and forms, and given limits; it is satisfaction from a limited point of view. Whereas the modern world leaves us unsatisfied; or where it leaves us satisfied, it is *vulgar*." Caution—tread lightly! Here we are perhaps approaching one of the august secrets of kitsch. An art of the limited and the canonical, of measurements attuned to a cosmic order, it nevertheless conceals a devouring, reckless movement. Whatever experiences the fragment as the whole, whatever reposes in the fragment with sated, steady, legal expression, is "vulgar." Then, like the desert wind, the inexhaustible *haine du bourgeois* rises, bringing vengeance. Yet kitsch has always accompanied art! Yes, but to pin down its shadow, process had to be expanded across the planet; the couple who are embracing and watching the sunset are supposed to remedy the absence of any model. Ancient kitsch hints at an even deeper secret: the guilt belonging to each thing that becomes an image—the echo of the violence of giving a name.)

．　．　．

Looking to the origins, Marx regarded the earth in two different ways: it was at once an "extension of the body" of man, and his "great laboratory," "arsenal," "working material." These antithetical modes recur often in his thought. On the one hand, there is an analogical chain of symbolic correspondences, in which the earth is enfolded as soon as it is considered an "extension of the body" of man (and thus we see that despite incessant secularization, terms like "heart," "brain," "flesh" remain symbolic poles). On the other hand, there is an Enlightenment-inspired dissociation, an experimental use of the whole, an absence of premises, represented in the image of the "great laboratory." But Marx's attention—and passion—are always directed at the second pole. The first, he realizes, obviously exists; but he is clearly too bored by it to specify its characteristics. For him it suffices to posit a state of *belonging,* both at the origin and (though here it is more problematic) at the end, as well as a considerable number of states of *separation* in all that occurs between those two stages. Marx analyzes these states of separation with a kind of tireless, turbulent, sensual pleasure, referring often and eloquently to something lost or to be recovered. But his eloquence fades, and he becomes suddenly distracted, as soon as he has the opportunity to clarify exactly what has been lost and what might be recovered. All this does not imply that Marx has given two incompatible definitions of the "land" of origin. The definitions are indeed discordant and contradictory, but they have always lived side by side in history: one is the latency of the other. Marx reveals his perceptiveness in the very fact that he posits them *together.* The euhemeristic gesture, the severing of correspondences, also takes place where the order of analogies has been established. Indeed, that order can be regarded as a conciliatory *reply,* a suturing of correspondences that ritually follows every act of severing.

"Fully developed individuals, those whose social ties are at the same time completely their own, who are born of communal relations which they control collectively—such individuals are products not of nature but of history. The degree and universality of the development of abilities in which *this* type of individuality becomes possible presuppose production based on exchange value. This production, together with universality, for the first time gives rise to the alienation of the individual from himself and from others, but it also creates the universality and all-sidedness of his relations and abilities. In earlier stages of development, the single individual appears fuller, because he has not yet realized the fullness of his relations and established them as an ensemble of powers and social relations independent of him. It is as absurd to regret this original fullness as it is to think that we must forever remain in our current state of emptiness. The bourgeois viewpoint has never gone beyond the antithesis between itself and this romantic viewpoint, and thus the latter will accompany it as its legitimate antithesis until the blessed end of the bourgeoisie." This passage exalts the metaphysical function of capital, which stands magnificently apart from everything else we know. Other apologists lack Marx's far-sightedness, and never dare attribute such evocative power to the commerce they are defending. The Universal itself, that spoiled firstborn child of the bourgeois era, is here considered the offspring of "production on the basis of exchange values"—and of nothing else. Marx disdains the communitarian connectedness of all prior stages (even though he is ready to shed a hypocritical tear for its lost "original fullness"), because he knows that those stages are inevitably *bornés,* limited. And for Marx, *Borniertheit* is the supreme defect, worse than any emptiness. It is a permanent threat, a hostile memory of the ghetto.

The "original fullness" is not *polútropos*, not "all-sided"; this is what Marx means. (But does Ulysses belong to that "origin" or not? A question which remains unanswered.) At the other end of history we see that, in an age when the bourgeoisie is flourishing most successfully, the essence of the bourgeois individual is indeed universal but completely empty, void, hollow, the result of an inexorable process of emptying. The anthropological question must then be posed in these terms: How are we to deal with that "total emptying" without yielding to some fatuous reference to the lost "original fullness"? (And here Marx means to nullify in one sarcastic sentence all the grand or petty reactionary criticisms aimed at the bourgeoisie.)

At this point the apparatus of dialectics, with all its deceptive aggressiveness, once again seems immensely useful. What development has emptied, development will refill. People will talk about the "universal development of individuals" instead of about the relations of production. Thus, instead of speaking of a real emptying, they will use a vacuous expression that nevertheless is tuned to the inclinations of a period which, more than any other, wants to "make it on its own." One need only avoid certain questions. What if the concrete (the individual) stubbornly refuses? And what if the universal will tolerate continued existence only in conditions of perfect emptiness? Around these same points, some masterly sleight of hand had already been performed by Hegel. Now Marx did the same, though his methods were cruder and he knew much less about the history of philosophy. And such legerdemain would be performed countless more times, with ever more brutal manners, by increasingly nefarious great-grandchildren, traveling cadres of the Third International, or the heirs of some black Byzantium, inhaling the sacrificial fumes of polytechnic schools while waiting to transform their savannah into a bloody scene à la Raymond Roussel, steeped in slaughter, to baptize a belated entry into History.

(The well-tempered crudeness of this doctrine guarantees it the sort of survival that harbors a threat for those who do not pay it homage. It is a special, *programmed* crudeness—programmed so that it can be efficiently applied as soon as possible. The concept is certainly crude, but it implies that there is a "process," in both the judicial and physical senses of the term. It helps the general process of what exists by subjecting it, among other things, to a trial, to *un procès*. The justice of history, which can also become "revolutionary justice" if circumstances are favorable, is a valuable expedient for setting in motion the procedures of praxis. The theory not only gave new theoretical dignity to praxis, but was already praxis in action, obviously camouflaged as Science. Here the word "materialism," with a herm's double sneer, historical and dialectical, performed irreplaceable services.)

Marx does not always abandon himself unrestrainedly to the worship of "development." Behind this word, he sometimes glimpses inevitable divergences. There are passages in which he comes dangerously close to asserting a full break between the two models of development, one perverse (that of capital) and one good (that which comes after capital); and in so doing he lets down his guard.

A society that is based on exchange value, and that has attained its complete fulfillment, can be defined thus: "Each individual possesses social power in the form of a thing [exchange value]." In the sentence that follows, the revolutionary leap is described with utmost concision: "Deprive the object of its social power and this power will have to be exercised by people over people." This notion is perfectly consonant with the thesis of Louis Dumont: if the primary characteristic of the Modern (but how many *primary* characteristics there are!) is that it ascribes supreme importance to the relationship between humans and things (the reverse of what obtains in other societies, which are primarily based on the relationship between humans), then abandoning the system of exchange value will mean restoring the preeminence of the relationship between humans. And here Marx gives one of many formulations of the stages of society, one that will never appear in handbooks of Marxism-Leninism. Here, in fact, the conceptual articulations emerge quite distinctly:

a. "Relations of personal dependence (at first entirely natural and spontaneous) are the first forms of society in which human productivity develops, but it does so only in limited ways and in isolated spheres." "Relations of personal dependence" are the characteristic, decisive element, as opposed to relations with things. And here dependence is entrusted to the *naturwüchsig*—solitary growth, forests and swamps. Development occurs "only in limited ways." Here it has a limit, a preestablished ambit, and in any case it does not comprise all exchanges. *Outside,* other modalities can and do exist.

b. "Personal independence based on *dependence on objects* is the second great stage. For the first time humans developed a system of social interchange, of universal relations, of diverse needs and universal abilities." The individual as a category first takes shape during this phase. An "individual" maintains relations of independence toward other subjects. But on one condition: that these relations coincide with a total dependence on things. "Individuals are subordinated to social production, which exists outside them, as a kind of destiny." This fate, which is embodied in the pure existence of things, is now called "social production." It is thus composed of things and of their production. Compared to form *a*, this form is an escape from the provincial—an expansion of borders to the universal, total, and general, in contrast to the singularity of the individual.

c. "Free individuality—based on the universal development of individuals, on their mastery of their communal and social productivity, and on their control of their social capacities—is the third stage." Here it is a matter of once again reversing the relationship between things and people, restoring things (and hence "productivity") to a state of subordination. The noose tightens: productivity must yield to another form of productivity, now called "the universal development of individuals." But what lies hidden behind this formula for proud freethinkers? "Production," the age-old name for this august, sacred *development* of Mankind, suggests only one course: to treat mankind itself as "human material." How then will the nascent "all-sided" man be constituted? He will be a parody of Anthropos—a progressive Anthropos, a ghastly hybrid of Monsieur Homais and the Homunculus of alchemy, produced by the application of a model (productivity as indefinite growth) to the increasingly "universal" subjects of society. They will be the only subjects that *improve themselves* perpetually! And we must remember that "improvement" was the word Adam Smith used to mean "development."

On this very delicate point, Marx repeatedly promises some clarification, but for unforeseen reasons such clarification must always be *postponed:* "(This last association, which purports to be based on the 'appropriation and control of the means of production,' is in no way arbitrary. It presupposes the development of material and intellectual conditions which at this point we cannot examine.)" We are still at this same point. But the denial is revelatory, as always. Marx immediately takes care to dispel the word "arbitrary" precisely because it contains the secret of the "new man," as if Marx has already glimpsed the repellent faces of the positive heroes who, a few decades later, would be produced with such enthusiasm. And they were surely not arbitrary, since they were useful. But they were constructed arbitrarily, as objects with exchange value had been in the past.

. . .

"In order to guarantee the exchangeability of the commodity, exchangeability itself is counterposed to it as an independent commodity." Like a new spice from the East, from those far reaches of the East which are the purest and most poisonous West, *exchangeability* comes on the market and quickly alters the face of reality. The same power that was already at work in the "arbitrariness of the sign," in the practice of convention, in every act of substitution (*x stands for y*), but did not yet possess the irreverence to formulate itself as an autonomous entity, now asserts itself—and dares to show that, instead of letting itself be subsumed and absorbed into *other* powers, it can subsume them itself and view them as its own partial applications. The master Aristotle had already said, "In reality everything can be exchanged." Certain platitudes slumber for centuries in the crevices of history, but when they awake, they become grinding, crushing jaws.

"Purely natural material has no *value* whatsoever. Since no human labor is objectified in it, it is pure material and exists independently of human labor. Value is only objectified; it has as little value as the elements of the universe themselves."

Since the social machine completely replaces the machine of the *stoicheïa toū kósmou*, it becomes necessary for nature itself and its elements, till then the supreme repository of power, to be stripped of authority and made indifferent to one another, inasmuch as they are "devoid of value," not animated by that breath from the origin that has now shifted into living labor.

The commodity is something that is added to immediate use. It entails a destruction of the immediate, but also restores it, through yet another process (exchange value is again transformed into use value). It is based on improper use of the object, the way a metaphor involves "improper" use of a word. As soon as an object acquires the *secondary* character of a commodity, the essence of commodity reveals the object as *primarily* commodity—that is, exchange value— and only at a certain point (the end of its circulation, the moment of its consumption) as an object of use. This is an inversion produced by exchange, but it is the basis of *every* exchange, unless the circulation takes place *within the same body*. And in the process of exchange the body of the community is inevitably wounded, when it comes into contact with the body of another community. The *derived* characteristics that hurl themselves against the origin, kick it aside, and overwhelm it in their play—though remaining, apparently, derived—are also *distant, liminal* characteristics (the first exchange is between community and community, on the border), which later reverberate in the body "with disruptive action."

The *excluded commodity* is a commodity that becomes a *general equivalent* and thus adds to its own particular use value a second kind of use value, which it acquires as a result of the fact that it has become a general equivalent. The excluded commodity becomes an object of desire in that it is equivalent to exchange. In addition to specific desires for single objects, there is a generic desire for exchange: "The excluded commodity as general equivalent is now the object of a universal need deriving from the same process of exchange, and has for everyone the same use value, that of being representative of the exchange value—in other words, being a general medium of exchange." By the detour of the *excluded commodity* we have arrived at a general object of desire, a unit for measuring use—and this is precisely, mockingly, the generic possibility of exchange. The heart of desire is not an object, but the possibility of exchanging objects.

The entire theology of the commodity unfolds in a process at the end of which exchange value is again transformed into use value. This process is *delay*, Freud's *Aufschub*, which generates all the phantasmagoria of commodities, "the gap that lies between purchase and sale." And this gap, this detachment, is the generic form of schism and duplicity. It "breaks down the local barriers of social interchange, which are long-standing and rendered sacred by tradition and foolish sentiment." It is "the general form taken by the rupture and separation of all the elements which were once united in this social interchange." It is the impossibility of innocence. The same can be said of the word, which is detached from interrelation, from kinship, from affinity with what it represents, since it is fixed above all in a simulacrum—writing—which is completely alien to the body and which is granted an incorruptible and autonomous existence, as happens with the "crystal of money."

Marx is a prisoner of the Enemy he attacks; his adversary's body falls on him and smothers him. Marx has the definitive vision of the *machine for demolishing limits,* which he calls capitalism, yet he questions not the *limit* but the *machine.* He wants to design a better machine, which will demolish limits without ever jamming, without crises. Like a great mechanic, he has a loving, passionate knowledge of the capitalist machine. Concerning the *limit,* he shares that machine's illusions. What offended him was not so much and not only the iniquity which capital engendered, but the fact that capital was preparing to become an *obstacle* to production, an antiquated and sclerotic form compared with the immensity of what was possible. Nobody has ever dreamed the dream of capital with as much faith as Marx was able to muster in his spirit. He was like a young man from the provinces who *takes seriously,* with despairing gravity, the customs of the metropolis—that is how Marx viewed capital. At times he felt like Rastignac on the hill of Père Lachaise, and then he unleashed in the world something that was to produce even more limitlessly than that old machine for demolishing limits. Capital had become his Madame de Beauséant. From her he had learned manners; it was she who had introduced him into society. But now she seemed to him withered, a bit ridiculous, doomed. He turned his gaze elsewhere, to the *débutantes* of the proletariat.

So far as development is concerned, Marx ultimately became more capitalist than capital itself. Sharp-eyed and obstinate, he looked everywhere for the limits of the power that demolishes limits. He wanted to reach the point from which he could look on capitalistic production as a form that was *borné,* timid, trapped in itself, and scorn it just as capital had scorned previous forms: "(The *most extreme form of alienation* . . . already contains *in itself*—though in an inverted form, upside down—the dissolution of all *limited presuppositions of production.* Moreover, it establishes the unconditional presuppositions of production, as well as the full material conditions for the total, universal development of the productive forces of the individual.)" Here a vibrant demonism is speaking, a desire for unlimited self-creation. Once absolute dissolution has been attained, once man has been totally expropriated, he imagines that the void can at last be filled with everything that man has never been. Marx's fury thus erupts not in a humanitarian idyll, but in a wild technological hallucination.

Marx rejoices: Capital "limits labor and the creation of value—by an artificial check, as the English put it. And it does so on the same grounds as and to the same extent that it posits surplus labor and surplus value. It therefore posits, by its very nature, a *barrier* to the creation of labor and value, a barrier that counteracts its tendency to expand them boundlessly. And inasmuch as it posits a barrier *specific* to itself and at the same time tends to overcome *all* barriers, it is a living contradiction." He has nailed the enemy to *its* limit. But the idea that *the* limit exists in nature and in the mind is something Marx refuses to consider.

"First of all there is a limit, which is inherent not in production generally but in production founded on capital." From this Marx deduces that capital "is not, as economists believe, the *absolute* form for the development of the forces of production." But such an "absolute form" does exist: this is Marx's dream, just as Hilbert's will be complete axiomatization. No Gödel intervened to undeceive him.

"We have seen that the sphere of circulation has a hole, through which gold (or silver—in short, the material of money) enters it as a commodity of specified value."

The "hole" is self-reflection. Out of all the objects that exist, there is always one that represents the representation of objects. And that single object is enough to compromise the order of all the others that have preceded it.

"A thing can be use value without being value. Such is the case if its usefulness for man is not mediated by labor. This is true of the air, of virgin land, of natural meadows, of the wood in the trees, and so on." From this paradox, which Marx formulates marginally in *Capital,* derives the entire articulation of a world. Let us follow the ceremony. The significant area is delineated: it is that of value. We touch its substance: it is labor. We seek the unit of measure: it is the time that elapses during labor. (Thus far, we're following Ricardo.) We observe its character: it is abstract labor, *sans phrase* (decisive addition by Marx)—an empty notion that puts a seal on the system at every point. ("La différence est le langage sensible de la ressemblance"—"Difference is the perceivable language of similarity," wrote Marcel Schwob.) It affirms the homogeneity of its elements and eliminates the unmeasurable, just as in Saussure the arbitrariness of the sign (in principle) allows language to exist as system, and just as in Freud the phallus, the primary signifier, allows exchanges of libido to take place and be counted. Ultimately this system, founded on the void, produces the totality of nature; but this time it is *worked nature*, ripened by the alchemical process of production (of goods, of signs, of ghosts).

Potlatch is based on the impossibility of *equal exchange;* the exchange must be unequal. Reciprocity is denied, since it is always an illusion. Only in the upside-down world of initiates do equivalents exist, because initiates communicate in a shared epiphany.

Equal exchange is mystical exchange—that of twins, of transparent speech. The machine of capitalism imposes *mystical exchange* as *usual exchange.* "Twins have the right speech, because it is equal. They have the same value. They are the same thing. The man who sells, the man who buys: they are also the same thing. They are twins."

The commodity as fetish can be viewed in two ways: as a deceptive superstition that continues to hover above the everyday secularized world, or as an everyday opportunity to appreciate the marvel of the fetish. Marx had the genius to perceive this marvel. But he harbored a deep resentment against the marvelous, because he knew it was only the beginning of the dreadful. And those who are exposed to the marvelous are not reliable, not usable. The slightest breath from the Powers will carry them off. Better to strangle the marvelous in its extreme form, to smash shop windows and destroy commodities. Then Marx could offer his gift to some truly dull-witted followers, meek and fervent; could teach them how to blow up the lock on a world from which every marvel has fled—or in which every marvel has been stabbed and lies dead on the ground, where it is pointed out to children as an enemy of the people.

༄

The Ruthlessness of Ricardo

A fraternal solidarity reigns between Marx and the cold, cruel theoreticians who defend capitalism. And this is the only feeling of solidarity that endures in Marx; toward the theoreticians of socialism, he displays mostly rancor and intolerance. Thus, he willingly agrees with Adam Smith regarding the distinction between productive and unproductive labor, and disparages David Ricardo's "sentimental adversaries":

"Ricardo rightly considers capitalist production the most generally advantageous of its time, the most advantageous for the creation of wealth. He wants *production for production's sake,* and this is *right*. If one wished to assert, as Ricardo's sentimental adversaries have done, that production as such is not the end, one would be forgetting that production for production's sake means nothing other than the development of humankind's powers of production, hence the *development of the wealth of human nature as an end in itself.*"

But the society desired by Marx has an aim that goes *beyond* capital—namely, the *"development of the riches of human nature,"* a movement toward that "all-sidedness" of the "total man" that so far has not been achieved. Capital, founded on the destruction of limits, is still *hesitant* about knocking them down; beyond capital lies the possibility that production for production's sake will assume its most radical, intense, and efficient form. Marx therefore wants to move the most lucid and ruthless notion of capitalist production (Ricardo's, in fact) into a context where capital would be engulfed because it has itself become an obstacle to production.

"Beyond a certain point the development of the forces of production becomes a barrier to capital; and thus the relationship with capital becomes a barrier to the development of the productive forces of labor."

The theory of the progressive decrease in the rate of profit serves primarily to establish a point of no return, where development finally hinders itself. Capital, which has been the very spearhead of development, thus becomes a "barrier," just as the economic relations dissolved by capital were barriers in prior stages. But if capital was the *subject* of that process of development, which now rebels against it, what will be the subject of the development that demolishes capital? At this point Marx presents the image of development as plan, as a sequence arranged by humans, who have reappropriated their means and their identities. But the primary characteristic of development is that it cannot be planned; it is a constant blind battering that takes place in the dark and that brings continually surprising results, because there is no knowledge *superior* to the workings of development itself. The other great power of modern society, *control,* here looms behind Marx's words, behind the painful images of men again assuming responsibility for their own fate, behind the popular prints of happy workers who become artists and fishermen and maybe even policemen. *Control* and *development* are, on the contrary, beasts that are locked together in a very slow struggle which will perhaps be mortal for both.

Ricardo and Marx were rival theologians, but both were "honestly" and "scientifically" devoted to the same God. Marx observes Ricardo's excesses with fond indulgence—excesses indeed, but inevitably in the right direction. "Ricardo, for example, who believes that the bourgeois economy deals exclusively with exchange value and that it is concerned with use value only exoterically . . ." Oh, noble error!

"Thus, Ricardo's ruthlessness is not only *scientifically honest* but *scientifically necessary* to his viewpoint. It makes absolutely no difference to him whether the development of the powers of production deals a death blow to real estate or to the workers. If this progress devalues the capital of the industrial bourgeoisie, so much the better. If the development of the productive power of labor reduces the value of permanent capital by half, it doesn't matter, says Ricardo. The productivity of human labor is doubled. This is *scientific honesty.* If Ricardo's viewpoint, as a whole, favors the interests of the *industrial bourgeoisie*, this is only *because* and *to the extent that* such interests coincide with those of the production and productive development of human labor. When these interests conflict with those of production, he is as *ruthless* toward the bourgeoisie as he is in other cases toward the proletariat."

Ricardo and Marx thus stood, respectively, on the side of the bourgeoisie and on the side of the proletariat, but only until those two classes could guarantee maximum productive development. And just as Marx imagined Ricardo setting himself implacably against the bourgeoisie, so we can imagine Marx setting himself implacably against the proletariat. For the objective, alas, was never anything less than man—indeed, the species; it was a good intention that Darwin's dreary catechism had already corroborated. Marx shook his head, irked: "That this development of the abilities of the human species, even if it initially occurs at the expense of most individuals and of entire classes of people, might ultimately abolish this antagonism and manage to coincide with the development of the single individual, and that the higher development of individuality might therefore be attained only through a historical process in which individuals are sacrificed—this is what they cannot understand." But Nietzsche understood it. In his last years he flung himself at times, like a visionary accountant, into plans and calculations concerning the classes, human types, nations, generations, that would have to be sacrificed—that would have to be docile material in an enormous experiment.

৵৻৽

The Crystal of Money

Within the world of analogy (which is, among other things, the world of qualities) we encounter emissaries of digitality (gold), and within the world of digitality (which is, among other things, the world of quantities) we encounter emissaries of analogy (gold).

First case: "What does a purely *quantitative* difference between things presuppose? That their *qualities* are identical. Hence, the quantitative measurement of various types of labor presupposes the equivalence, the identity, of their quality." But if you want to represent convention (and hence the suppression of qualities), you cannot rely, initially, upon something conventional (paper money). What you need is a material that becomes more precious as it approaches the cancellation of differentiating qualities, as it comes closer to pure exchangeability. Divisibility, uniformity, and invariability are the emissaries of digitality, and they introduce themselves in gold. ("The only qualities necessary to make a measure of value perfect are that it should itself have value, and that this value should be itself invariable," wrote Ricardo; but a *single quality* suffices to undermine the reign of quantity.) And Marx is irritated with naïve people who do not understand this: "The study of precious metals as subjects of money relations, indeed as their incarnations, is by no means a matter that lies outside the realm of political economy, as Proudhon believes, any more than the physical composition of paint and marble lies outside the realm of painting and sculpture." Finally: "The precious metals [should be] uniform in their physical qualities, so that equal quantities of them should be so far identical as to present no ground for preferring one to the others. This does not apply, for example, to equal numbers of cattle and equal quantities of grain."

Second case: gold as an emissary of analogy within the world of digitality. With growing surprise, we become aware that the annihilation of qualities, a process that Marx incessantly describes in the *Grundrisse* and in *Das Kapital,* is continually compared to the process of alchemy, which produces qualities. C-M-M-C and M-C-C-M (where the letters stand for "commodity" and "money") are the economic translations of the alchemical terms *caput mortuum* and *quinta essentia,* and money replaces the philosopher's stone. "It is as though, for example, the discovery of a stone granted me possession of all the sciences, irrespective of my individuality." Thus, in this alien country, gold retains its entire majestic array of solar and regal associations, serving as the vibrant hub of a hierarchical system of correspondences. At the center of a neutral land, undifferentiated and conventional, we find the most ancient splendor.

For many centuries every thing, every being, appeared and moved accompanied by its own Double. Indeed, there was a time when the dominant presence was the Double, of which the single being was merely an indication. Then Doubles gradually began to disintegrate and disappear. Ultimately they took refuge in the nocturnal part of nature and were acknowledged only in sporadic and sinister fashion. But new Doubles, of another species, began to spread. This species was the exchange value that multiplied and superimposed itself on the forms of all things. There was actually a Double that was transformed immediately into a thing and that corresponded to no body at all. This was money. And the fact that it lacked a body to which it could bind itself endowed it with a longer life. "All commodities are perishable money; money is the imperishable commodity."

There are two movements:

a. Everything is usable material. The subject is a procedure.
   Absolute conventionalism. What acts is the void that dictates the terms of the experiment. It outlines the object and works on it.
b. Everything is interrelated. Universal interdependence.
   Resonance. If you touch one element, you affect all its kin.
   But which are its kin? A prior knowledge is implied, a canon.

We cannot do without either of these two movements, in any of their articulations. Marx believes that in the "tribal" phase (namely *b*), *a* is concealed but operates as an invisible corrosive. In the post-historical phase, only the action of *a* is generally recognized by society; *b* leads a wild clandestine life, but still radiates its power over everything.

Money is the *sign of representation,* the sign of the dominion achieved by the system of representing (hence the system of convention, of substitution, of "standing-for," of the interchangeable) over the system of corresponding (the system of analogy, of nondiscursiveness, of association, of uniqueness, of the symbol—in the sense of the Eleusinian Mysteries). Marx's discovery pertains to the way in which exchange value passes from minor and marginal power to primary and central power—to *capital* power—in the modern world. All forms of life now bear the imprint of the fulfillment of this process; everything exists *under the sign* of exchange value. Once the implications of this passage have been absorbed, all talk of structures and superstructures is pure *blabla* (a word invented by Céline), ready for the Soviet encyclopedia. There is no need for a superstructure that corresponds to some conditioning structure. It is enough to say that we live *under the sign* of exchange value, and that exchange value is the economic *name* of a power that is otherwise manifested in substitution, in convention, in all forms of representation generally.

Exchange value is an ever-present aspect of reality but is always somewhat concealed, always to some extent interstitial or peripheral, an element that has long lived "in the pores of society," like the Jews—and exchange value, for Marx, *is the Jew* of every society. Over many centuries (Marx's account ranges from ancient Greece to industrial Europe and Balzac), exchange value becomes *the essential aspect* of reality, the element to which everything *refers,* the basis of perception, with which every detail is imbued. This world—in which things, in order to be, must be exchanged—is the world that Marx, and only Marx, has thoroughly described in all its alchemical phases: C-M-M-C, money as *caput mortuum;* M-C-C-M, money as *quinta essentia.* It is the world in which we blithely live, and which has always kept us wrapped in an invisible film. Marx comes to our aid not with crude, humanistic, repellent, vainglorious, legislated-fun concepts of the just society, which *must* come, but rather with his irreplaceable description of the society of substitution and exchange, just as it exists today, now, everywhere, established and continually expanding.

When real estate and landed property first become enveloped in money, the Immutable realizes that it is subject to the unstable power of exchange. This symbolic transition is already perceptible in the seventeenth-century pamphleteer Edward Misselden: "Where before money was invented, there was an Exchange, or Permutation in movable and mutable things onely, as Corne, Wine, Oile, and the like: and afterwards in immovable and immutable things, as Houses, Lands and the like; there was a necessity of money, to value such things with money as could not be exchanged. And so by degrees all things came to be valued with money, and money the value of all things." If *everything* is divisible (since everything is translatable into money, and money *is* divisible), nothing inalienable exists anymore. And what is indivisible? Quality. But quality, because it is integral to the object, obeys the rule that applies to all objects—namely, that they are translatable into prices. Therefore it will command, at most, a higher price. Quality becomes *luxury*—and as such becomes manipulable, divisible, and exchangeable. Prestige, which was the origin of every value, the primeval exuberance, becomes the value of the superfluous.

Quality: the heir of prestige. The unit for measuring prestige cannot be ascertained. Prestige is a force that manifests itself through emblems, ordeals, combinations with other forces. We do not have a unit for measuring force—at least, the force that Giordano Bruno was still dealing with but that was no longer of concern to Newton.

The space of images vanishes as soon as the "crystal of money," the *Geldkristall,* is put into it; and the closing of this space seems to herald an invasion of immediate reality by images, a *coniunctio* that would lead back to the origin. But this does not happen. The crystal of money refracts only the images of circulation (commodities). Its hidden face, the one that opens onto the world of images like a porthole onto the ocean, is opaque; on that side the crystal of money is undifferentiated. The opposite happens among the elements of circulation: when money is inserted in their midst, when the crystal is placed in the empty space of circulation, as a "universal equivalent," changes take place that affect the entire inexhaustible series of goods. These goods, which until then could assume any form whatsoever, are now subject to certain rules. They must fulfill at least three requirements:

1. they must be easily divisible (*contrary to* unity);
2. they must be uniform within each single specimen (*contrary to* the composite);
3. they must be identical across all specimens (*contrary to* difference).

The refracted light that comes from the crystal imposes these characteristics—*its own* characteristics—on everything which wants to be transformed in that light. And by this means, it radically changes the nature of the images in circulation. They cease to be *fetishes*—unique, irreplaceable, fundamental concretions of power—and become replaceable things, whose value lies precisely in their replaceability. Nevertheless (and here black magic comes into play once again), the spell of the fetish does not disappear. Instead of merely surrounding the individual circulating images, it envelops the entire process.

Money provides the most obvious example of inversion; the world becomes *too* esoteric. Hypostatic images commonly become autonomous, but now, in addition, they actually become *objects*. Money is palpable currency, a banknote that wears out. Thus, the overwhelming power of the image is confirmed—the image that actually succeeds in being transformed into a thing, whereas previously it was pure, invisible, mental presence. But now that this thing exists, the door that leads to the realm of images is closed. Money comes to occupy the only *empty place* in the circulation of the real ("It is deposited always in a place of circulation that has been cleared of goods")—the *hole* that afforded access to images: "We have seen that the sphere of the circulation of commodities has a hole through which gold (or silver—in short, the material of money) enters as the commodity of a given value." Now that space is closed; its seal is a glittering crystal. All the metamorphoses converge toward and bounce back from that point. They can no longer hint at events that take place beyond themselves, because everything now takes place on this side—between their protean material and the crystal, between the crystal and the multiplicity of forms.

"Circulation becomes the great alembic of society: all is thrown in, only to reemerge as the crystal of money." What happens? A certain relationship among subjects, like the circulation of goods, produces a natural deposit, a concretion, a crystalline commodity that reflects all the others and becomes indispensable to their circulation. This crystal is not an image; it exists, since it is an object.

And to it as object are attributed the properties of the global process of the circulation of commodities. Double inversion, *chassé-croisé* of money: a *thing* is conceived as the concretion of a *process* (commodities). The crystal of money becomes the unique subject, but its uniqueness represents *replaceability* itself. Another paradox of the inversion: the modern fetish is not only that which appears unique, but that which is replaceable, reproducible, and alienable to the greatest degree. Hence Baudelaire's fascination with prostitution. Prostitution is the guarantee of total alienability, just as the sacred guaranteed the untouchable. In the age of inversion, the sacred is *protected* by its own prostitution.

"Where money is not in itself the community, it necessarily dissolves the community." As exchange value becomes dominant and as the prevailing relationship between goods and money becomes inverted (from C-M-M-C to M-C-C-M), money becomes the community. It embodies in one subject the *nexus rerum* that henceforth would be undecipherable in the world outside it—the world of "horrid chance." Thus does inversion take place here: the process of Convention inherits the function of the Canon, takes on the majesty and the powers of the regime it has overthrown.

❧

History Experiments

The central role that sacrifice played in archaic societies has been assumed by experimentation.

The cruel priests who raised the knife over the altar are now the authors of conspiracies and plots.

Any discussion of experimentation should be prefaced with a passage deleted from *Die deutsche Ideologie* (*The German Ideology*): "Thus far we have chiefly been examining a single aspect of human activity, *the way in which man shapes nature*. Another aspect is *the way in which man shapes man*."

Post-history is inhabited by men who believe in "good causes," in "man," in "society," in many other hypostases. But it is ruled by a mocking (and perhaps transcendental) being for whom *all is material, interchangeable, exploitable*—a perpetual manipulator who invents forms and throws them away, who quickly tires of common materials and is always looking for untried ones, who excavates the rain forest of the Amazon and drills pack-ice to add flavor, an exotic aroma, to the *kykeon*, the broth served in the Mysteries.

The unnameable present.

Marx speaks of post-history when he mentions the passage from "history" to "universal history"—an experimental phase of history in which everything forms a single body, in which nothing is external to society and everything acts on everything else, as in the resonant primordial cosmos. Its empirical foundation is the world market, since this market is an escape—an exit with no possibility of return—from *Borniertheit*, from local narrowness. The world market reinvents a kind of *fate* (just as post-history in general reactivates all the archaic categories, which now apply to a reality that *inverts* the one in which they were created.)

"The more the original isolation of the various nations is destroyed by the progressive perfecting of the modes of production, of commerce, and of the division of labor which emerges spontaneously [*naturwüchsig*] among nations, the more history becomes universal history. Thus, for example, if an Englishman invents a machine that leaves countless workers in India and China without bread and disrupts entire ways of life in those countries, such an invention becomes a fact of universal history."

"Whence it follows that this transformation of history into universal history is surely not just an abstract operation of 'self-consciousness,' of the spirit of the world or some metaphysical phantasm. Rather, it is an entirely material, empirically verifiable operation of which each individual is proof, inasmuch as he walks and stands still, eats, drinks, and gets dressed." But nothing is more metaphysical than this "purely material operation." And one may say that the true fulfillment of metaphysics—perhaps even its return to the Mystery in which everything takes place in a wordless pageant, a mute display of objects—is manifested precisely in what Marx describes as the "transformation of history into universal history."

The societies we study in books, the societies that make up the past and that have left a motley heap of detritus or have vanished almost without a trace, like bird tracks, all obeyed the need to negotiate, clash, and be reconciled with what lay outside themselves. And from that Outside they drew the flower of their strength. Or else they were inherited by the Despot, who administered them to *his* ends—the ends of an individual opposed to everything. The society into which we were born is the first in our planet's history that strives to be sufficient unto itself and that can compare itself only to itself. The names of the entities Outside exist now only in dictionaries, except for the word "nature"; but "nature" today designates primarily a sequence of social events or, at most, accidents. For this reason, too, we must look for a different name for this kind of society. We may call it "post-historical," signaling that compared to this society, all history now seems a landscape of ruins, an endless contagion.

In 1908, during twelve weeks of clairvoyance, Alfred Kubin glimpsed the first post-historical city: Pearl.

Historical transformations (the events described in history books) occur *in opposition to* an apparently stable order. This is an order of substances, of correspondences, of analogies—the invisible, omnipresent, inevitable axis of the world.

Post-historical transformations are inherent in the experimental character of order, which presents this characteristic of itself as stable.

Many people in the nineteenth century accused the new age of "materialism"; today we realize how naïve they were. In fact, the gnosis of the modern age, clandestine and imperious, assumes that all is spirit and that the spirit is the most malleable of materials.

"It's nothing but *x* plus *y*": this axiom, more than any other, is today worthy of being called a Commonplace. We hear it repeated in many different forms. It's the wisdom of the man in the street and the shrewdness of the psychologist. It accompanies the perpetual smile of the researcher: "Life? There's nothing very amazing about it. It's physics plus chemistry." And then we hear a second voice, which Bloy has taught us to recognize in Commonplaces. For something to be "nothing but," a part of it must be useless, negligible, reduced to nothing; specifically, its very appearance, the *letter,* must be replaceable by its components. But this formulation at once gives rise to doubt—the suspicion that the world before us is a world of manifest esotericism, that it has rejected the nexus with the exoteric, that the letter is no longer a protective sheath but the secret meaning.

"Capitalism" is the economic term for an immense upheaval in the brain—for the dominance that exchange, and hence digitality, achieve over all things. Every other principle becomes an island within it, just as there are tribal islands within the global market. Socialism itself, fraternal enemy of capitalism, stems from capitalism the way a Salvation Army leaflet harks back to the verses of Isaiah. In theory, that is. In practice, when one applies socialism in order to correct the intrinsic evils of capital, it immediately produces still greater evils, but without undermining those it is aiming to remedy. And this time the evils are more odious, because they are more human. In the cruelty of capitalism an element of ordeal remains: money. In socialism—which has the most inappropriate goal, namely to put everything into man's hands—there is no longer any obscure, discriminating, extrahuman element such as money. In its place appear new priests: informers.

Within Chinese society, within all societies, the park of the Son of Heaven once epitomized all nature in miniature. Now all nature is our park, and we do not know what it epitomizes.

.   .   .

A perplexity peculiar to post-history: "When a single impression awakens in us a mathematician, a child, a poet, a painter, a philosopher—a dozen languages, kinds of adjustment, series of discrete acts—it is quite understandable that we should be perplexed."

In Russia, law is an imported article. Like all exotic curiosities, it stirs the imagination and attracts devotees. But the background to which it is applied is hostile to it. Two possibilities thus present themselves: either law is immediately expelled, because it strives to corrupt the genuine prosperity of the country; or else it is assimilated, but in such a way as to be forever held in contempt. In the few months he held power, Czar Peter III (who used to play with toy soldiers, and once had a mouse court-marshaled and hanged for daring to scale two cardboard forts), decided to introduce the code of Frederick the Great into Russia—a code that had already been in force in Prussia for several years. "But," Claude Rulhière notes, "whether because the translators were inexperienced or because the Russian language has no expressions for legal concepts, there was not one senator who managed to understand the code. And in that vain attempt the Russian people saw only a sign of contempt for their customs and a mad attachment to foreign ways." At the outset of the age that continually wanted to *explain* history, Frederick's enlightened and military law was replaced by Marx's law of the developmental phases of productive forces. But both served chiefly to perfect the methods of the Bureau of Secret Affairs, which Peter the Great had established to reform the nation's customs through a sophisticated police system. This bureau continued to function with zeal and foresight under various names, from Ochrana to the KGB—offering, among other things, the only undeniable example of the effects of progress in Russia.

There was a muted moment, between the death of Hitler and the death of Stalin, when the nations of the world, still dazed, prepared to take their places obediently in the new order. Post-history had blossomed; now a tropical luxuriance was in store. In those years, objects proliferated. They were (as a Hermetic philosopher would have said) "subtle" objects, which were to the objects previously used what the subtle body is to the gross body in alchemy. A new age was slowly taking shape, and its characteristic mechanisms were beginning to move. Between the Algerian war and the assassination of John F. Kennedy, the first stages of the game were laid out. And soon everything was wrapped up in it and was taking part in it, as naturally as Coca-Cola cans were used, along with nails and broken glass, to decorate fetishes, as if they had always been intended for that purpose.

The period between 1945 and the present could conceivably be rendered in two parallel histories: that of the historians, with its elaborate apparatus of parameters, discussing figures, masses, parties, movements, negotiations, productions; and that of the secret services, telling of murders, traps, betrayals, assassinations, cover-ups, and weapons shipments. We know that both accounts are insufficient, that both claim to be self-sufficient, that one could never be translated into the other, and that they will continue their parallel lives. But hasn't this perhaps always been the case—at least since the Old Man of the Mountain loosed his men throughout the world? Indeed, it was like this for a long time. But the secret in those days was secret, and glimpses of it were erratic and exclusive; it was a presence that could be discerned but not grasped—a secret presence, in fact. Secrecy had not yet been absorbed into the secret services. This would not take place until the age of pure "post-history," a term that is used here as a makeshift name, intended only to show our inadequacy in the face of the unnameable present—the era that began in 1945.

The metaphysical meaning of the secret services lies in the words that designate them: "secret services" because they appropriate secrecy, *all* secrecy. Their meaning lies in their loathsome and dizzying conquests, but even more in the fact that they have violently forced secrecy to become apparent, too visible, as blatant as an advertisement posted on every corner. All secret services share a mission that is far more important and far more effective than all their conflicts: the annihilation of secrecy.

Post-history: the darkening epiphany in which hypostases solidify, become palpable bodies, and then elude perception as never before.

Their contagion casts doubt on the substance of all bodies. When the secret is in the letters of the word, the letter confounds. It is no longer read, but only reproduced.

"Hidden power," "secret organization," "conspiracies," "string pulling," "plot," "double dealing": these are words, mental gestures, that belonged to gnosticism. At one time, they were still illuminated by the oblique light of the Templars; today they designate murders, worldwide frauds, blackmail, abuses of power. Crime assumes the cast that once belonged to perennial heresy—to gnosticism.

The secret agent is enveloped in his own peculiar squalor, which has begun to find expression in the language of fiction. Yet why should that squalor have such a penetrating character? Because the secret agent usurps the place of secrecy—and Psyche is sadly disappointed when she realizes that the monster is no longer secrecy, but the agent who has been assigned to eliminate it.

❧

Praxis, a concept that is clear to every Jesuit, could be seen as brazen wickedness only in the narrowminded cities of Germany, where "time falls drop by drop, and never interrupts solitary reflection with the slightest sound." Only amid the clumsy highmindedness of the northern provinces, so stolid and respectably morose, could such extravagance make leaves and dust swirl to the point where the possessed citizens took up their spades to mix blood and earth. Marx's term "praxis" presupposes a material that demons can infiltrate—namely, "a profound tranquillity. Every now and then people made a bit of a racket in favor of certain ideas, but gave no thought to their application. It seemed as if thought and action never had any relation to each other, and that truth, for the Germans, was like the statue of Mercury known as Hermes, which has neither hands for grasping nor feet for advancing." Madame de Staël, thanks to her experience of society, sensed all this immediately, but was born too soon to converse with Marx, who would have identified philosophy with the missing hands and feet.

Czar Nicholas I played the role of matchmaker in the long and bitter relationship between the intelligentsia and praxis. Around 1840, early in that "important decade between 1838 and 1848" (as Pavel Annenkov dubbed it), the Russian authorities thought it advisable to direct young people yearning for the West toward German universities rather than toward Paris, the seat of all corruption and revolution. In Germany, they supposed, a modicum of decency had been preserved, under the mystical despotism of Friedrich Wilhelm IV. But if the intention (in the ominous words of the minister Uvarov) was to delay Russia's intellectual development by fifty years, history would once again take its cue from the shrewd determination of police forces and rulers and turn this scheme into a joke. In Berlin, to be sure, barricades and insurrections belonged to the realm of evil. But that German city lacked even the shady charm of dissipation, the *vie moderne,* the nervous accounts in the newspapers; it had none of the volatile blend of fever and cynicism that Baudelaire breathed every day. It had none of the clandestine presence of the Faubourg Saint-Germain or the conspicuous presence of the grisettes. Snobbery had not yet corroded the raw substance. Germany lacked something: it had not lived enough. Germans associated ideas with tension; and the more virulent this tension, the more powerful their visions of the "action" or "praxis" into which these ideas could be transformed—visions that were fascinating and overwhelming because of their sheer exoticism. The young Engels, already an excellent reporter, explained, "In Berlin today, if you ask anyone with the faintest idea of the mind's power over the world to identify the battlefield where the struggle for control of German public opinion both in religion and in politics—and hence for the control of all Germany—is taking place, he will reply that this battlefield is the university, and to be specific, lecture hall 6, where Schelling gives his courses on the philosophy of revelation." In that auditorium a young Russian aristocrat, Mikhail Bakunin, was observed shouting his admiration for the philosopher. He had come to Berlin in 1840 as if to a "New Jerusalem," with money his friend Alexander Herzen had given him. In the vast country from which he came, his associates were already speaking excitedly of Schelling and Hegel, even in the most far-flung regions. By 1830 Ivan Kireyevksy's letters from Berlin were transmitting signals, and every post-Hegelian pamphlet was being devoured by far too many greedy eyes. Nothing is more fertile than misunderstanding. In Germany, the longing to embark on "action" naturally assumed the very academic features (pedantry, remoteness from real life) that Marx and Engels would later ridicule in *The Holy Family* and other works. In Russia it was the biological heritage of the "superfluous men": ruined and degraded nobles, individuals corrupted by reverie, geometric loci of subtle psychic dissociation—the Russian disease, later the essence of the Russian novel! These people were, in short, the most precious component of the intelligentsia. They, too, so hopelessly excluded from any chance of an academic life, saw "action" as the sole Fata Morgana, capable of guiding their latent, savage violence in *one* direction, without scattering it in the intoxicating abjection of private life.

The point of contact—midway even in a geographic sense—was a little book by a Polish nobleman, August Cieszkowski, titled *Prolegomena zur Historiosophie* (Prolegomena to Historiosophy), published in 1838. It was a fatal shard of the Hegelian legacy. In just a few pages, which dissected history by triads in accordance with the Master's teachings, Cieszkowki releases the genie of "praxis"—an apparently naked, secular word in which the new image of the Paraclete emerged. First, he draws inferences from an assertion that in those days sounded plausible: *"Today thought has been thought to its uttermost end."* What stage comes next? What "transition" is opened up? "It is the recognition that, as we have said, consciousness is not the highest element but must progress by rising above itself, even *by emerging from itself.* Such is the content of the transition, which reveals itself as the need for a *substantial* unit of being and thought that is no longer simply *in itself and for itself* but must produce a substratum *outside itself.*" Behind its coded façade, this language descended from Hegel is quite concrete: the "substratum" is nothing but the new material, the *technical material,* which is timidly seeking a name. But it cannot blossom until the will moves definitively away from the Napoleonic catechism and into places that had previously been forbidden it: *"Now the absolute will must attain that height of speculation to which reason had once been elevated . . . Philosophy, abandoning the point of view that is most proper to it and consonant with it, will move on to a terrain that is alien to it but upon which its development entirely depends, namely the abso-*

lutely practical terrain of the will." Thus, it became inevitable that the relationship between thought and will would radically change: "According to Hegel, the will is only a particular mode of thought; but this is an erroneous idea. On the contrary, thought is a constituent element of will, because will and action are, in fact, *thought returning to being.*" The dream of a "complete reconciliation with reality in every area of life" which obsessed the young Hegelian Bakunin (and a great many others scattered throughout Europe) could therefore come true, if people put their faith in the magic of this unheard-of elementary word: "praxis." The fact that behind it, barely concealed, lay the "will to will" in which Heidegger would recognize the emblem of "nihilism" (and hence of "technology") could not have been evident, since no one had had much experience with technology. Nevertheless, Cieszkowski formulated the greatest regulatory maxim of the new age: *"Nihil est in voluntate et actu quod prius non fuerit in intellectu"* ("There is nothing in the will or in action that was not already in the intellect"). As a decisive consequence, "The will must pursue its phenomenological course as reason hitherto pursued its own. For its part, political life *[Staatsleben]* will have to assert its universal dominion, as art and philosophy have done, one after the other." And here the concreteness suddenly becomes brutal: "In the future, philosophy will have to consent to being essentially *applied.* Just as the poetry of art has passed into the prose of thought, so philosophy will have to descend from the heights of theory into the field of praxis." Philosophy, in its ultimate, "applied" form, agrees to die. But first it penetrates every object, as we now know from experience.

In the hidden recesses of history, an anomaly was in the making: a "new migration," no longer of barbarians toward the spirit but of the spirit toward the barbarity of nature, which yearned for deliverance. An obscure process, "which is foreshadowed by a fermentation, indeed to some extent by a decomposition." (And wouldn't Marx and Engels soon afterward speak of the "decomposition of the Hegelian system?") At the end of this alchemical process, the *coniunctio* would once again appear—in this case via the abrogation of the *Trennung,* that odious "separation" which had already so tormented Lessing and, after him, all the cruel and tender souls of the Romantic movement. "Thus is celebrated the absolute *peace* between interiority and exteriority. This peace ensures their joint victory, both outside and inside, rescuing perceptible appearance from the contempt in which it was held." The tangle of Cieszkowski's arguments enmeshed those who would soon become contending intellectual powers: Marx (in a letter of 1882 he denied that he had read Cieszkowski, but it is hard to believe him), Nietzsche, and Stirner. Concealed in the dream of that unreal peace, they were still waiting to emerge from it—to separate and clash.

⚜

The Artificial Barbarian

". . . we who not only think and speak aphoristically but also live *aphorisménoi* and *segregated,* like aphorisms in life without communion with men, without taking part in their sufferings and their joys; we who are not consonant in the din of life but solitary birds in the silence of night."

Stirner is one of the many signs that reveal the end of education. Cast out from the school of the Absolute Spirit, as the master Hegel had wished, he was unable to acquire any of the tacit gestures and minute vocal inflections that had built civilization and that in the end, out of discretion, claimed to be nothing more than slight residues of Taste. By this point, all he had left was the obsessive rosary of the idea or the howl of the aphasia to which he finally abandoned himself, the hammering (as at one's temples) of the silence that extends beyond the emptied idea.

Stirner speaks incessantly of ghosts and phantoms. And as he speaks, everything becomes tangled in the malevolent spell that his shrill, insolent, unstoppable voice would like to break—indeed, to mock. But no one had closer relations with ghosts than Stirner. Even now, we are more likely to encounter him among ghosts than among philosophers. It has been said in some quarters that Stirner is not a fit subject for respectable philosophers; if they touch Stirner's words, they'd better wash their hands. Even his name is scarcely mentioned seriously, evoking the image of a magician in top hat and frock coat rather than the dignity of a thinker. Stirner continues to be exiled from our culture, even though hundreds and hundreds of volumes have been dedicated to him.

Many remember Stirner only because Marx and Engels devoted so many caustic pages to him in *The German Ideology,* rather as Eugen Dühring is remembered chiefly because of Engels' book *Anti-Dühring* (though in this case it would be more merciful to forget both Dühring and the Anti-Dühring). There are, however, a few people who love him to such a degree that they will love no others for fear of diminishing him. They venerate him—the very man who wanted to devour the sacred and dispel veneration. Sometimes they tend toward a gentle dementia, at other times toward a cold fury. At any moment, somewhere in the world, there is a small press that is busily printing a new edition of *Der Einzige* (*The Ego and Its Own,* in one English version), often along with an edition of *Thus Spoke Zarathustra.* Universities pay no attention to these facts. They have forgotten that it was Stirner who disfigured them once and for all with his slashing strokes. They consider his work a good dissertation topic. But to treat Max Stirner only within one of the countless histories of the neo-Hegelians or of anarchism is already an invitation to the writer to avoid this monstrosity. Stirner then becomes a "position," always an extreme one, the ultimate of something. To be sure, some readers have become aware of the monstrosity, absorbing it or rejecting it, in any case not concealing it. But the anonymous body of culture has not acknowledged it. Having reached a stage of its life when (like everything else) it claims autonomy, this body secretes within itself new substances, and soon new entities: artificial barbarity, the artificial barbarian. Max Stirner announces them, explains them. And immediately he becomes ghostly. Stirner's presence is thus clearest in two authors, the first of whom does not mention him at all and the second of whom speaks of him in a text he will never publish: Nietzsche and Marx. We cannot understand much of their writing unless we read it as an impatient, sometimes feverish murmur addressed to a phantom who is persecuting them: Stirner. Marx and Nietzsche have never had much to say to each other directly. Still, they communicate like two people who are not acquainted but who have a dream (a terror) in common. And so they must meet at least in the angry, conspiratorial, ruthless, grim, circular fight with their phantom—a struggle that binds them like convicts in the same prison. These two early, self-conscious proponents of an "experimental philosophy" reencounter in Stirner a secret aspect of their thought, but the very aspect they did not want to acknowledge, in view of its consequences. In the course of their lives, we see them make continual patient efforts to hide this affinity, to elude the gloomy silence of the man who had preceded them in the intoxicating betrayal of thought. The boldness of Marx and Nietzsche descends in a direct line from the earlier, unsurpassable boldness of Stirner. "It took an *eiserne Stirne* [literally an 'iron brow,' meaning shamelessness] to write *Der Einzige,* and one could almost believe that the author, for this very reason, chose the name Stirner."

For a long time, thought had been waiting to be degraded. But first a person wicked enough to help in the process had to be found. Someone who had "the taste and the genius for provocation" (such as Saint Paul, Nietzsche, or Joseph de Maistre) and the courage to take an unprecedented step: to link, from one end to the other, with a delicate clasp, metaphysics and mad ravings. The task fell to a teacher in Madame Gropius' school for well-born young ladies, a man who wrote for the Berlin gazettes in the years just prior to 1848 and who signed his articles "Stirner."

Later, many people declared what others had supposed but had not dared to say: that metaphysics in general was mad raving. A hypothesis suited to the coarseness of the times. A more insinuating hypothesis, to which people paid little attention, was that mad raving was metaphysics. Stirner generously contributed to muddying the waters of thought forever. After him, it became a purely administrative matter to decide who was a philosopher and who wasn't. Every one of Wittgenstein's sentences implies contempt for the profession of philosophy. Valéry recorded his intellectual experiments in dozens of notebooks every morning between five and eight, but he took great care not to speak of them during the day, when he was visiting salons, attending meetings of the Académie, or dining *en ville*. Musil camouflaged himself among scientists who, with a faint smile, took part in the social gatherings of the Spirit. Mad raving swathed them all in benevolence, received them in its capacious folds.

They said they were witnessing the advent of disenchantment. But that disenchantment had survived for centuries—some even said millennia! The world endured: it remained enchanted. Stirner describes how a disenchanted entity *ought* to live—and his irony stems from his recognition that such an entity does not exist. If it did, it would be classified by disenchanted scientists as a throwback to archaic times: mute, violent, unpredictable, protean. Without verifiable identity. Unique. *Einzig.*

The division of people into Platonists and Aristotelians can be formulated in another way, perhaps even more precisely: people can be divided into those who think the world is sustained by magic and those who do not. Among the latter, many have the bad habit of thinking that magic is a practice based on illusion (being at the same time an interesting prelude to science). But Wittgenstein made it clear: what is magic is not *how* the world is, but the fact *that* it is.

Marx's rancor toward the petty bourgeoisie originates in his classical tastes. Forms, for him, must be closed and precise. Profiles must stand out against an empty, unimportant background. The aristocrat has such a profile, as does the bourgeois (so long as he holds to the virtues and vices that shape him)—and so, finally, does the worker. But in the middle, between these forms, lies the most irreparable evil. For Marx, the petty bourgeois are the *Lumpen* of the bourgeoisie—and the *Lumpen* are evil incarnate. They disturb him because they are metamorphic, malleable, lacking a physiognomy of their own; thus, they are capable of becoming anything, irrespective of the classifications established by history. In those damp sands of bitterness, ambition, resentment, and delirium, he saw Bolsheviks and fascists already being born. There was nothing wrong with the Bolsheviks; the acid bath of the Cause would suffice to make them unrecognizable. The revolutionary, by definition, has no origin ("he does not even have a name," says the catechism of Nechayev); he has only a purpose. But it was the countless other proliferating species that frightened Marx and seemed to him beyond control, like a sea of jellyfish. In Stirner he recognized the herald of that poisoned host. That *single individual* of Stirner's certainly did not offer an anthropological model for the petty bourgeois (as Marx and Engels, out of polemical shrewdness, claimed it did). It represented something far more fearsome: the breakdown of the schema of classes, the chaotic irruption that spoiled the sacred drama of history in the penultimate act. This was the prime unforgivable sin—and this is enough to explain the fury of Marx's attacks on Stirner.

On the basis of a thorough Hegelian education, Stirner prepares for gratuitous terror; on the basis of a razor-edged dandyism, Barrès prepares for immersion in blood's wisdom. Bourget sees the young Barrès of *Un Homme libre* as a "delicate nihilist" who belongs to an "aristocracy of the nerves" and who mocks the world, which has already reached the "puberty of silliness" (Huysmans). All he can do is breathe the odor of the stables and ask that everything "become part of the race again." The mediator will be a little backward girl, Bérénice. We are told that she "adopted as her doll a little gilded statue of Our Lady, which opened at the womb to reveal the Trinity." The past, race, blood are all grasped when the ego of the delicate nihilist has become utterly enfeebled, when the barbarity produced by experimentation on the little man needs to cling to an order. (That Ego was distilled in the latter part of the nineteenth century, in preparation for the "boys of 1889." Previously, only a hint of that aesthetic arrogance had been felt; afterward, its flavor would disappear, or would mingle with the many flavors of the masses—but it would lose that hint of the clandestine, the sequestered, and the depraved.)

One of the chief characteristics of *Der Einzige* is its brutality. But it is a reasoned brutality, arrived at through education—or rather, through the most ambitious pedagogic system that the West has produced, the only one that has ever claimed to absorb, incorporate, and subsume everything, in the fury of *Aufhebung*. The teachers of German idealism made painstaking, heavy-handed conceptual efforts to eliminate anything immediate, vigorous, elusive, and violent that might arise. Even Stirner's enemies admit that he had a venomous gift for thoroughness. The question then becomes how, at the pinnacle of culture, the unknown land of *artificial barbarity* can suddenly beckon. It is a realm to which Stirner introduces us with the faint smile of the teacher opening the door of his classroom, where the young ladies of Madame Gropius are waiting.

Why should we keep hanging about Hippel's tavern, amid the beer stains and sawdust? Many upheavals and collapses have taken place since then, and most of us have forgotten all about it. Yet it is undeniable that through the agency of the negligible Stirner, and still in the jargon of the Absolute Spirit, the protective sheath of culture was punctured for the first time. It was through him that a global and irreversible *loss of dignity* took place, and then became our foundation. Since then, a certain barbarity has imbued even the most cultivated speech; it is a new prerequisite for sensitivity, for thought. It would thus be useful to us if we could bring it back into the light in all its crudeness. Today's world derives from Marx, Freud, and Nietzsche (who were, after all, respectable individuals who cared about good manners and knew very well that such manners should be kept, even if "critique of the existent" could—should—finally abolish them); but it stems to an even greater degree, and unwittingly, from Stirner. It cannot know this, not only because "paternity is always uncertain" but because every paternity at this point must be spurious. Here Stirner settles the matter in obscurity, as befits a petty clerk of Nothingness: "The civilized being of the immense cities returns to the wild state—that is, to a state of isolation—because the social mechanism allows him to forget the need for community and to lose his feelings of connection to other people, which were once kept alive by his wants. Every improvement in the social mechanism renders useless certain acts, certain ways of feeling, certain attitudes toward communal life."

They expected him to come from the distant East, sporting wispy Mongol mustaches, a necklace of bones, and a fur cloak spattered with marrow and blood. Instead he made his appearance in Berlin, as a teacher in a boarding school for well-born young ladies. His jacket was impeccable but threadbare; he had oval spectacles and a shy, mocking profile. When his friends started brawls at Hippel's, he kept to one side, at the far corner of the table. While he sat writing in his musty room, one could occasionally hear a cry born of over-wrought nerves, something very much like barking. After the publication of *Der Einzige,* Stirner's daily life in Berlin (where by that time everyone actually wanted to forget Hegel) became something exotic—something that we can only speculate about, like Rimbaud's life in Harar. It later transmigrated into its two definitive forms: the silence of Bartleby and the "death ship" described by Traven.

In order for Stirner to be born, the Big City must exist. The ghost of the enemy of ghosts belongs to Hippel's Berlin tavern, where the Freien, the Free Ones, gather; but it belongs even more to the St. Petersburg underground, to the belly of Paris, to the mountains of garbage in London, to the death ships that swallow their passengers without documents and without names in the port of Antwerp. Its place is with a certain type of disorderly crowd: feverish autodidacts, slave-laborers of the pen, rootless men ready for anything, discredited bourgeois, dispossessed aristocrats, the damned of the earth who have been cast out from the bush, the swamps, or the desert to stand under the marble ceilings of the Polytechnics of another continent, the swelling crowd of those whose most profound knowledge is of public humiliation and private exaltation. In hotel registers Nietzsche identified himself as a "university professor," though he would never again hold that position, and though with every passing year he felt he was becoming more like those teeming phantoms. He could even have assumed a role among them—in fact, had already chosen one: that of the "respectable criminal." He abhorred that aggressive and rumpled company, yet he knew that ultimately they would be an appreciative audience for his books. He chased them away in every manner possible, relying to the end on good manners. But he could not erase all the signs of affinity; there were too many. Dostoyevski once jotted down in a notebook with curiosity and disgust (next to sums of money that had never arrived or that had already been spent) that *man no longer had a profile,* and that for a long time he himself had already been surrounded in his room by a hostile swarm of those presences; indeed, he belonged to them and had betrayed them. He consummated this lengthy betrayal in his novels, which are often shaken by the convulsive excitement of someone who is too close to what he is writing, like a policeman compiling a report on a massacre in which he has taken part.

Stirner is the barbarian who comes from one of Germany's provincial little states and bursts into the center of the metaphysical Empire. The same tools that helped Hegel absorb every vestige of barbarity into the Spirit now serve to dismantle the spirit, to uproot it from every terrain, to bore into the anthropological soil of the Enlightenment. The true "philosophy of the hammer," which Nietzsche would never succeed in practicing because he was too unalterably polite, is achieved in the brief, punchy, aggressive sentences that make up *Der Einzige*.

Stirner's *egoist* denies all dependence; but every sort of dependence is a root, terrestrial or celestial. The egoist is an uprooted man who for the first time recognizes himself as such. He roams the cities, a complete stranger to everyone and everything. The words that invade his mind, the desires that assail him—everything is something that he can use or throw away. The only thing that is *his own* is the act of taking or chasing away. He is the man from underground who plunders metaphysics.

We do not have, and certainly never could have, any letters from Stirner that would be as moving as Nietzsche's letters from the college of Schulpforta asking for Schumann scores. So far as culture is concerned, there is something physiologically tainted and corrupt in Stirner, something that poisons him from the start.

Stirner's premise is that the process of secularization is unable to consume or extinguish the sacred, as it claims to do. It merely shifts it. And the power that it assumes is all the more devastating and uncontrollable since it no longer has a name, and cannot be recognized for what it is.

What is it about Stirner that people have been unable to forgive? Not so much the numerous openly criminal statements that he scatters like oriental spices in his cuisine of neo-Hegelian iteration. Not so much his formulations of the "egoist" and the "unique," so incompatible with and irreducible to any practical rationality. But certain rapid sentences such as, "Our atheists are pious people," which crowns a demonstration that no one has been able to refute. Stirner has described our world, which is scourged by a critical process that "advances without respite" toward absolute disenchantment, as in fact profoundly sanctimonious. Who, indeed, is more sanctimonious than a healthy layman—so conceited and credulous about his own principles? And what about those haughty atheists, who are all convinced that a supreme mystic like Giordano Bruno was one of them? The Church, which burned him, had a far more accurate knowledge of his true character. But the atheists have even dedicated a monument to him, as if he were the Unknown Soldier. And the champions of the Enlightenment? If they really exist, they should first of all give up their credulity toward Reason. These are the new "pious people," the bigots who are not even protected by ceremonial mediations, by the arcane pragmatism of a church. They let themselves be ruled not by sacrament but by a few capitalized words: Society, Humankind, Man, the Species. (These were the ones the nineteenth century preferred, and they continue to run wild today, even though many others have joined them.) Such people do not know the premises on which they act and do not like it if some irreverent sophist queries them on the subject. If they are forced to reveal these premises, they come up with a rather paltry vision. Fragments of Banality and scrolls of Commonplaces decorate the pedestal of their Principles and Values—which were better off covered with their superstitious practices. These, after all, are not always murderous: at times they have a certain inane mildness.

Suspended between the oppressed masses and the oppressing masses, Stirner anticipates Lautréamont's sneering comment on poetry that "must be made by all, not by one." But he applies it to philosophy. In *Der Einzige* we are invaded by thoughts that for a long time never had the slightest hope of finding refuge in books. Brute thoughts. This breach of protocol is an unforeseen effect of democratic rule. Lautréamont the chronicler will explain it this way: "Doubt always used to have minority status. But in our century it is in the majority. We absorb violation of duty through our pores." Doubt slashes at every thought that raises its head. But its blade grants its victims an easy resurrection. Those thoughts quickly reappear—as opinions.

Where do Marx and Engels cheat when they speak of Stirner? Almost everywhere. With a book like *Der Einzige,* in which paradox is the *object of the text,* and in which all is incongruous and aberrant with respect to any traveled path, one need only pretend not to notice that the incongruity, paradox, and aberration are not accidents but the very aim of the discourse; one need only refuse to see that this raving is nothing but the definitive propaedeutics to silence— and the work of destruction is done. Then one can calmly say that *Der Einzige* is incongruous, paradoxical, aberrant, and raving. One can even say this in two or three pages. And the fact that Marx and Engels repeat it for more than three hundred reveals, at the very least, their bad conscience. It also reveals their farsightedness. United at this point by the Holy Bond of the Cause, they could not refrain from fiercely attacking *the* book that more than any other mocks the Cause, the Bond, and especially the Holiness of Cause and Bond. Assuming (but only for the sake of argument) that the force of their "critique" had already succeeded in dispelling any sacred aura, this does not mean that Marx and Engels were prepared to demonstrate that fact exoterically. The working class needed holy images; the Cause would stand as a guarantor of proper feeling, of ordered and hardworking lives devoted primarily to self-denial, in preparation for the struggles and conflicts with the Enemy. Never would it be revealed that Free Thinking, the creature whose mind was finally purged of every chimera, was the true church mouse of modern times. Even a small amount of Stirner's prussic acid would be enough to produce incurable spasms in the mighty torso of the Worker—that deplorable anthropological figment on whom Marx and Engels built their labor practices, which the fervent "engineers of the soul" would eventually replace with different ones. In the molten lead that flowed from Stirner's book, in its obsessive repetitions and unseemly arguments, Marx and Engels, who now claimed to speak for all workers, saw the emergence of a different and fearsome mass of proletarians. Not Pellizza da Volpedo's workers, striding proudly to be gunned down by mustachioed officers, but the infernal, shapeless mass of the *Lumpen:* incorrigible vagabonds, incapable of class loyalty, rootless from the womb, violent, inarticulate, disrespectful enemies of labor and learning—those whom the newspapers called, with a shudder, "the dregs of society." It was the underground emerging into the open; and this ghostly "reserve army" threatened to stifle the proletariat before the proletariat could snuff out the bourgeoisie.

The accursed separation, the *Trennung* that already tormented Lessing's Freemasons, was thus also cleaving the immaculate fortress of the proletariat. It was a barely visible lesion, a malignant crevice that swallowed up anyone who strayed from the correct line. From that obscure chasm, years later, the damned of the earth would reemerge, now forming a network without frontiers, comparable only to the one that capitalism cast over the planet. Eluding any reliable census, like rats, they had at their disposal the most evasive and destructive weapon: dumb refusal, the repudiation of all forms of society. The secret torment of Marx and Engels in devising their practical systems was not so much the bourgeoisie, that adaptable class which from the outset had been as eager to self-destruct as it was clever about restoring itself; their worry was the *Lumpenproletariat*—the detritus of all classes, the "apotheosis of rootlessness," from which one could expect an array of damaging, unpredictable attacks on behalf of class interests. The *Lumpen* threatened the historical succession of the classes, that saving schema which justified the current wretchedness and formed the basis of the radiant future. If the proletariat was not the *final* class, the definitive class, the one that would make human destiny *weltgeschichtlich,* that would give it a global dimension—if the proletariat had to fight internally to distinguish itself from *another* proletariat, that of the *Lumpen*—then the whole plan seemed imperiled. The course of historical Providence no longer converged toward *one* final point, but risked being swallowed up and destroyed by boundless, inexhaustible dissociation.

This, then, was the threat Stirner posed, but no one could admit it openly, because the very act of recognizing it would expand its existence. Marx and Engels never explicitly say they are fighting Stirner for these reasons; they try to shove him back among the harmless Berlin philosophers, describing him, against all appearances, as "the weakest and most ignorant of that philosophical brother-hood." In *The German Ideology,* too, the references to the *Lumpen* problem are hasty and curt—but they are all the more significant: "Stirner consistently identifies the proletariat with pauperism, whereas pauperism is merely the condition of the proletariat in a state of ruin, the lowest level to which the now defenseless proletarian descends in his confrontation with the pressure of the bourgeoisie. Only the proletarian who has been robbed of all his energy falls into pauper-ism. See Sismondi, Wade, and so on. In the eyes of the proletariat, for example, 'Stirner' and his like may well be paupers but will never be proletarians." The proletarian thus incarnates the respectability of poverty, and would never receive a pauper into his home. The reasons for this genuine class hatred are obscure; Marx and Engels tell us only that the "ruined proletarian" has no more "energy." Sufficient reason, one might say, for the not-yet-ruined proletarian to trample on him. But is it really true that the "ruined proletarian" has no more energy? Rather, doesn't he have a far more insidious energy, an energy that no longer allows itself to be channeled? Best to skip over this; and such is the tactic that Marx and Engels employ. It's true that even afterward the insults to the *Lumpen* were violent, but they were always accidental and sporadic. Marx and Engels did their best to disguise the fact that their ultimate criterion for the "human" was its organizability. But the habit of contempt remained. It is enough to see the proud disdain with which Rosa Luxemburg, years later, put her comrades on their guard: "The proletariat is the last class of bourgeois society to appear on the scene with revolu-tionary aims. It cannot be overwhelmed by an even more radical social stratum which exceeds the goals that the workers have con-sciously set. The only social stratum that lies below the proletariat— the level of the disinherited social parasites, comprising prostitutes, professional criminals, and every sort of obscure and marginal ex-istence—is not a revolutionary factor; on the contrary, it is counter-revolutionary." And Lenin, with his usual nonchalance, would deal with the consequences of that hatred, shoring up the dam against the recurrent anarchic tide: "Anarchism results from despair. It's part of the mind-set of an intellectual who has gone off the rails, or a representative of the *Lumpenproletariat;* it is not typical of a proletarian." Thus, people simply assumed once and for all what the *correct psychology* of the proletarian should be, not to mention that of the intellectual who stays on track.

But even then, Marx and Engels had not included Russia in their calculation. To speak of someone with contempt as narrowminded petty bourgeois, or as a raving pauper of the intellect, was not an effective argument in a country where the poisonous flowers of the intelligentsia were budding from outcasts of all classes, and where raving was becoming eminently "practical." From his wretched boardinghouse in Berlin, Stirner was in direct communication with the Russian underground. No one more perfectly embodied the "unique" than the underground man who made his voice heard. And although Stirner's obsessive arguments resulted in the yearned-for aphasia, the voice from underground has never ceased: it has infused all discourse, disfigured all seriousness, mocked all eminence, pursued history down every dark passage. It was in Russia that Stirner's hidden face would surface, the one that Marx refused to recognize. All the Hegelian apparatus, the academic disputes, the pretense to expounding a "philosophy" were only papier-mâché castles, superfluous and ostentatious—fit for provoking solitary laughter, like the shameful memories that haunt Dostoyevski's Man from Underground (a "collegiate assessor" by profession): the yellow stain on his trousers, his urge to jostle the arrogant officer on Nevsky Prospekt, the dull faces of his former schoolmates. In Dostoyevski, *Der Einzige* would find its epigraph: "Gentlemen, you must forgive me for philosophizing like this; I have been underground for forty years."

Superstitious and clearsighted, Marx feared the power that comes with loss of class—a power that always casts a shadow over the proletariat's radiant ascents. A person who loses class does not move from one class to another; rather, he moves from a class, with its distinctive customs and dress, to an unspecified place that has no shape or affiliations, a place that is no longer inside but *opposite* society. In the *Grundrisse,* Marx concisely sketched the genealogy of the individual in the history of capital; but the individual (that unmanageable character) eluded him as an empirical concept. That welter of psychological forces, cut loose from everything, was no longer a material that could be easily shaped. At most, it might give rise to the terrorist. Furthermore, the individual was the one who initiated the break from the most oppressive faith that Marx shared with his—and our—times: faith in Society. Even in the Paris of Balzac, from the servants' quarters to the drawing rooms, we see many instances of humiliation and progressive degradation. But in Balzac, losing class never produces the "Russian effect." The majestic *comédie* still dominates, involving a very long series of steps and fractions of steps, which one can ascend or descend. The dark center is Vautrin, the keen-eyed ex-convict and policeman, who represents omnipotence *from below*. He alone can wear all masks with impunity, because he is the god who visits his victims incognito. Other people can wear many masks in succession, but they are constrained and oriented by their role of the moment. In Dostoyevski, in contrast, a gelatinous mass blurs the outlines. Everything is unstable—and a secret pact binds instability to abjection. His characters tend to lose (or lost at the outset) their connections: to their families, to their class, most of all to society and to their feelings. With unnerving abruptness, they can reverse their emotions at any moment. They flow without banks, almost indifferently—both innocent and depraved, pitying their victims even as they torture them, veering suddenly from tears to the wildest, most contemptuous laughter.

Der Einzige was one of the books in the young Dostoyevski's library. It also circulated among the Petrashevskys, the perversely naïve group of subversives that would disband before the rifles of Nicholas I's officers, and then scatter among the "houses of the dead." But in the Dostoyevski-Stirner relationship we find something far more serious than a legacy of ideas: Stirner's anthropological *monstrum* will continue to live in Dostoyevski's novels. *Der Einzige* infuses psychology with a powerful reagent, something that causes a break from everything proposed as Law: above all, identity (the system of equivalents), as well as roles, class conventions, established sentiments. Likewise, in Dostoyevski a sudden upheaval disfigures the image of what is supposed to be human. The characters no longer have precise outlines; something vague, abrupt, and capricious is invading every individual. The psyche, like a vapor, escapes through every crack and envelops the city. The entity that

Stirner calls the *unique* is primarily a shapeless hollow. From that hollow Dostoyevski summons a teeming mass of faces: Raskolnikov, Kirilov, Ivan—and the Man from Underground, who in his quintessential anonymity somehow incorporates them all.

Dostoyevski inhabits the underground as Zarathustra inhabits his mountain cave, but he will not receive any "supermen" there. Instead, he awaits Stirner's *Unmensch,* the individual who eludes the domesticated canon of the human, which humanist torturers, cultivators of "science and common sense," try to impose on people, convinced they are doing good. Hence his sober, subversive questions: "What makes you think that man either can or *should* be changed in this way?" "Mightn't it be possible that man likes things other than his well-being?"

Having arrived in Russia and abandoned his Hegelian cloak, Stirner couldn't help making a speech "concerning sodden snow." The Underground Man takes his tone from that sarcasm, which readers of *Der Einzige* had not even noticed when the book first appeared, so little did those Berliners know about life. And now that tone reaches a climax: "We find it painful to be men—real men of flesh and blood with *our own private bodies;* we're ashamed of it, and we long to turn ourselves into something hypothetical called the average man. We're stillborn, and for a long time we've been brought into the world by parents who are dead themselves; and we like it better and better. We're developing a taste for it, so to speak. Soon we'll invent a way to be begotten entirely by ideas." The style has become more insinuating, but we instantly recognize the voice of the unique. Here, too, as in Stirner, an element of deliberate brutality overwhelms us, an unnatural immediacy that rebels against *l'homme de la nature et de la vérité* (who is *l'homme dans toute la vérité de la nature* at the beginning of Rousseau's *Confessions*). The Underground Man is, in fact, an alchemical product, "born from a retort" and "not from the womb of nature." But artifice makes him even more violent, because it makes him more civilized ("civilization develops only the range of sensations—nothing more"), and it deprives him of the innate stupidity of men who "are convinced more quickly and more easily than others that they have found a firm foundation for their actions." While he tosses and turns in his fetid sheets, the Underground Man, consummate product of Western culture, retains the bad habit of trying to devise an epistemology. With a shard of diamond, he cruelly scratches the diaphanous matter of thought. He discovers he is a victim of the *bottomless,* Shestov's *bespotchvennost* (*Bodenlosigkeit* in German; *déracinement* in the French translation by Boris de Schloezer) and loudly vents his rage: "Where are the prime causes on which I might rest? Where are my foundations? Where shall I ever find them?" Like Stirner, the Underground Man has "founded his cause on nothing" and rails in his shrill, insistent voice.

Behind the bitterness, the insults, and the silences, Marx and Stirner share a fundamental experience that marks their lives: the *spiritualization* of the world. In the nineteenth century, greedy science and tenacious philosophy (which out of secular modesty was now called "critique") exiled shadows, hypostases, ideas, symbols, auras, categories, and emblems from the world, anatomizing reality in the harsh light of the dissection room. The bourgeoisie was rejoicing as the Spirit (*Geist*) extended ever farther and became ever more superfluous, since people had no more need for it except when they unveiled monuments. Machines were humming incessantly (although not in backward Germany); and because *Geschichte* had become *Weltgeschichte,* because all "history" was now "world history," remote peoples were destroyed by the blind movements of these machines, and by the rise and fall of the Stock Exchange. Utter disenchantment pervaded the world; people stumbled over haloes in the mud on teeming roadways, while the great body of the nineteenth century was unwittingly performing its harsh experiment on itself, convinced it was doing something entirely different (more than anything else, it thought it was "shedding light"). As all this was occurring, two young Germans, petty bourgeois with a natural tendency to degenerate into *Lumpen* (Stirner was twice imprisoned for debt, and Marx was arrested in London on suspicion of thievery as he went to pawn his wife's silver, which bore the Argyll coat of arms), looked around and saw a stately dance of ghosts. They shared the prevailing belief of those days: that ghosts were a sign of evil. (Guénon noted that, by a disturbing coincidence, spiritualism began to spread like an epidemic in the United States in 1848. He saw this as a necessary counterweight to the barricades in Europe, which themselves merely signaled a modern development on the stage of history: the entrance of a new character, Chaos.) Their gaze became fixed on, captivated by, those ghosts. But they resisted; and they scorned those around them who carried on in ignorance, convinced they were now living in an empty world. *"Hypostases non fingo!"* the possessed Stirner declared from his teacher's desk at the school for young ladies, as a mass of categories was pressing him to the wall. To this refusal to give shape to hypostases, a refusal that was far more radical and effective than its ancestor, uttered by Newton, Marx replies with a shrug, "Bah! How can one believe that thought determines reality, when it is reality that determines thought!" (implying a whole rosary of concomitant chiasmata). And he points to the concrete, into which one must pack accounts, banks, warehouses, working hours, customs regulations, gold, bonds, and marauding ships. But he is feigning this disgust: his most rigorous application of Stirner's attack on hypostases will come years later, in the first book of *Das Kapital*. There, Stirner's words will find the experimental validation that Marx himself had impatiently denied. Once reality is stripped of metaphysical veils and reduced to the naked process of production-circulation-consumption (from which all other processes derive and on which they are modeled, according to the axioms stated by Engels), it is precisely *then* that we see the great dance of ghosts, the final mutation of *Geist* into *Poltergeist*. They snatch up the wardrobe and the chairs, the women and the lengths of cloth, which cease to be possessions and instead become possessed. Thus, the only immediate successor to Stirner, the only loyal follower who saw clearly what the master had seen only indistinctly and who applied it rigorously to the concrete, is the Marx of *Das Kapital* and the *Grundrisse*.

A later follower, impelled by similar premises, was to wander a long time before formulating that violent initial imperative into a strategy. This follower was Nietzsche. Once he had recognized the unreal character of every hypostasis and the malevolent power of those fictions, he did not withdraw into the barbarian inarticulateness of the "unnameable" and the "unsayable." Instead, he saw fictions—and hence hypostases—everywhere, not only in every word and every action, but in every form and process of nature. And he chose to experience *all* fictions by accepting them as such. This procedure, which constantly shifts the outlines of forms, is the only one that can prevent appearance, no matter how sumptuous and striking it may be, from being gradually petrified into essence.

In time, everything finds its way into the history of philosophy. In 1866, after twenty years of almost total obscurity, Stirner was mentioned in two books that would long remain standard reference works: Johann Edward Erdmann's *Grundriss der Geschichte der Philosophie* (Outline of the History of Philosophy) and Friedrich Albert Lange's *Geschichte des Materialismus* (History of Materialism). In fact, Stirner's reputation would rise as a result of this latter "history," in which *Der Einzige* emerged from a regenerative silence as a "notorious work." But Lange somehow allowed himself to be awed by Stirner, offering an assessment that proved to be decisive: *Der Einzige,* he claimed, was "the most extreme book we know."

The "magic of the extreme" was once again exerting its power. ("The magic that fights for us, the eye of Venus, which captivates and blinds our adversaries—this is the *magic of the extreme,* the seductive power exerted by all that is most extreme. We immoralists—we are *the most extreme.*") In the summer of 1887, while reading Lange's work at the British Museum, a young Scot named John Henry Mackay came upon Stirner's name for the first time, in the sentence quoted above. He made note of it. A year later, when he read *Der Einzige,* it seemed to him that mankind had found its liberator in Stirner. Soon he set off in pursuit of this prodigious author, who was at that time unknown. Marx and Engels had built, piece by piece, "Marxism" and the "Marxist" (clearly taking care to denigrate Marxists later). Stirner does not build any such individual as the "Stirnerian," even if he left useful hints for building him; he would come into being, irrepressibly, on his own. The prototype was that somewhat ridiculous and bombastic Scot, who would be followed by countless others, from the workers of the black terror to the dandies of *La Revue blanche.* Devoting himself to the research for Stirner's biography, Mackay mobilized all the powerful forces of spiritualist kitsch ("for this book is life itself"), which at that moment was rising to heights that it would never see again. And Stirner sparked yet another paradox: "On the one hand we have Stirner's book, the product—perhaps too mature, and extremely blasé—of a long evolutionary process. Lacking the slightest ingenuousness, it was the last remnant of crumbling Hegelianism, which was burying itself in critique and contemptuous laughter. And on the other hand there is Stirner's biographer, Mackay—a fellow with a childish heart full of ingenuousness, and with a lovely, warm spirit. Yet he hasn't a drop of humor or critical ability." The destroyer of the "Cause" was now becoming the noblest of all "Causes," to be announced to the world by every means; he was an object of sacrifice, of self-denial, of unswerving devotion. First Mackay, and then those embarrassing Stirnerians, would become living examples of the "pious atheists" that Stirner had mocked in his book.

In the course of his mission, Mackay soon noticed something strange. He had published an announcement asking anyone who had had some connection with Stirner to get in touch with him. There were few responses. The trails vanished the moment they were revealed. Mackay received news of people who had died or moved away, and learned of archives that were now dispersed. Raising his head with puzzled pride, Mackay asked, "Can it be that a life of such greatness was nevertheless lacking in great external experiences?" Well, yes. Although Stirner as ghost seems to have done his best to expunge the traces of his documented life, and although we have not a single portrait of him (except the sketch drawn by his enemy Engels) and not more than a signature in his handwriting, the little that remains seems flooded by a beam of intense light: the light of squalor and penury, of an anonymous and humiliated life, which occupies no more than a few lines in municipal registries and scholastic archives. The only sources, in fact, that were open to Mackay.

The research for the biography lasted years. Not until 1898 did a Berlin publisher issue the work, entitled *Max Stirner: Sein Leben und sein Werk,* which to this day has remained the only biography of the Unique. Meanwhile, the "case of Stirner" had opened up an infamous coda to the "case of Nietzsche." And just as Nietzsche's sister, Elisabeth, took care of him in Weimar and allowed only a few carefully chosen guests to see him sitting glassy-eyed in his chair, wrapped in a long, heavy, white garment, so the pathetic Mackay wanted to be the First Apostle of Stirner. But in every sect there are disputes over precedence. Mackay was bitter because the philosopher Eduard von Hartmann claimed to have "rediscovered" Stirner in his *Philosophie des Unbewussten* (Philosophy of the Unconscious; 1869) and in his *Phänomenologie des sittlichen Bewusstseins* (Phenomenology of Moral Consciousness; 1879), whereas it was obvious that Hartmann wanted to exalt Stirner only in order to belittle Nietzsche. Mackay was also angered by Paul Lauterbach's preface to the economy edition of *Der Einzige* in the Universal-Bibliothek series from Reclam publishers (1893), which heralded Stirner's triumphal readmittance to the company of authors who must be read.

To point out, as Lauterbach did quite knowledgeably, those authors to whom Stirner seemed "akin" was for Mackay an act of lèse-majesté, because to him it was obvious that Stirner was the "Good Tidings of Great Joy." The only fact that could give Mackay joy was that by now Benjamin Tucker and his friends, the "individualist anarchists," were already active in the United States. Stirner's legacy, Mackay warned, was in their "loyal and strong hands," a bit the way Marx and Engels entrusted theirs to a proletariat whom they obliged to be rough and straightforward.

Although Mackay accorded Nietzsche a certain respect, it seemed unfair to him that Stirner's return to prominence should have come on the coattails of Nietzsche's success. How could anyone, asked Mackay, compare this "confused spirit, eternally vacillating, constantly contradictory, buffeted almost helplessly between truth and error, with the profound, clear, calm, and superior genius of Stirner?" It was "an absurdity, not even worth serious refutation." Infusing his adjectives somewhat dull-wittedly with good intentions, Mackay constructed a portrait of the Unknown Great Man. The more his research on Stirner's life fell back into the void, into insignificance, the more fervidly he drew an image lacking any relation to verifiable reality. He piled votive offerings around the miraculous image of the first thoroughly impious man the world had ever known. In keeping with his style, and to prevent "these external traces of the great life from being erased," Mackay soon devoted himself to memorial tablets. In the spring of 1892, with the support of Hans von Bülow, the only person who had known both Stirner and Nietzsche, he had such a tablet mounted on the façade of the house on Philippstrasse in Bayreuth where Stirner had died. On a slab of granite, which had been acquired cheaply because it was marred by an almost invisible crack, these words were carved: "In this house / during his last years / lived Max Stirner / (Dr. Caspar Schmidt, 1806–1856) / creator of the immortal work / *Der Einzige und sein Eigentum* / 1845." In the course of his research, Mackay would later discover that Stirner had never been awarded the title of doctor of philosophy—or, if truth be told, even that of high school professor. On his grave, only the name Max Stirner appeared. A longer inscription would have cost 469 marks, but the collection effort had succeeded in raising only 438.

Ida Overbeck: "Once, when my husband was out, Nietzsche stayed and talked to me for a while, telling me about two strange characters he was dealing with at that time—people with whom he felt a kinship. As is always the case when one finds some internal rapport, he was animated and happy. Some time later he found a book by Klinger in our house. My husband had not found Stirner in the library. 'Ah,' said Nietzsche, 'I was mistaken about Klinger. He was a Philistine; I feel no affinity at all with him. But Stirner—with him, yes.' A grave expression darkened his face. And as I looked attentively at his features, they changed again. He waved his hand, as if to drive away or repel something, and murmured: 'Now I've told you, and I didn't want to speak of it. Forget it all. They will talk of plagiarism, but I know you won't.'"

Why does thought need hypostases? Because it knows that within thought lies powers that surpass it. The hypostasis is an act of homage that thought offers to the realm of images. Those allegorical figures with their vacant, somber gaze, statues that circumscribe the precinct of the intellect, are the last heirs of the angels and the great zodiacal animals, which once plundered thought without restraint. Even today they stand in a circle among the rank weeds, and soon everyone will forget that they ever served a purpose. Why, in fact, should thought be enclosed within boundaries? Vague rectilinear movements draw it toward an unknown that is supposedly of the same nature as the known. The statues are receding, covered with moss, before some anonymous vandal can decapitate them. In the pond in the center of the park, the water lilies float silently. Beneath the water's surface lurks a dark life-form that soon will execute the master of the garden.

· · ·

Paradoxes: In order for all to become process, all had to become thing. (*Thing* is what is at our disposal; *process* is a power that can have anything at its disposal.) And in order for all to become thing, all had to be definable, limitable, ultimately *separable* from all.

Thing is that which can be administered, has a distinct outline, is detached from the rest. Hypostases are formed in such a way as to allow this specifying and fixing of the psyche's turbulence. But people attributed hypostases with a surplus of power in relation to the subject, making them capable of using, rather than usable. It was then necessary to forget that such power existed. Reason, once again, showed plenty of zeal for accomplishing this; but its life was at stake, or rather its tranquillity. For centuries, science has aggressively made fun of angels, with precisely this defensive aim.

"The spirit dwells in heaven and dwells within us; we poor things are, in fact, nothing but its 'dwellings.' If Feuerbach proceeds to destroy its heavenly dwelling and forces the spirit to move in with us bag and baggage, I'm afraid that we, its earthly apartments, will be badly overcrowded." The prosaic nature of this move corresponds to Stirner's perpetually mocking attitude. It puts the sublime into immediate contact not so much with the humblest as with the median—with that weary, daily ordinariness that is now thought to contain every heaven and hell. Thus, barely twisting Feuerbach, Stirner spins the whole scene around. No longer do we have the well-meaning speculative theses of a flourishing association of workers; now we are confronted by an unprecedented anthropological case, which disturbs every classification. In the table of variants within which the relationship between sacred and profane is usually inscribed, we finally come upon a novelty: one of the opposing terms, the profane, has met up with a gypsy caravan crammed with knickknacks and has the audacity to invite the gypsies to live in its Biedermeier apartments, merely because one of them insists he is a distant relative. Feydeau could easily make a farce out of all this, and Stirner realizes as much. So he presents this epoch-making event as a moment of confusion: a family is flustered at the arrival of a crowd of guests, more numerous and more demanding than anticipated. But this comic domestic scene still contains portents. The sacred demands a vessel; its vaporous and penetrating power can be countered only by someone who knows how to contain it (with objects, supports, constructions, rites, formulas). In the bourgeois *intérieur,* nothing is ready for such a task: the knickknacks wink, the scattered little boxes spring open, the curtains shudder, the wallpapers wrinkle, the tablecloths shriek. The Guest passes through, leaves some traces of his presence, withdraws toward the attic, is deposited in Odradek (as Kafka hinted). From this point on, in the eyes of the child who will become Walter Benjamin, every object in the room becomes a totem. Putting an ear to one of them, you can still hear the rustling of that Guest passing by. The walls are covered with tattoos.

"What do we gain if, for a change, we shift the divine from outside ourselves to inside ourselves? *Are we* what is in us?" In those days, the blaring trumpets of the Human were announcing continual conquests. All sorts of things were being hoarded, and the individual smugly contemplated his growing store of possessions. But *who* appropriated *what*? And what was the difference between appropriating a category of thought and possessing a letter of credit? Possession seemed a kind of first step toward appropriation, which in turn could be considered complete when it absorbed, without any residue, the appropriated entity. *"Ablatio omnis alteritatis et differentiae"* ("elimination of every type of otherness and difference"), Nicholas Cusanus had written. But he was referring to the godlike soul, which is assimilated to divinity; whereas now the point is to assimilate ourselves to something that by definition is alien to us. Yet even without divine intervention, which always maliciously complicates things, and also without any secular possession, appropriation still encounters difficulties.

Our own body is already alien to us. We can use it, or we can be obscurely overpowered by it; in any case, we treat it like a multitude of aliens. And the mind itself—couldn't it perhaps look at itself as *another* thing? Indeed, isn't this an inherent characteristic of it? What else is the glorious "self-awareness" to which the Spirit soared, if not the total fulfillment of that capacity?

Let us go still farther back: What is one's *own*? In the answer to this question all the ambitions, all the secret intentions of thought are revealed. We open the *Upanishads* (but in Stirner's time no one was aware that Schopenhauer had just begun teaching how to open them). In the three words of the *tat tvam asi*, that which is one's *own* declares itself to be the discovery of identification. The alien is one of the countless fruits of nonknowledge, which blocks the circulation of the *own* within itself. And that self is the whole. Yet nonknowledge remains that which is immediately proper to us: our own. Paradoxes of a thought teeming with gods. In those days Feuerbach's emancipated Reason had barely incorporated the gods, and had done so, moreover, in the euphemistic form of the "divine." Obviously Feuerbach's subject had different aims from the subject of the *Upanishads*, which in any case Feuerbach had not read. What sort of *own* was he looking for then? In fact, for a model of Man full of good sentiments and virtues. But Feuerbach here is a pretext, and it is surely not in his moderate Reason that we should seek the reply of an age without gods. Reason without premises (every premise is an alien) has narrowed it down to the field of inquiry in which it develops its greatest strength: logico-mathematical inquiry. *Own* is a sentence that belongs to a formal theory. A formal theory is a sequence of transparent statements, in the sense that each of them is defined in all its elements and, through deduction, can be traced back by means of rules of deduction to a minimum number of initial statements (the axioms). The formal system is a multiplicity in which everything is proper, is *own*, and cannot be anything else. But we know from Gödel's incompleteness theorem that for formal theories (including arithmetic), there exists no effective procedure that allows one to ascertain whether or not a generic statement belongs to the theory itself.

Thought without premises thus encounters an impassable difficulty in the process of appropriation. And the theorem that reveals this problem is perhaps *the* thought from which that thought hangs by imperceptible threads. But it is not certain that the formal system was constructed primarily for the sake of appropriating logical consistency. Even thought from which the gods are absent has its paradoxes. In fact, the most striking thing about the formal system is its power. Arithmetic, which is the formal system on which Gödel proved his theorem, cannot assert its own consistency. But arithmetic acts. And a formal system that functions is also a machine that produces and expands power. To return to the construction of the formal system: What characterizes it within the sentences? First, it lacks premises: the formal system considers everything outside itself as equal to zero. Second, it is arbitrary: in a formal system, any true statement can be taken as the initial sentence of a theory, provided that every constituent element is defined without residue. (In reality, there is always a remainder. In the proposition $a = b$ it is the form of the signs a, $=$, and b. "In the beginning was the sign," Hilbert said, and his statement—unwittingly?—hints at the fact that the arbitrary can make everything transparent except itself.) The reduction of the context to zero and the arbitrariness of the signs in the formal system are two procedures that generate boundless power. Their application is not limited to the sphere in which such procedures are displayed in their pure form—namely, the logico-mathematical sphere. Without the subject's knowing it, these procedures function in all the spheres in which thought lacks premises. They act in the most impure and blatantly inconsistent forms; they are always more or less subtle *simulations* of formal systems. But their aim is not consistence, which even the formal system cannot possess within itself. These simulations strive for power—and they achieve it, often to an extent that goes far beyond predictions. (They do this precisely because they are simulations, so that their elements blend with empirical data. Thus, they are not transparent—even if it is agreed that they are, so long as the simulation holds.) The formal system can be a grandiose means of control, although it will inevitably encounter, at a certain point in its development, a basic, uncontrollable element. But the hope is that this element will not cause too many practical problems. In fact, in the years since Gödel formulated his theorem, arithmetic has never ceased to provide its services. In simulated formal systems the uncontrollability manifests itself in much more obvious and drastic forms, even with regard to pure functioning. But until that moment, the intoxication of power is immense. In this intoxication, thought without premises finds its formulation of the proper, of one's *own*. *Own* is that which belongs to the sphere in which a form of power can be exercised. Power is measured by the capacity to control. Control is produced by simulating pure formal systems, or by mixing simulations with pure formal systems. But are *we ourselves* the formal systems that act in us?

. . .

The confiscation of the divine by the human, that act of prudent management demanded by the age, resulted in some big surprises when it came time to take inventory. Among the items in stock were not only Goodness and Power—those virtues that appealed to everyone—but also a number of rather antiquated yet imposing commodities. *Ego sum qui sum* had been the first statement of the divine, which now had to find a new home. Feuerbach would not have dared, would not have known how to venture this far; but it is from this very point that Stirner sets forth, with morbid consistency. The fact that the whole *Einzige* is primarily an immense tautology (and a mocking aberration at that—a tautology constructed with all the tools of dialectics) stems from the act of transposing the biblical *Ego sum qui sum* to the adult European of the nineteenth century. Here, too, we find proof of a certain ineptitude on the part of the progressive minds of the day. Those orators who were so hostile to religion believed that the religious was a collection of Virtues, and that the time had come to make a public park of them. They, of all people, were unable to accept the obvious: that the religious contains inexhaustible reserves of ambiguity and atrocity—more than enough to shatter the narrow secular psyches of the professors, engineers, lawyers, notaries, and public servants who wanted to appropriate it. And this indeed took place. Madmen would be born—ineffable, inexpressible, unique—supplied with prodigious power that was caged in ghostly bodies shaken by spasms. Teratology became tautology, and this engendered a feeling of exhilaration.

Why is the "unique" unique? Many of Stirner's readers have taken the term in its psychological sense: deploring it or exalting it, they assumed it referred to the preciousness of the ego. But first of all, the ego of the unique exists only as a negative and destructive power. On this point, Stirner deliberately severed relations with idealism just as sharply as Marx did. "When Fichte says, 'The ego is all,' this seems in perfect harmony with my positions. Yet the ego is not all; rather, the ego *destroys* all. And only the ego that dissolves itself, the ego that never is, the *finite* ego, is truly ego. Fichte speaks of the 'absolute' ego, but I speak of myself, of the perishable ego." Stirner's ego is the negation that produces and abolishes in rapid alternation, tending toward an impossible simultaneity. Those who read Stirner seeking confirmation of the substantiality of the subject will find, on the contrary, a deserted, silent hollow. Why "unique" then? Instead of Feuerbach's universal and "all-sided" Little Man (who was later bequeathed to Marx and since then has hovered over history), Stirner wanted to make the unique a hircocervus—a fabulous monster, half goat, half stag, that would evoke all the horror of fairy tales. The unique—disinherited and reduced to rags by a process that uses everything and lets only what is usable exist—is the delirium resulting from the fact that the pauper *takes the place of* the process that has reduced him to his state of poverty. This is, in fact, a pure substitution: the subject changes but the functioning is not impaired. The unique, too, uses everything and replaces everything. He does not succeed, however, in replacing the cipher of himself—his compulsion to behave in the same way as the process whose place he has taken. Similarly, the principle of substitution cannot change places with another principle. At the very center of the despotic regime of substitution, there is something that escapes it: the unique (the pauper-despot), who has become identified with the process itself. The process, like the unique, is irreplaceable. Ultimately, the regime of exchange clashes with itself as subject—and as a subject that cannot be exchanged, unique, immeasurable. This immensely productive paradox is the motor that hums constantly in our ears.

The Own and the Alien. If we wish to keep this awkward couple together, our best course would be to expunge one of its terms (the second, the bad one) in favor of the other. This is what Marx intended when he equated communism with the "destruction of alienness"—"with the communistic regulation of production and the destruction of alienness implicit in it." But this method was suspect from the very start. It entailed too much love for Society, that arrogant avatar of the Whole. Stirner—who was likewise inclined toward paranoia and brutality, but gaudy and crude forms of them—saw that among historical figures only God (and the despot who models himself on Him) manages to blur the distinction between own and alien. All is alien to him because it is not God; all is his own because God is "all in all." Why not apply the same criterion to the untethered, wandering ego that refused to find a place in Hegel's architecture? Like God, this ego would be the supreme egoist—the only egoist who could make his thing-cause (*Sache,* in German, means both) coincide with the whole, thus exceeding the usual limitations of the egoist, who can move only in his own dominions. But once the ego expands in this aberrant way, who would even think of the own and the alien, except as a remote recollection of the desks in a Berlin classroom? On the contrary, we are now approaching assimilation to "the most prostituted being of all" (as Baudelaire says)—namely, God, *"l'être par excellence,"* who, because of his love, never tires of going out of himself (*"sortir de soi"*) and cannot but go out into himself. Marx also foresaw this possibility: "General prostitution appears as a necessary stage in the development of the social nature of personal dispositions, abilities, capacities, and activities. Stated in gentler terms, it is the universal relationship between usefulness and use." Stirner takes this action to its extreme: let us use all as our own, and we will be used by all in all. Maximum ownership (all is our material) coexists with maximum alienness (we are material used by all); and both are intertwined with universal prostitution, many steps beyond Sade, still encumbered by feudal memories of sovereignty. In the good old days of Kant, distinctions between what was one's own and what was alien could still be decided according to statute. But now everything is simultaneously both—especially the ego, which demands that all be at its disposal, and which is at the disposal of all.

The blind rage that Marx directs at the *Lumpen* continues in his anger at unproductive workers. Maintaining with paleo-bourgeois zeal the distinction made by Adam Smith, Marx includes among such workers all the "rabble, from the whore to the pope." In the *Grundrisse,* the work that digs the grave for the whole majestic concept of productive labor (since it hypothesizes the phase we are approaching today, when the productive worker is ultimately transformed into "foreman and regulator of the productive process"), Marx's unshakable loyalty to the metaphysical structure of production—far more than to its historical manifestation—is apparent. It will drive him to rhetorical extremes when he defends Smith's distinction from servile economists who want to persuade the bourgeoisie "that it is productive labor if someone picks the lice off his head or strokes his penis, since the latter motion may enliven the blockhead the next day at the shop counter." Marx is concerned not only with a technical distinction, which is useful if you want to highlight the specificity of salaried labor ("a form that replaces the earth as the terrain upon which society rests"). Much more important, in his view, is to ally oneself with the process of capital in its murderous hostility toward the unproductive powers, who nevertheless embody the unmeasurable: sacrament, pleasure, sovereignty. And here, in the silent simultaneity of their monologuing notebooks, Baudelaire replies. Whereas Marx had lowered the sacrament to prostitution, Baudelaire elevates prostitution to a sacrament: "L'amour, c'est le goût de la prostitution" ("Love is a passion for prostitution").

Whore, Pope, *Lumpen:* it is this Trinity of prostitution that Baudelaire, too, was identifying. (He wrote his *Fusées* between 1855 and 1862; Marx's *Grundrisse* dates from 1857–1858.) In their sovereignty, they are all *vicars* of God: "L'être le plus prostitué, c'est l'être par excellence, c'est Dieu" ("The most prostituted being of all is the being par excellence—namely, God"). Since they rule only a certain part of the manifest world, they cannot attain the global and eternal prostitution that is the mark of the divine. Whether the *Lumpen* then present themselves as paupers, dandies, or poets makes little difference. They are, in any case, beings without dignity (if anything, they have majesty). What deprives them of dignity is precisely their contact with something extrasocial and self-sufficient, true *nefas:* pleasure, the invisible, the gratuitousness of art. (The writer belongs to the *Lumpen* as soon as he speaks of *l'art pour l'art*—art for art's sake. It is his insolent retort, in a cracked falsetto, to the power that has stripped him of authority. Since he no longer has a function and has been banished from Court, he spurns every function.)

❧

A *New* Frisson

Nerves and the Modern find their definitive voice in Baudelaire's notes (even though the Goncourts will later write, with shameless vanity, "We were the first to write about the nerves)." At a time when the German Romantics are still talking about ideas, Baudelaire blends theological asides with the smells of the streets, the nausea of manifestos, urban happenstance, itemizations of debts, and recipes using Icelandic lichens. It's as if a side-curtain were shockingly pulled aside to reveal the person, while on stage the same old performance continues. We glimpse his obsession with the names of newspaper editors, his "listes de canailles" ("lists of scoundrels"). Burke's sublime, the "delights of chaos and immensity," is now encamped at the crossroads, and at every step there are yawning chasms of the sort that visitors to Switzerland, on their Grand Tour, once made it a point to see. The individual walks under "the square sky of solitudes," through the prairies of the mind. At times "the voice of the adjective penetrated my bones."

Nerves first emerge as a historical subject with Baudelaire's generation. As if previously nerves weren't actually a part of the human body—didn't give those jolts, those shocks, that are now savored with alarm and delight. Here is the first sign that the network of the Body has become the ultimate abode of the Spirit—once resonant, then luminous, then all-enveloping, then aura-like, then vaporous, finally just nervous. And this transition to the body is inevitably accompanied by the urge to *experiment* on the body. But the Spirit cannot be an object of work and study unless it has some fixed location—a site that becomes the meeting point of all praxes, all aestheticisms (which are blueprints for huge industrial enterprises, the first blossoming of the imposing apparatus of the media, from the rooms of Huysmans' Des Esseintes to the palace courtyards of

Cecil B. De Mille), all positive sciences, all organizations, all peda-
gogies. The new thought of the age converges toward a single point:
henceforth, people don't want to *have a certain kind of thought;* they
want to *act on all thought,* and then evaluate the thought that emerges.
The most convincing action will supposedly be the most effective.
And for that very reason, the most effective action will be considered
a consequence of right thought, just because it is effective.

In December 1861, the treacherous Sainte-Beuve advised Baudelaire
to write a letter in which he would formally seek nomination to the
Académie. It was to be addressed to the current Secrétaire Perpétuel
de l'Académie Française, Abel Villemain, who by virtue of his position was the perfect embodiment of Baudelaire's notion of stupidity,
or *la Sottise* ("I have a passion for *la Sottise*"). Baudelaire wrote the
letter amid much agitation and with many double meanings. ("To
tell the truth, I'm soliciting your votes now primarily because if I
decided to wait and solicit them only when I felt worthy, I would
never solicit them." Note the "grammatical dance," in which the verb
solicit occurs three times in one sentence.) When Baudelaire paid
the obligatory call on Vigny, one of the Forty, the latter shook his
big aristocratic head. It was a *faux pas,* he declared, unforgivable. All
too often he had heard his colleagues whisper, "We'll make that
fellow bow and scrape, and then we won't appoint him." Meanwhile
he made a mental note: "Baudelaire seems of no literary consequence,
except as the translator of that philosophical novelist [Poe]. Has the
distinguished, suffering look of a studious and diligent man." But
Baudelaire still had to see the enormous Villemain, *enormis loquaci-
tas:* "The hatred of a *mediocre* person is always an *immense* hatred."
He listened as the man lectured him "with indescribable solemnity"
about *Les Paradis artificiels:* "La Toxicologie, Monsieur, n'est pas la
Morale!" ("Toxicology, my dear Sir, is not Morals!"). In masterly fashion, Baudelaire transcribed the sentence inserting two harsh capital
letters. Ever childish, he said to himself, "I'll make him pay dearly
for this." They took leave of each other with the following words:
"*Villemain, insisting:* 'I have never had the slightest originality, Monsieur.' *Baudelaire, insinuating:* 'Monsieur, how would you know?'"

Uno Harva (Holmberg)

"The act of pouring or sprinkling fermented mare's milk on the back of the sacrificial animal recalls a custom followed in the Volga region. Water is poured on the victim, to see if the sacrifice pleases. The animal's shudder indicates a positive reply. At least, it is said that the Yellow Uigurs do this. On the back of the sacrificial lamb, they customarily pour 'white water' (*ak su*)—that is, water mixed with milk—and the shudder it provokes is considered proof that the sacrifice is pleasing to the god. Furthermore, the Mongolians have a word, borrowed from the Chinese, that denotes the act of pouring brandy or water in the ears of a sacrificial pig. So we see that they, too, observe a similar custom."

Karl Meuli

"'Shake yourself promptly!' Aristophanes' Trygaeus cries to his sacrificial ewe. That is, she must give her consent by nodding her head. The Delphic god had said it quite clearly to Euscopos: only a sheep that spontaneously consents can be a proper sacrifice. Even in Plutarch's time, this rule was still scrupulously observed; Daphnis, for example, pours milk and wine on the head of his sacrificial animals, as was done to obtain the required sign of assent. Water could also be poured into the victim's ear. For sacrifices at Delphi, a shake of the head was not enough: the animal had to shudder, so that the Pythia could utter the prophecy."

Baudelaire: "The sacrifice is complete only with the *sponte sua* of the victim."

"[Baudelaire] was also proud of this sentence, which had been written to him by a great poet: 'You have endowed the sky of art with a kind of macabre light—you have created a new *frisson.*'" Baudelaire was proud of those words not only because they had been written by Hugo (about whom he harbored no illusions: "He woos everyone, and *treats as a poet* anyone who comes along"), but because they were *those* words: the "new shudder" was the *nouveau* which "au fond de l'Inconnu" ("at the bottom of the Unknown") encountered the shudder—hence the most ancient, the too familiar (and therefore effaced), memory of sacrifice. After that, the encounter is repeated every day, like the sudden irruption of leopards into the temple: "In the end it can be foreseen and becomes a part of the ceremony."

❧

Behind the Windowpane

Max Ophuls tried to make it understood with multiple references in his shots: a grille, a pane of glass, a half-drawn blind, a lace curtain, a drapery that the lens skims over. Or perhaps simply a jumble of objects that distance and encircle the characters. Or even the vast fringe of darkness enfolding them. Later, in an impromptu talk on the radio, he finally referred to the text that gives the most concise definition of the film image: "The person who looks in through an open window never sees all the things that are seen by someone who looks in through a closed window. There is no object more profound, more mysterious, more fertile, more tenebrous, more dazzling than a window illuminated by a candle. What one sees in the sunlight is always less interesting than what happens behind a windowpane." This is the tone of Baudelaire, but also of Ophuls, his cinematic heir. The screen image appears in an age when mental images tend to invade the streets and change into brute perceptions, acceptable to any empiricist. In the course of this invasion, some are caught on the screen—and there they live on, leading a double life. Their esotericism, the foundation of great cinema, wants to keep them in contact both with their mental origin and with their final release into the streets. The latter process is represented by Baudelaire's "open window," by the illusion of a continuity between inside and outside, of a life that is rediscovered intact in two dimensions. But the other path, which returns to the origin, leads from the screen image back to the mental image, hence to the image "behind a windowpane," which appears to "someone who looks in through a closed window." The "windowpane" of the mind can be the surface of a mirror or the transparency of lace or the frame provided by the objects and the darkness: all signals of an imperceptible, unbridgeable distance between the world and its reflection, between the two perpetual sources of imagery. "Behind the windowpane," the light emanating from persons and things is no longer a light of nature but the radiance of the surface itself: the radiance of Psyche.

Meanwhile, "the illness of which Flaubert died has still not been analyzed." In Berlin, Laforgue circled around this point, as his voice, skipping impertinent passages here and there, traversed the pages that the empress Augusta asked him to read. He gracefully accepted his role as slightly chlorotic lady-in-waiting, guardian of ennui like "the clock in a deserted railway station." But in his physiology the great philosophical terms, always high-sounding (Will! Renunciation! Schopenhauer! Hartmann!), underwent a rich mutation, degenerating into illustrations from a biological atlas. The concepts huddled quietly behind a sheet of glass, no longer turned toward the Platonic Plain of Truth but suspended in the Berlin aquarium. "Confronting the dull, sated, wise, Buddhist gaze of the crocodiles, the pythons (the ophidians), etc. How well I understand those old races of the Orient who had worn out all meanings, all temperaments, all metaphysics." And there was something that went even further: "The ideal is these sponges, these starfish, these plasmas in the cool, opaque, utterly dreamlike silence of water." It was the piano of Debussy covering a now exhausted thought, corroding it beneath its layer of sound.

⋙⋘

In that "critical age in which some turn to the ironic and the acerbic, others to the insipid and the cloying, and others still to the vulgar," in this first official age of the bourgeoisie, the years of Louis-Philippe and of disillusion, a curtain edged in black, though still transparent, descends to separate the present from the past. The present, true, is a bit intimidating, if for no other reason than because it is big, massive; but it no longer has the aesthetic decorum of history. A new dimension of dreariness is born. For the first time, delicate individuals are assailed by the presentiment that the world around them might be definitively ugly. History, on the other hand, as some insinuate, means scenery, costumes, and overwhelming passions. And at this point, every historian tends unwittingly to transform himself into a Ludwig II of Bavaria in disguise, speaking aloud with the Names in the archives. Spiritualism, after 1848, becomes a basis for even the most rigorous studies. Until a historian of today, Robert Darnton, recognizes in that tendency, as if it were something obvious, the special vocation of his discipline: "The reconstruction of worlds is one of the historian's most important tasks. He undertakes it, not from some strange urge to dig up archives and sift through old paper, but because he wants to talk with the dead."

After the fall of Napoleon an insidious, imprudent feeling begins to spread: that passions, great gestures, and the soul's abiding tensions henceforth belong to the stage or to the past, and no longer to the events of the day. A profound sense of inadequacy and a vague tinge of the mediocre now seem to accompany every apparition like a tax. And so every feverish Julien Sorel daydreams about the battles of Napoleon as the definitive picture of the past, and every Joseph Delorme will nourish his hypochondria on the repudiation of the present. A new breed of beings is concerned primarily with eliminating every one of its surfaces that adheres to the world. To sever bonds, to estrange the heart—in short, to sabotage. From the dandy to the nihilist conspirator, to the young Barrès, to the esotericist white or black, to Louis II, to the fugitive who seeks the Orient, between spleen and bitterness, silent exaltation and heightened perception, solitary points appear on all sides, faint lights that make up the constellation of contempt: these are the Pléiades of Gobineau, the calenders, wandering dervishes who tell interconnected tales, kings' sons who are often born in little apartments and at times are disfigured by fate. They meet at the table of an inn, on their restless Grand Tour, and the exchange of a few sentences is enough to alert them: perhaps that stranger whom they have just met, that artist who does not let his hair fall to his shoulders, who dresses like everyone else, who naturally obeys the dictates of good manners, whose outer appearance makes no claims—perhaps he, too, is a king's son. So it happened, Gobineau tells us, that Conrad Lanze met Wilfrid Ore on the Arona boat, after climbing the Saint Gotthard amid dust and rhododendrons with Louis de Laudon, whom he had met two weeks before in Zurich, where they "had immediately become fond of each other."

If we really must find a distinction between what can be said of the Modern and everything that we encounter in previous ages, might it not perhaps be a certain ability to let oneself be carried away by form or gesture, and to ignore limitations even when explicitly defending them—to invade every off-limits area, perhaps on the pretext of guarding it against all violations? Why does Joseph de Maistre seem to us so close to his hated Voltaire? Why does Pascal converse so fraternally with the most unbelieving moralists? It is a certain way of *not looking to the consequences,* of acting on the impulse—and with the pleasure—of a haphazard, rapacious, heedless movement: *eris palpans in meridie.*

Sainte-Beuve achieved his even-tempered and balanced tone at the cost of a continual surfeit of the black humors in his system: his capillaries became poisonous corals. Severed, they are found in the *Cahier vert* that Sainte-Beuve hoped would fall "only into friendly hands" (though so far it has fallen only into indifferent hands). Few have noticed how he used the "darkest part of the palette, very black and very thick," which also served to preserve the sort of gossip that could not be published, *par bienséance,* and to congeal some clots of a confession that could never have been dissolved in speech, likewise *par bienséance.* In compensation, those isolated words conceal in their laconic spareness a pathos that suspends them in the void, or against the background of his "arsenal of vendettas," like the spare chapters of the only novel Sainte-Beuve ever wrote: The Cautious Journey of a Delicate Soul toward Desolation:

"All my organs have become so decayed and are, so to speak, in such a *threadbare* state, that I cannot press on any of them."

"Lately, rereading Theocritus, I felt *my pastoral soul* stirring again within me, that soul of the golden age which so many layers of bronze, earth, and lead have covered."

.   .   .

"Our heart has all the skins of the snake—seven double folds, like impenetrable shields."

"I was a petty thief as a youth; as an old man, I shall be a pirate. Oh, how I would have preferred to be a good literary gentleman, living on his estate as a poet!"

"No corruption is worse than that of soft-hearted people and mystics."

"I am the vainest and weakest of beings, and my combined weaknesses are precisely what gives me the air of a wise man: they all undo one another."

"Living in an immense city, in a century of corruption and overweening ambition, amid a literature of insatiable pretentions, unspeakable vices, offenses to decency, and widespread filth, I have worked from the beginning to cultivate within myself, to the greatest extent possible, the faculty of contempt.

"Having done this, after a while one needn't think about it any longer; one has already moved on to indifference."

"Why have I ceased to love nature, the countryside? Why have I ceased to love strolling along little paths? I'm well aware that they are unchanged, but now *there is no longer anything beyond the hedge.*"

On September 7, 1847, Sainte-Beuve wrote to Collombet: "Chateaubriand is more silent than ever: he lives in a dream. His fine mouth still smiles, his eyes weep, his broad brow in repose has all its majesty. But what is inside and underneath? Is anything there?"

Madame Récamier, after an unsuccessful cataract operation, was now almost blind, and lived in darkness. Outside: the barricades of 1848, the abdication of Louis-Philippe, the Republic proclaimed. The visitor groped his way along as he entered the great drawing room of the Abbaye-aux-Bois, where for years the furniture had stood in geometric and hierarchical patterns. The shutters were closed, the curtains drawn. From the door, a shaft of light penetrated the gloom, but it was too dim to guide the visitor's steps. Madame Récamier's voice had to come to his aid, suggesting that he proceed toward the great screen that concealed her armchair. Chateaubriand sat beside her, unalterably taciturn.

❦

Bien-Aimé

Louis XV knew from the start that he was a "roi de perdition" (a "king of perdition"), no matter what he did. And this knowledge gave him the harsh, cold intolerance which trembling courtiers perceived in him when he was still a child. His most primal emotion, even more than boredom, was vexation: vexation at finding himself at one of those points where the pincers of history are on the verge of closing and allow no play whatsoever. It was as if his existence had run its entire course even before he lived it. He felt that he could not have been other than dissolute, inert, scornful. And that even if his will had attempted to rebel, it would have been destroyed and no one would have been surprised, just as it was his lot to destroy, to no one's surprise, the privileged position of certain of his subjects.

Madame du Hausset records that laughing was painful for him: at most he made an effort to smile. And that smile meant: we grant you everything, provided you do not demand our attention. With grim pedantry, which effaced his natural elegance, he would repeat the same stories over and over, never finding anyone willing to tell him how boring he was. People have credited him with many rather banal witticisms and have praised their cleverness, whereas they cite some of his most devastatingly lucid statements as evidence of his obvious unworthiness. He was obsessed by "les rois fainéants" ("the idle kings"); and Cardinal Fleury, who forced him to remain inactive yet exhorted him to maintain a certain façade of activity, once committed the imprudence of speaking to him on the subject. "One day I went so far as to tell His Majesty that kings had been dethroned in France for their idleness. It seemed to affect him deeply. He made no reply; but two days later he remarked to me, 'I've been thinking about what you said concerning some of my predecessors who were deposed. Pray tell me: When the nation deposed them, were they allotted large pensions?'"

". . . he appeared at the far end of Versailles' little suites like a large and sullen and mournful child, with something in his spirit that was arid, spiteful, sarcastic . . ."

The Parc aux Cerfs, whose very name invited resentful subjects to dream of endless and cloistered wantonness, was "a rather modest house with a tiny garden, bounded by the rue des Tournelles (a cul-de-sac) and the rue Saint-Médéric. It comprised four bedrooms and some small sitting rooms, and could house at most two or three women; indeed, it seemed made to accommodate only one." The house bore that name because it was located in an area on the outskirts of Versailles where, in the days of Louis XIII, there had been a park containing wild animals. It was inhabited not by thousands of full-breasted *gopī* (cowherd girls) pining for Krishna but by one or two girls at a time, ever prepared for the visits of an unknown nobleman who sometimes passed for a Polish gentleman and who forgot to take off his cordon bleu. And every now and then, for a few months, the house was empty. It was there that absolutist whim finally laid the foundations of a very bourgeois institution: the kept woman. Even Madame de Pompadour, who supervised those pleasures and later dealt with childbirths and pensions, did not fail to coin a regulatory maxim for countless future ménages of lower rank: "It is his heart I'm after." As for the rest, she gave it up with relief. She would never again have to eat chocolate with triple vanilla and truffles every day for breakfast, to rouse her "exceedingly cold temperament," since "men, as you well know, attach great importance to certain things."

Louis XIV says, "L'Etat, c'est moi" ("I am the State"). A courtier says to Louis XV, "Tout cela est à vous" ("All this is yours"). This is Villeroy's satanic statement, which Hugo singled out in *La Pitié suprême* to establish the motif of the dour compulsion toward omnipotence. It's when he grows tired of verses like "Sanche! Alonze! Clovis! Sennachérib! Cambyse!" that Hugo succeeds in defining the chronic state of Louis XV as none of the king's contemporaries had been able to: "Une stupide joie avec un vaste ennui" ("A stupid joy and a vast boredom"). Only Louis XV's enemy, his opposite, had unresentful words for him on the king's death, when even the coffin could not properly contain the pestilential remains, which were hastily and unceremoniously transported to Reims at night, to the accompaniment of jests and pranks. Only Frederick the Great managed to state, in a letter to Voltaire, what was sadly obvious: that the doomed man was *un honnête homme* whose sole fault was that he was king. With sorrowful urbanity, the Cardinal de Bernis had written something similar in a letter that is a threnody for the Seven Years War: "I love the king, and I grieve for him with all my heart. An *honnête homme* capable of friendship and desiring only good, he allows evil to be fomented and to cloud the splendor of a reign that could have been glorious and peaceful."

"Every dynasty comes to an end with a king who neglects governing and devotes himself to licentiousness. Nature announces his ruin through inauspicious omens (such as comets, double suns, earthquakes, floods, diseases). In China, as we know, it is through the people that Heaven reveals its determination to withdraw its mandate (*ming*) from the ruling monarch (revolution, songs of inspired youths). The king's debaucheries are not, however, simply an expression of immoral impulses. They express his desire to seize for his own profit all possessions, all power . . .

"The 'rois de perdition,' in their arrogance, wanted to touch Heaven by building nine-storey towers, but also by digging deep shafts. Their behavior can be understood as an extreme exaggeration of a morality of normal celebration (one thinks of the peasantry's winter drinking bouts). What is wrong is not the act itself, but its immoderateness. It consists of doing always and to excess what can and must be done only at certain times."

We shall never with certainty know much about his licentiousness, just as we shall never with certainty know much about his childish games. But one account tells us that, when he was seven, his courtiers entertained him by filling a vast hall with sparrows and then suddenly releasing some hawks, which mutilated the little birds with their sharp beaks. According to another account, "The king had a white fawn that, since he had fed and raised her himself, would eat only from his hand and loved him very much. He had her taken to La Muette and said he wanted to kill her. He chased her off, fired at her, and wounded her. The fawn dragged herself toward him and nuzzled him. He again had her placed at a distance, shot at her a second time, and killed her. The act seemed very cruel. Other, similar stories are told about him, concerning some birds he keeps at Passy."

In politics, Louis XV had one constant objective: to conspire against his own government. He is the first king to have chosen to act as his own agent provocateur. The Secret du Roi was a form of "parallel" policy that often ensnared and strangled Louis XV in his own secrecy. The Duc de Broglie, who was the first to try to reconstruct this vain high-wire act, a novel of multiple deceits, recalls a typical moment. In 1773, Louis XV, plotting behind the scenes with Sweden, "achieved a state of complete satisfaction: dealing with a matter that was half diplomatic and half military, he succeeded in hiding one part from his minister of war, the other part from his minister of foreign affairs—and the whole, finally, from the usual confidant of his secret policy. Three mysteries were furthered simultaneously, none related to the others. This was the crowning achievement of his system and a masterpiece of its type." Then, when Louis XV managed to deceive even his secret confidants by partly tipping his hand to his ministers, who had always served as his dupes, a sort of paralyzing peace gently touched him. All external objectives dissolved as he revealed the game that forced him to risk everything and always gamble against himself, and hence to betray even the traitors he had chosen. The conspiracies, overlapping one another, were neutralized—leaving the useless sovereign at the center, alone. Whether he studiedly avoided action like a hypochondriac or, on the contrary, feverishly devised secret maneuvers, in any case his every act was damned at its origin, which rendered it futile.

Among the bastard children of Louis XV, the son of Mademoiselle de Romans was privileged to have an allusive name. On a certain

December day, the king dispatched from Versailles one of his rare personal notes, which has since passed through the hands of many collectors: "I was well aware, *ma grande,* that when you left, you had something in your head, but I could not guess exactly what it was. I do not want our son to be given my name on the baptismal certificate, but neither do I wish to make it impossible for me to acknowledge him in a few years' time, if it pleases me to do so. I should like, therefore, for the certificate to show the child's name as Louis Aimé or Louise Aimée, son or daughter of Louis le Roy or of Louis Bourbon, whichever you prefer . . . I also want the godfather and the godmother to be poor folk, or servants; other sorts of people will not be considered."

"Ma grande" Louis XV called her, because in Mademoiselle de Romans (according to the penetrating eye of Sophie Arnould) "nature, abandoning her own rules of good taste, had amused herself by creating a great exaggeration. Mademoiselle de Romans was well made, and everything about her was perfectly proportioned, but that perfection was colossal . . . Next to her the king himself, though a very handsome man, looked like a schoolboy or a half-king." Too often Louis XV went to visit her in Passy, and too often he sent a carriage with six horses to fetch her. Choiseul was beginning to worry about the possible political consequences, and Madame de Pompadour was alarmed. Only the Maréchale de Mirepoix could find words to reassure her: "I am not going to tell you that he loves you more than her; and if at the wave of a magic wand she were transported here and dined with us this evening and all were aware of her tastes, perhaps you would have some cause for worry. But princes are, first of all, men of habit. The king's affection for you is the same that he has for your private rooms, for all that surrounds you. You are suited to his ways; you know all about him. He never feels any embarrassment with you, is never afraid of boring you. How could he have the courage to uproot all this in a single day, to rearrange his life so thoroughly, and make a public spectacle of himself by altering the décor to such an extent?" But fear was mingled with curiosity: after the bastard's birth, it was said that Mademoiselle de Romans went to the Bois de Boulogne covered in lace, with the infant in a wicker basket, and nursed him there, sitting by a secluded path. One day Madame de Pompadour, making the faithful Madame du

Hausset walk ahead of her and concealing her own face with her bonnet and with a handkerchief she held to her mouth, pretended to be casually strolling along that path in the Bois. Mademoiselle de Romans was nursing the baby; she had drawn back her jet-black hair and fastened it with a diamond-studded comb. Madame de Hausset approached and said, "'What a pretty child!' 'Yes,' she replied, 'I can say so myself, though I am the mother.' Madame, who was clinging to my arm, trembled, and I did not feel very sure of myself. Mademoiselle de Romans asked me, 'Do you live nearby?' 'Yes, Madame,' I answered. 'I live at Auteuil with this lady, who at the moment has a terrible toothache.' 'Ah, I feel very sorry for her; it's an ailment that I, too, have often suffered.'"

The king soon grew weary. His archers came to take away the child, who was to be raised far from his mother. There were many letters, querulous and insinuating, from the mistress fallen out of favor. But at Versailles, long before Hollywood, Busby Berkeley's maxim was à propos: "There's no comeback for a has-been." All the mother could do was await the son's future: when Louis XV died, she sent the new king her son's baptismal certificate—and the fourteen-year-old Abbé de Bourbon was received at Court. His figure reminded many of the slender and well-proportioned physique of Louis XV. While waiting for appointment to some rich abbey, the bastard was sent to Rome to Cardinal de Bernis, the last of the four great cardinals who for a time had governed France. Now, in his palace on the Corso, he welcomed visiting French noblemen. He lodged the Abbé de Bourbon with attentiveness, with affection, with that "mixture of geniality, refinement, nobility, and simplicity" which made Madame de Genlis declare him "the most agreeable man I have ever known." But in Paris they had already begun to forget the young abbot of royal blood. There was no further talk of abbeys—and they neglected to send him money. He wandered around Italy. Bernis, his last patron, complained, "He is the Wandering Jew. It pains me to see a man with such a name roaming idly from one Italian inn to another. Either he should have been forbidden to bear an illustrious name or that name should be respected in his person. I confess that in this matter, as in some others, my ideas are somewhat old-fashioned; but then, I myself am old-fashioned." The Abbé de Bourbon died in Naples, of chicken pox, during his aimless wanderings.

Some time afterward, Madame Louise, a Carmelite nun and the Abbé de Bourbon's half-sister, told how she had met the Abbé Turlot, who had looked after the abbot on his deathbed: "The other day we talked again about the poor Abbé de Bourbon . . . So the world goes: he has been dead for six months and no one gives a thought to him anymore. I should so like to have a little epitaph composed for him, if only to remind people that he existed. I must speak to someone about it." Less than a year later Madame Louise herself died, and her plan came to nothing.

❧

For a long time images were part of a cosmic liturgy which followed the sun in its course through the Zodiac. And for a short time they inhabited the ceremonies that accompanied the sun of sovereignty. Having descended from the heavens, they settled in one of Versailles' mezzanines. There they remained, often abandoned, like a tiresome country cousin who talks about people no one has ever heard of. They were dislodged from that humiliating segregation the moment the revolutionary mob began rioting. Some ended up on pikes; others were exalted in Egyptian rituals. It was not clear whether everything was tending toward triumph or toward persecution. In fact, the movement was toward both—but there was no longer any *templum*. With the belt of the Zodiac now undone, each image wandered through ever vaster cities, forgetting its tribe, ready to let itself be lured and looted everywhere: in drawing rooms and abbeys, in pressrooms and satanic mills, in ruins, American forests, suburbs. A new life, uncontrolled, clandestine, and contagious, was beginning for them. For years they met at the crossroads of the mind, and at times recognized a certain family resemblance, the imprint of a shared past. But no sooner had they paused than a violent gust would drive them on, down other alleyways, in ceaseless migration.

> We used to smile at the shorn hedges,
> at the curved Chinese roofs,
> at the porcelain curls,
> at the silk trains;
> yet in moments

of empty weariness,
raising a hand to our head,
we felt something missing there:
a dusty wig.

(For a long time it had not been clear what belonged to the *templum* and what did not. A perpetual grumbling came from the most recent centuries, from that unique and by then immense *fin de siècle* that had begun with the libertine aridity and the already criminal recklessness of the Régence or—if we want an earlier cosmic background—with the "untuned" heaven of Donne and the forsaken "degrees" lamented by Ulysses in *Troilus and Cressida,* a *fin de siècle* perhaps now on the brink of its ultimate end. A breath of modernity ready to disperse. It was hard to circumscribe that grumbling, to find a frame sufficiently polite and well designed, and yet not too visible, as a frame must be, but made of a substance that might then be revealed, to the lingering eye, as a pigment of the painting itself. At this point, Talleyrand appeared. Had not Brichot said, in the class-rooms of the Verdurin salon, that he had been the first of the *fin de siècle?* Talleyrand offered another advantage as well: that of having not ideas or, still less, opinions, but an obscure, murky residue of the knowledge which only "hints.")

᪥

A Visit to Picpus Cemetery

The rest home for single ladies, which was managed by nuns devoted to the perpetual adoration of the Sacred Heart, was not far from the Rothschild hospital, where the outskirts of Paris woo the wasteland. In the courtyard, the Brother and Sister were sitting on a wooden bench. The considerate Brother was paying a visit to his Sister, a guest at the home. Above her melancholy, somewhat prominent eyes, her hair was still done in the style of a mannish spinster, while around her wrists and her neck some surviving family jewels defended the dignity of the lady *en retraite*. The Brother was waiting for the right moment to talk about bills and receipts. From his pocket he produced a case for rings, which was empty. He handed it to his Sister; perhaps she had some use for it. Slowly, his Sister ran her finger over the silk lining. "It's well preserved," she said. But they had to pretend to talk of other things, too. They were sitting on the bench waiting for the gatekeeper, who guided small groups of visitors through the cemetery of the "Victims of the Revolution," just beyond the gate of the rest home.

"Who owns the cemetery?" the Brother asked.

"The Société Immobilière et Civile de l'Oratoire du Cimetière de Picpus," his Sister said. "They're the heirs of the victims, and the only ones who can be buried in the cemetery. They're the families of the aristocracy."

"But aren't people other than aristocrats buried there? While I was waiting, I went into the chapel and looked at the list of those who lie in the communal graves. The victims seem to have come from all walks of life. Merchants, lawyers, commoners . . ."

"Ah, yes. By then, they had done away with almost all the aristocrats . . ."

"There must have been a lot of settling of scores—jealousies, denunciations, and so on."

"They took them from the Nation in wagons. There are one thousand three hundred and six."

"At the end of the war, too, there must have been a lot of settling of scores, a lot of jealousies and denunciations. By that time, they just killed them and said no more about it."

A lady from the rest home interrupted them.

"Oppressive weather today. So sultry."

"Yes, it's been stifling for two days," the Sister said.

"It's nice to receive visits."

"My brother . . ."

"I have a sister myself. But she only comes when it suits her."

There was a tremulous smile on the Brother's moist pink face, which was darkened by gray shadows. He had not shaved carefully. His suit, too heavy, was of the kind that is no longer sold in shops.

"Brothers are better than sisters," he said. "Because they concern themselves with solving practical problems and try to help when they can."

Another waiting visitor sat down on the bench, a frail little old man wearing a light-colored cloth cap. Smiling, he bared his long, yellow teeth; there were only three of them, widely spaced. For several years he had been visiting the historic sites of Paris, and on that oppressive August day it was the turn of Picpus cemetery. He had no interest in beauty; his only concern was history.

"I'm for history, one hundred percent," he would repeat whenever possible. Cemeteries and plaques were history and nothing but history, and thus he was in favor of them. At the end of the tour, the gatekeeper, a dour homesteader from Algeria who had been driven from his land and who often confused his lost Africa with the ancien régime, devoted a few words to the sixteen Carmelites of Compiègne who had died for their faith on July 17, 1794. He also mentioned the books of Lenotre, which were on display in the porter's lodge for anyone who wished to purchase a memento. Then for the first time the little old man addressed the Brother: "But we mustn't forget that the Carmelites were the curés' whores. And so . . ."

For a moment there was a Jacobin glint in his sharp eyes. The Brother smiled, knowingly. But his Sister was already urging him to follow her toward a gate that led to the rest home's garden. Shortly afterward, the group broke up.

༄

The symbol, for us, is continually submerged and exposed by the "mnemic wave." During the Enlightenment it was relegated to secret societies and ceremonies, between Cagliostro and Sarastro; but with the advent of German Romanticism, it starts to shake off this confinement. Friedrich Creuzer mentions the Cabiri. The first great antiquarian of archetypes lists them in Part Two of *Faust*. Johann Jakob Bachofen speaks of swamps and graves. In academic publications, the ones naïve littérateurs consider most remote from life's delicate substance, scholars accumulate materials that seethe with life, compiling thousands and thousands of myths, rituals, and fairy tales in just a few years. Then comes an explosion of interpretation. New schools of thought clash with one another: the Solars, the Lunars, the Astrals, the Diffusionists, the Evolutionists, the Tellurics. Like proliferating tribes, they find their chiefs, their witch doctors, their victims. They dream of tortuous migration routes, rebirths from Blood and Earth, descents from the Astral Bodies, totemic university chairs, skeleton keys. They are shaken by salutary upheavals; they speak in the name of science. A renowned authority on ghosts, C. G. Jung, understands, with his Swiss shrewdness, that whatever he may do he should never give up speaking in the name of science. Yet there *is* no science. In private, Jung writes gnostic apocrypha, which he will analyze in public as psychotic documents. In public, he analyzes psychotic documents, restoring them to academia's vast library—still virtually unknown to anyone who is not at least a university assistant or an independent scholar—where the myths, rituals, and fairy tales have been amassed. He establishes links; he verifies (wants to verify) correspondences and coincidences. He records everything, in the name of science. He has found the *laissez-passer* that will allow him to survive: every few pages, he says that the entire forest of the past is a "psychological reality." And what is God, what are all the gods, if not a "psychological reality"? By this crude device, Jung smuggled hundreds of myths and images out of the university libraries, conveying them into the minds of his patients and his readers. But this was merely a convenient ploy. In its exoteric aspect, it was the *laissez-passer* that the world needed. In its esoteric aspect, it said something that once again separated the symbol from the word: as "psychological reality," the symbol was connected with a *state of consciousness*. And states of consciousness could no longer be turned into, reduced to, transparent meanings. A state of consciousness can relate to language, but it cannot be replaced by language. Thus, along this dubious path, the symbol was returning to life, was once again breathing.

"Industry penetrates the dream and shapes it to its image, all the while becoming as fantastic as the dream itself." Sainte-Beuve wrote this in 1839, commenting on the new phenomenon known as "industrial literature." Images were now being revealed as a new object of production: advertising, the novel, and the visions of cranks who wanted to obtain patents for new inventions were growing simultaneously, all obeying the same impulse. (The new form of the novel was in fact a result of the confluence of the "novel for maidservants" and the "genteel novel," the latter of which was striving to elevate itself to the "honor of the three sous" claimed by Stendhal. When there were so many avid readers, "directors of lending libraries cut every volume of a novel in two, and rent each half for three sous a day.") Just as in the old days the fertile earth had nourished the social body with its inherent productivity, so now the movements of images left to their own devices created an invisible perpetual motion, the unceasing hum of the city. But the mutation of images accompanied an equally radical mutation of industry; the experimental sphere of industry now comprised the entire psyche, before the psyche itself was even named. By a process of osmosis with that new psychic material, industry was assimilated to the "dream." The neat plates of the *Encyclopédie* were no longer enough. Behind every artisan's workshop a camera obscura now opened, ready to enfold all society in a shadowland that is never troubled by crises of overproduction.

∽✤↶

The Organization Wouldn't Like It

The most recently devised and most frequently used form of the death sentence is precisely this sentence: "The organization wouldn't like it." It expresses perfect ideological neutrality. From Hollywood's film noir to the Lubyanka to the old Mediterranean mafia, all "organizations" agree when it comes to this succinct phrase.

"Organization": we encounter this menacing word on all sides, at both the top and the bottom of the ladder. It has become *the* metaphysical word—or rather, it is the word into which all metaphysics appears to have migrated, like a family of decayed aristocrats who now occupy a three-room apartment in a housing project. Yet from that squalid vantage point, they seem to wield a power they have never before enjoyed.

For centuries, societies have been organized—but, as it were, haven't realized it. They spoke of other things, perhaps; they spoke of order. And now a chasm has opened up between order and organization. The latter is born when all traces of order have been lost, or when order survives as a mere will-o'-the-wisp. Organization is always based on itself, on nothing, on pure operation. Order is always based on another order, of which it is the image, the visible twin.

At the origin of organization: the conspiracy.
At the origin of the conspiracy: the secret society.
At the origin of the secret society: initiation.
At the origin of initiation: the origin.

The Italian Quattrocento, forced to seek some sort of equilibrium because of the constant friction among its overly confined city-states, prefigures the subsequent history of Europe—a history in which Italy would no longer play a part, except as an instrument. Machiavelli was born at the center of that vast workshop in which the new notion of equilibrium was being tested, and this is why he is so far ahead of other Europeans. With the advent of the Reformation, and hence with the disavowal of the hierarchic principle (Church *and* Empire), equilibrium—the equivalent of *pax* in a sphere dominated by pure play and interacting forces—becomes the sole remaining criterion of reference. The political theory of the seventeenth century will be devoted primarily to absorbing the immense and brutal novelty behind that noble euphemism: the equilibrium which could almost be seen as a secularization of the *harmonia mundi*. Inspired by this secular rage, let us turn to the gentle Archbishop Fénelon for a mild yet merciless statement of why such equilibrium is necessary:

"Not only are neighboring states compelled to deal with each other reciprocally according to the rules of justice and good faith; but, for the sake of their private security and the common interest, they must also construct a kind of society and general republic.

"We should acknowledge the fact that, in the long run, the greatest power always dominates and overturns the others, if the others do not unite to act as a counterweight. People cannot hope that a superior power will remain within the confines of careful modera-tion, or that, from a position of strength, it will desire only as much as it could obtain from a position of weakness. Even if a prince were enough of a paragon to make such admirable use of his prosperity, this wondrous situation would come to an end with his reign. The natural ambition of sovereigns, the flattery of advisers, and the prejudice of entire nations prevent us from ever believing that a nation capable of subjugating others would refrain from doing so for whole centuries. A kingdom that could boast of such extraordinary justice would be an ornament to history and a marvel whose like we would never see again."

This is a billowing European gloss on a passage by Thucydides: "We believe by tradition so far as the gods are concerned, and see by experience so far as mankind is concerned, that, according to a law of nature, everyone inevitably exploits all the power at his disposal."

Civil war, "the worst kind of war," marks the beginning and the end of the modern era. The vengeful, mocking epiphany of the god Terminus, it suddenly puts a limit on what had claimed to be the negation of limits. The modern age is magnificent when it submits a truth claim to relentless criticism and then, as a result of that criticism, withdraws the claim. The modern age is murderous, and immensely effective as such, when it claims to have discovered a truth. Carl Schmitt has definitively shown that when people were striving to escape the fury of the wars of religion, the act that saved them all was their renunciation of the *justum bellum*. The delicate transition from the *justa causa belli* to the *justus hostis* thus ensured that, "amazingly, for two hundred years, there has been no war of annihilation on European soil." In that brief period the *jus publicum Europaeum* was combined with the modern state—the *machina machinarum,* the "first modern machine and the concrete premise of all other technical machines." Then *la guerre en forme,* war according to a set of rules—that cruel game which was nevertheless redeemed by the severity of its rules—conferred a new unity on a certain spatial sphere (a certain part of Europe) and made it coincide with the locus of civilization itself. But the game broke down from inside: in August 1914 Europe embarked on a war which seemed like many other dynastic disputes yet which immediately proved to be the first technical war, meaning that by its very nature it could never be a *guerre en forme.* Thus also emerged the revolution, final variant of the war of religion and the ultimate type of civil war. The modern form of truth, the most effective and most destructive form, is tautological: that which is revolutionary is just, because it is revolutionary. In this way the question of the *justa causa belli* is tabled again and finds a brisk reply. When the Islamic summons to holy war rings out in Iran, it will be one of the many farces and endless misunderstandings provoked by the West's envelopment of the world; it will already be a parody of the revolutionary war—and the Western intelligentsia will have no difficulty in recognizing it as its own. At least, at the beginning . . . The full and radiant truth of faith is subjected to the procedural and tautological truth of the extreme West, at the very moment the West is being repudiated. At least, at the beginning . . .

Just as Benjamin viewed Baroque tragic drama through the window of the Expressionist morgue, so Schmitt saw wars of religion in terms of Rathenau's bloodstained fur coat, the incursions of von Salomon's outlaws, and the carts loaded with banknotes during the Weimar Republic's inflation. He thus perceived a pattern that until then had never been so exactly perceived: the unstable constellation of the *jus publicum Europaeum* was always preceded and followed by massacre, which initially was called a war of religion and today has many names—primarily because there is no longer any way of precisely distinguishing a *guerre en forme* from total war, and total war from civil war, and civil war from revolutionary war, and revolutionary war from "global civil war," which incorporates and retains all the preceding categories. Korea and Vietnam were the first examples of remote and circumscribed civil wars involving the two great powers, with a military apparatus equal or superior to that which had been employed in the world wars. The Arab-Israeli war was both a civil war and a war of race and religion, and established a theater of permanent negotiation for the powers. Terrorists hijack airplanes (or merely blow up airline offices) thousands of kilometers away from the enemy. Such actions sarcastically remind us that the *nomos* has been completely uprooted from any soil, and that today's order rests on nothing and hence has no borders; but they also imply that at any moment and in whatever place, the killing of some *hostis injustus,* predetermined or chosen at random, belongs to the events of the theater of war.

. . .

An acrobatic episode in Talleyrand's political history is the period during which he headed the provisional government, in 1814. At that moment all Europe seemed suspended from a single point—namely, his bedroom on the mezzanine of his palace on the rue Saint-Florentin. By then, Talleyrand was already the flotsam of three different tides: bishop of the ancien régime, sacrilegious drafter of revolutionary texts, minister of Napoleon. But no one dared to say this—and Alexander I slept in safety a few meters above him. Vitrolles, who observed Talleyrand with blatant curiosity (though also with devotion, because he still sensed in him the presence of "mysteries that the uninitiated can never penetrate"), notes: "It is difficult to form an idea of what the provisional government was. It was all contained in Monsieur de Talleyrand's bedroom, on the mezzanine of his palace. Some clerks who had been gathered under the direction of Dupont de Nemours, the last and best of the economists, made up the office staff, and Roux-Laborie was the assistant secretary-general. Monsieur de Talleyrand kept the room open to all his acquaintances, men and women, and the conversations of the many people who came and went were the real deliberations on the affairs of state. A number of more or less witty articles were to be printed in the newspapers; these became the most important business, a process that was called 'shaping opinion.' Furthermore, myriad ideas were always occurring to the people who came and went, and when one of them happened to attract the Prince de Talleyrand, he would turn it into a decree. The members of the government would sign it on faith when they in turn came to visit their premier." All the cumbersome liturgy of power is here dissipated in continuous chatter, which is open to anyone who passes through. Yet sovereignty remains, like an intact crystal, even if now it is hidden under the many pillows of the Prince. It will be a long time before Europe sees it again in so bold a form—so close to aura and miasma, its primordial state. A few months later, at the Congress of Vienna, sovereignty already seemed corroded by a certain lack of inner substance. A morganatic kinship links the monarchs of the Congress of Vienna and the deputies of the Weimar Republic. And soon thousands of people will light torches in the Nuremberg stadium to summon from the darkness the vanished essence of sovereignty, before bathing it in blood to enliven its ghostly pallor.

The *esprits forts* of the eighteenth century became the Homais of the nineteenth century and the prevailing opinion of the twentieth.

So far, only two attempts have been made to build a world beyond nihilism. The first was during the Hitler years: reunion of blood and earth, defeat of the Hebraic acids of the intellect. The second was during the Stalin years: gaining access to the "kingdom of liberty," engineering of the soul.

One day the United States discovered that it was an empire. But it didn't know what an empire was. It thought that an empire was merely the biggest of all corporations.

If the profane—that is to say, the profaner—devours what is sacred, then sacred and profane will merge in an unprecedented blend that will make it impossible ever to separate them.

At one time, only the immeasurable had value. Now, only value is measurable; and nature, which has no value, has once more become immeasurable.

One of democracy's achievements: extending to everyone the privilege of access to things that no longer exist.

The inevitable political choice offered today: Shall we be governed by money or by informers? Ah, but money is so much more amiable and absent-minded.

The founding idea of all progressive thought has an air of great common sense. It was summarized in a few lines jotted down by Hugo in 1830, a happy date for rational progressive thought: "The republic, in my opinion, is the sovereignty of society over society: protecting itself with the national guard; judging itself with juries; managing itself with city administration; governing itself with the electoral college." How could we want anything more obvious, convincing, straightforward? Hence the surprise, the helpless bewilderment, in the twentieth century when society finally did become "sovereign over society" and was immediately shown to be not a democracy or a republic, as Hugo had hoped, but an experimental theocracy, whose first priest-engineers were named Lenin and Hitler. Many others followed, more similar to anonymous officials. All this appears to stem from an unexplored mechanism of the mind whereby the word "sovereignty" drags all the gods in its train. And if the gods can no longer be named, it will drag in its train only the Inquisition in the name of God, which is now its own name. A disenchanted sovereignty *cannot* exist, just as arithmetic *cannot* not contain undecidable propositions. Our entire political future depends on the investigation of such a theorem of sovereignty, which is still a long way from seeming evident, convincing, well defined.

The Moscow Gatekeeper

Andrei extended his hands toward the warmth of the tea. Through the gatehouse window he could see the assistant director, Anatoli Lozovski, whose pallor was accented by two little red patches on his cheeks—"a genuine Kremlin complexion," people called it. (Lozovski set foot inside the institute not more than two or three times a year, and his appearance was always cause for alarm.) Andrei remembered the days when those who walked behind the coffins were expressionless, drained of all feeling, because they were prepared to die in the everyday events of the revolution. Words, since then, had sedimented into a kind of sludge, sticky at first, but now hardened and covered by a light (almost invisible) layer of dust. Coming out of the city's cramped, musty rooms, you felt as if you'd stepped into the streets of some town in Asia. But not for long; even there, you couldn't escape the ghosts of the remote, ice-covered monasteries, each enclosed within an eight-meter-thick wall. Prisoners (among them Andrei's son, detained since the age of fifteen) languished in that solitude, before they were buried at the foot of the wall, just as the carcasses of domestic animals were buried in barnyards. Sitting in his gatehouse before the offices filled up, and feeling thick-headed at that early hour, since he had not yet had his first drink, Andrei gazed out the window at the yellowish-gray wall and sensed the torpor of that neglected space overgrown with weeds. Like most people, he was attracted by distances, as if every faraway, invisible thing were suffering from his absence and calling to him. But he had become suspicious of those chasms that opened in him every few moments as naturally as you would close a door. Here, alcohol didn't affect you the way it did in imperialist countries. It served chiefly to limit his perceptions; to fill up gaps; to establish a continuous and oppressive current enabling him to carry out unobtrusively his duties as gatekeeper; and above all to help him get through the night, when he felt drawn back to the steppes—to those vast, fondly remembered places where twenty years ago he had worked as an Improver. But actually the most dangerous time for him was the early morning, that wrenching moment when he was liable to be stricken by sobriety. And sobriety was closely bound to hatred, which did not come naturally to him but which he could not help absorbing through the walls. Hatred disturbed him; he could not anchor it to the ocean bed. Often he would regain his balance with a thought: here he was, living in the gatehouse of the Gorky Literary Institute (in September 1929 Gorky had written to him from Moscow, "Despite the great sensitivity with which you depict characters, you still color them ironically, so that readers see them less as revolutionaries than as mental defectives"); and this was the closest he could come, here in the city, to the life he most respected. He had always wanted to be one of those pensive men stationed in the lodges at railway crossings. The railway lines, bordered by their embankments, had always seemed to him calm and intelligent in their isolation. Here in the gatehouse, of course, he never saw a locomotive. If he did, there would no doubt be a familiar face in the engineer's cab: that of his father, Platon Platonov, a railway mechanic, who had been the first to tell him that the Resurrection of the Bodies would take place in the graveyard for machines. Repairing locomotives: a heavenly job. But such work would never be given to him, not only because of his tuberculosis and his drinking but also because it would have been improper to entrust Soviet transport, regarded as "the tracks for the locomotive of history" (he recalled a little poster he'd seen on a pole in Central Asia), to a *podonok* ("scum," Stalin had written in the margin of one of Andrei's stories in 1931).

"Talking to yourself is an art; conversing with others is a pastime," Andrei thought, opening the closet where the brooms and rags were kept. His wrinkled body, calm and inexpressive, was coming more and more to resemble that tiny spectator who lives inside every man, playing no part in his actions or his sufferings, always tranquil and unmoved, always the same. The tiny fellow's task is to see and to bear witness, yet he has no voting rights in the man's life, and no one knows the reason for his solitary existence. "*I* see, too," Andrei thought, "but I could never say that I see." That little corner of consciousness is illuminated day and night, like the gatehouse to a great apartment building. The gatekeeper is always watching; he knows all the inhabitants of the building, but not one of them ever consults him about personal matters. They enter and leave; the gatekeeper-spectator follows them with his eyes. A tenant may come out of the building and leave his wife there, yet is never jealous of the gatekeeper. The latter sometimes appears sad in his impotent wisdom, but he is always polite and reserved. He is the eunuch of the man's soul. He lives elsewhere. When there is a fire, he calls the firemen and observes the course of events from outside. "Who would ever think that, before becoming this creature, I was an engineer, that I took part in the great reclamation, and that I wanted to make the waters of the Yellow Springs rise again, so as to bring socialism to the steppes?"

❧

(. . . to listen to a story that is a person, time changed into space, a space that expands and coils in time, resting on a false present, a radiant hollow facing an echoing past; not knowing where your feet are sinking, but surrounded by noble architectural remnants, no more solid than a filmy layer covering other surfaces, whose enamel no one will mar; traversing them, we once again find ourselves on contemporary soil, brimming with ephemeral, overlapping memories—but like visitors this time, alien to this and every other ground.)

The misadventures of homo naturalis. He gives off an odor through the mere act of living; his gestures are brusque and awkward. He strolls about and listens, a captive of his own curiosity, yet is often overcome by sudden fits of drowsiness. He cautiously sniffs in every corner before settling there temporarily. Lewd with kitchen maids, too nearsighted to perceive distant fates, sentimental beneath his rough yet delicate hide, he reminds us of the loneliness of childhood. Sidestepping is a necessity for him, in his thoughts as well as in his carnal pleasures. He distrusts their origin. Gliding, never stopping at any point, breaking up the ground because it consumes his legs. Distracted and inconsequential, he would like to be seen as a grateful and happy spirit; but he lets himself be caught saying certain ugly words that leave traces of acid, accompanying these words with a self-deprecating laugh and disguising them with false politeness. He likes to touch the rancid crust that cannot be cleansed from the bottom of one's being. It's as if he were in a barrel, his vision obscured on all sides; he curls up in himself, shaken by the irrepressible laughter of *homo deiectus,* and severs all his links to the outside with nervous little scissors. His laughter is the kind that seizes you by the throat—the kind that seized Molière on stage, just before he suffocated.

❧

Wake for Montaigne

It was up to Mademoiselle de Gournay to weep, as a matter of ceremony. Everyone else was conversing in tones scarcely lower than usual, summing up and digressing: ah, the Roman matrons, the murderous physicians, the mail-coach horses, the position of the thumbs, the futility of the human condition, the cannibals, the back rooms of loneliness . . . Those who were present thought Montaigne was absent—and none of them had bothered to pay superstitious homage to his face, which was decorously set off by a little collar of Flemish lace, near his book, in the casket of aromatic cherry wood. But suddenly Montaigne began to speak, and insisted that they answer him, as custom requires when people are conversing in polite society.

"And now—doesn't everything become immense?" Sainte-Beuve said finally, his eyes alive with a glint of fanaticism that was quite alien to him and that alarmed some of the ladies. "This conversation, which we are now conducting amid intervals of silence, will never cease. The speaking presence of the dead man in our midst, whom we were burying with honor, clearly means that we shall still be obliged indefinitely to comment on and listen to every nuance of our moods. And the eternal chatter of the details dismays me."

"You, of all people." From behind his back came the voice of that raving man from the *Soirées* of St. Petersburg. "My dear friend, you who wept so copiously in the vale of tears, who welcomed Good Friday with a hearty dinner *chez* Magny, who listened magnanimously to everything that was specific and concrete, that was bound to the moment and to discretion . . . Now it's you—yes, you—who are the first to sense that a hateful veil is descending over these little pleasures, these errant distractions of the intellect, far more and much earlier than over the vast storms of passion." Sainte-Beuve turned and replied, "Nothing is innocent—I'm well aware of that. And least innocent of all is our sensitivity to and pleasure in nuance, which have always moved us and within which we have moved . . . But after all, even when you were with the chevalier and the senator on your terrace, facing the Neva, your words merely continued the whisperings from your *cabinet de lecture;* they changed only the background, which you preferred obscure and barbaric, since you expected a lightning bolt from heaven . . . Whereas we, out of delicacy, out of uncertainty, had given that up from the beginning. And now I daresay the lightning bolt and the whispering will remain inseparable for a long time . . . Nothing clear-cut is in store for us." Sainte-Beuve replied, gradually lowering his tone of voice to the one the ladies recognized. His face once again assumed its habitual expression, which reminded them of an old, soft cat. Only a flush around the ears betrayed him. But soon the conversation resumed on several sides, and became indistinct.

Much later, a thin, stern, carelessly dressed man rose to his feet. As if in conclusion, he said, "Remorseless confessions addressed to no one, for the sake of entertainment, pleasure, boredom. Ever since you first emerged from Montaigne's little tower, from its rooms inscribed with aphorisms, and ever since you dispersed throughout the world to haunt cafés, drawing rooms, attics, and basements, weeds have obscured every straight and narrow path. *Ibidem* a dense forest has sprung up, dark and poisonous—fatal to all dreamers who doze off in its vast shade. A forest of death, akin to that gloomy expanse of myrtle and cypress mentioned by Virgil (*Secreti celant calles* . . .), desolate home of suicides, where silently and with sylvan eye many of our dear ones founder, gazing scornfully like Dido on prudent Aeneas, who did not invoke the Ego but bound it in a tight bundle (*atque inimica refugit in nemus umbriferum*). What lured you into that darkness, if not the charm of a detail, an invincible and unspeakable singularity, which you loved to explore and which you entered like stubborn watchmen, like marmots in their stony burrows? Whoever was drawn to that life was devoted from the outset to the discontinuous; he was the enemy of all *aequalitas,* was an observer (worshiper?) of abrupt forces, was incapable of holding a long breath that could envelop every part. Gusts of wind, ribbons, tiny barbs, spores, crevices, quavering sounds, exasperated nostalgias: little by little you have transformed yourselves into the cluttered bottom of a drawer."

☙

Ja'far Sâdiq (d. 765) once said, "Our cause is a secret veiled in a secret, the secret of something that remains veiled, a secret that only another secret can reveal. It is a secret about a secret that is satisfied by a secret."

O***: We were under the glass dome of the station. Petersburg. I still have the list of addresses. There I'll find the names of the dead. Damp air from the parks, redolent of leaf mold; the odor of the abandoned greenhouses and trellised roses in the orangeries. Then come the heavy fumes from the dining car, the acrid cigars, the burned gaskets of the railway coaches, the maquillage of the crowd. Thought: scatter it, devastate it, so that it will be reminded of its furtive and lethal existence. Literature: How many unpleasant traits did people ascribe to you, as if you were a flighty woman who thinks of nothing but new clothes? Will you still sometimes open your door to the being that no longer frequents philosophy texts, that lies wordless among the algorithms? Perhaps then it will again be possible to say, "I have cast my life to the winds of heaven, but have kept my thoughts. They are not much. They are everything, they are nothing—they are life itself."

When he was a student in Königsberg, he was twice convicted of theft. He became "manservant," secretary, and ultimately the lover of Duchess Anna; then an autocrat, when Anna became empress. He treated the Russians like plantation slaves. His name was Ernst Johann von Bühren, and he was a member of the minor Baltic nobility, but he liked to give the impression that his name was Biron, as if he were descended from that illustrious French family. After causing many people to be deported, he was deported himself, along with his immediate family, his brothers, and some friends, for the crime of "repeated lèse-majesté." He was brought back from Siberia at the wish of the mad Czar Peter III. With him came the beautiful Lopuchina, who had had her tongue cut out, and many others, including his mortal enemy Marshal Münnich, who had had a prison built for Biron and where he himself was confined for twenty years. The czar wanted Biron and Münnich to drink a toast in his presence. He raised his glass, but then walked away after someone whispered something to him. Thus, "those two old enemies were left face to face, glass in hand, not saying a word, their gaze fixed on the spot where the emperor had vanished. A few minutes later, satisfied that the emperor had forgotten them, each looked at the other and measured him with his eyes. They set down their glasses without having taken so much as a sip, and turned their backs on each other." Petersburg was crowded "with interesting people—interesting, at least, because of their lengthy misfortunes." These *revenants*, brought back from the dead by the grace of Peter III's benevolent whim, went as soon as possible to the city's vast warehouses. "According to national custom, these were the repositories of all confiscated goods—sad collections of the ruins of favor, where you could see, arranged in chronological order, all the flotsam of those famous shipwrecks. The people went searching in the dust for their precious furniture, their diamond-studded medals and decorations, the gifts by which even monarchs had once secured their credit. But often, after vainly hunting about, they saw that their possessions had been appropriated by the favorites of the current regime." Rulhière noticed Biron wandering around Petersburg: "On summer nights he was virtually alone in the streets, strolling about the city where he had once held sway, and where everything he encountered asked him to account for the blood of a brother or a friend."

***: They're not so much thoughts as the edges of thoughts. Like memories—piercing because one can never possess them completely. They draw near and then fade, crests of the mnemic wave. They shun all connectives, seeking a lacuna, a space in which to breathe between one thing and the next, just as they do in their life as recollections. The question whether they are others' memories (what others?), or ours, or no one's becomes confused beyond a certain threshold and then impossible to clarify ever again. Henceforth they live together in the same cloud of dust. They speak among themselves like family portraits in a dimly lit corridor.

In a letter to Gershom Scholem, Benjamin refers to his book on Paris and its arcades (the *Passagen-Werk*) as the "old, half-apocryphal, somewhat rebellious province of my thoughts." The book would take its "tone" from the essay on postage stamps in *Einbahnstrasse* (One-Way Street), where he discusses collectors "who are interested only in canceled stamps." According to Benjamin, such collectors are perhaps "the only ones who have penetrated the mystery," for cancellation is the "occult part of the stamp," its "nocturnal face." History, as it is presented by orthodox historians, is for him an uncanceled stamp—prosaic in its clarity. Whereas the postmark, which "covers the people's faces with bloody streaks" and opens "chasms between whole continents," is the invisible hand of time, which willfully imposes an indelible black mark on a landscape of tropical palms. And it is this wound that enhances the Eros of the stamp and of history, a wound that enchants us in its "lacy white tulle dress: the scalloped edge."

For Benjamin, the transition from dreaming to wakefulness was symbolized by the comb, which traces a path through the maze, through the hair that has become tangled during the night. "Combing: in the morning, the comb is the first thing that dispels dreams from the hair. Combing is a mother's job," he said to Fränkel, who was assisting him in a mescaline session. The comb meets the resistance of *"indéfrisable"* hair, such as hairdressers displayed in their windows in the arcades. Tangled hair must be approached shrewdly, because it is "only with shrewdness that we extricate ourselves from the realm of dreams." Thus, the comb that Benjamin discusses will be the attribute of the sirens, the Pecten Veneris, the *kteís* (which is at once "comb" and "vulva"), the comb that appeared in the mysteries of Themis. Because of its feminine quality, this comb both untangles and evokes dreams. Benjamin's shrewdness is that of the wily Odysseus, who not only listens to the Sirens but wields their ceremonial object as a weapon, using it to guide him out of the dream, yet without denying it, ensuring its complicity in a pact. Literature is that slow, cautious, shrewd progress of the comb: "In the comb we find consolation, a way of making unhappened what has happened."

Like a true gnostic, accustomed to persecutions and disguises, Benjamin wanted to hide beneath the cloak of a dialectical materialist and be attacked as such, so that he could survive as a gnostic, unharmed. But every policeman's soul is trained to recognize the *foetor gnosticus*; there is always some zealot ready to point the finger at him, in his office at the *Soviet Encyclopedia*. Benjamin, in Moscow, suffered only harassment. Lying on his bed, in a shabby room, he munches sugared walnuts and reads Proust, guarded by his invincible, aching childhood.

· · ·

In 1879 Marianne North donated 832 oil paintings to the Royal Botanic Gardens, Kew—images of flowers and plants she had seen in Brazil, New Zealand, Borneo, Chile, India, California, Australia, Singapore, Jamaica, Tenerife, and other places. They were hung very close to one another, as in a painting by Teniers or in some giant stamp album. Dense, intricate carvings framed the windows of the lofty gallery that ran around the two rooms (when the weather was bad, only a dim light fell on the tropical splendors). The walls were paneled with the 246 types of wood she had gathered on her travels. Some portions were inlaid with flower designs. Among the painted plants were the four that now bore her name: *Northea seychellana, Nepenthes northiana, Kniphofia northiae, Crinum northianum.* Only one of her wishes was not granted: she had wanted tea to be served there, in those rooms that were like an island of mirrors in the middle of the park. But the botanical authorities would not allow it: "No refreshments in Kew Gardens." Marianne North titled her two-volume autobiography *Memories of a Happy Life.*

Talleyrand's art belongs to metamorphosis, hence to monstrosity. The sentimental moralism of the nineteenth century could not understand it: corruption and political about-faces are not enough to achieve monstrosity. But the eyes of Aimée de Coigny—among the most feminine eyes ever to gaze upon Talleyrand—recognized the frightening and delicate moments at which he underwent his protean changes: "In our childhood we were told about fairies who for a period of time were compelled to relinquish their glittering forms and assume other, repellent shapes. Just like them, Monsieur de Talleyrand is subject to sudden metamorphoses, which are brief but frightening. At such times, the sight of respectable people irritates him and he becomes hateful toward them. I was afraid, I don't know why, of finding him in this state, which I call his 'snakeskin.' But I was pleasantly surprised to see him open and gracious."

Léon Daudet—in the days when Edmond de Goncourt still called him *"grand gamin,"* though he was already sporting the black velvet cap of a fashionable student—had a dream. He dreamed that the pathologist Charcot came to him with some of Pascal's *pensées* and a brain: Pascal's brain. Charcot pointed out to him "the cells those thoughts had inhabited. They were absolutely empty, and looked like the cells of a dried beehive."

⚜

The Wolf-Man Remembers

I was born where the earth of Odessa
is blacker.
French governess, Austrian tutor.
I ploughed across Europe with my doctor,
and an assistant for card games.
Many years later I found myself off limits
in the dead zone with my easel.
Allied forces, Russian forces—
they all wanted to arrest me.

⚜

You want to see Europe? Go to Spa: "There's no better observation point than the baths and springs." The Prince de Ligne had a saber wound, and wanted to see; as always, he was curious, idle, indifferent to his own affairs, impulsive because he knew his luck was good. What he saw was the shifting allegory of Europe, signed by a continental Hogarth—the improbable, precarious world that history had reared and then abandoned to the current. "I come to a great hall, where I see amputees preening like swans and cripples strutting like peacocks; ridiculous names, titles, faces; amphibians of Church and society skipping and gamboling behind English columns; hypochondriac lords sadly strolling; Parisian sluts entering with great bursts of laughter, thinking to pass themselves off as charming and nonchalant, and hoping thereby to become so; young men of all countries acting as if they were English and thinking themselves so, speaking through clenched teeth and dressed as footmen, with their hair done in greasy black curls and Jewish-looking sidelocks falling about their dirty ears; French bishops with their nieces; an accoucheur wearing the order of Saint Michael; a dentist wearing the order of the Spur; dance teachers and singing coaches in the uniforms of Russian majors; Italians in the uniforms of Polish colonels, walking Polish bear cubs; Dutchmen who consult the newspapers for the latest exchange rate; thirty self-styled Knights of Malta; ribbons of every color, left and right and in the buttonhole; medals of every shape and size, worn all over the chest; fifty Knights of Saint-Louis; old duchesses returning from their walk, with great canes à la Vendôme and powder and rouge three inches thick; a few marquises returning from card games in the country; dreadful and suspicious faces amid mountains of ducats, devouring all the money that was tremblingly staked on the gaming table; one or two electors in hunting garb, sporting gold chevrons and knives; a few princes in disguise, who wouldn't have been any more impressive under their real names; a few old generals and officers retired for wounds they never received; some Russian princesses with their physicians; some Palatine or Castilian women with their young almoner; a few Americans; some local burgomasters; escaped prisoners from every jail in Europe; charlatans of every stripe; adventurers of every species; abbés from every country; some poor Irish priests, tutors to young men from Liège; a few English archbishops with their wives; twenty sick people dancing madly for their health; forty lovers, or presumed such, sweating and agitated; and sixty women dancing the waltz, displaying various degrees of beauty and innocence, ability and flirtatiousness, modesty and voluptuousness."

THE CHEVALIER DE B***: The most amazing thing about history is how easily it disappears. The dead are truly wiped away; their monuments are used merely to regulate traffic; their books are grassy country graves. Every person who lives is the barbarian of what has just lived. If we look into the past, we find only a stubborn reverberation of images, a droning of harsh voices. And in between are vast opaque zones without sound. The invisible are grateful to us if we perceive this awesome distance, this majestic muteness. They reserve their greatest contempt for those who treat the past with cordial familiarity.

.   .   .

"What can thought do now?" the Master asked. "Hide," he answered, and disappeared.

Conversation is an art which its great masters—and great mistresses—considered lost even as they were speaking. Madame de Staël's lament over the irretrievable loss of a certain tone is the continuation, decades later, of Madame du Deffand's lament. It would be useless, therefore, to search for a moment in which that fleeting essence had not already vanished. But we can determine what caused this irreversible dissipation. It was *husbands*—as Stendhal declared, with touching passion. If we had to formulate in a few words the immeasurable difference in manners between the age of Louis XVI and that of Louis XVIII, we would say this: Prior to the reign of the guillotine, ladies appeared in society by themselves, whereas just a few years later (in a trend started by Napoleon, who "in 1804 made *pruderie* fashionable") it was impossible to see a young lady in a drawing room without being "sure to discover her husband playing cards in some corner. This eternal and constant presence of the husband, no doubt praiseworthy and highly moral, dealt a mortal blow to the art of conversation . . . The husband repressed the freedom of mind that gives rise to mischief, innuendo, and witty wordplay, which, though innocent in themselves, cannot flourish in the presence of an *authority established by law.* That is to say, in wit, satire, gaiety—in the whole comedy of society—a spirit of *opposition* is inevitably manifest. Many people make fun of established authority; they are, by their very nature, rebellious. To say nothing of the constraint that the eternal presence of a particular person imposes on the imagination. How can you tell a story or relate an anecdote if you're within earshot of a witness who will notice any embellishments you may add to achieve a certain effect or enliven your tale? Could you interject into a conversation, with that necessary air of spontaneity, the spicy things you've gathered during the day, if you're being observed by a person who perhaps was accompanying you? It's impossible. Once the husband enters the room, the art of conversation flies right out the window." Talleyrand was always surrounded by women who paid no attention to their husbands, in the Stendhalian sense, and often in every other sense as well. It all started in Reims, the day of his first great venture into society. "Beginning with the coronation of Louis XVI, I developed ties with several women remarkable for their various gifts—women whose friendship has never for a single moment ceased to cast a spell over my life. I refer here to the Duchesse de Luynes, the Duchesse de Fitz James, and the Vicomtesse de Laval." Some were his mistresses; some disappeared over the years and others were added, but it was as if the latter had always been near him. They were insolent and adventurous at the outset, decrepit and frivolous at the end. But they always kept watch like bodyguards, enclosing the Prince in a magic circle of soft draperies.

Fénelon soon realized how difficult it was to be a Taoist at the French court. *L'esprit*—in other words, mind, intelligence, wit—had just rejected the uncontrollable power within it that *ubi vult spirat,* that flows everywhere, so as to become a cross between dogged studiousness and rustling libertinism. Everything, whether it was etymology or a bit of gossip, had to be submitted to its hostile scrutiny. It was an invisible observer, though people claimed to see everything from its point of view. An astounding psychologist who scorned psychology, Fénelon immediately understood the endless process that held sway over the new devotees of the "I, which is the god of profane persons." It was a system that, like a set of gears, would keep them rolling toward Nietzsche and Freud, those tireless genealogists lurking at the threshold of every birth and every history, ready to unveil all (but Nietzsche ultimately saw that all was veil). And at that point, only shreds of the Ego would remain. No one who followed that path could ever find peace, because "the Lord is not to be found in agitation." Fénelon adumbrates the whole story of the Enlightenment in a few lines: "Whoever wants to be certain that he is always acting according to reason, and not according to passion or whim, would never have time to act. He would spend his entire life dissecting his own heart and would never attain what he desires; for he could never be sure that whim or passion, under false pretenses, wasn't making him do what he seemed to be doing out of pure reason."

In his letters, Fénelon explained that mortifying and punishing oneself (and most of all giving in to "scruples") were less important than doing something far more difficult—namely, extinguishing all respect for *l'esprit*.

Where *l'esprit* is, there is the I. And "the I, which must be renounced, is not an indefinable something or a ghost in the air. It is our intellect as it thinks; it is our will as it wants, in its own way, out of self-love." *L'esprit* divides into two rival breezes and two rival lights; and each breeze immediately extinguishes the other's light. "Reasoners, scholars without faith, extinguish the inner spirit as the wind extinguishes a candle." "I have always noticed that your esteem for *l'esprit* is rooted in your heart and that you never let it go. Yet this is precisely what the spirit of grace extinguishes first, when it is allowed to act freely." A single image dominated Fénelon's conduct: the image of water, a feminine water that has no form of its own but assumes every form—protean, transparent, flavorless. The archbishop was the water that flowed in the interstices of Versailles. Saint-Simon, who could read physiognomies the way Fénelon could penetrate minds, saw his face as a mobile and liquid surface: "This prelate was tall, thin, well built, and pale. His nose was large, and his eyes poured forth a stream of fire and intelligence. His face was like no other I have never seen—you couldn't forget it, even if you'd seen it only once. It contained everything, but opposites did not clash within it. It had gravity and charm, seriousness and gaiety; in it you sensed the doctor, the bishop, and the great gentleman. Refinement, intelligence, grace, decorum, and above all nobility floated on that surface, and in his entire person." It should not be surprising that this exterminator of *l'esprit* possessed such an abundance of it, even if he was "a man who never wished to have more *esprit* than those with whom he was speaking." This, in fact, was his art of dissembling. Enemy of "all extremes, even of the good" (since all of them "can become affected and overrefined"), he displayed his great wit and intelligence only to seem more mediocre, closer to the ordinary courtier, who was at all times avid for *l'esprit*. In his social perfection, to which Saint-Simon paid homage, Fénelon had discovered a vehicle through which he could transmit, intact and disguised, that nameless, formless "background" of everything, which intelligence and subtlety were constantly dispersing. "Nothing can equal the courtesy, the discernment, the pleasure with which he received everyone." But that immaculate hospitality was the stage for a work of vast destruction: "Be a true nothing, in everything and everywhere; but do not add anything to this pure nothingness. On nothing, there can be no hold. And it can lose nothing. True nothing never resists, because it has no *I* to worry about." It is "incredible," Saint-Simon remarks of Fénelon, "to what extent he became the idol of military men."

The *Lumpen,* shrilly evoked by Stirner, nested in every crevice of society. They were the shadow of history—measureless, oppressed, mute existence. They were "the immense renegade of Yesteryear" visible behind the weight of the "past, which will not go away," a past that tears off bits of the present "with its black nails" and "vomits up its old night." But this was only the beginning. Stirner was not well acquainted with nature, beyond Charlottenburg. When the *Lumpen* stole their way into it, moving up from underground to till the soft earth, he could no longer follow them. He fell silent. Victor Hugo, who had become a poet of materiality by practicing spiritualism, took Stirner's place. The epos of the *Lumpen* flowed from his mouth, that *"bouche d'ombre."* The world of séances and trances had given Hugo a shabby metaphysics, but also one rich in all-inclusive images that mingled his well-meaning attitude with the evil meanings of Maldoror, until it achieved a sparkling neutrality. In the swirl of metamorphoses every object, every plant, every pebble proved to be a place of expiation, every landscape a penitentiary, a reliquary. Replying to the Marquis Coriolis d'Espinouse, who reproached him for falling "into utter Jacobinism," Hugo insolently spoke of "the ancient rheumatism we call royalty." But his was the shattering hilarity of darkness, which presupposed an apparition: "The entire dreadful prison full of outcasts rises before us." In his walks on Jersey, among the rocks and heather, he saw that the prison full of outcasts was the cosmos itself. "Yes, your untamed universe is the convict of God. / The constellations, dark letters of fire, / Are the brand of the prison on the world's shoulder." The cosmos, which had been desiccated by the crude mechanists, came to life again, watered with souls. It lived in every dustmote, but was like an endless jail of phantoms. "The shadowy archipelago of prisons glows with light." Those who had been expelled from society—the *Lumpen,* the *gueux*, the beggars—were now the hosts in an even larger dwelling, receiving the great and the kings of the earth. Caiaphas is a thorn, Pilate a reed, Alaric a "scarlet-throated" volcano. "Grains of sand are kings, blades of grass are emperors," all nailed into a palpable form which moans, but which can also be a chair or a window ledge. Hugo announces the existence of "the pariah universe." Hofmannsthal's expert ear would detect, in the more than one hundred fifty thousand lines Hugo wrote, a few words that he had branded: *fauve, hagard. Fauve* is the universe as the "convict of God." And after a brief outpouring of other lines, Hugo writes, "L'univers est hagard." A word from falconry, *hagard* derives from *Hagerfalk*, which is a wild falcon that is too ferocious to let itself be tamed. Over time, the word has acquired new meanings: "gaunt," "tormented by a sinister presence"—meanings that also apply to the *Lumpen*, the wild falcons that wander the city streets. But now those streets are etched on the domed vault of the heavens.

The *Liber Mundi* that the monk was contemplating had luminous, clearly inscribed letters. Every creature in it was copied from the great Koran: the cosmos. Every blade of the cloister's grass found its place on the written page, because "nature has only one scripture" and everything obediently led back to that scripture. Every book Saint Jerome opened on the lectern was in a sense the same book; every letter filled his cell with a hum of correspondences, while the meek lion lay at his feet, keeping watch over a harsh savannah of parchments. Reading was the act that absorbed all others, even the liturgical gestures. In the syllables of the hymns, one could find excerpts from a reading of the seasons, bookish recollections of the celestial cycles. Sainte-Beuve, a moody young man from the provinces, had abandoned his medical studies because a literary career was opening up for him. From the beginning he had lent an ear to every voice, but he could not quite understand the meaning of the verb "to believe." Yet he became aware that a "parasitic religiosity" was inhabiting him, like a treacherous outsider. Incapable of any kind of faith, he observed in himself, with a naturalist's wonder, the vibrations of a "Christian *sensibility*." He was one of those beings whom he had once described: "A sober life, a misty sky, some mortification of desire, a reserved and solitary manner—all this penetrates them, softens them, and leads them imperceptibly toward belief." But something that leads people toward belief is quite different, quite remote, from something that imposes belief. Indeed, in his case it excluded belief. The elegiac Sainte-Beuve, who used to gaze at the bleak courtyard behind his study, soon became the *rôdeur* who prowled the streets of the great city, consumed by the presage of a feminine softness; the *railleur* who shrewdly found his way through editorial offices; the *causeur* who laced his conversation with tiny drops of flattery or venom. And something told him that this complex of vices formed the cornerstone of literary civilization—that they would allow nothing to be worshiped but themselves. With the spontaneous cynicism of an inventor of forms, Sainte-Beuve for many years used that "Christian sensibility" to keep himself in tune with Port-Royal. But it was a question of ear, certainly not one of doctrine. He found himself admiring Bayle for a certain "basic indifference," and for his ability to maneuver on any terrain, provided it was typographic. "He is not afraid of *mésalliances*; he goes everywhere, roaming the streets, inquiring, accosting people. Curiosity lures him on, and he does not deny himself the pleasures he is offered." It was a curiosity all the more avid for being based on an essential indifference—a case of fidelity to an irrepressible infidelity. Was he a skeptic? Or a mystic? Whatever the case, something about Bayle reminded Sainte-Beuve of himself. In both of them, everything ultimately stemmed from a single experience: reading. This insinuating mania did not even strive to rediscover, in the transparency of the page, the characters of the *Liber Mundi*. It expected only that idle books by unknown writers might furnish some idle reply: "Would you be so kind as to tell me / In which pile of clutter, in which nook, / I might find some record / Of Monsieur Malherbe's long stay / In Carpentras, or of how Ménage looked / When he played his role *chez* Sévigné? / Did Monsieur Conrart know Latin / Better than Jouy? Did he use fewer quill pens / Than Suard? Did Doctor Guy Patin own more than ten thousand volumes?" But one day Sainte-Beuve sensed he was approaching something that seemed to be his own point of equilibrium. It was an unwelcome vision, which he yielded to out of pure weariness. In a way, he was like those monks who compiled herbaria and who after all did not really interest him: for them, *everything was book*. But in him liturgical devotion was disguised as "basic indifference," a readiness to read those endless and now somewhat soiled letterforms—to read them everywhere, without selection, without plan, without close attention, without hope of finding the beginning or the end of the book, which actually no longer existed. "Perhaps from a secret need to justify my indolence, or perhaps from a deeper understanding of the principle that *in the end everything is the same,* I have come to a certain realization. I now see that whatever I do—whether I work in my study on a lengthy text or scatter myself in many articles or spread myself about in society, whether I allow my time to be consumed by the importunate, by the needy, by appointments, by the life in the streets, by anyone and anything, no matter what—I never cease doing one thing: namely, reading a single book, an infinite, perpetual book. It is the book of the world and of life, which no one reads to the end and of which the wisest decipher only a certain number of pages. All the pages I come across, I read—zigzag, backward. What's the difference? But I never stop. The richer the blend of colors and the more frequent the interruptions, the more I advance through this book, in which you always find yourself in the middle. But the most valuable thing is to have read around in it, in all sorts of places."

What are the dead for us, if not—first and foremost—books? Among all forms of prehistoric religion, the strangest and most difficult to understand in our own day seems the cult of the dead, the constant presence of the dead in every aspect of life. To a prehistoric man, in contrast, our strangest and most mysterious form of worship would be our use of books. Yet these two forms of belief converge. Concretized as portable objects that accompany us—our parasites, persecutors, comforters—the dead have settled on the written page. Their power has never diminished, even though it has been wondrously transformed.

◌◌

Voices from the Palais-Royal

Restif: ". . . this center of a big city's chaos."

Richelieu chose the spot with his usual gift for finding a body's center of gravity. That long quadrangle, known in those days as the Palais-Cardinal, then the Palais-Royal, then the Palais-Marchand, then the Palais-Egalité, then the Jardin de la Révolution, then once again the Palais-Royal, was the center of the center, the heart of the vast body of *la civilisation* which had been appropriated after eighteen years of rivalries and cabals. Weighty figureheads and stone anchors jutted from the ancient façade, evoking the cardinal's authority over oceans, rivers, and trade.

In the pool of the central fountain, little Louis XVI once came close to drowning. In those days, Anne of Austria was occupying Richelieu's place, and Mazarin had only to cross the garden of the Palais-Cardinal to go from his residence, the Hôtel Turbeuf, to the queen's apartments. The future Sun King was not yet ten and spent long hours with the daughter of one of his mother's maids. He called her "queen Maria" and played king and queen with her in the kitchens of the palace.

Among the many and varied works of Louis-Sébastien Mercier is a description of what Paris might be like in the year 2440. "A Dream If Ever There Was One," says the subtitle—but like all rational utopias, this Paris is suffused with Tedium and Integrity. In the theater, the only surviving plays are full of admonitions and positive characters; Mercier liked the idea of a perpetual Zhdanovian Corneille, but had strong misgivings about Racine, because he, "after making his heroes effeminate, made his spectators effeminate, too." The streets are constantly illuminated, and the libraries have been purged of every harmful book. The "dangerous agitation" of the Jews, who have been aggressive and rapacious because of a lack of "vigilance in the preceding centuries," has at last been stopped. It has taken "wisdom, constancy, and firmness to quell that ardent fanaticism," but the Jews have ultimately been reduced to "earning their living in absolute tranquillity," a state that Mercier does not elaborate on. Yet his gaze encompassed more than this pedantic utopia. He also had the eye of a voracious *flâneur;* and at the end of his *Tableau de Paris,* after one hundred twenty-two chapters on puppies and *roués,* on Bicêtre and obscenities in the churches, on *modistes* and parliament, he introduces us to that incomparable place, that essence of the West, which imbued the entire city with its vague magnetic force: the Palais-Royal.

"A spot unique on the globe. Visit London, Amsterdam, Madrid, Vienna—you will see nothing similar. A prisoner could live here without ever being bored, and would think of freedom only after several years. It's precisely the sort of place that Plato considered appropriate for a prisoner, a place where a man could be held without a jailer and without violence, in sweet and voluntary chains. People call it the 'capital of Paris.' You can find everything here. Put a twenty-year-old fellow with fifty thousand livres a year in this enchanting spot, and he would never—could never—leave it. He would become like Rinaldo in the palace of Armida. And just as that hero saw his days and his glory almost slip away in such a place, our young man would lose his, and perhaps his fortune as well. Henceforth he would find pleasure only here; he would be bored anywhere else. This charming spot is a little city of luxury enclosed in a big city—a temple of voluptuousness from which glittering vice has banished even the ghost of modesty. There is no pleasure garden in the world more prettily depraved; here laughter abounds, and innocence blushes."

"Whatever you desire, you're sure to find it here. You'll find lessons in physics, poetry, chemistry, anatomy, languages, natural history, etc., etc. The women here have renounced the pedantic seriousness of the old Hôtel de Rambouillet. They flirt with the sciences, which they view as toys and which amuse them as much as their little poodles or parakeets."

.   .   .

"Here you can see everything, hear everything, know everything—there's enough to turn a youth into a little savant. Yet here, too, libertinage takes hold of undisciplined young people, who later circulate in polite society and introduce a tone unheard of elsewhere: indecency without passion. Here libertinage is eternal. Its temple is open at every hour of the day or night, and at every sort of price."

"In the shops, all the fripperies of fashion are displayed side by side with the most precious and enduring jewels."

"All day long, the cafés are crowded with men who have only one occupation: to tell or to hear news—which becomes completely distorted, since each teller alters the words according to his circumstances."

"The Palais-Royal is draining the life from the other neighborhoods of the city, which have begun to look like sad and uninhabited provinces."

". . . this labyrinth of ribbons, gauze, tassels, flowers, dresses, masks, rouge boxes, packets of six-inch-long pins."

There is a place where all the dispersion and fragmentation of Paris, all its scent of pleasure and money, expand and condense within the confines of a single palace, as in a bright shell. It is the Palais-Royal, which became the Palais-Marchand when the debts and the miserliness of the Duc d'Orléans led to the opening of shops, dens of depravity, perfumeries, and gambling halls under its arcades. On the threshold of the Revolution, those arches were a magnet for Rumors, the armillary sphere of courtesans, the glow of murderous coals. Before Colette and Cocteau gazed out from its windows, which today afford a view of nothing more than children shouting and playing, two rivals kept watch from them in the darkness—guardians of one of the most credulous and indifferent men who ever lived: the lord of that castle, the Duc d'Orléans, later Philippe-Egalité. They were Madame de Genlis, who "always yielded rapidly to a man's advances, in order to avoid the scandal of a flirtation," and Choderlos de Laclos, who spent his days deep in intrigue and who recommended "wicked love affairs" as a "useful training ground for the wicked politician."

One of the truly perfect *incipits* of literature conveys the irresistible attraction of the Palais-Royal: "Around five o'clock in the afternoon, no matter what the weather, it's my habit to stroll in the Palais-Royal. I'm the man you always see sitting alone on d'Argenson's bench, lost in thought. I converse with myself about politics, love, matters of taste, questions of philosophy. I abandon my mind to all its libertine urges. I leave it free to pursue the first idea, wise or foolish, that occurs to it—just as in the Allée de Foy our dissolute young men will pursue a flighty-looking courtesan who has a laughing face, a lively eye, and an upturned nose, then leave her for another, approaching them all and not staying with any. My thoughts are my whores." Here Diderot formulates a poetics of thought that is the converse of the one advocated by the *Encyclopédie*—and that is far more radical in opposing the past. Here the most stubborn of sins, the *delectatio morosa*, is not only defended but exalted to the level of method. A long series of witnesses thought they had to extirpate this sin before they could even begin to approach thought; now it becomes the primordial medium of thought itself. And the Palais-Royal is the mnemotechnical locus of this thought. A nameless subjectivity, comfortably ensconced in the midst of chaos, follows threads of words and drifting images; it builds tiny edifices of paper, gazes at ribbons, buckles, shawls ruffled by the breeze under the arcades; it notices little shudders, immerses the mental word in the external din, opens itself to imperious, unexpected lights and shadows; it lets itself go, pays no attention to where it is headed—does not even think that its wanderings might soon lead it back to d'Argenson's bench, with no memory of where it has been.

The Palais-Royal is a locus of rumors and "profound idleness," a universal storehouse, a promise of perpetual availability, a no-man's-land where the police never set foot (such is the power of the Orléans), a park of the Son of Heaven, a *paradisus inversus,* a "vast flesh-market," a herald of the industrial phantasmagoria that Benjamin will find in the arcades. It is the image of an unpurged *bonheur,* childish and cruel, which keeps refining its own pleasure and strives to wed it to destruction. The first liturgical act of the Revolution was performed there, on July 12, 1789: two wax busts (of Necker and the Duc d'Orléans) were removed from the Hoffmann-like collection of Curtius' waxworks and borne along in a procession. "At the sight of that ghostly pair," noted a witness, "the populace indulged in wild conjectures." Those conjectures were followed, two days later, by the taking of the Bastille. Throughout the Revolution, events would be nurtured by the ghosts that swarmed in the Palais-Royal.

The Galeries de Bois, the Camp des Tartares, the Cirque: these are some of the lost places of the Palais-Royal. Under its arches one could find great muslin scarves, almanacs with the descriptions and prices of available women, and thirty-one gambling establishments. In 1790 the National Assembly received a "petition from the two thousand one hundred public women of the Palais-Royal." They wore gold and silver earrings shaped like little guillotines. La Chevalier, one of the most sought-after "nymphs," was the daughter of the Dijon executioner. Restif gratified his mania for classification, which already resembled Fourier's, by compiling a list of the "prostitutes of the *allée* of sighs," the "sunamites," the "*converseuses.*" There was Boutonderose, always dressed in linen; Dorine, a philosopher of distinguished manners, generally dressed in pink-lined muslin; Elise, "a woman tailored by Sensuality more than by the Graces"; Pyramidale, a handsome brunette; Sensitive; Amaranthe; Barberose. Among the denizens of the Camp des Tartares there was a Prussian giantess, Mademoiselle Lapierre, two meters twenty centimeters tall; the beautiful Zulina, a nude, reclining odalisque, actually a life-size wax statue covered with imitation skin; the enormous Paul Butterlbrodt, who weighed two hundred thirty-eight kilograms. The shops sold "Roman dresses à la Clio," "Greek chemises," and "Thessalonian jackets" which could be opened by untying a single knot. Women sported new hairstyles, known as "*à la sacrifiée*" and "*à la victime.*" In the aristocrats' private apartments that were now on the second floor of the galleries, the "women of the world," those ten or so great courtesans, received guests, attended by little black servants and set off by magnificent social display. These women were "the real danger." They were a far greater threat than the "nymphs," who led their clients to attic niches rented by the minute—rooms scattered in the vast maze of corridors, beyond the sumptuous halls where the little ivory roulette ball was spinning. Sensual enticements assailed the brain: the perfume of warm flesh, powdered and rouged; smells from the wide-open kitchens, where game was hanging from pegs and where hungry men gathered—"calamitous dogs," as Baudelaire described them, "those who wandered alone through the winding ditches of the immense cities," those "who slept in a ruin on the outskirts and came every day, at a set time, to receive food at the door of a Palais-Royal kitchen."

With the intent gaze of a naturalist, Hippolyte Taine bends down to examine the Palais-Royal and recognizes the flora that is peculiar to the new age: the poisonous burgeoning of the *déclassés,* who jam and corrode the rudimentary gears of every class struggle. "Center of prostitution, gambling, idleness, and pamphleteering, the Palais-Royal attracts all the rootless people who drift about in a big city and who, having neither profession nor family, live only for curiosity and pleasure. They're steady customers of the cafés, habitués of gambling dens, adventurers, *déclassés,* errant or superfluous sons of literature, of art, of the bar, lawyers' clerks, students, misfits, *flâneurs,* foreigners, and rooming-house residents. It is said that there are forty thousand of them in Paris." Michelet decried the Palais-Royal of the Orléans as a "house where everything is false." That arid, intoxicating fever could have developed only in a place devoted to a *karma* of voluptuous gambling, cold exasperation, and deceit—powers that belong to the realm of exchange. But when the liturgy of the Revolution began, the roles were reversed: the *déclassés* of the Palais-Royal, who speculated on rumors, became the voice of the people; they filled the galleries of the assemblies and intimidated the provincial delegates. Ultimately came the Council of State, which Napoleon installed in the palace of the Orléans, thus putting the seal of administrative control on that house teeming with ghosts. There, one evening in 1787, the young officer Bonaparte had accosted a pale "nymph," even though "he was more aware than anyone of the wretchedness of their condition." "You must be very cold. How can you keep walking about out here?" he said. "Ah, sir, it's hope that keeps me going; I must see the evening to its end." There were also fires, restorations, barricades; but between the modern State and the

Palais-Royal, no understanding was allowed. When Bonaparte rose to power, the first rumor that emanated from the Palais-Royal said that the general was preparing to deport the girls of the palace to Egypt. "What a horrible thought! Damn! That's not how deportations are done!" said Bonaparte with a show of indignation, as soon as the rumor was reported to him. And he began stroking the head of Rustan, his beloved slave. Today the palace is filled with silence, broken only occasionally by an echoing footstep. There is a public garden, isolated chairs, children. Colette was once making her way home on a chilly day when she encountered, between the colonnade and the wall, "a constant current of air moving in a zigzag. It comes from the Palais-Royal square and divides into two streams, one filling the rue de Montpensier, the other penetrating the galerie de Chartres. In summer it makes the dust swirl; in autumn, in the same spot, it whips up a maelstrom of prematurely fallen leaves."

In the Palais-Royal people laugh, because "the comical is one of the clearest signs of Satan in man"—an undeniable trace of original sin. The mark of the Orléans, their obligatory scorn for everything, is even impressed on the perfect symmetry of their palace. But its garden is also the retreat of the Old Man of the Mountain, the point at which civilization is most "turbulent, overflowing, mephitic." Walking through the streets of Paris, Baudelaire imagines Bernardin de Saint-Pierre's Virginie, who moved Napoleon even in his last days on St. Helena (as emperor he had said to Bernardin, "You should give us a *Paul et Virginie* every six months"). She who is "the perfect symbol of absolute purity and innocence" seems to the poet "still dewy with the ocean mist and gilded by the tropical sun, her eyes filled with great primeval images of waves, mountains, and forests." She, too, proceeds toward the Palais-Royal. And there, "by chance, innocently," Virginie sees displayed in a shop window a "caricature full of anger and resentment, the kind of image that only a bored and perceptive civilization can make." Perhaps a scandalous picture of the despised *Autrichienne?* Or a scene of depravity in the Parc aux Cerfs? Virginie realizes she is looking at the unknown: "That engraving will leave her with a strange malaise, something resembling fear." As we observe Virginie observing the Palais-Royal caricature, we hear Baudelaire's subdued laughter close by, along with his parting words:

"For the phenomena engendered by the fall will become the means of rescue."

The West has dreamed of being encyclopedia and brothel, stage and museum, Eden, university, seraglio. That dream was realized once, in the Palais-Royal. But the dream was afraid of itself. It accompanies us now, held in suspension.

༄

Mundus Patet

A shadow-line separates us from every ancien régime: the moment at which the unique Palais-Royal was broken up into a multitude of arcades. The galleries of royalty, the "superb arcades of the cardinal's palace" celebrated by Corneille, were invaded by shops, gambling dens, cafés, brothels. The gardens were full of the city's prattle; the Voices caught fire. Everything unfolded in a quadrangular epiphany—a final dissipation before the curtain came down on the Theater with a Cast of Thousands. In that indiscreet swarm, each man—from the libertine aristocrat to the ignorant rustic—found his designated place among the numerous pleats of the courtesans' hierarchic fan. When Napoleon installed the Council of State in the Palais-Royal, the place was already inhabited by invisible carcasses—and it was preparing to abandon those remains to an enemy power: the Administration. A few years later—first secretively, then frenziedly—the arcades began to open their mouths toward the streets of Paris. The essences of the Palais-Royal, which had withdrawn into the shadows, returned; they dispersed throughout a stifling, artificial space and multiplied within the city. Benjamin's perceptive eye would have seen those mouths as entrances to the Hades of the new world, *facilis descensus Averni*. "In ancient Greece, people knew of places that gave access to the Underworld. Our whole waking life is a land where at certain hidden points we descend into the Underworld—a land full of scarcely visible places out of which dreams flow. During the day we pass by them, suspecting nothing; but once sleep comes, we quickly head back to them. Groping in the darkness, we lose our way in those obscure passages. In daylight, the labyrinth of the city's streets resembles consciousness, and the arcades (the tunnels that lead to the city's past) flow into them without attracting attention. But at night, among the dark masses of buildings, the denser blackness of the arcades stands out, frighteningly. The belated passerby hastens past them, unless we have encouraged him to venture through those narrow alleyways." Paris in its industrial prehistory, after the insolent spectacle of the Palais-Royal, found traces of the *mundus* in the darkness. In the days when Rome was founded, and even before the city was given a name, it was the custom to dig a "round pit" called the *mundus*. According to Plutarch, the pit was filled with "the first fruits of all that is good according to tradition and necessary according to nature." And the pit was considered a door leading to the underworld (*deorum tristium et inferum quasi ianua*). Such was the case, too, in the arcades: the first fruits of merchandise were crowded together in motley displays, under glass ceilings, amid little marble tables and cast-iron columns. Just as "the soil of Rome was sown with the mouths of Hell," Paris was riddled with chambers of venality where "on one side gaslight Sirens sang, and, on the other, oil-lamp odalisques delighted the eye." But the adventures that mingle here are primarily the adventures of objects. Timid yet despotic, enveloped in the stagnant air of the shop windows, they soon abandon themselves to illegitimate crossbreeding. They discover "occult affinities: palm plant and dust mop, hair dryer and Venus of Milo, prostheses and letter-writing manuals are all found here together, after a long separation." In a passage from Cato quoted by Festus, we read: "The *mundus* takes its name from the *mundus* [vault of heaven] that rises above us. And as I have learned from those who have entered it, its form is indeed like that of the *mundus* on high." In an arcade, the celestial and subterranean vaults do not exist, except in the milky light reflected in its shopfronts and allusive windowpanes. The prudent Romans believed it unpropitious to begin a war on one of the three days of the year when the pit full of first fruits was open. *"Mundus patet,"* they said ("The *mundus* is open"). Parisians under the Restoration and under Louis-Philippe viewed the arcades chiefly as a practical and lucrative means of attracting people who wished to idle about, sheltered from the elements. To Benjamin they seemed a collection of oneiric fragments that we would like to visit after we have awakened. Writing about the arcades, he repeated one of the gestures that was essential to the founding ritual of Rome: after the *mundus* had been dug, Plutarch says, "everyone brought a handful of earth from his native province and threw it among the first fruits, mixing everything together." The earth of German Romanticism at last encountered what it did not yet know: the Big City.

Despite what Benjamin says, the great book inspired by the arcades is not so much Aragon's *Peasant of Paris* (bewitching though it is), but Céline's *Death on the Installment Plan*, with its stories of the Passage des Bérésinas (actually the Passage Choiseul), where Céline's mother had a shop. She mended lace, often for frivolous and wealthy clients who were quick to shoplift dainty bits of trimming, concealing them in a flutter of sleeves; the only food she cooked was pasta with butter, so that no odors would permeate her delicate merchandise; she moved anxiously and haltingly around the stifling shop, since she was lame in one leg. But Benjamin did not include *Death on the Installment Plan* among the disparate sources for his book on the Paris arcades; perhaps he had not even read it. From the outset, Benjamin was defensive and suspicious when it came to Céline; obviously forcing the comparison, he grouped him with Benn and Jung as a proponent of "clinical nihilism in literature," which he planned to discuss in a lecture. But these writers are linked less by that incessantly talked-about "nihilism" than by the alarm bells Benjamin heard in their works: behind Jung's academic, pseudo-scientific prose, erratic and aggressive images hovered—images that could not be translated into dialectics. Benn, he realized, was sneering at culture, much as Brecht did at the opposite end of the spectrum. But Benjamin had already decided to submit to Brecht's harsh ferule, and he thus rejected all other alternatives. In Céline, ultimately, all was swept along from the beginning by a dark current that overwhelmed every island of momentary refuge, every possibility of another history that was not the *"petite musique"* of gradual decomposition. Yet if there is a poetics of the arcades—if those highly artificial places have what one might call a secretion, an essence—it is what little Destouches, the morose boy in the shop's back room, absorbed silently from his mother: "My mother still works. I remember that in the arcade, when she was younger, there was always an enormous heap of lace to be mended, a prodigious peak towering over her table—a mountain of work that would bring only a few francs. It never ended. She had to do it, so that we could eat. It gave me nightmares, and her as well. I've never forgotten it. Like her, I always come to my table and see an enormous pile waiting for me—a pile of Horror that I would like to patch up before having done with everything."

⚓

Historians are unanimous in criticizing the ease with which Talleyrand made money through his negotiations. He obtained substantial sums, called *douceurs,* from a wide variety of sources. Even his contemporaries were curious to know the details of how he so insolently lined his pockets. Paul-François Barras devotes seven pages of his *Mémoires* to a list of the "diplomatic gratuities and affairs of Talleyrand, Prince de Bénévent"—a list that he claims to have obtained from Madame de Staël. Adding up the various sums through the year 1815, he arrives at the majestic figure of 117,690,000 francs (excluding the negotiations that Talleyrand conducted by means of his wife or his emissaries).

But no historian has managed to prove that Talleyrand conducted some important negotiation solely because of the *douceurs* he would receive. He made others give him money, a great deal of money, to do what he would have done in any case. In this he followed the lead of his friend-enemy Mirabeau. Talleyrand, more than anyone else, clearly understood that history had moved from the world of *douceur* to that of *douceurs.* Consequently, he felt it was time to make a change in the diplomatic practice of accepting *douceurs,* which had a long-standing tradition: he no longer took "snuffboxes or jewels, as was the custom, but only cash." To him, a snuffbox would have been insulting and superfluous. Money, in contrast, was the surest way of hiding oneself, a means of keeping the world at a distance and of blinding it with a cloud of golden dust that rendered it temporarily helpless. Only one clear and very strict rule linked the age of *douceur* with that of *douceurs*—a rule that Talleyrand stated one day for Vitrolles, to explain why Bourrienne had not been appointed prefect of police: "What do you expect? Bourrienne wasn't here. He was returning from Hamburg in a rickety carriage. At the outskirts of Paris a wheel broke, and while it was being repaired he lost twenty-four hours. That's what it means to be a poor devil. And Bourrienne, even if he had an income of two hundred thousand livres, would still be a poor devil. You see, above all else, you must never be a poor devil." This was his gloss, profane and precise, on the biblical precept, "Unto every one that hath shall be given."

The *douceurs* would later quickly vanish at the gambling table, in his misguided speculations and his ongoing project of perfecting his *savoir vivre*. Carême remained his cook, however. Three times Talleyrand had to auction off his beloved library. The last time, at a sale in London, the 3,465 items of his *bibliotheca splendidissima* brought him 210,000 francs. He was then sixty-two years old. On the day of Talleyrand's death, the newspapers were full of solemn and inane reflections. Stendhal, who was in Marseilles, read them with irritation. That same evening he dashed off an essay of his own on Talleyrand's death, "out of impatience . . . [and] out of indignation at all the pompous sentiments." He was "dead tired," and in his mind whirled the image of a Spanish dancer, Dolores Seral, for whom he had just expressed his admiration. But the first sentence of his personal epitaph for Talleyrand, which he never finished, burns away all intellectual haziness and reveals the delightfully disreputable truth: "Monsieur de Talleyrand was a man of infinite wit who always happened to be short of money."

While Johann Caspar Schmidt was growing up in an obscure corner of Germany—before he became Max Stirner, author of the only Western book to present the idea of revolt in its chemically pure state—the elderly Talleyrand was engaging in lengthy conversations with Dorothée prior to his long sleepless nights in which "one thinks of so terribly many things." Once he dwelt on his memories of the seminary: "I was so unhappy that I spent the first two years at the seminary almost without speaking to anyone. I lived alone, in silence. In my free time I withdrew to the library, where I sought out and devoured the most revolutionary books I could find, feeding on the history of rebellions, sedition, and upheavals of all countries. I was angry at society, and did not understand why I couldn't occupy the position that naturally belonged to me—why I was deprived of it simply because I was afflicted by a childhood infirmity."

"Angry at society": these are words that no one would expect to hear from Talleyrand's lips. Yet they are confirmed, with subtle differences, by what Talleyrand wrote in his *Mémoires*: "In the seminary, I suffered from a sadness that few other sixteen-year-olds can have felt. I sought no one's acquaintance. I did everything sullenly. I resented my superiors, my parents, all institutions, and especially the power that people gave to the social conventions to which I had to submit.

"I spent three years at Saint-Sulpice seminary, almost without speaking. They thought I was haughty, and often reproached me for it . . . I was merely a decent young man, extremely unhappy and inwardly enraged . . . The library of Saint-Sulpice, enriched by Cardinal de Fleury, was vast and well chosen. I spent my days there reading the works of the great historians, the moralists, and a few poets, as well as the private lives of a number of statesmen. I devoured travel accounts. A new land, the dangers of storms, the tale of a disaster, descriptions of countries where one could see the effects of great changes, sometimes of upheavals—all this held a strong attraction for me. Sometimes my own situation seemed less unalterable, when I compared it to those great shifts, those great shocks, which modern navigators described so often in their writings." Talleyrand made some clever modifications: whereas he spoke of "rebellions" and "sedition" in private conversation, he referred to "travel accounts" and "storms" in his published memoirs. But weren't they, after all, the same thing? Weren't they just so many forms of the "torrent" that prevents us from ever settling in a safe place? Traces of Max Stirner's adolescent years survive only in a few notes that his professors made in their record books, at boarding schools that were surely not as distinguished as the seminary of Saint-Sulpice. But all of *Der Einzige* is infused with the memory of long, violent daydreams of revolt. Stirner and Talleyrand, when they came out into the open, both found themselves obliged to forge ahead into a dizzying nothingness. Stirner belonged to nothingness from the beginning, and was to represent it in all its purity and claims to absoluteness. Talleyrand's nothingness was born of his exclusion from his "natural position," which for him continued to exist amid all the upheavals; it was a legitimate place, representing an order that neither storms nor rebellions could disturb. He never lapsed, however, into the crude naïveté of thinking that order could be identified with some social system. Yet any social system was obliged to hint at that order. This was a reflection of Saint Paul's enigma, "Non est enim potestas nisi a Deo" ("There is no power which doesn't come from God"). Throughout his life he felt a premonition. He perceived, as if scenting a faint perfume, that behind the world, behind the raging of its waves, stretches an inaccessible "hidden ocean," heavenly and terrestrial, where the last vibrations of the waves converge. There in that hidden ocean, together with Dawn, had appeared—and still stood—the prop that separates and steadies Heaven and Earth: the ṛta.

Talleyrand's last negotiating table was his deathbed. As always, he had prepared that debate well in advance, and without anyone's noticing. When his wife (who became obese but who had formerly been a voluptuous adventuress in India) finally died, Talleyrand said laconically, "This greatly simplifies my position." It was a sign that he was beginning to make his last moves. Cold and impassive, as his legend demanded, he worked out his deliberate game over more than three years. One day he remarked casually to Dorothée, "'I wouldn't mind seeing the Abbé Dupanloup . . . He's our confessor,' he added with a half-serious smile." A few weeks later the abbé was invited to the Hôtel Saint-Florentin, where he heard the Prince recall what the dying Fénelon had said about Saint-Sulpice ("I know nothing more apostolic, nothing more venerable"). He, too, had been educated at that seminary, in his morose and dreamy adolescence, when he was trying to be a "little Bonaparte"—years which he now claimed had been the happiest he had ever known. Through the Abbé Dupanloup and Dorothée, here acting as his minister, the sovereign Talleyrand negotiated with the Church in the last four months of his life and arrived at a "formula for atonement." Two obstacles had to be overcome: first, as bishop he had voted for the impious civil constitution of the clergy and had ordained some constitutional bishops; second, after being demoted to the lay communion by a brief of Pius VII, he had married, breaking the unrescinded vow of sacerdotal chastity. A number of papers, repeatedly revised, passed back and forth between the Hôtel Saint-Florentin and the archbishop of Paris, Monseigneur de Quélen, a staunch Breton who for years had begged the Prince to perform this act of contrition. In the context of these negotiations, the Prince's last public appearance takes on a meaning of its own. Wearing a close-fitting black frock coat and a flowing lace cravat, the eighty-four-year-old Talleyrand, looking like a *merveilleux* of the Directory, was "carried in the arms of two liveried manservants" up the steps of the Institut de France to deliver the eulogy for an undistinguished diplomat named Reinhard. Once again, he had a precise and clear-cut reason for making this speech, which might have seemed a whimsical tribute. It was to be his "farewell to the public," delivered in his most perfect style. ("It's just like Voltaire! The very best of Voltaire!" Victor Cousin repeated after the speech, with enthusiastic gestures and the awkward excitement of a scholar.) But above all, it was to be an allusion. In his summary of the life of Reinhard, Talleyrand emphasized, with superb clarity, the importance of Reinhard's theological studies, the same sort of studies that had guided the speaker in his youth. Launching into a detailed list of the great theologian-diplomats who had graced the history of France, the Prince remarked that the art of diplomacy, when seen from a certain angle, looked like a branch of the study of religion. "I heard him say that he considered himself one of the foremost theologians of his time," a faithful observer, Baron von Gagern, had written years earlier. Talleyrand now revealed the rationale that underlay his paradoxical claim. Copies of his eulogy on Reinhard were delivered the next morning to Monseigneur de Quélen and to the Abbé Dupanloup.

It is pointless to wonder if Talleyrand's desire to recant was "sincere." It would be like wondering if the final documents of the Congress of Vienna were "sincere." To be sure, his initial impulse to begin negotiations was not religious but ceremonial. In his last years, Talleyrand foresaw the danger that lay ahead: after his death, he could be denied a religious burial; he might be granted nothing more than a wretched civil funeral. This was his sole fear. He said to his physician, "I'm afraid of only one thing: impropriety." All his life

Talleyrand had been scandal itself, but that scandal had always had the power of conferring order, of eluding every *inconvenance*. And now, at his death, that precarious image risked breaking down in the face of the Church's solemn refusal. In his last performance, he would appear as a man expelled from the most ancient order. Reading Fénelon, Talleyrand paused at one passage: "Let us cast a glance at the Church, at that visible society of the children of God which has been preserved through the ages: it is the kingdom without end. All other powers rise and fall. Having amazed the world, they disappear." Talleyrand wrote in the margin, "Very beautiful!" His place was in the kingdom without end. "I realize I have to do something to placate Rome," he said to Dorothée.

But a recantation could also render his whole life vain, by denying it. And here Talleyrand's political genius proved itself one last time. In politics, actions themselves are less decisive than the time at which they are performed. A politician is someone who has time on his side. And Talleyrand always had an abiding faith in the power of time. Postponement was the esoteric weapon of his policy. This time, Talleyrand decided to push it to its limit, namely death. "Most things get done by not being done": this is a purely Western translation of the *wu wei* of Lao-Tzu, and Talleyrand's ruling maxim. It was another secret that he would one day confide to Gagern. Now the maxim was given its strictest application: one must allow things to be done at the last moment before death, and even *decide* that they happen in this way. In his death agony, on the penultimate day of his life, Talleyrand four times but with great politeness rejected the invitation to sign his recantation. At last he said that he would sign it early the next day, between five and six. At dawn on that May morning, as the clock was striking six, he signed the document, after Dorothée, pronouncing each word distinctly, had slowly read the two pages of text, in the presence of illustrious witnesses. More than a recantation, it expressed his submission to the authority of the Church; its *verba generalia* cloaked all offensive memories.

To postpone this act until precisely the right moment in his death agony was his ordeal. Tormented by the "enormous sore" caused by his anthrax, which made it impossible for him to lie on his back, he was supported in the arms of two men who were replaced every two hours; his shoulders rested on a pillow "that was hung from the ceiling with ropes." Talleyrand was a gambler to the last: he made a wager on the hour of his own death, staking everything on his last moment of lucidity. His final act would be, once again, a signature. A minimal act, but the only one that could stand for the whole. Next to his signature (CHARLES-MAURICE, PRINCE DE TALLEYRAND, which had appeared at the bottom of all the great treaties of the age), and set as close as possible to it, there was to be the seal of an unchallenged authority—the seal of death. And so it was: nine hours after signing his name, Talleyrand died. Ensuring the minimum interval between his signature and the seal of death guaranteed him against any attack. But when the document reached Rome, the Holy See deemed it insufficient. If Talleyrand had survived for a few more days, he would have had to undergo the humiliation of signing again—and of signing a far more stringent text. Now it was too late. Talleyrand could no longer correct himself, could no longer condemn himself with the words imposed by the Church, which would have marred the sovereignty of his style. The Prince had already received the sacraments; he had died—as he had specified in the first words of his will—"in the bosom of the Roman Catholic Apostolic Church." Yet the Church never publicized the fact that the Pope considered Talleyrand's recantation inadequate. For a long time those pages remained on the desk of Gregory XVI, among his most precious documents. Then they vanished. The maternal Vatican archives contain no trace of them.

The theological struggle, the true *agōnía*, ended with a statement of breathtaking insolence and wisdom, which was recorded by a single witness, Prosper de Barante. When the Abbé Dupanloup approached the Prince to administer extreme unction, Talleyrand held out the backs of his hands to him, saying, "Monsieur l'abbé, remember I am a bishop." On that long-ago day when Talleyrand had been ordained a bishop, he had been anointed on the palms. Now his hands were to be anointed on the other side, so that they would be entirely covered. With that act, Talleyrand acknowledged that the arbitrary will of his parents, which had forced him to undergo spiritual investiture, had actually been more clear-sighted than any design of his. He had been forced to protect the sacred, wrapping it in scandal—through "a revolution that has been going on for fifty years," as he said in the text he had just signed. But now he held out the backs of his hands for anointment. He who for so many years had been the very image of the devil acknowledged that, at the outset, his soul had been sold to God.

In the relentless attack on Talleyrand, Chateaubriand thought he had outdone everyone else in the field by commenting on his death as follows: "Monsieur de Talleyrand, called before the supreme tribunal many times over the years, was stubbornly disobedient. At the behest of God, death sought him and finally found him. If one were to look closely at this life, which was as rotten as Monsieur de Lafayette's life was healthy, one would have to confront a disgust I am incapable of overcoming. Pestilent men resemble the corpses of prostitutes: the ulcers have so corroded them that they cannot be used for dissection." But there was someone who went even further: Sainte-Beuve. True to his style, he gave vent to harsh invective, but concealed himself in the poisonous whisper of a postscript: "God save us from the *douceur* of corrupt men, if any of their important interests is at stake."

"It can be said that, like the kings of France, Talleyrand died in public," after signing his recantation. Precisely at eight o'clock Louis-Philippe appeared, accompanied by Madame Adélaide. He was wearing a brown coat and shiny boots, and was holding his hat nervously in his hand. Looking *"tant soit peu bourgeois"* ("a little bit bourgeois"), he gazed at the Prince's old, somewhat faded dressing gown and his high forehead. Talleyrand dispelled all awkwardness by introducing those present to the king, in the order established by protocol, right down to his first valet, Hélie. In the hours that followed, a small crowd collected in the drawing room next to the dying man's bedchamber. A number of politicians, "some with powdered heads, some with bald heads, gathered around the blazing fire. Their animated conversation—although, by the good taste and feeling of him who directed it, conducted in a low tone—filled the apartment with its unceasing murmur." Colmache, the Prince's secretary, was observing the throng. He saw Montrond, Talleyrand's old companion in his vices and speculations, sitting off to one side, alone and sad: Montrond "sat silent and sorrowful, apart from the rest, apparently lost in thought, paying no attention to the various details of the scene which was being enacted around him, and which, had it been elsewhere, would not have failed to call forth some of the sharp and bitter traits of satire for which he is so much dreaded." The beautiful Duchesse de V. was lying on a divan by the window, surrounded by "a bevy of young beaux, all robber-like and *'jeune France,'* kneeling on the carpet beside her or sitting low at her feet on the cushions of the divan." As soon as the whisper went around that the Prince had died, the rooms immediately emptied: "One would have thought that a flight of crows had suddenly taken wing, so great was the precipitation with which each one hurried from the mansion, in the hope of being first to spread the news among the particular set or coterie of which he or she happened to be the oracle." Only the truly faithful remained, those who perhaps mourned the Prince most deeply: his servants. Each maintained the routine to which he was accustomed. All of a sudden, Colmache saw the cook appear: "Punctual to the hour in the morning at which he had for so many years been summoned to receive his orders, now followed by his bevy of *marmitons,* with their snow-white costumes and long carving-knives, [he walked] with solemn step to the foot of the bed, and kneeling down with cotton cap in hand, breathe[d] a short prayer. Each sprinkled the corpse with holy water, and then the whole procession withdrew in the same silence with which they had entered."

⚬⃨

Letter from Petersburg

Monsieur le Chevalier,

I'm writing to you after a hiatus of fourteen months, during which I've had no correspondence with anyone. The Neva, which is flowing before me, seems in the meanwhile to have carried me even farther away. Through the taffeta curtains I catch the scent of Kamchatka.

As you well know, my spells of rage and intransigence have always been mitigated by my innate cheerfulness; but under the yoke of vain and constant suffering, this buoyancy has now well-nigh vanished. In the evenings I summon my carriage and, almost forcing myself, go to call on those same ladies who once enchanted me. My head feels overburdened, weary, *flattened* beneath the enormous weight of *nothingness.* Nowadays I converse chiefly with myself, even if such unsociable behavior disgusts me. But one has to do something. So I shut myself away and read, with an ecstasy that makes me shiver; at night I often hear myself railing aloud at people who are dead, yet hideously vital. And the harsh world of politics is always invading my mind, mingling with all my ideas and turning them into poison. My most recent pleasurable experience occurred a few months ago: I went to see the remains of a mammoth found inside a block of ice at the mouth of the Lena. Although polar bears had partly devoured the carcass, I was able to touch it, to stroke it—that irrefutable witness to the Flood, that promise of the coming Fire which tortures and moves us with its inevability. Its ear was still covered with fur. Five or six times I put my nose to its flesh. The most extravagant voluptuary inhaling the most exquisite Oriental perfume could never know such delight as I derived from the fetid odor of that putrefied, antediluvian meat. *Quod semper, quod ubique, quod ab omnibus.* In the presence of that carcass I felt that the sweetness of dogma—the emerald spindle on which all of my sensations are wound—was still gently vibrating. Then I went back to conversing with the cupboards. Faced with the unspeakable ridicule of modern philosophy, my certainties are like that mammoth, intact in its mountain of ice. And like that carcass, I allow myself to be torn slowly to pieces by the polar bears of my solitude. There's only one thing I'd like to know, my good chevalier: What are people talking about in Paris these days?

Your
Senator from St. Petersburg

Sainte-Beuve shows us how the *bon mot* became the *fin mot*—the ultimate, concealed truth—and how the *fin mot* proved to be so bitter that, out of decency, people generally avoided saying it; eventually it became confounded with too many other *mots*. Otherwise the laborious trudging along life's road might have ended in hopeless paralysis. "You have to keep some of your illusions, some of your faith in the progress of life. When you know the *fin mot* too well, nature removes you from the stage, because you would prevent the drama from proceeding."

"To put some *thoughts* into people's heads every now and then, so that people will pass them around: 'As we read in Lichtenberg, in Meister, in Mencius . . .'" Sainte-Beuve's greatest concern was to "pass them around"—to insinuate into his articles those thoughts, those little sentences, that most belonged to him, but without attributing them to himself, so that they wouldn't be conspicuous. Otherwise they would have been too salient—and their delicacy would have suffered from the exposure. He felt that an author must wait for readers who will be able to penetrate the outer layers, perceive the hidden vibrations. But over the years, Sainte-Beuve's circumspection has become self-defeating. We find it difficult to see beneath the surface of his writings, and feel somewhat irritated that he should be so deaf to certain writers whom he could not—would not—recognize (this was the charge that Proust leveled at him). Meanwhile we forget to consider his own work with the same far-sighted gaze we accuse him of denying to others.

No one had greater respect for the conventions of literary life than Sainte-Beuve. Even as he lay dying, he dictated a few polite lines in response to an article by Caro. ("Such gentleness! What balm! How many essential truths come to light, not without some slight remorse!") In no one else did those conventions produce so much poison. Some of this venom went into the posthumous *Cahiers*, fragments of intense color; and some of it, in the three years from 1843 to 1845, emigrated to Switzerland, where Juste Olivier's *Revue Suisse* published the searing *Chroniques parisiennes* by an anonymous writer (Sainte-Beuve). But as the author wryly noted, "Paris concerns itself only with what is published in Paris." So it happened that, two weeks after reverently hailing Chateaubriand's *Vie de Rancé* in the *Revue des Deux Mondes* ("When it comes to Monsieur de Chateaubriand, the critic can no longer act as a critic; he merely gathers flowers along his way and fills his basket"), the same pen greeted the book with sarcasm in the *Revue Suisse*. Sainte-Beuve remembered clearly how Chateaubriand's hollow tones had resounded in his literary youth. He recalled how Chateaubriand had stood beside Madame Récamier, who "every day conceived a thousand charming ways of eliciting and renewing praises for him"—praises that the melancholy old man never wearied of: "From all sides she gathered new friends and admirers around him. She tethered us all to the foot of his statue with a golden chain." For a long time Sainte-Beuve had been a shy acolyte at the delightful shrine of the Abbaye-aux-Bois. Chairs would be arranged in circles, like planetary orbits, and Chateaubriand would enter with the manuscript of the *Mémoires d'outre-tombe* wrapped in a silk scarf. The young critic had been paralyzed by the glory of the master and by Madame Récamier. Never once in those years had he been able to hint at what already seemed obvious to him: that Chateaubriand had less to do with religion, politics, and thought than with the corrosive cult of two jealous powers: literature and women. All the more reason for Sainte-Beuve to shudder, since he recognized a similar inclination in himself; but it was confined to his study, or to a room of the Bibliothèque Mazarine, or scattered in the wanderings of an anonymous Parisian *rôdeur*—in any case camouflaged forever by a scholarly grisaille, with the housekeeper in the shadows, holding the purse. And this inclination had remained in its niche for years, with no American forests, no thick aristocratic walls, no travels in the Holy Land or along the lagoons. His soul, breathing the fragrance of Joseph Delorme's prematurely withered verses, had taken "only a single journey: that from Amiens to Paris, perhaps with an excursion to Rouen during holidays from the Ecole de Médicine." But now the English papers were calling Chateaubriand "the good old man." Sainte-Beuve maliciously translated this as *"le vieux bonhomme"* ("the simple old fellow") and twisted the knife: "This means he has been crowned both with laurel and with a stocking cap."

The gout-ridden Chateaubriand had dictated the *Vie de Rancé* from his iron bed in his room on the rue du Bac, where the only other piece of furniture was a white wooden chest with a broken lock. He had culled quotations from the seventeenth-century volumes brought to him by a repulsive Breton secretary, and then had mixed them up with his own irrepressible memories, which continued to surface in that second *outre-tombe*, since he had already completed the *Mémoires,*

and his loyal guardians Madame de Chateaubriand and Madame
Récamier had feared that their beloved's imagination would have no
further outlet. Now confronted with the *Vie de Rancé,* that ghostly
and still sensuous delirium, Sainte-Beuve could announce to the
Swiss with the brutality of a gossip columnist, "Chateaubriand's
Rancé is a disappointment." Then he clarified: "Those of us who are
at a distance and who thus feel less obligatory deference than others
must admit frankly that this book, which we thought would be
simple and austere, has become, as a result of the author's negligence
and lack of seriousness, a genuine piece of bric-à-brac. The author
flings everything into it, scrambles everything, empties all his cupboards." He continued, with a sneer, "The most charming and frivolous images are continually flying out, hovering in every corner and
behind every column of the cloister. One carefree wit remarked the
other day that the book is truly like the temptation of Saint Anthony:
there are so many devils in it, and such pretty ones! In certain parts,
it seems as if La Trappe must have passageways leading to the wings
of the Opéra stage."

The Trappists were not pleased either: the book, which Chateaubriand had written as an homage to the founder of their order, the
great reformer Armand de Rancé, and as an act of penance for his
own transgressions, had nothing pious about it. Indeed, it unleashed
a horde of demons on La Trappe. The monastery's secretary sensed
that underlying the book was "a foolish belief in certain slanderous
and improbable tales." The Abbé Dubois, an austere historian who
had written a study of Rancé, accused Chateaubriand of perversely
and obstinately ignoring "whatever did not fit into his novel." And
this is true: the *Vie de Rancé,* Chateaubriand's last wandering, is
scarcely an edifying biography. It was his final surrender to free—
even wild—association, a perverse rummaging in his own memory
that stirred up shadows among the ruins of time. Their movement
is abrupt, intemperate, erratic. One feels the strain behind the virtuous *pensum* and the attraction of an overflowing monologue. The
prose juxtaposes facts, quotations, and recollections like so many
stones that are held together only by their moss. Utterly lacking in
coherence and consistency, it ranges from lulling gentleness to cruel,
sharp insights. The book is devoted to the man who had dared to
write, "We live in order to die. This is God's plan: He grants us the

joy of experiencing the light, only to deprive us of it." Yet the *Vie de Rancé* expresses a consuming regret for every moment of lost life and leaves us in a state of mind incompatible with serenity. It is a farewell that, behind the mask of contrition, pursues memories of sin. Nothing is more murky than the restlessness and tedium of an old man.

Finally, Chateaubriand made use of a blasphemous superstition in his book, and this was doubtless what the stern secretary of the convent was alluding to. It was the story concerning the severed head of the Duchesse de Montbazon—a tale that had been making the rounds for nearly two centuries. Mistress of the young Rancé, she was "one of the most beautiful creatures you ever set eyes on"; "at every ball, she outshone all the other women." Tallemant assures us of this, even though she was not to his taste, since she had "breasts twice the desirable size. To be sure, they were beautiful, white, and firm, but it was all the more difficult to conceal them." The Cardinal de Retz characterized her by saying that he had "never seen anyone who maintained so little respect for virtue while living steeped in vice." She was presented at Court at an early age, and had a passion for love affairs and money, which she often mixed together; at such times, "greed tempered her debauchery, but did not get in its way." She claimed that at thirty she'd no longer be good for anything— there would be nothing left to do but throw her in the river. She was thirty-five when the wedding of Princess Marie was celebrated, yet her beauty was still matchless. Rancé, fourteen years younger than she, was already an abbé when he fell in love with her. On the day he was introduced to her, he had long curly hair, two emeralds at his wrists, a diamond on one finger, a sword at his side, and two pistols in his saddle, and was wearing a violet doublet made of exquisite fabric. Daniel de Larroque, in his pamphlet "on the true reasons for the conversion of the abbé of La Trappe," which he published in 1685 and intended as an attack on Rancé, claimed that the turning point in Rancé's life came with the sudden death of Madame de Montbazon: "I have already said that the abbé of La Trappe was a ladies' man and had several love affairs. The last was with a duchess famed for her beauty, who, after narrowly escaping death while crossing a river, met with it a few months later. The abbé occasionally liked to sojourn in the country, and thus was not in Paris when this unforeseen death occurred. His servants, who knew of his passion, took care to keep the news of the sad event from him. He learned of it only on his return . . . He went straight up to the duchess's apartments, where he was allowed entry at any hour; but instead of finding the pleasure he anticipated, the first thing he saw was a coffin. He knew it was his beloved's—he saw her bloodstained head, which had rolled from beneath the cloth with which it had been carelessly covered. It had been severed from her body because the coffin was too short, and this way there was no need to get a new and longer one." Others said that Rancé stole Madame de Montbazon's head—that he had it with him throughout the stages of his conversion, and even kept it in his cell during all his austerities in the cloister. Years later, it was rumored that the head was displayed in the room of Rancé's successors at La Trappe. Portraits of Rancé often depict a skull among the papers, folio volumes, and crucifixes. This skull, in whose silence the rule of La Trappe was condensed, would thus be not an image of death but an irreplaceable fetish, a reminder of the woman who "so often had bent over the bosom of life."

The impudent Chateaubriand pretends to examine the credibility of this legend with a philologist's accuracy. He even proposes a plausible explanation: the duchess was decapitated for the purposes of anatomical study, and not because some stingy person wanted to save the price of a coffin. His conclusion, in any case, is clear: "All poets have adopted Larroque's version; all religious men have rejected it." Here the waters divide and flow in different directions. Chateaubriand's last book, which was supposed to present him to the world as a penitent, actually contained his most wicked revelation: in this case and always, he would ally himself with those who believe more in legend than in religion, with those for whom religion is itself a legend. He at last admitted that he was primarily a writer. Before taking his leave, he placed Madame de Montbazon's head in the cell of the reformer of La Trappe. It was truly his last piece of bric-à-brac. Then he shut his cupboards.

"What have you been doing these past forty years?"
The Trappist's lips parted an instant to break the silence: *"Annos aeternos in mente habui"* ("I was thinking of the years in Eternity").

. . .

MONSIEUR DE SAINT-LOUIS: I have always been a soldier, and I was still in command of my regiment, which served under Turenne, when I visited La Trappe for the first time. The monastery was located in my part of the country, tucked away among hills and ponds, in the ancient forest of Le Perche. Great solitary leaves glided over the water as if over a surface of lead. I had never seen an area so devoid of life, unless it was at the Escorial. I had been informed that Rancé, our Monsieur de la Trappe, was being threatened by people who opposed his reforms, which paid homage to silence. I offered him my services, to defend him. He did not refuse my offer; he did not accept my offer. He did not even smile. Time passed, and I sold the command of my regiment to Villacerf's eldest son. I returned to Rancé, asking that he admit me to La Trappe. He housed me in a building that he had constructed outside the walls of the monastery. One day he said something to me that was to guide my actions for more than thirty years: "Make a Rule for yourself. It can be as lenient as you wish, but you must adhere to it." And once he said (giving me a glimpse of the gentleman who had loved Madame de Montbazon, the most beautiful woman of our time and the most shameless in vice) that I, with my long experience of the world, must already know the humiliations awaiting me; for the men we live among in this world are the instruments God has chosen to humiliate us, and in a single instant we can often suffer all the mortifications that a monk endures only in the course of many years. For a long time I was desperate and never left my lodgings, just outside the precincts of the true Rule. But one day, amid that silence, I saw the world pass by on a breath of wind. It was light, insubstantial, hollow. The Rule had done its work. Then I was happy again to be with my weapons, in a remote garrison at the ends of the earth, where you can still hear snatches of a soldier's song and the rumble of a rolling cask, while waiting for the clamor to end.

NOTES

NOTES

Notes are keyed by page number.

1 "a difficult man to follow": Duchesse d'Abrantès, *Salon de Monsieur de Tal-leyrand*, in *Histoire des salons de Paris* (Paris: Ladvocat, 1838), vol. 6, p. 1.

2 "ampler space for the gods": *Śatapatha Brāhmaṇa* (tr. J. Eggeling), I, 4, 1, 23.

4 *"uncertainty about people's identity"*: L. Bloy, *L'Ame de Napoléon*, in *Oeuvres* (Paris: Mercure de France, 1966), vol. 6, pp. 266–267.

4 "a Napoleon was needed": Ibid., p. 306.

4 "general homogeneity": Letter from Lavater to Goethe, November 1773, in W. Goethe, *Werke* (Zurich: Artemis, 1954), vol. 13, p. 108.

5 "Nature forms man": W. Goethe, *Aus Lavaters Physiognomischen Fragmenten*, in *Werke*, vol. 13, p. 33.

5 "our Weimar modesty": Sulpiz Boisserée, in *Goethes Gespräche, 1817–1832*, in W. Goethe, *Werke*, vol. 13, p. 434.

5 "supreme diplomat of the century": W. Goethe, *Collection des portraits histo-riques de M. le baron Gérard*, in *Werke*, vol. 13, pp. 993–994.

7 "utterly common": Duchesse de Dino, *Chronique de 1831 à 1862* (Paris: Plon, 1909), vol. 1, p. 248.

7 "Goethe, the Talleyrand of art": Sainte-Beuve, "Molière," in *Oeuvres de Molière* (Paris: Paulin, 1835), vol. 1, p. 248.

7 "Sainte-Beuve disliked argument": Barbey d'Aurevilly, *Goethe et Diderot* (Paris: Lemerre, 1913), p. 116.

7 "Sainte-Beuve had a flash of inspiration": Ibid., p. 274.

8 "gazing at himself in a mirror": Ibid., pp. 60–61.

8 "He loved the worldly life": Duchesse d'Abrantès, *Histoire des salons de Paris*, vol. 6, pp. 5–6.

8 "The benefits he enjoyed": Ibid., p. 6.

8 "There was only one course": *Mémoires du prince de Talleyrand* (Paris: Cal-mann Lévy, 1891), vol. 1, p. 124.

9 "age of revolutions": Sainte-Beuve, "Mirabeau et Sophie," in *Causeries du lundi* (Paris: Garnier, 1926), vol. 4, p. 1.

9 "that you are": *Chāndogya Upaniṣad*, VI, 8.

10 "India wound up becoming Germany": V. Hugo, "La Vision d'où est sorti ce livre," in *La Légende des siècles* (Paris: Gallimard, 1891), p. 10.

10 "wall of the centuries": Ibid., p. 8.

11 *"Expressa nocent"*: Duchesse d'Abrantès, *Histoire des salons de Paris*, vol. 6, p. 2.

11 "sagging corners of his mouth": Chateaubriand, *Mémoires d'outre-tombe* (Paris: Gallimard, 1958), vol. 2, p. 901.

11 "collection of every vice": *Mémoires de Barras* (Paris: Hachette, 1896), vol. 3, p. 134.

12 "Talleyrand, prince of": G. Flaubert, *Dictionnaire des idées reçues,* in *Oeuvres* (Paris: Gallimard, 1975), vol. 2, p. 1022.

13 "boulevards crowded with people": *Lettres et papiers du chancelier comte de Nesselrode, 1760–1815* (Paris: A. Lahure, n.d. [1908]), vol. 2, p. 114.

15 "*Principles* are fine": Talleyrand, *Mémoires* (Paris: Plon, 1982), p. 443.

15 "origins of the Wahnungwe": L. Frobenius, *Erythräa* (Berlin: Atlantis, 1931), pp. 149–150.

17 "descendant of one of the oldest families": E. Dumont, *Souvenirs sur Mirabeau* (Brussels: Hauman, 1832), p. 250.

17 "*a name and a coat of arms*": Talleyrand, *Mémoires,* p. 34. Subsequent citations come from the same source: "great houses," p. 35; "pharmacy," p. 36; "birth-right," p. 37; "silk dress adorned with lace," p. 37; "chest that held the linen," p. 37; "heredity of feelings," p. 38; "enlightened civilization," p. 36; "more scientific pharmacies," p. 37.

20 "smile of the multitude": Sainte-Beuve, "Mémoires du général La Fayette," from *Portraits littéraires,* in *Oeuvres* (Paris: Gallimard, 1960), vol. 2, p. 164. Subsequent citations come from the same source: "the idol of honor," p. 146; "Lafayette's primary motive," p. 148.

22 "I possess the secrets of many men": Balzac, *Le Père Goriot,* in *La Comédie Humaine* (Paris: Gallimard, 1971), vol. 2, pp. 940–941.

22 "a cold, impassive face": Stendhal, *Souvenirs d'égotisme,* in *Oeuvres intimes* (Paris: Gallimard, 1955), p. 1451. Subsequent citations come from the same source: "hero from Plutarch," p. 1452; "basic elegance," p. 1453; "polite as a king," p. 1453; "remember everyone's name," p. 1451; "all intriguers," p. 1452; "little nieces," p. 1458.

23 "Lucien had to endure": Stendhal, *Lucien Leuwen,* in *Romans et nouvelles* (Paris: Gallimard, 1972), vol. 1, p. 854.

Note for Lucien

25 "games my pen is playing": Stendhal, *Souvenirs d'égotisme,* in *Oeuvres intimes* (Paris: Gallimard, 1955), p. 1503.

25 "pulling out his watch and sighing": *Mémoires du Comte Alexandre de Tilly* (Paris: Jonquières, 1929), vol. 1, p. 224.

25 "I'm told it still lives": Ibid., p. 225.

26 "boring as an Italian *opera buffa*": Laclos, *Lettres inédites* (Paris: Mercure de France, 1904), p. 167.

26 "softened": Stendhal, *Souvenirs d'égotisme,* p. 1512.

26 "novelistic devices": Laclos, *Lettres inédites,* p. 239.

26 "coat of the new world": Chateaubriand, *Mémoires d'outre-tombe* (Paris: Gallimard, 1958), vol. 1, p. 293.

27 "the happiness of the human race": Ibid., p. 292.

27 "What a temple!": Letter from Hegel to his wife, September 30, 1827, in *Briefe von und an Hegel* (Leipzig: Duncker & Humblot, 1887), vol. 1, pp. 271–272.

27 "When I visited my mother": Talleyrand, *Mémoires* (Paris: Plon, 1982), p. 63.

28 "consistently light manner": *Mémoires de Madame de Rémusat* (Paris: Calmann Lévy, 1880), vol. 1, p. 196.

To Live in the Stream

28 "the torrent of *affaires*": Saint-Simon, *Mémoires* (Paris: Gallimard, 1958), vol. 4, p. 718.
29 "born bored": Ibid.
29 "in the person of Bonaparte": Talleyrand, *Mémoires* (Paris: Plon, 1982), p. 764.
29 "embarking on new adventures": *Souvenirs du baron de Barante* (Paris: Calmann Lévy, 1901), vol. 3, p. 550.
30 "*permanent* state": A. de Tocqueville, *L'Ancien Régime et la Révolution,* in *Oeuvres complètes* (Paris: Gallimard, 1971), vol. 2, p. 349.
30 "to achieve its ends": Ibid., p. 337.
30 "to study and be trained": Ibid., p. 338.
31 "the tempest itself": Metternich, *Mémoires documents et écrits divers* (Paris: Plon, 1881), vol. 3, p. 445.
31 "avalanche of statesmen": Letter of January 4, 1821, ibid., p. 447.
31 "some serious reflections": Chateaubriand, *Mémoires d'outre-tombe* (Paris: Gallimard, 1958), vol. 1, p. 938.
32 "the embraces of these dead": Ibid., p. 907.
32 "mad, sweet France": Sainte-Beuve, "Chateaubriana," in *Chateaubriand et son groupe littéraire sous l'Empire* (Paris: Garnier, 1948), vol. 2, p. 347.

Exempla Voluptatis

33 "no longer knew what was happening": Chateaubriand, *Mémoires d'outre-tombe* (Paris: Gallimard, 1958), vol. 1, p. 92.
33 "it was a slave who welcomed me": Ibid., p. 217.
34 "a nest of swans": Ibid., p. 425.

The Great Ball

35 "*spoils taken from the defeated*": "Mémoires de Frédéric de Gentz," in Metternich, *Mémoires, documents et écrits divers* (Paris: Plon, 1881), vol. 2, p. 474.
36 "this report is correct": Ibid., pp. 474–475.
36 "the cause of the people": Talleyrand, *Mémoires* (Paris: Plon, 1982), p. 769.
37 "improvement after its fall": B. Constant, *De l'esprit de conquète et de l'usurpation,* in *Oeuvres* (Paris: Gallimard, 1979), pp. 1003–1005. The five foregoing quotations come from the same source.
38 "if the sovereign does not cede it": "Instructions pour les ambassadeurs du Roi au Congrès," in Talleyrand, *Mémoires,* p. 671.
38 "mystical community of states": G. Ferrero, *Ricostruzione* (Milan: Garzanti, 1948), p. 165.

Treacherous Trifles

40 "long habit of dissipation": Fénelon, *Correspondance* (Paris: Ferra Jeune–Le Clere, 1827), vol. 6, pp. 211–212.

40 "breaches the world has made": Ibid., p. 218.

40 "pleasures of social conversation": Ibid., p. 227.

40 "monstrous confusion": Pascal, *Pensées*, in *Oeuvres complètes* (Paris: Gallimard, 1976), p. 1210.

41 "disparate or distant events": L. Bloy, *L'Ame de Napoléon*, in *Oeuvres* (Paris: Mercure de France, 1966), vol. 5, p. 292.

41 "terrible danger": Ibid., p. 306.

41 "born of vanity": Talleyrand, *Mémoires* (Paris: Plon, 1982), p. 156.

42 "great measures, *coups d'état*": B. Constant, *De l'esprit de conquête et de l'usurpation*, in *Oeuvres* (Paris: Gallimard, 1979), p. 1050–1051.

Sad Glory

43 "Horrible and grand": Napoléon, *Lettres d'amour à Joséphine* (Paris: Fayard, 1981), p. 99.

44 "proof of his ability": B. Constant, *De l'esprit de conquête et de l'usurpation* (Paris: Gallimard, 1979), p. 1052.

44 "impenetrable silence": F. von Gentz, "Journal de ce qui m'est arrivé de plus marquant dans le voyage que j'ai fait au quartier-général de S.M. le Roi de Prusse, le 2 d'Octobre 1806 et les jours suivants," in *Mémoires et lettres inédits du Chevalier de Gentz* (Stuttgart: L. Hallberger, 1841), pp. 280–281.

45 "ideas of the economists": *Mémoires de G.-J. Ouvrard, sur sa vie et des diverses opérations financières* (Paris: Moutardier, 1827), vol. 1, p. 135.

45 "royalty could not do without it": Ibid., p. 128.

45 "he did not create them": Chateaubriand, *Mémoires d'outre-tombe* (Paris: Gallimard, 1958), vol. 2, p. 908.

46 "a path that has no end": *Mémoires de G.-J. Ouvrard*, vol. 1, p. 59.

46 "the breaking point": Talleyrand, "Mémoire au Conseil Exécutif provisoire sur les rapports actuels de la France avec les autres Etats de l'Europe," in G. Pallain, *Correspondance diplomatique de Talleyrand: Le Ministère de Talleyrand sous le Directoire* (Paris: Plon, 1891), p. xiii.

47 "great families of the empire": Talleyrand, *Mémoires* (Paris: Plon, 1982), p. 326.

47 "greeted with the utmost pleasure": Ibid.

47 "so decidedly *écriveuse*": Sainte-Beuve, *Madame de Genlis*, in *Causeries du lundi* (Paris: Garnier, 1926), vol. 3, p. 25.

47 "in the houses": Talleyrand, *Mémoires*, p. 327.

47 *"We shall see!"*: Ibid.

47 "like glory": P.-L. Roederer, *Mémoires sur la Révolution, le Consultat et l'Empire* (Paris: Plon, 1942), p. 173.

48 "without their husbands": Stendhal, correspondence of February 10, 1826, in *New Monthly Magazine*, in *Courrier anglais* (Paris: Le Divan, 1935), vol. 2, p. 479.

48 "the order of the day": Stendhal, correspondence of February 1, 1825, in *New Monthly Magazine*, in *Courrier anglais*, vol. 2, pp. 256–257.

51 "have never gone the rounds of Paris": Stendhal, correspondence of April 1827, in *New Monthly Magazine*, in *Courrier anglais*, vol. 3, p. 338–342.

51 "precursor of this demon": L. Bloy, *L'Ame de Napoléon*, in *Oeuvres* (Paris: Mercure de France, 1966), vol. 5, p. 301.

51 "proud and filthy beggars": Ibid., p. 316.
51 "first modern regular armies": C. Schmitt, *Theorie des Partisanen* (Berlin: Duncker & Humblot, 1975), p. 12.
52 "interested third party": Ibid., p. 78.
52 "sacrifice of the poor": L. Bloy, *Histoires désobligeantes* (Paris: Crès, 1914), p. 223.
52 "faults of Bonaparte's mind": *Mémoires de Madame de Rémusat* (Paris: Calmann Lévy, 1880), vol. 3, p. 265.
53 "a famous code": L. Bloy, *Le sang du pauvre* (Paris: Stock, 1922), p. 31.
53 *"Begging is forbidden"*: Ibid., p. 34.

"The Mysterious Strength of Legitimacy"

54 "fear of the violated rule": G. Ferrero, *Potere* (Milan: Comunità, 1947), p. 34.
54 "power to exorcise fear": Ibid., p. 52.
54 "mysterious strength of legitimacy": Letter from Talleyrand to the Duchess of Kurland, July 25, 1820, in G. Lacour-Gayet, *Talleyrand* (Paris: Payot, 1931), vol. 3, pp. 107–108.
55 "a good chance of lasting": [C.-M. de Villemarest], *Monsieur de Talleyrand* (Paris: J. P. Roret, 1834), vol. 1, p. 168.
55 "theological insurrections": M. Stirner, *Der Einzige und sein Eigentum* (Stuttgart: Reclam, 1972), p. 29.
55 "the things of this world": L. Dumont, "La Genèse chrétienne de l'individualisme," *Le Débat,* 15 (September–October 1981): 143.
55 "archetype of the will": Ibid., p. 142.
56 "not of this world": Ibid., p. 144.
57 "its base function": *Mémoires de la comtesse Potocka* (Paris: Plon, 1911), p. 65.

The Origins of Sweetness

58 "sacrificed to Baal": Frazer, *The Golden Bough* (London: Macmillan, 1976), p. 810.
58 "betrayal through a kiss": L. Wittgenstein, "Bemerkungen über Frazers *Golden Bough*," in *Synthese* 17 (1967): 249.
59 "achieved an extreme sweetness": Sainte-Beuve, *Chateaubriand et son groupe littéraire sous l'Empire* (Paris: Garnier, 1948), vol. 1, p. 38.
60 "kindly spirits of the dead": L. F. Céline, *Mort à crédit* (Paris: Gallimard, 1962), p. 501.
60 "their explanations": L. F. Céline, "Lettres à ses amis," in *Cahiers Céline* (Paris: Gallimard, 1979), vol. 5, p. 198.
60 "speak more softly to things": L. F. Céline, *Mort à crédit,* p. 501.
62 "Congress will not have its seat there": J. de Maistre, *Considérations sur la France* (Paris: Rusand, 1829), p. 111. Subsequent references come from the same source: "simply does not exist," p. 94; "indefinable quality," p. 104; "Providence *erases,*" p. 31.

Eulogius

63   "*intersignes*": L. Massignon, *Le Voeu et le destin,* in *Opera minora* (Beirut: Dar Al-Maaref, 1963), vol. 3, p. 697.

63   "make a scholar of me": C. Nodier, *Souvenirs, épisodes et portraits pour servir à l'histoire de la Révolution et de l'Empire* (Brussels: Hauman, 1835), vol. 1, p. 1.

63   "highly learned editor": Ibid., p. 2.

63   "logic of extermination": Ibid., p. 14.

63   "pink-footed pastorale": L. Bloy, *La Chevalière de la mort,* in *Oeuvres* (Paris: Mercure de France, 1966), vol. 5, p. 52.

64   "moisten my eyebrows": C. Nodier, *Souvenirs,* p. 18.

64   "curse of Alsace": Metternich, *Mémoires documents et écrits divers* (Paris: Plon, 1880), vol. 1, p. 7.

64   "insignia of his position": Ibid., p. 8.

64   "violence against my opinions": Ibid.

64   "foothills of the Jura": C. Nodier, *Souvenirs,* pp. 3–4.

65   "supper at Madame Tesch's": Ibid., p. 5.

65   "nothing that bound the heart": Ibid., p. 6.

65   "*moderatism* of the Convention": Ibid., p. 15.

66   "Robespierre's messenger": J. Michelet, *Histoire de la Révolution française* (Paris: Gallimard, 1977), vol. 2, p. 679.

67   "everyone stopped": C. Nodier, *Souvenirs,* p. 27.

67   "await further orders": Ibid., p. 28.

68   "the more it is itself": J. Michelet, *Histoire de la Révolution française,* vol. 2, p. 995.

69   "Brittany and the Vendée": Ibid., p. 993.

70   "they are growing flowers": Ibid., pp. 993–994.

L'Autrichienne

70   "*intersignes*": L. Massignon, "Bi-centenaire et naissance de Marie-Antoinette," in *Opera minora* (Beirut: Dar Al-Maaref, 1963), vol. 3, p. 685.

71   "pleasure-loving lady": W. Goethe, *Dichtung und Wahrheit,* in *Werke* (Zurich: Artemis, 1954), vol. 10, pp. 399–400; idem, *The Autobiography of J. W. von Goethe,* trans. John Oxenford (New York, 1969; London, 1971), pp. 393ff.

71   "the queen herself and her court": Goethe, *Dichtung und Wahrheit,* p. 400.

74   "always implacable": Prince de Ligne, *Mémoires,* in *Mémoires et lettres* (Paris: Crès, 1923), p. 88.

74   "insipidness of good company": Stendhal, *Souvenirs d'égotisme,* in *Oeuvres intimes* (Paris: Gallimard, 1955), p. 1486.

The Woodsman and the Fisherman

75   "progress of the human spirit": Talleyrand, "Mémoire sur les relations commerciales des Etats-Unis avec Angleterre," in *Mémoires* (Paris: Plon, 1982), p. 227.

76   "the spot he has dwelled in": Ibid.

76   "create only cosmopolitans": Ibid., p. 228.

Goethe in Venice

78 "wedding of France": J. Michelet, *Histoire de la Révolution française* (Paris: Gallimard, 1977), vol. 1, p. 414.

78 "that sacred moment": Ibid., p. 412.

78 "innocence and credulity": Ibid., p. 427.

79 "No temple would have sufficed": Ibid., p. 409.

79 "he took part in hope": Ibid., p. 410.

79 "He who is raised": Ibid., p. 418.

80 "shaded by a palm tree": Words of Moreau de Jonnès, ibid., pp. 706–707.

80 "Here it is!": G. Avenel, *Anacharsis Cloots* (Paris: Champ Libre, 1976), p. 112.

82 "come as soon as you can": A. Cloots, *Ecrits révolutionnaires* (Paris: Champ Libre), 1979, pp. 53–54.

82 "to destroy it would be vain": [C.-M. de Villemarest], *Monsieur de Talleyrand* (Paris: J. P. Roret, 1834), vol. 1, p. 306.

83 "fourteenth of July": *Mémoires et relations politiques du baron de Vitrolles* (Paris: Charpentier, 1884), vol. 1, p. 451.

84 "Burn this letter": Letter by Talleyrand published in full in [C.-M. de Villemarest], *Monsieur de Talleyrand*, vol. 1, pp. 315–318.

84 "making anyone laugh": L. Madelin, *Talleyrand* (Paris: Flammarion, 1944), p. 46.

85 "prophetic symbol": J. Michelet, *Histoire de la Révolution française*, vol. 1, p. 414.

85 "prior guilt": Ibid., p. 420.

85 "dwindles into unity": Ibid., p. 423.

85 "becoming a policy": Ibid., p. 543.

85 "the fiercest royalists": Ibid., p. 698.

85 "frightening simplicity": Ibid., p. 697.

86 "climb up there so proudly": Ibid., p. 698.

86 "an animated mountain": Words of Moreau de Jonnès, ibid., p. 706.

87 "cunning and ambitious": Gouverneur Morris, *A Diary of the French Revolution* (London: Harrap, 1939), vol. 1, p. 108.

87 "very hot": Ibid., vol. 2, pp. 222–223.

On Taste

89 *"homme d'esprit":* Letter from Madame du Deffand to Horace Walpole, December 2, 1770, in *Horace Walpole's Correspondence with Madame du Deffand and Wiart* (New Haven: Yale University Press, 1939), vol. 2, p. 489.

89 "beginning of Jean-Jacques": Sainte-Beuve, "Hamilton," in *Causeries du lundi* (Paris: Garnier, 1926), vol. 1, p. 94.

89 "perfect *honnête homme*": Ibid., p. 93.

90 "exhibit on French industry": [H. de Latouche], *Album perdu* (Paris: Aux Marchands de Nouveautés, 1829), p. 171.

90 "understanding all history": Sainte-Beuve, "Les regrets," in *Causeries du lundi*, vol. 6, p. 403.

91 "was not human": Chateaubriand, *Mémoires d'outre-tombe* (Paris: Gallimard, 1958), vol. 2, p. 10.

91 "some postponement": Talleyrand's instructions to General Andréossy, in G. Pallain, ed., *Correspondance diplomatique de Talleyrand: La Mission de Talleyrand à Londres en 1792* (Paris: Plon, 1889), p. 151.

92 "write to us": Chateaubriand, *Mémoires d'outre-tombe*, vol. 1, p. 975.

92 "choose a new ministry": *Mémoires et relations politiques du baron de Vitrolles* (Paris: Charpentier, 1884), vol. 3, p. 228.

92 "not sufficiently veiled": Letter from Talleyrand to the Duchess of Kurland, September 25, 1815, in "Archives Talleyrand," in G. Lacour-Gayet, *Talleyrand* (Paris: Payot, 1931), vol. 3, p. 44.

92 *"for prospect"*: Sainte-Beuve, "Le Cahier vert," in *Cahiers* (Paris: Gallimard, 1973), vol. 1, pp. 119–120.

92 "reign of the sword": Sainte-Beuve, *Port-Royal* (Paris: Renduel, 1842), vol. 2, p. 42.

93 "energetic and shrewd": Sainte-Beuve, "Le Cahier vert," p. 80.

93 "living on his estate as a poet": Ibid., p. 169.

Metamorphoses of Style

93 "greatness and majesty": *Lettres choisies du Seigneur de Balzac* (Leiden: Elseviers, 1652), p. 350.

94 "perfect ineptitude": Sainte-Beuve, *Port-Royal* (Paris: Renduel, 1842), vol. 1, p. 50.

94 "turns of phrase": Sainte-Beuve, "Le Cahier vert," in *Cahiers* (Paris: Gallimard, 1973), p. 120.

95 "spoils it for others": Sainte-Beuve, *Port-Royal,* vol. 1, p. 50.

95 "which always reappeared": Ibid., p. 69.

95 "not as far from Guez de Balzac as he thinks": Ibid., p. 55.

96 "skeletal structure": Ibid., p. 53.

96 "flora of all harvests": Sainte-Beuve, "Le Cahier vert," pp. 103–104.

96 "imposes on reality": M. Proust, *Contre Sainte-Beuve; By Way of Sainte-Beuve,* trans. Sylvia Townsend Warner (London, 1958), p. 127.

96 "made over and absorbed": Ibid.

96 "imprint of what we are on what we do": R. Daumal, "Dialogue du style," in *Les Pouvoirs de la parole* (Paris: Gallimard, 1972), p. 265.

97 "on the same level as conversation": Proust, *Contre Sainte-Beuve,* p. 78.

97 "different school of thought": Ibid., p. 81.

97 "not separating the man and his work": Ibid., p. 76.

97 "practicing Christianity": Sainte-Beuve, "Le Cahier vert," p. 100.

98 "not allowed to see": Ibid., p. 58.

98 "an Ovidian metamorphosis": Ibid., p. 100.

98 "the common run of intellectuals": Ibid., p. 124.

99 "like a highwayman": J. G. Eckhart, "Des seel. Herrn von Leibniz Lebenslauf," in *Murr's Journal zur Kunstgeschichte und allgemeinen Litteratur* (Nuremberg, 1779), vol. 7, p. 200.

99 "monkey-like air": *Mémoires de Madame de Hausset, femme de chambre de Madame de Pompadour* (Paris: Firmin-Didot, n.d. [1882]), p. 101.

Belated Nostalgia for Sorrow

101 "domain of the Occident": Talleyrand, *Mémoires* (Paris: Plon, 1982), p. 76.

101 "she is repugnant to me": Comtesse de Kielmannsegge, *Mémoires sur Napoléon I* (Paris: Victor Attinger, 1928), vol. 1, pp. 131–132.

101 "correct her feet and legs": *Journal des Goncourt* (Paris: Charpentier-Fasquelle, 1894), vol. 7 (1885–1888), p. 210.

102 "I achieve it": Madame de Staël, *Delphine,* in *Oeuvres complètes* (Paris: Firmin-Didot, 1838), vol. 1, p. 378.

102 "arrive at the bottom of everything": Madame de Staël, letter to Talleyrand, February 28, 1809, in *Lettres (1778–1817)* (Paris: Klincksieck, 1970), p. 383.

102 "dozing out of habit": *Mémoires de Madame de Rémusat* (Paris: Calmann Lévy, 1880), vol. 3, p. 325.

102 "would have been better to suffer": Ibid., p. 327.

103 "Over this belated nostalgia for pain": F. Blei, *Talleyrand* (Berlin: Rowohlt, 1932), p. 19.

The Languor of a Park in Berry

103 "to make an end of it": Talleyrand, fragments published in B. de Lacombe, *La Vie privée de Talleyrand* (Paris: Plon, 1910), p. 249.

103 "I am prepared for everything": Ibid., p. 250.

103 "struggle against necessity": Talleyrand, from the "Archives Broglie," in G. Lacour-Gayet, *Talleyrand* (Paris: Payot, 1931), vol. 3, p. 310.

104 "There is nothing less aristocratic": Letter addressed from Madame the Duchess of Dino to the Abbé Dupanloup, May 10, 1839, in Duchesse de Dino, *Chronique de 1831 à 1862* (Paris: Plon, 1909), vol. 1, p. 239.

104 "the spies fell asleep": *Mémoires de Aimée de Coigny* (Paris: Calmann Lévy, 1902), p. 165.

104 "society itself that is ending": Talleyrand, from the "Archives Broglie," p. 293.

105 "Little triangular brackets": Barbey D'Aurevilly, *Le Chevalier des Touches,* in *Oeuvres romanesques complètes* (Paris: Gallimard, 1977), vol. 1, p. 749.

105 "as grumpy, solemn, and pedantic": Ibid., p. 790.

106 "in the abstraction of his madness": Ibid., p. 870.

106 "to display to the people": J. Flammermont, *La Journée du 14 Juillet 1789* (Paris: Société de l'Histoire de la Révolution française, 1892), p. 105.

Around Port-Royal

107 "the atheist is quiet": J. de Maistre, *De l'Eglise gallicane* (Paris: Rusand, 1821), p. 105.

108 "a theological club": Ibid., p. 40.

108 "especially women": Ibid., p. 52.

108 "naturally in revolt": Ibid., p. 32.

108 "considering it dead": Ibid., p. 102.

108 "cornerstone of the edifice": Ibid., p. 107.

108 "toy soldier of the Holy Spirit": Baudelaire, "De l'essence du rire," in *Oeuvres complétes* (Paris: Gallimard, 1976), vol. 2, p. 526.

109 "authorities of the universe": J. de Maistre, *De l'Eglise gallicane*, p. 107.
109 "revealed Bonaparte to himself": E. M. Cioran, *Essai sur la pensée réactionnaire* (Montpellier: Fata Morgana, 1977), p. 71.
109 "belongs entirely to Hobbes": J. de Maistre, *De l'Eglise gallicane*, p. 28.
114 "how lovely and captivating": From the manuscript version of the "Relation de la captivité de la mère Angélique de Saint-Jean," in Sainte-Beuve, *Port-Royal* (Paris: Renduel, 1842), vol. 4, p. 142.
114 "pure fragrance": Ibid.
114 "indistinguishable from religion": Ibid., p. 151.
115 "separate them gently from their background": Ibid., p. 152.

Among the Ruins of Kasch

125 "swimming in happiness": L. Frobenius, "Brief aus dem Ostsudan," in *Vom Schreibtish zum Äquator* (Frankfurt: Societäts-Druckerei, 1925), pp. 411–412.
126 "Kaschitic Ocean": Ibid., p. 414.
127 "you would not understand it": L. Frobenius, *Atlantis* (Jena: Diederichs, 1923), vol. 4, p. 8.
127 "traces of a chivalric tradition": L. Frobenius, *Monumenta Africana* (Frankfurt: Societäts-Druckerei, 1929), pp. 293–294.
128 "questions about where we come from": L. Frobenius, *Atlantis,* vol. 4, p. 4.
128 "the Kasch of the East": Ibid., p. 21.
128 "anywhere in world literature": L. Frobenius, *Kulturgeschichte Afrikas* (Zurich: Phaidon, 1933), pp. 273–274.
130 "a *marriage* with the god of the Oven": M. Granet, *Danses et légendes de la Chine ancienne* (Paris: Presses Universitaires de France, 1959), vol. 2, pp. 500–501.
134 "the kingdom of Chou could call itself safe": *Chuang Tzu,* XXI.

Elements of Sacrifice

135 "dwells in the depths of the sky": *Ṛg Veda*, X, 93, 5.
136 "reality is the sacrifice": *Maitrāyaṇi Saṃhitā*, 1, 10, 11.
137 "sacrifice is the ritual act par excellence": R. Guénon, *Etudes sur l'hindouisme* (Paris: Editions Traditionnelles, 1966), p. 263.
137 "The victorious Horse": *Ṛg Veda*, I, 163, 12.
137 "the axe will not cause lasting harm to your body": Ibid., I, 162, 20.
138 "gods before the gods": *Tāṇḍya-Mahā-Brāhmaṇa*, 25, 8, 2.
138 "considered themselves above sacrifice": *Taittirīya Saṃhitā*, 6, 3, 4, 8.
139 "Never, not for a single instant": *Bhagavad Gītā*, III, 5.
139 "Thus turns the wheel": Ibid., III, 16.
139 "cause the world's creatures to perish": Ibid., III, 24.
143 "spilled copiously over the altars": Lucretius, *De rerum natura*, V, 1200–1201.
143 "the social and the supernatural": S. Weil, *Cahiers* (Paris: Plon, 1970), vol. 1, p. 263.
143 "enslavement to society": Ibid., p. 27.
144 "kinsman of the Sun": *Mahā-karmavibhaṅga*, 1.
144 "those who prepare traps": *Majjhimanikāya*, XXVI.
144 "because hunger is death": *Bṛhad Araṇyaka Upaniṣad*, I, 2, 1.

146 "from suffering, knowledge": Aeschylus, *Agamemnon,* 177.
146 "The notion of the negligible": S. Weil, *Cahiers,* vol. 1, p. 143.

Law and Order

150 "from flesh and from blood": Porphyry, *De abstinentia,* II, 46, 2.
150 "sorcery": Ibid., I, 28, 1.
150 "Detachment can be achieved through violence": Ibid., I, 32, 1.
150 "sacrifice of thought": Ibid., I, 45, 4.
150 "taken from other beings": Ibid.
150 "train ourselves to die to others": Ibid., II, 61, 8.
150 "dead to the law": Galatians, 2:19.
150 "dead to sin": Romans, 6:2.
150 "race of philosophers": Porphyry, *De abstinentia,* II, 26, 3.
151 "abundance of the things being sacrificed": Ibid., II, 15, 3.
151 "impassive soul": Ibid., II, 61, 1.
151 "payment of taxes": Ibid., II, 61, 2.
151 "The essential function of sacrifice": R. Guénon, *Etudes sur l'hindouisme* (Paris: Editions Traditionnelles, 1966), p. 194.
152 "A householder has five slaughterhouses": *Manu-smṛti* (tr. G. Bühler), III, 67–71.
154 "he conversed with the stars": C. Lullier, *Mes cachots* (Paris: Published by the author, 1881), p. 205.
154 "you may appropriately sacrifice it": Oracle no. 537, in H. W. Parke and D. E. W. Wormell, *The Delphic Oracle* (Oxford: Basil Blackwell, 1956), vol. 1, p. 365; vol. 2, p. 214.
155 "life being guilty": J. de Maistre, "Eclaircissement sur les sacrifices," in *Les Soirées de Saint-Pétersbourg* (Paris: Librairie Grecque, Latine et Française, 1821), vol. 2, p. 395.
156 "Art is magic": T. W. Adorno, *Minima Moralia* (Frankfurt: Suhrkamp, 1951), p. 428.
158 "Molière's inexhaustible comment": R. Girard, *Des choses cachés depuis la fondation du monde* (Paris: Grasset, 1978), p. 428.
158 "not the whole people": John, 11:56.
158 "No one has done better": R. Girard, *Le Bouc émissaire* (Paris: Grasset, 1982), p. 164.
158 "except at the expense of a victim": Ibid., p. 208.
159 "Who will immolate whom?": R. Girard, *La Violence et le sacré* (Paris: Grasset, 1972), p. 177.
159 "there must be consent and joy": Baudelaire, *Mon coeur mis à nu,* in *Oeuvres complètes,* ed. Pichois (Paris: Gallimard, 1975), vol. 1, p. 683.
160 "stay in their pen": *Chuang Tzu,* XIX, 6.
160 "has no value": K. Marx, *Das Kapital,* in *Marx Engels Werke* (Berlin: Dietz, 1970), vol. 25, p. 660.
160 "Death is hunger": *Śatapatha Brāhmaṇa,* X, 6, 5.
160 "white bones": Hesiod, *Theogony,* 500.
160 "killing always means killing oneself": S. Weil, *Cahiers* (Paris: Plon, 1970), vol. 1, p. 152.

161   "the repository of all truth": Baudelaire, *Mon coeur mis à nu*, p. 678.

161   "anthropological intuition": R. Girard, *Des choses cachés depuis la fondation du monde*, p. 90.

163   "hidden ocean": *Ṛg Veda*, VIII, 41, 8.

163   "resonant substance": M. Schneider, "Le Rôle de la musique dans la mythologie et les rites des civilisations non européennes," in *Histoire de la musique*, Encyclopédie de la Pléiade (Paris: Gallimard, 1960), vol. 1, p. 213.

164   "are called immortal": *Iliad*, V, 341–342, trans. Richmond Lattimore.

164   "a means to die": Plutarch, *Septem sapientum convivium*, 160 B, 1–2.

165   "boil like a pot": Job, 41:31.

165   "darting flames on all sides": *Bhagavad Gītā*, XI, 16–17.

167   "Machiavellianism of the people": Reported in H. Taine, *Les Origines de la France contemporaine: La Révolution* (Paris: Hachette, 1890), vol. 2, p. 69.

167   "a cancer that could affect the rest of the body": Ibid.

167   "exterminate one-third of the population": Ibid., p. 70.

168   "the modern *well-being* of the French": J. Burckhardt, *Historische Fragmente* (Basel: Benno Schwabe, 1942).

168   *"nusquam interrupta connexio":* Macrobius, *In Somnium Scipionis*, I, 14.

169   *"Orate sine intermissione":* Thessalonians I, 5:17.

170   *"sanguine taurorum et hircorum":* Hebrews, 10:4.

The Doctrine of the Forest

171   "The road of heaven has become visible": *Ṛg Veda*, I, 46, 11.

171   "raised the prop in bottomless space": Ibid., I, 24, 7.

171   "a vast road for the sun": Ibid., I, 24, 8.

171   "measured the first creation": Ibid., VII, 41, 10.

171   "measuring magic": L. Silburn, *Instant et cause* (Paris: Vrin, 1955), p. 22.

171   "the sky and the earth still farther away": *Ṛg Veda*, X, 113, 5.

171   "enshrouding them in darkness": Ibid., X, 113, 7.

171   "watery residence": J. C. Heesterman, *The Ancient Indian Royal Consecration* (The Hague: Mouton, 1957), p. 149.

172   "links all states of existence": R. Guénon, *Symboles fondamentaux de la Science sacrée* (Paris: Gallimard, 1962), p. 400.

172   "he who knows this thread": *Bṛhad Araṇyaka Upaniṣad*, III, 7, 1.

172   "hidden ocean": *Ṛg Veda*, VIII, 41, 8.

172   "everyone's friend": *Śatapatha Brāhmaṇa*, IV, 1, 4, 8.

172   "the other world": Ibid., XII, 9, 2, 12.

173   "meek law": A. Stifter, Preface to *Bunte Steine*.

174   "no support during the night": L. Stilburn, *Instant et cause*, pp. 401–402.

175   "represents in his person the cosmic drama": J. C. Heesterman, *The Ancient Indian Royal Consecration*, p. 6.

175   "blend of arrogance and greed": L. Dumont, "Le Renoncement dans les religions de l'Inde," Appendix B in *Homo hierarchicus* (Paris: Gallimard, 1906), p. 335.

175   "ravines of sacrifice": *Śatapatha Brāhmaṇa*, IX, 2, 3, 12.

176   "relationship of mortals among themselves": C. Malamoud, "Terminer le sacrifice: Remarques sur les honoraires rituels dans le brahmanisme," in M.

Birardeau and C. Malamoud, eds., *Le Sacrifice dans l'Inde ancienne* (Paris: Presses Universitaires de France, 1976), p. 156.

176 "Rudra's part": *Śatapatha Brāhmaṇa*, I, 7, 4, 9.

177 "the body of the sacrificer can return to its owner": C. Malamoud, "Terminer le sacrifice," p. 194.

177 "taking over death and impurity": J. C. Heesterman, "Brahmin, Ritual and Renouncer," p. 4.

177 "responsible for all the innovations that India has known": L. Dumont, "La Genèse chrétienne de l'individualisme," *Le Débat*, 15 (September–October 1981): 126.

179 "element of otherworldliness": Ibid., p. 144.

Archives and Will-o'-the-Wisps

182 "like a researcher after a good day in the Archives Nationales": R. Cobb, "Becoming a Historian," in Cobb, *A Sense of Place* (London: Duckworth, 1975), p. 19.

182 "penetrate into the inner room": Ibid., p. 20.

182 "the most unknown of all histories": L. Bloy, *L'Ame de Napoléon*, in *Oeuvres* (Paris: Mercure de France, 1966), p. 271.

184 "to construct, then to pillage": R. Cobb, "L'Affaire Perken," in Cobb, *A Sense of Place*, p. 76.

184 "a program of virtue": R. Cobb, *Reactions to the French Revolution* (London: Oxford University Press, 1972), p. 20.

185 "the bureaucratic Terror": Ibid., p. 19.

The Demon of Repetition

187 "the cyclomania of our being": P. Valéry, *Cahiers* (Paris: Gallimard, 1973), vol. 1, p. 313.

187 "as mortally circular as the diurnal rotation": Ibid., p. 175.

187 "years of intense work": S. Freud, *Jenseits des Lustprinzips,* in *Freud-Studienausgabe* (Frankfurt: Fischer, 1975), vol. 3, p. 228.

187 "mystical": Ibid., p. 263.

187 "ultimate things": Ibid., p. 268.

188 "I found myself back in the square": S. Freud, *Das Unheimliche*, in *Freud-Studienausgabe*, vol. 4, pp. 259–260.

188 "involuntary repetition": Ibid., p. 260.

188 "the age up to which he will be permitted to live": Ibid., pp. 260–261.

189 "analytic treatment of neurotics": Ibid., p. 261.

189 "the shortest path to its final shape": Freud, *Jenseits des Lustprinzips*, p. 247.

190 "possessed by some 'demonic' power": Ibid., p. 231.

190 "a sense of the disturbing": S. Freud, *Das Unheimliche*, p. 244.

191 "seems to serve the death instincts": Freud, *Jenseits des Lustprinzips*, p. 271.

191 "do their work unobtrusively": Ibid.

191 "has not hitherto been clearly recognized": Ibid., p. 248.

191 "return to the inanimate state": Ibid.

191   "spared hesitation and indecision": S. Freud, *Das Unbehagen in der Kultur,* in *Freud-Studienausgabe,* vol. 9, pp. 223–224.

192   "the living substance to die": Freud, *Jenseits des Lustprinzips,* p. 248.

192   "more circuitous detours": Ibid.

192   "die only in its own fashion": Ibid., p. 249.

192   "something of the sort exists": W. Goethe, *Gespräche mit Eckermann,* in *Werke* (Zurich: Artemis, 1954), vol. 24, p. 399.

193   "The tradition of all past generations": K. Marx, *Der achtzehnte Brumaire des Louis Bonaparte,* in *Marx Engels Werke* (Berlin: Dietz, 1970), vol. 8, p. 115.

194   "surely been revolutionaries more wicked": A. de Tocqueville, *Souvenirs,* in *Oeuvres complètes* (Paris: Gallimard, 1971), vol. 12, p. 115.

194   "a parody of other revolutionary scenes": Ibid., p. 139.

194   "tragedy peformed by provincial amateurs": Ibid., p. 75.

194   "eternal revision": J. Burckhardt, *Historische Fragmente* (Basel: Benno Schwabe, 1942), p. 205.

196   "over it the enamel": G. Benn, *Altern als Problem für Künstler,* in *Gesammelte Werke* (Wiesbaden: Limes, 1962), vol. 1, p. 577.

196   "alive and constantly changing": Chateaubriand, *Mémoires d'outre-tombe* (Paris: Gallimard, 1958), vol. 1, p. 182.

197   "thronged with giggling women": Ibid.

197   "abandoned halls of the Alhambra": Ibid., p. 183.

197   "principle of neuronic *inertia*": S. Freud, "Entwurf einer Psychologie," in Freud, *Aus den Anfängen der Psychoanalyse, 1887–1902* (Frankfurt: Fischer, 1975), p. 306.

197   "principle of constancy": Freud, *Jenseits des Lustprinzips,* p. 270.

198   "repeat the same course of life": Ibid., p. 247.

198   "tension": Ibid., p. 248.

198   "figurative languages": Ibid., p. 268.

198   "specimens of the external world": Ibid., p. 237.

198   "sampling it in small quantities": Ibid.

198   "protective shield": Ibid.

198   "outer layer": Ibid.

198   "to some degree inorganic": Ibid.

199   "a similar fate": Ibid.

199   "projection": Ibid., p. 239.

199   "a species such as the butterflies or the orchids": O. Spengler, *Der Untergang des Abendlandes* (Munich: Beck, 1927), vol. 1, p. 27.

200   "through the midst of the sea": Exodus, 14:16.

200   "protected by thine hand": Book of Wisdom, 19:7–8.

200   "the waters he called the Seas": Genesis, 1:10.

201   "the draining of the Zuider Zee": S. Freud, *Neue Folge der Vorlesungen zur Einführung in die Psychoanalyse,* in *Freud-Studienausgabe,* vol. 1, p. 516.

201   "never touched by any religious uneasiness": C. Lévi-Strauss, *L'Homme nu* (Paris: Plon, 1971), p. 615.

201   "up to others, not us, to deal with it": Ibid., p. 597.

201   "a maniacal and desperate side": Ibid., p. 608.

201   "cadenced by pauses and repetitions": S. Freud, *Zwangshandlungen und Religionsübungen,* in *Freud-Studienausgabe,* vol. 7, p. 14.

202 "its most sharply delineated aspects": C. Lévi-Strauss, *L'Homme nu*, p. 603.
202 "constitutes the essence of ritual": Ibid.
203 "categories, laws, and axioms": Ibid., p. 608.
203 "accentuating every kind of ambiguity": Ibid.
203 "a source of amazement": C. Lévi-Strauss, *La Pensée sauvage* (Paris: Plon, 1962), p. 295.
203 "in the realm of continuity": Ibid., p. 296.
203 "a means of abolishing difference": Ibid., p. 308.
204 "it represents this as continuous": Ibid., p. 301.
205 "represents a special discourse": Ibid., pp. 301–302.

Goethe's Birthday

205 "with tears in his eyes": F. von Gentz, in *Goethes Gespräche, 1817–1832*, in W. Goethe, *Werke* (Zurich: Artemis, 1954), p. 38.
205 "because of the exchange rate": W. Goethe, *Briefe, 1814–1832*, in *Werke*, vol. 24, p. 677.
205 "repeated puberty": W. Goethe, *Gespräche mit Eckermann*, in *Werke*, vol. 24, p. 677.
206 "Then I got drunk for nothing": Eduard Genast, in *Goethes Gespräche, 1817–1832*, pp. 39–40.

Sacrificial Crumbs

206 "a mask over his head": Boccaccio, *Decameron*, IV, 2.
207 "The ice was all around": S. T. Coleridge, "The Rime of the Ancient Mariner," lines 59–60.
207 "Upon a painted ocean": Ibid., lines 117–118.
208 "devoured in less than three minutes": Marquis de Sade, *L'Histoire de Juliette*, in *Oeuvres complètes* (Paris: Tête de Feuilles, 1973), vol. 9, p. 14.
208 "plus lubriquement": Ibid., p. 15.
208 "every sailor a butcher": H. Melville, *Moby-Dick*, ch. 67.
209 "sanctum sanctorum of the whale": Ibid., ch. 78.
209 "white phantom": Ibid., ch. 69.
209 "lost in infinite perspectives": Ibid.
210 "zone of the Ecliptic": G. de Santillana, "La Storia da riscrivere," in *Reflections on Men and Ideas* (Cambridge, Mass.: MIT Press, 1968), pp. 319–320.
210 "accepted Copernican theory": F. Yates, *Giordano Bruno and the Hermetic Tradition* (London: Routledge and Kegan Paul, 1964), p. ix.
210 "something else implied in it": Ibid.
211 "the true and only 'inhabitants'": G. de Santillana, "Riflessioni sul fato: Fato antico," in *Reflections on Men and Ideas*, p. 326.
211 "this tendency to retrograde movement is innate": Plato, *Politicus*, 269 c–d.
211 "we call heaven and world": Ibid., 269 d.
211 "from its own proper movement": Ibid., 269 e.
212 "drama of the incommensurables": S. Weil, *Sur la science* (Paris: Gallimard, 1966), pp. 216, 245.

212   "their most marvelous triumph": S. Weil, *La Source grecque* (Paris: Gallimard, 1953), p. 156.

213   "includes a corresponding theory": R. Guénon, *Etudes sur l'hindouisme* (Paris: Editions Traditionnelles, 1966), p. 263.

213   "confirms superstition": Baudelaire, *Mon coeur mis à nu,* in *Oeuvres complètes,* ed. Pichois (Paris: Gallimard, 1975), vol. 1, p. 680.

214   "the reservoir of all truths": Ibid., p. 678.

214   "each individual in his own language": R. Guénon, *Les Principes du calcul infinitésimal* (Paris: Gallimard, 1946), p. 39.

215   "between the Torah and the Tao": W. Benjamin, "Paralipomena zu Kafka," in *Gesammelte Schriften* (Frankfurt: Suhrkamp, 1977), vol. 2, part 3, p. 1219.

216   "Terrible things . . . Enough": F. Kafka, *Briefe* (Frankfurt: Fischer, 1959), pp. 333–334.

217   "man enough to be that man": W. Benjamin, *Briefe* (Frankfurt: Suhrkamp, 1966), vol. 2, p. 803.

217   "Trappists make him a butcher": V. Hugo, *Choses vues, 1830–1848* (Paris: Gallimard, 1972), p. 439.

217   "another horse, which replaces the previous one": U. Harva, *Die religiösen Vorstellungen der altaischen Völker* (Helsinki: Werner Söderström, 1938), p. 218.

218   "no smoke without god": R. Hamayon, "Il n'y a pas de fumée sans dieu," *L'Ethnographie,* 118, nos. 74–75 (1977): 171.

The Anti-Romantic Child

219   "a sensitive and thinking being": J. Bentham, "The Philosophy of Economic Science," in *Economic Writings* (London: Allen and Unwin, 1952), vol. 1, p. 82.

219   "between Punishments and Crimes": Ibid., pp. 117–118.

219   "The only common measure": J. Bentham, fragments published in "Appendix 2," in E. Halévy, *La Formation du radicalisme philosophique* (Paris: Félix Alcan, 1901), vol. 1, p. 412.

219   "speak a mercenary language": Ibid., pp. 412–414.

220   "money being the current instrument": Ibid., p. 406.

220   "beyond which pleasure cannot go": Ibid., p. 408.

220   "between sum and sum": Ibid.

221   "the great *subversive*": J. S. Mill, "Bentham," in *Mill on Bentham* (Cambridge: Cambridge University Press, 1980), p. 42.

221   "the chief subversive thinker": Ibid., p. 44.

221   "on his fellow creatures": Ibid., pp. 62–63.

221   "the forms are innumerable": A. Blanqui, *L'Eternité par les astres* (Paris: Baillière, 1872), p. 12.

Limits

223   "sacred limit": K. Marx, *Grundrisse der Kritik politischen Ökonomie* (Berlin: Dietz, 1974), p. 440.

223   "beyond the point of departure": Ibid., p. 438.

224   "unlimited vitality of capital": R. Luxemburg, "Die Akkumulation des Kapitals," in *Gesammelte Werke* (Berlin: Dietz, 1975), vol. 5, p. 276.

224   "mere child's play in comparison": Ibid., p. 274.

224 "a single identical faith": E. Canetti, *Masse und Macht* (Hamburg: Claasen, 1952), p. 563.

Process

224 "the richness of its substance": G. W. F. Hegel, *Phänomenologie des Geistes* (Hamburg: Meiner, 1952), p. 563.

Glosses on Marx

226 "wealth the aim of production": K. Marx, *Grundrisse der Kritik politischen Ökonomie* (Berlin: Dietz, 1974), p. 387.
226 "creates the best citizens": Ibid.
227 "and that of his own nature": Ibid.
227 "produces his totality": Ibid.
229 "it is *vulgar*": Ibid., p. 388.
230 "working material": Ibid., p. 376.
231 "blessed end of the bourgeoisie": Ibid., pp. 79–80.
233 "Each individual possesses social power": Ibid., p. 75.
233 "in isolated spheres": Ibid.
233 "universal abilities": Ibid.
234 "a kind of destiny": Ibid., p. 76.
234 "the third stage": Ibid., p. 75.
234 "at this point we cannot examine": Ibid., p. 77.
235 "an independent commodity": Ibid., p. 114.
235 "everything can be exchanged": Aristotle, *Politics*, I, 9, 1257, a, 16.
235 "elements of the universe themselves": K. Marx, *Grundrisse*, p. 271.
236 "with disruptive action": K. Marx, *Zur Kritik der Politischen Ökonomie*, in *Marx Engels Werke* (Berlin: Dietz, 1970), vol. 13, p. 36.
236 "general medium of exchange": Ibid., p. 34.
236 "between purchase and sale": Ibid., p. 77.
236 "tradition and foolish sentiment": Ibid.
236 "this social interchange": Ibid.
237 "productive forces of the individual": K. Marx, *Grundrisse*, p. 414.
238 "a living contradiction": Ibid., p. 324.
238 *"production founded on capital"*: Ibid., p. 318.
238 "commodity of specified value": K. Marx, *Das Kapital*, in *Marx Engels Werke* (Berlin: Dietz, 1970), vol. 23, p. 131.
238 "the wood in the trees": Ibid., p. 55.
239 "They are twins": M. Griaule, *Dieu de l'eau* (Paris: Editions de Chêne, 1948), p. 238.

The Ruthlessness of Ricardo

240 *"as an end in itself"*: K. Marx, *Theorien über den Mehrwert*, in *Marx Engels Werke* (Berlin: Dietz, 1970), vol. 26, part 2, pp. 110–111.
240 "the productive forces of labor": K. Marx, *Grundrisse der Kritik politischen Ökonomie* (Berlin: Dietz, 1974), p. 635.
241 "only exoterically": Ibid., p. 540.

242   "he is as *ruthless* toward the bourgeoisie": K. Marx, *Theorien über den Mehrwert*, p. 111.

242   "this is what they cannot understand": Ibid.

The Crystal of Money

243   "presupposes the equivalence": K. Marx, *Grundrisse der Kritik politischen Ökonomie* (Berlin: Dietz, 1974), p. 90.

243   "should be itself invariable": D. Ricardo, "Absolute Value and Exchangeable Value," in *The Work and Correspondence of David Ricardo* (Cambridge: Cambridge University Press, 1966), vol. 4, p. 361.

243   "painting and sculpture": Marx, *Grundrisse,* p. 90.

243   "equal quantities of grain": Ibid.

243   "irrespective of my individuality": Ibid., p. 133.

244   "the imperishable commodity": Ibid., p. 67.

245   "the pores of society": Ibid., p. 387.

246   "and money the value of all things": E.M. [Edward Misselden], "The Circle of Commerce or the Balance of Trade," in *Defence of Free Trade* (London: Nicholas Bourne, 1623), p. 94.

246   "crystal of money": K. Marx, *Das Kapital,* in *Marx Engels Werke* (Berlin: Dietz, 1970), vol. 23, p. 145.

247   "has been cleared of goods": Ibid., p. 127.

247   "commodity of a given value": Ibid., p. 131.

247   "the great alembic of society": Ibid., p. 145.

248   "dissolves the community": Marx, *Grundrisse,* p. 136.

248   "horrid chance": F. Nietzsche, *Also sprach Zarathustra,* part 2: "Von der Erlösung."

History Experiments

249   *"the way in which man shapes man"*: K. Marx and F. Engels, *Die deutsche Ideologie,* in *Marx Engels Werke* (Berlin: Dietz, 1970), vol. 3, p. 36.

249   "a fact of universal history": Ibid., p. 45.

250   "eats, drinks, and gets dressed": Ibid., p. 46.

252   "we should be perplexed": P. Valéry, "Tel quel," in *Oeuvres* (Paris: Gallimard, 1962), vol. 2, p. 706.

252   "mad attachment to foreign ways": C. Rulhière, "Anecdotes sur la Russie," in *Histoire de l'anarchie de Pologne* (Paris: Nicolle et Desenne, 1807), vol. 4, p. 341.

254   "time falls drop by drop": Madame de Staël, *De l'Allemagne* (Paris: Garnier-Flammarion, 1968), vol. 1, p. 117.

254   "nor feet for advancing": Ibid., p. 121.

255   "the philosophy of revelation": F. Engels, *Anti-Schelling,* in *Marx Engels Werke,* suppl. vol. 2, p. 163.

256   *"to its uttermost end"*: A. Cieszkowski, *Prolegomena zur Historiosophie* (Berlin: Veit, 1838), p. 85.

256   "a substratum *outside itself*": Ibid., p. 99.

257   *"terrain of the will"*: Ibid., pp. 114–115.

257   *"thought returning to being":* Ibid., p. 120.

257   *"non fuerit in intellectu":* Ibid., p. 121.

257   "as art and philosophy have done": Ibid., p. 122.

257   "into the field of praxis": Ibid., p. 129.

257   "foreshadowed by a fermentation": Ibid., p. 153.

257   "the Hegelian system": Marx and Engels, *Die deutsche Ideologie,* p. 17.

258   *"peace* between interiority and exteriority": Cieszkowski, *Prolegomena,* p. 128.

The Artificial Barbarian

258   "birds in the silence of night": S. Kierkegaard, *Enten-Eller* (Milan: Adelphi, 1977), vol. 2, p. 116.

260   "chose the name Stirner": G. Daumer, *Das Christenthum und sein Urheber* (Mainz: Kirchheim, 1864), p. 135.

260   "the genius for provocation": E. M. Cioran, *Essai sur la pensée réactionnaire* (Montpellier: Fata Morgana, 1977), p. 9.

262   "delicate nihilist": P. Bourget, preface to *La Discipline* (Paris: Nelson, n.d.), p. 8.

262   "aristocracy of the nerves": Ibid., p. 7.

262   "become part of the race again": M. Barrès, *Le Jardin de Bérénice* (Paris: Emile-Paul, 1910), p. 210.

262   "to reveal the Trinity": Ibid., p. 64.

262   "boys of 1889": Bourget, preface to *La Discipline,* p. 5.

263   "certain attitudes toward communal life": P. Valéry, *Cahiers* (Paris: Gallimard, 1973), vol. 2, p. 1452.

266   "Our atheists are pious people": M. Stirner, *Der Einzige und sein Eigentum* (Stuttgart: Reclam, 1972), p. 203.

266   "advances without respite": Ibid., p. 158.

266   "must be made by all": Lautréamont, *Poésies II,* in *Oeuvres complètes* (Paris: José Corti, 1958), p. 386.

266   "We absorb violation of duty": Ibid., p. 373.

269   "that philosophical brotherhood": K. Marx and F. Engels, *Die deutsche Ideologie,* in *Marx Engels Werke* (Berlin: Dietz, 1970), vol. 3, p. 168.

269   "will never be proletarians": Ibid., p. 183.

269   "it is counter-revolutionary": R. Luxemburg, *In revolutionärer Stunde,* in *Gesammelte Werke* (Berlin: Dietz, 1975), vol. 2, p. 34.

269   "not typical of a proletarian": V. I. Lenin, *Der Anarchismus* (Berlin: Dietz, 1953), p. 20.

272   "begotten entirely by ideas": F. Dostoyevski, *Notes from Underground,* trans. Andrew R. MacAndrew (New York: Signet, 1961), p. 203.

273   "Where shall I ever find them?": Ibid., pp. 36–37.

275   "notorious work": F. A. Lange, *Geschichte des Materialismus* (Iserlohn: Baedeker, 1886), p. 292.

275   "the most extreme book we know": Ibid.

275   "we are *the most extreme*": F. Nietzsche, "Nachgelassene Fragmente (Herbst 1887 bis März 1888)," in *Werke* (Berlin: W. de Gruyter, 1970), vol. 7, part 2, p. 176.

275   "this book is life itself": J. H. Mackay, *Max Stirner: Sein Leben und sein Werk* (Berlin: Published by the author, 1914), p. 158.

276 "hasn't a drop of humor": K. Joël, *Philosophenwege* (Berlin: Hermann Hey-felder, 1901), p. 234.

276 "great external experiences": Mackay, *Max Stirner,* p. 6.

277 "loyal and strong hands": Ibid., p. 21.

277 "not even worth serious refutation": Ibid., p. 19.

277 "external traces of the great life": Ibid., p. 8.

278 "I know you won't": "Erinnerungen von Frau Ida Overbeck," in C. A. Bernoulli, *Franz Overbeck und Friedrich Nietzsche: Eine Freundschaft* (Jena: Diederichs, 1908), vol. 1, pp. 238–239.

279 "will be badly overcrowded": Stirner, *Der Einzige und sein Eigentum,* p. 35.

280 "*Are we* what is in us?": Ibid., p. 34.

283 "the perishable ego": Ibid., p. 213.

284 "destruction of alienness": Marx and Engels, *Die deutsche Ideologie,* p. 35.

284 "all in all": Stirner, *Der Einzige und sein Eigentum,* p. 5.

285 "*sortir de soi*": Baudelaire, *Mon coeur mis à nu,* in *Oeuvres complètes,* ed. Pichois (Paris: Gallimard, 1975), vol. 1, p. 692.

285 "relationship between usefulness and use": K. Marx, *Grundrisse der Kritik politischen Ökonomie* (Berlin: Dietz, 1974), p. 80.

285 "from the whore to the pope": Ibid., p. 183.

285 "foreman and regulator": Ibid., p. 592.

286 "enliven the blockhead": Ibid., p. 184.

286 "the terrain upon which society rests": Ibid., p. 188.

286 "c'est le goût de la prostitution": Baudelaire, *Fusées,* in *Oeuvres complètes,* vol. 1, p. 649.

286 "L'être le plus prostitué": Baudelaire, *Mon coeur mis à nu,* p. 692.

A New Frisson

287 "We were the first": *Journal des Goncourt* (Paris: Fasquelle, 1902), vol. 3 (1866–1870), p. 248.

287 "listes de canailles": Baudelaire, *Mon coeur mis à nu,* in *Oeuvres complètes,* ed. Pichois (Paris: Gallimard, 1975), vol. 1, p. 694.

287 "chaos and immensity": Baudelaire, *Fragments divers,* in *Oeuvres complètes,* ed. Le Dantec (Paris: Gallimard, 1954), p. 1282.

287 "the square sky": Baudelaire, *Poèsies de jeunesse,* in *Oeuvres complètes,* ed. Pichois, vol. 1, p. 206.

287 "voice of the adjective": Baudelaire, *Titre et canevas,* ibid., p. 594.

288 "a passion for *la Sottise*": Baudelaire, "Canevas des 'Lettres d'un atrabilaire,'" ibid., p. 781.

288 "I would *never* solicit them": Baudelaire, letter to A. Villemain, December 11, 1861, in *Correspondance,* ed. Pichois (Paris: Gallimard, 1973), vol. 2, p. 194.

288 "grammatical dance": Baudelaire, *Titres et canevas,* p. 594.

288 "then we won't appoint him": A. de Vigny, from an unpublished daybook, fragment published by Claude Pichois in Baudelaire, *Correspondance,* vol. 2, p. 751.

288 "studious and diligent man": Ibid.

288 "always an *immense* hatred": Baudelaire, "L'Esprit et le style de M. Villemain," in *Oeuvres complètes,* ed. Pichois, vol. 2, pp. 192, 194.

288 "La Toxicologie": Baudelaire, letter to Victor de Laprade, December 23, 1861, in *Correspondance,* vol. 2, p. 199.

288 "make him pay dearly": Baudelaire, letter to Madame Aupick, December 25, 1861, in *Correspondance,* vol. 2, p. 203.

288 "how would you know?": Poulet-Malassis, in *Baudelaire devant ses contemporains,* ed. W. T. Brandy and C. Pichois (Paris: U.G.E., 1967), p. 162.

289 "observe a similar custom": U. Harva, *Die religiösen Vorstellungen der altaischen Völker* (Helsinki: Werner Söderström, 1938), p. 567.

289 "the Pythia could utter the prophecy": K. Meuli, *Griechische Opferbräuche,* in *Gesammelte Schriften* (Basel: Schwabe, 1975), vol. 2, p. 995.

289 "the *sponte sua* of the victim": Baudelaire, *Titres et canevas,* p. 598.

289 "you have created a new *frisson*": T. Gautier, *Souvenirs romantiques* (Paris: Garnier, 1929), p. 267.

289 "He woos everyone": Baudelaire, letter to Manet, October 28, 1865, in *Correspondance,* vol. 2, p. 539.

290 "becomes a part of the ceremony": F. Kafka, "Betrachtungen über Sünde, Leid, Hoffnung und den wahren Weg," in *Hochzeitsvorbereitungen auf dem Lande* (Frankfurt: Fischer, n.d. [1982]), p. 31.

Behind the Windowpane

290 "no object more profound": C. Baudelaire, *Le Spleen de Paris,* in *Oeuvres complètes,* ed. Pichois (Paris: Gallimard, 1975), vol. 1, p. 339.

291 "illness of which Flaubert died": J. Laforgue, letter to Ephrussi, April 9, 1882, in Laforgue, *Mélanges posthumes* (Paris: Mercure de France, 1903), p. 258.

291 "deserted railway station": J. Laforgue, "Pensées et paradoxes," ibid., p. 16.

291 "Buddhist gaze of the crocodiles": J. Laforgue, "Paysages et impressions," ibid., p. 16.

291 "dreamlike silence of water": Ibid.

291 "others still to the vulgar": Sainte-Beuve, "Le Cahier vert," in *Cahiers* (Paris: Gallimard, 1973), p. 91.

292 "he wants to talk with the dead": R. Darnton, *The Literary Underground of the Old Regime* (Cambridge, Mass.: Harvard University Press, 1982), p. v.

293 "fond of each other": J. de Gobineau, *Les Pléiades* (Paris: Plon, 1963), p. 34.

293 "only into friendly hands": Sainte-Beuve, "Le Cahier vert," p. 57. The quotations that follow come from the same source: "palette," p. 58; "vendettas," p. 124; "organs," p. 316; "Theocritus," p. 342; "heart," p. 114; "thief," p. 169; "Corruption," p. 352; "vainest," p. 200; "immense city," pp. 136–137; "nature," p. 273.

294 "Is anything there?": Charles-Augustin Sainte-Beuve, *Lettres inédites à Collombet* (Paris: Société Française d'Imprimerie et Librairie, 1903), p. 238.

Bien-Aimé

296 "allotted large pensions": H. Walpole, *Memoirs of the Reign of King George the Third* (London: Lawrence and Bullen-Putnam, 1894), vol. 2, pp. 169–170.

296 "arid, spiteful, sarcastic": E. and J. de Goncourt, *La Duchesse de Châteauroux et ses soeurs* (Paris: Charpentier, 1879), p. 48.

296   "made to accommodate only one": E. and J. de Goncourt, *Madame de Pompadour* (Paris: Fasquelle, 1903), p. 151.

296   "It is his heart I'm after": *Mémoires de Madame du Hausset, femme de chambre de Madame de Pompadour* (Paris: Firmin-Didot, n.d. [1882]), p. 79.

296   "attach great importance": Ibid., p. 71.

297   "Sanche! Alonze! Clovis!": V. Hugo, *La Pitié suprême* (Paris: Calmann Lévy, 1879), p. 4.

297   "Une stupide joie": Ibid., p. 20.

297   "glorious and peaceful": Cardinal de Bernis, letter to Count Stainville, March 31, 1757, in *Mémoires et lettres de F.-J. de Pierre Cardinal de Bernis* (Paris: Plon, 1878), vol. 2, p. 198.

297   "done only at certain times": R. A. Stein, "Présentation de l'oeuvre posthume de Marcel Granet: 'Le Roi boit,'" *L'Année sociologique*, 3 (1952): 63–64.

298   "birds he keeps at Passy": *Chronique de la Régence et du règne de Louis XV ou Journal de Barbier*, 1st series, 1718–1726 (Paris: Charpentier, 1866), p. 212.

298   "masterpiece of its type": Duc de Broglie, *Le Secret du Roi* (Paris: Calmann Lévy, 1878), vol. 2, p. 421.

299   "will not be considered": Letter of Louis XV, published in E. and J. de Goncourt, *Portraits intimes du XVIII siècle*, 1st series (Paris: Charpentier, 1878), p. 259.

299   "a schoolboy or a half-king": S. Arnould, from "Papiers inédits de Sophie Arnould," ibid., p. 260.

299   "altering the décor to such an extent": *Mémoires de Madame du Hausset*, p. 146.

300   "I, too, have often suffered": Ibid., p. 147.

300   "the most agreeable man": *Mémoires inédits de Madame la Comtesse de Genlis* (Paris: Colburn, 1825), vol. 3, pp. 32–33.

300   "I myself am old-fashioned": Letter from Cardinal de Bernis, in F. Masson, *Le Cardinal de Bernis depuis son ministère* (Paris: Plon, 1884), p. 383.

301   "must speak to someone about it": Letter from Madame Louise to Cardinal de Bernis, September 3, 1787, in P. Sommervogel, "Gustave II et le cardinal de Bernis," in *Etudes religieuses, historiques et littèraires par des Pères de la Compagnie de Jésus*, 4th series, vol. 4 (1869), p. 198.

A Visit to Picpus Cemetery

304   "mnemic wave": A. Warburg, "Burckhardt-Übungen (1927)," published in E. H. Gombrich, *Aby Warburg* (London: Warburg Institute, 1970), p. 274.

305   "as fantastic as the dream itself": Sainte-Beuve, "De la littérature industrielle," in *Portraits Contemporains* (Paris: Calmann Lévy, 1889), vol. 2, p. 448.

306   "three sous a day": Stendhal, "Projet d'article pour *Le Rouge et le Noir*," in *Romans et Nouvelles* (Paris: Gallimard, 1972), vol. 1, p. 702.

The Organization Wouldn't Like It

308   "we would never see again": Fénelon, "Supplément à l'examen de conscience," in *Ecrits et lettres politiques* (Paris: Bossard, 1920), pp. 79–80.

308   "all the power at his disposal": Thucydides, *Historiarum*, V, 105.

308 "the worst kind of war": C. Schmitt, *Ex captivate salus* (Cologne: Greven, 1950), p. 30.

308 "there has been no war of annihilation": C. Schmitt, *Der Nomos der Erde* (Berlin: Duncker & Humblot, 1974), p. 123.

308 "all other technical machines": C. Schmitt, *Gespräch über die Macht und den Zugang zum Machthaber* (Pfullingen: Neske, 1954), p. 26.

309 "global civil war": Schmitt, *Der Nomos der Erde,* p. 271.

310 "the uninitiated can never penetrate": *Mémoires et relations politiques du baron de Vitrolles* (Paris: Charpentier, 1884), vol. 1, p. 316.

310 "came to visit their premier": Ibid., p. 326.

311 "the sovereignty of society over society": V. Hugo, *Choses vues (1830–1848)* (Paris: Gallimard, 1972), p. 110.

Wake for Montaigne

318 "turned their backs on each other": C. Rulhière, "Anecdotes sur la Russie," in *Histoire de l'anarchie de Pologne* (Paris: Nicolle et Desenne, 1807), p. 336.

318 "their lengthy misfortunes": Ibid., p. 338.

319 "the favorites of the current regime": Ibid., p. 339.

319 "the blood of a brother or a friend": Ibid., p. 334.

319 "province of my thoughts": W. Benjamin, *Briefe* (Frankfurt: Suhrkamp, 1966), vol. 1, p. 470.

319 "tone": Ibid., p. 462.

319 "interested only in canceled stamps": W. Benjamin, *Einbahnstrasse,* in *Gesammelte Schriften* (Frankfurt: Suhrkamp, 1977), vol. 4, part 1, p. 135.

320 "chasms between whole continents": Ibid.

320 "lacy white tulle dress": Ibid.

320 "Combing is a mother's job": W. Benjamin, *Über Haschisch* (Frankfurt: Suhrkamp, 1972), p. 131.

320 *"indéfrisable":* W. Benjamin, *Das Passagen-Werk,* in *Gesammelte Schriften,* vol. 5, part 2, p. 1213.

320 "In the comb we find consolation": W. Benjamin, *Über Haschisch,* p. 131.

321 "to see him open and gracious": *Mémoires de Aimée de Coigny* (Paris: Calmann Lévy, 1902), p. 239.

322 "the cells of a dried beehive": *Journal des Goncourt* (Paris: Charpentier, 1895), vol. 8 (1889–1891), p. 53.

The Wolf-Man Remembers

322 "no better observation point": Prince de Ligne, *Mémoires,* in *Mémoires et lettres* (Paris: Crès, 1923), p. 94.

323 "modesty and voluptuousness": Ibid., pp. 92–93.

324 "made *pruderie* fashionable": Stendhal, correspondence of November 1824 for the *London Magazine,* in *Courrier Anglais* (Paris: Le Divan, 1936), vol. 4, p. 16.

324 "Once the husband enters the room": Ibid., p. 18.

325 "ties with several women": Talleyrand, *Mémoires* (Paris: Plon, 1982), p. 50.

325 "the god of profane persons": Fénelon, "Lettres spirituelles," in *Oeuvres spirituelles* (Paris: Le Clere, 1802), vol. 4, p. 37.

325 "not to be found in agitation": Ibid., p. 301.

325 "seemed to be doing out of pure reason": Ibid., p. 120.

326 "out of self-love": Ibid., pp. 209–210.

326 "as the wind extinguishes a candle": Ibid., pp. 124–125.

326 "when it is allowed to act freely": Ibid., p. 291.

326 "entire person": Saint-Simon, *Mémoires* (Paris: Gallimard, 1958), vol. 4, p. 606.

326 "affected and overrefined": Fénelon, "Lettres spirituelles," vol. 3, p. 409.

326 "the pleasure with which he received everyone": Saint-Simon, *Mémoires*, vol. 4, p. 607.

327 "True nothing never resists": Fénelon, "Lettres spirituelles," vol. 4, p. 144.

327 "the idol of military men": Saint-Simon, *Mémoires*, vol. 4, p. 608.

327 "vomits up its old night": V. Hugo, "Ecrit en 1846," from *Les Contemplations*, in *Oeuvres poétiques* (Paris: Gallimard, 1978), vol. 2, p. 680.

327 "utter Jacobinism": Ibid., p. 671.

327 "ancient rheumatism": Ibid., p. 679.

327 "rises before us": Ibid., p. 678.

327 "on the world's shoulder": V. Hugo, "Ce que dit la bouche d'ombre," from *Les Contemplations,* p. 815.

327 "glows with light": Ibid., p. 821.

328 "blades of grass are emperors": Ibid., p. 819.

328 "the pariah universe": Ibid., p. 821.

328 "L'univers est hagard": Ibid., p. 819.

328 "only one scripture": W. Goethe, *Wilhelms Meisters Wanderjahre*, in *Werke* (Zurich: Artemis, 1954), vol. 8, p. 40.

328 "parasitic religiosity": J. Levallois, *Sainte-Beuve* (Paris: Didier, 1872), p. 13.

328 "Christian *sensibility*": Sainte-Beuve, *Chateaubriand et son groupe littéraire sous l'Empire* (Paris: Garnier, 1948), vol. 1, p. 72.

329 "imperceptibly toward belief": Ibid.

329 "basic indifference": Sainte-Beuve, "Du génie critique et de Bayle," from *Portraits littéraires,* in *Oeuvres* (Paris: Gallimard, 1960), vol. 1, p. 983.

329 "the pleasures he is offered": Ibid., pp. 984–985.

329 "ten thousand volumes": Sainte-Beuve, "Mes livres," from "Joseph Delorme," in *Poésies complètes* (Paris: Charpentier, 1855), p. 80.

330 "in all sorts of places": Sainte-Beuve, "Notes et pensées," in *Causeries du lundi* (Paris: Garnier, 1926), vol. 11, p. 442.

Voices from the Palais-Royal

331 "center of a big city's chaos": Restif de la Bretonne, *Les Nuits de Paris* (Paris: Aux Trois Compagnons, 1947), p. 306.

331 "made his spectators effeminate": [L. Mercier], *L'An deux mille quatre-cent-quarante* (Paris, 1786), vol. 1, p. 352.

332 "absolute tranquillity": Ibid., vol. 3, p. 181.

332 "innocence blushes": L. Mercier, *Tableau de Paris* (Paris: Pfluger, 1904), vol. 3, pp. 131–132.

332 "their little poodles or parakeets": Ibid., p. 132.

333 "at every sort of price": Ibid., p. 136.

333 "the most precious and enduring jewels": Ibid., p. 137.

333 "according to his circumstances": Ibid.
333 "sad and uninhabited provinces": Ibid.
333 "labyrinth of ribbons": Ibid., p. 138.
333 "the scandal of a flirtation": Talleyrand, *Mémoires* (Paris: Plon, 1982), p. 120.
334 "the wicked politician": J. Michelet, *Histoire de la Révolution française* (Paris: Gallimard, 1977), vol. 1, p. 126.
334 "My thoughts are my whores": Diderot, *Le Neveu de Rameau,* in *Oeuvres* (Paris: Gallimard, 1969), p. 395.
334 "profound idleness": Mercier, *Tableau de Paris*, vol. 3, p. 138.
334 "vast flesh-market": E. and J. de Goncourt, *Histoire de la société française pendant la Révolution* (Paris: Quantin, 1889), p. 183.
335 "wild conjectures": J. Dusaulx, "L'Oeuvre de sept jours," in *Mémoires sur la Bastille* (Paris: Librairie des Bibliophiles, 1889), p. 190.
335 "tailored by Sensuality": [Restif de la Bretonne], *Le Palais Royal* (Paris: Au Palais-Royal, 1790; and Brussels: Christiaens, n.d.), vol. 1, p. 14.
335 "the real danger": Goncourt, *Histoire de la société française pendant la Révolution,* p. 184.
336 "at the door of a Palais-Royal kitchen": Baudelaire, *Le Spleen de Paris,* in *Oeuvres complètes,* ed. Pichois (Paris: Gallimard, 1975), vol. 1, p. 361.
336 "there are forty thousand of them": H. Taine, *Les Origines de la France Contemporaine: La Révolution* (Paris: Hachette, 1890), vol. 1, pp. 41–42.
336 "everything is false": Michelet, *Histoire de la Révolution française,* vol. 1, p. 126.
336 "wretchedness of their condition": *Napoléon inconnu: Papiers inédits (1786–1793), publiés par Frédéric Masson et Guido Biagi* (Paris: Ollendorf, 1895), vol. 1, pp. 181–182.
337 "prematurely fallen leaves": Colette, *De ma fenêtre,* in *Oeuvres complètes* (Paris: Le Fleuron, 1950), vol. 12, p. 361.
337 "signs of Satan": Baudelaire, "De l'essence du rire," in *Oeuvres complètes* (Paris: Gallimard, 1976), vol. 2, p. 350.
337 "overflowing, mephitic": Ibid., p. 528.
337 "primeval images of waves": Ibid., p. 529.
337 "bored and perceptive civilization": Ibid.
337 "something resembling fear": Ibid.
338 "the means of rescue": Ibid., p. 528.

Mundus Patet

339 "venture through those narrow alleyways": W. Benjamin, *Das Passagen-Werke,* in *Gesammelte Schriften* (Frankfurt: Suhrkamp, 1977), vol. 5, part 2, p. 1046.
339 "necessary according to nature": Plutarch, *Vita Romuli,* XI, 1.
339 "the mouths of Hell": A. Pagniol, *Recherches sur les jeux romains* (Strasbourg: Publications de la Faculté des Lettres de l'Université de Strasbourg, 1923), p. 9.
339 "delighted the eye": Benjamin, *Das Passagen-Werke,* p. 1045.
339 "after a long separation": Ibid.
339 "that of the *mundus* on high": Cato in Festus, *De significatione verborum,* ed. Lindsay, p. 144, 18–21.
340 "mixing everything together": Plutarch, *Vita Romuli,* XI, 1.

340 "clinical nihilism in literature": W. Benjamin, *Briefe* (Frankfurt: Suhrkamp, 1966), vol. 2, p. 731.

341 "before having done with everything": L. F. Céline, "Lettres à des amies," in *Cahiers Céline* (Paris: Gallimard, 1979), vol. 5, p. 263.

341 "diplomatic gratuities": *Mémoires de Barras* (Paris: Hachette, 1896), vol. 4, p. 257.

341 "only cash": H. C. Freiherr von Gagern, "Herr Talleyrand und sein Verhältnis zu den Deutschen," in *Mein Antheil an der Politik* (Leipzig: Brockhaus, 1845), vol. 5, p. 204.

342 "never be a poor devil": *Mémoires et relations politiques du baron de Vitrolles* (Paris: Charpentier, 1884), vol. 3, p. 128.

342 "all the pompous sentiments": Stendhal, "Monsieur de Talleyrand," in *Mélanges de politique et d'histoire* (Paris: Le Divan, 1933), pp. 111, 117.

342 "short of money": Ibid., p. 111.

342 "so terribly many things": "Lettre adressé par Madame la duchesse de Talleyrand à l'abbé Dupanloup," May 10, 1839, in Duchesse de Dino, *Chronique de 1831 à 1862* (Paris: Plon, 1909), vol. 1, p. 239.

343 "a childhood infirmity": "Documents de Monseigneur Dupanloup," text published in B. de Lacombe, *La Vie privée de Talleyrand* (Paris: Plon-Nourrit, 1910), p. 281.

343 "described so often in their writings": Talleyrand, *Mémoires* (Paris: Plon, 1982), pp. 44–45.

344 "Non est enim potestas": Romans, 13:1.

344 "simplifies my position": "Lettre adressée par Madame la duchesse de Talleyrand," p. 233.

344 "with a half-serious smile": "Récit fait par l'abbé Dupanloup de ses relations avec Monsieur de Talleyrand," in Lacombe, *La Vie privée de Talleyrand*, p. 345.

344 "nothing more venerable": Ibid., p. 351.

345 "two liveried manservants": Sainte-Beuve, "Talleyrand," in *Nouveaux lundis* (Paris: Calmann Lévy, 1884), vol. 12, p. 107.

345 "The very best of Voltaire!": Ibid., p. 110.

345 "one of the foremost theologians": [H. C. Freiherr von Gagern], *Mein Antheil an der Politik* (Stuttgart: Cotta, 1823), vol. 1, p. 105.

345 "I'm afraid of only one thing": Sainte-Beuve, "Talleyrand," p. 112.

346 "Very beautiful!": Lacombe, *La Vie privée de Talleyrand*, p. 287.

346 "something to placate Rome": "Récit fait par l'abbé Dupanloup," p. 368.

346 "Most things get done": [Freiherr von Gagern], *Mein Antheil an der Politik*, vol. 1, p. 128.

346 "enormous sore": Letter from Pauline de Périgord to a friend, in G. Lacour-Gayet, *Talleyrand* (Paris: Payot, 1931), vol. 3, p. 401.

346 "hung from the ceiling with ropes": Ibid.

348 "cannot be used for dissection": Chateaubriand, *Mémoires d'outre-tombe* (Paris: Gallimard, 1958), vol. 2, p. 905.

348 "the *douceur* of corrupt men": Letter from Sainte-Beuve to Nefftzer, March 8, 1869, in Sainte-Beuve, "Talleyrand," p. 132.

348 "Talleyrand died in public": Sainte-Beuve, "Talleyrand," p. 114.

348 *"tant soit peu bourgeois"*: M. Colmache, *Revelations of the Life of Prince Talleyrand* (London: Henry Colburn, 1850), p. 342.

348   "its unceasing murmur": Ibid., p. 345.
349   "for which he is so much dreaded": Ibid., p. 346.
349   "young beaux, all robber-like": Ibid.
349   "a flight of crows": Ibid., p. 348.
349   "the same silence with which they had entered": Ibid.

Letter from Petersburg

351   "When you know the *fin mot* too well": Sainte-Beuve, "Le Cahier vert," in *Cahiers* (Paris: Gallimard, 1973), p. 168.
351   "put some *thoughts* into people's heads": Ibid., p. 88.
351   "Such gentleness!": Sainte-Beuve, *Correspondance* (Paris: Calmann Lévy, 1878), vol. 2, p. 391.
351   "what is published in Paris": Sainte-Beuve, "Mathieu Marais," in *Nouveaux lundis* (Paris: Calmann Lévy, 1884), vol. 9, p. 17.
351   "fills his basket": Sainte-Beuve, "Chateaubriand (1844)," in *Portraits contemporains* (Paris: Calmann Lévy, n.d.), vol. 1, p. 49.
352   "with a golden chain": Sainte-Beuve, "Madame Récamier," in *Causeries du lundi* (Paris: Garnier, 1926), vol. 1, p. 135.
352   "holidays from the Ecole de Médecine": Sainte-Beuve, "Joseph Delorme," from *Premiers lundis,* in *Oeuvres* (Paris: Gallimard, 1960), p. 379.
352   "with a stocking cap": Sainte-Beuve, *Chroniques parisiennes* (Paris: Calmann Lévy, 1876), p. 154.
353   "*Rancé* is a disappointment": Ibid., p. 221.
353   "empties all his cupboards": Ibid., p. 222.
353   "the wings of the Opéra stage": Ibid.
353   "whatever did not fit": Abbé Dubois, *Histoire de l'abbé de Rancé et de sa Réforme* (Paris: Ambroise Bray, 1866), vol. 1, p. 113.
354   "outshone all the other women": Tallemant des Réaux, *Historiettes* (Paris: Gallimard, 1980), vol. 2, p. 217.
354   "breasts twice the desirable size": Ibid.
354   "steeped in vice": Cardinal de Retz, *Mémoires* (Paris: Gallimard, 1961), p. 159.
354   "greed tempered her debauchery": Chateaubriand, *Vie de Rancé*, in *Oeuvres romanesques et voyages* (Paris: Gallimard, 1969), vol. 1, p. 1377.
355   "he saw her bloodstained head": [Daniel de Larroque], *Les Véritables Motifs de la conversion de l'abbé de la Trappe* (Cologne: Dumarteau, 1685), p. 78.
355   "the bosom of life": Chateaubriand, *Vie de Rancé*, p. 1023.
355   "religious men have rejected it": Ibid.

Calasso, Roberto.
[Rovina di Kasch. English]
The ruin of Kasch / Roberto Calasso;
translated by William Weaver
and Stephen Sartarelli.
p.   cm.
ISBN 0–674–78026–4
I. Weaver, William, 1923–   . II.
Sartarelli, Stephen, 1954–   . III. Title.
PQ4863.A3818R613   1994
853′.914—dc20
94–5383
CIP